W. W.
PRESCOTT

ADVENTIST PIONEER SERIES

George R. Knight, Consulting Editor

Published volumes:
James White: Innovator and Overcomer,
by Gerald Wheeler

Joseph Bates: The Real Founder of Seventh-day Adventism,
by George R. Knight

W. W. Prescott: Forgotten Giant of Adventism's Second Generation,
by Gilbert Valentine

To order, call

1-800-765-6955.

Visit us at

www.reviewandherald.com

for information on other Review and Herald® products.

W. W. PRESCOTT

Forgotten Giant
of Adventism's Second Generation

GILBERT M. VALENTINE

REVIEW AND HERALD® PUBLISHING ASSOCIATION
HAGERSTOWN, MD 21740

The author assumes full responsibility for the accuracy of all facts and
quotations as cited in this book.

Bible texts credited to RSV are from the Revised Standard Version of the
Bible, copyright © 1946, 1952, 1971, by the Division of Christian Education of
the National Council of the Churches of Christ in the U.S.A. Used by permission.

This book was
Edited by Gerald Wheeler
Copyedited by Delma Miller
Designed by Trent Truman
Electronic makeup by Shirley M. Bolivar
Typeset: 11/14 Berkeley Book

PRINTED IN U.S.A.

09 08 07 06 05   5 4 3 2 1

R&H Cataloging Service
Valentine, Gilbert Murray, 1947-   .
    W. W. Prescott: Forgotten giant of Adventism's second generation.

    1. Prescott, William Warren, 1855-1944.   I. Title.
                            B

ISBN 0-8280-1892-8

DEDICATION

To Gail

William Warren Prescott

*"I have…seen in him some of the rarest gifts
possessed by any man in our ranks."*
—A. G. Daniells to W. C. White, 1908

*"We have but few men of Prescott's ability,
and with ability come peculiarities of temperament."*
—I. H. Evans to A. G. Daniells, 1910

*"I am convinced that you are blessed with large executive
ability…I feel that the interests of the cause are safe in your hands."*
—A. G. Daniells to W. W. Prescott, 1916

*"The wildest and most unsafe man that has ever
undertaken to pose as a leader of this denomination."*
—J. H. Kellogg, 1904

*"The more I am associated with Brother Prescott,
the more I am convinced that he is not only a Christian but
a gentleman in the first degree. He is so free from anything like
harshness. He tries to take a fair view of everything,
so that one cannot but like him."*
—S. H. Lane to A. G. Daniells, 1902

*"You sometimes allow your mind to center upon
a certain train of thought, and you are in danger
of making a mountain out of a molehill."*
—E. G. White, 1908

"The most overpowering personality I ever met."
—H.M.S. Richards, 1980

A NOTE ON SOURCES AND ABBREVIATIONS

I N THE interests of space, references have been made as economically as possible. At the same time, the information given should be sufficient to enable those who wish to check an interpretation or follow up an inquiry to do so. Abbreviations have been used for people's names and for organizations in the interests of brevity and uniformity. Where individuals or organizations are referred to only once, the full name is given. Names that are referenced more than once are abbreviated as per the following list. More complete references may be found in the author's Ph.D. dissertation. "William Warren Prescott: Seventh-day Adventist Educator," Andrews University, 1982.

While some secondary sources have been helpful in providing contextual material, this study has relied largely on primary materials such as personal and official correspondence, memorandums, committee minutes, magazine articles, reports, and other manuscripts. Materials for the early years may be found in special collections such as those at Dartmouth College or in other Historical Society Collections in New England.

Much of the material for Prescott's years after 1885 is to be found primarily in either one of the two extensive and carefully indexed archival collections maintained in the headquarters building of the General Conference of Seventh-day Adventists at Old Columbia Pike, Silver Spring, Maryland, in the United States of America or in the Heritage Room at Andrews University. Other helpful sources were located at Union College and at Avondale College. In the main, letters and minutes and other documents concerning denominational issues are to be found in either the Ellen G. White Estate in Washington, D.C., or in the General Conference Archives. Because the two archival collections are geographically adjacent to each other and overlap to some degree, the specific collection or file groups of documents have not been indicated except where it is felt that the location may not be obvious or could not be assumed.

The archives of the General Conference of Seventh-day Adventists include correspondence, minutes, and papers of the General Conference committees and various other organizations, as well as some specialized files. Located in very close proximity to the General Conference archives is the large collection of materials that comprises the Ellen G. White Estate. This collection houses not only the published and unpublished letters and manuscripts of Ellen G. White but also the voluminous correspondence files of W. C. White and, later, his son Arthur L. White. The files also contain extensive incoming correspondence from the General Conference leadership and other church personnel involved in the life and ministry of Ellen White and in the later work of the White Estate trustees. The White Estate also maintains a large number of document files that bring together topical collections of documentary items on a broad range of specific subjects.

LIST OF ABBREVIATIONS

AFJK	Alfred F. J. Kranz
AGD	Arthur G. Daniells
AJB	A. J. Breed
ALB	Alonzo L. Baker
AOT	Asa O. Tait
AP	Alice Perrine
ATJ	Alonzo T. Jones
AUCSM	Australasian Union Conference session minutes
AUHR	Andrews University Heritage Room
AWS	Arthur W. Spalding
BCCBdMin	Battle Creek College board minutes
BCCFacMin	Battle Creek College faculty minutes
CBH	Carlyle B. Haynes
CCC	Clarence C. Crisler
CEH	Claude E. Holmes
CFV	C. F. Vaugh
CHC	C. H. Chaffee
CHJ	Charles H. Jones
CHW	Charles H. Watson
CKM	C. K. Meyers
CMS	C. M. Snow
CPB	Calvin P. Bollman
CT	Charles Thompson
CVL	Clarence V. Leach
CWF	Charles Willaim Flaiz
CWI	Charles W. Irwin
DAR	Dores A. Robinson

DTJ	Dan T. Jones
DWR	Drury W. Reavis
EAS	Edward A. Sutherland
EEA	Elmer E. Andross
EGS	E. G. Sauer
EGW	Ellen G. White
EJW	Ellet J. Waggoner
EKV	Emmett K. Vande Vere
EMC	Emmanuel Missionary College
EMCBdMin	Emmanuel Missionary College board minutes
ERP	Edwin R. Palmer
EWF	Eugene W. Farnsworth
FDS	Frank D. Starr
FG	Frederick Griggs
FMW	Francis M. Wilcox
FWH	Frank W. Howe
GAI	George A. Irwin
GBS	George B. Starr
GBT	George B. Thompson
GC	General Conference
GCAr	General Conference Archives
GCCMin	General Conference Committee minutes
GCOMin	General Conference officers minutes
GEH	George E. Hutches
GIB	George I. Butler
GMV	Gilbert M. Valentine
HCL	H. Camden Lacey
HEO	Howard E. Osborne
HFS	Homer F. Saxton
HMSR	Harold M. S. Richards, Sr.
HNS	Harriett N. Smith
IAF	Irving A. Ford
IHE	Irwin H. Evans
JAB	John A. Burden
JEF	John E. Fulton
JEW	J. Edson White
JHK	John Harvey Kellogg
JLMc	James L. McElhany
JLS	John L. Shaw
JNL	John N. Loughborough
JSW	Judson S. Washburn
JWW	J. W. Watt
LAS	Leon A. Smith
LCC	L. C. Chadwick
LEF	LeRoy E. Froom

LFT	Lewis Francis Truby
LHC	Lewis Harrison Christian
LHW	Lynn H. Wood
LRC	Louis R. Conradi
LTN	Leroy T. Nicola
MCW	Milton C. Wilcox
MEK	Milton E. Kern
MLA	Milian Lauritz Andreasen
NJW	Nels John Waldorf
NZT	Nelson Zane Town
OAJ	Ole A. Johnson
OAO	Ole A. Olsen
OWD	Opal Wheeler Dick
PM	*Protestant Magazine*
PTM	Percy T. Magan
RAU	R. A. Underwood
RCP	Roscoe Celester Porter
RH	*Review and Herald*
RHPABdMin	Review and Herald Publishing Association board minutes
RMK	Robert M. Kilgore
RPK	Rochelle P. Kilgore
RSD	Robert Sloane Donnell
SDAES	Seventh-day Adventist Education Society
SDAPABdMin	Seventh-day Adventist Publishing Association board minutes
SM	*Student Movement*
SMc	Sara McEnterfer
SNH	Stephen N. Haskell
ST	*Signs of the Times*
TEB	Tyler Edwin Bowen
UC	Union College
US	Uriah Smith
WAC	William A. Colcord
WAS	William A. Spicer
WBW	William B. White
WCG	W. C. Grainger
WCGM	William C. G. Murdoch
WCW	William Clarence White
WEC	William Ellsworth Cornell
WEH	Warren Eugene Howell
WHB	William H. Branson
WHH	W. H. Holden
WMR	William M. Robbins
WTK	Walter T. Knox
WWF	William Ward Fletcher
WWP	William Warren Prescott

CONTENTS

CONTENTS

A WORD TO THE READER

FOR MOST contemporary Seventh-day Adventists, the name W. W. Prescott draws a blank look," notes *Adventist Review* editor William G. Johnsson. "Yet on any reckoning," he observes, Prescott "was a towering figure" in the life of the Advent movement.[1] The professor was not, in fact, noticeably taller in a physical sense. Nonetheless, he stood giantlike, casting an imposing presence astride a formidable stretch of denominational life.

Professor Prescott's active working career in the church spanned an unusually long period of 52 years—from 1885 to 1937—effectively embracing the entire second generation of the Adventist Church. He lived and worked through an era that witnessed some of the most important and critical developments in the history of the denomination. His life and work is of particular interest because he was so personally and intimately involved with many of these crucial issues. A study of Prescott's life, therefore, offers unique, valuable and often surprising insights into numerous chapters in the development of the church. It throws light on the struggles to grow denominational institutions, on important reorganizational developments, on the expanding mission of the church, and on the maturing of its theological perspectives. Such a study also opens windows onto the political conflicts, the personal quarrels, administrative struggles, and often-intense theological and educational debates that swirled through the church for much of this fascinating period.

As the denomination's most highly educated and articulate educational administrator during the formative period of Adventist education, the professor gave a distinctive Prescott mold to a number of important Adventist colleges. As the first General Conference educational leader, he also gave a distinctive shape and direction to the educational system as a whole. Adventist education still bears his legacy. At a later time he became one of the leading architects involved in the organizational restructuring of the church, and shortly after that he led in the reforming and the relocating of the church's flagship publishing house and in the process set a mold for the church's publishing work worldwide. That distinctive shape also still survives.

Surprisingly, however, shortly after Prescott's death in midcentury at 89 years of age, the Prescott name rapidly deleted itself from denominational memory. The professor quickly became a forgotten giant. A major reason for this amnesia seems to have been that the good professor had been so often associated with the disturbing of the status quo. In his later years, in the 1930s and early 1940s, a period of marked conservative consolidation in the church, some leaders perceived him to be just a troublemaker who made too many of the new generation of leaders uncomfortable. It was easier to simply forget him.

And it was true. Contention and debate swirled around W. W. Prescott almost throughout his entire career as one of Adventism's most charismatic and influential leaders. And, to a certain extent, his name still carries a little of the aura of controversy. Why? Because even though more than 60 years have passed since his death, many of the issues that so agitated the professor (such as righteousness by faith, the eternal deity of Christ and the Trinity, the nature and authority of Ellen White's inspiration, the interpretation of Daniel 8, and the reliability of modern translations of the Bible) are still very much alive in the church.

Prescott's role as one of the church's most forceful and prolific theological writers and one its most dynamic preachers had made him a dominating force in the reshaping and restating of Adventist theology for more than 30 years around the turn of the century. When convinced of an idea or convicted over some issue, he was not one who was afraid to speak his mind. Thus he sometimes polarized audiences of his fellow ministers.

Prescott believed that the church could change and should change. Just as the Advent movement must grow in size, so, he believed, it must grow in its biblical understanding. Doctrine was not static. Clearer concepts of truth must be adopted. Wrong ideas needed to be discarded. Adventist schools should likewise improve. Higher standards, fresh ideas, a more Christocentric curriculum—all were a must. Both Adventist preaching and teaching needed to change. They must both be progressive.

For Prescott, to live was to grow, and to grow was to change. Wherever change was taking place in the church, the professor always seemed to be at the forefront. He was what modern social psychologists call a "change agent." If there was a debate or some difference of opinion in the church, one could be sure Prescott was not far away.

The lingering shadows of controversy surrounding Prescott's name has unfortunately obscured the 52 years of widely varied and extremely valuable denominational service he gave in the classroom, the pulpit, and the editor's chair, as well as from behind numerous presidential desks. Pulpit, pen, and chalk were the tools of the professor's trade, and with them he labored to reshape and reform biblical understandings and teachings for the second generation of Adventists. His lifelong burden was that the church be molded to be more clearly Christocentric in its understanding of Scripture, in its statement of doctrine and in its proclamation. To a large degree, that shape also still endures.

William Prescott was a religious educator. Trained as a teacher in the rigors of the classics, he was, in his early 30s, also ordained as a pastor. Throughout most of his long career he was simultaneously both elder and professor, successfully merging the two roles into one. In a sense he was the embodiment of the integration of faith and learning, of ministry and teaching, of religion and education. This unique blending of the gifts of preaching, writing, and teaching in an educational ministry enabled him to have a more lasting impact in shaping the life and thought of the church than would have been possible otherwise. His impact on the church, however, was more than just the result of being a good preacher, writer, and teacher. According to his colleague and friend, General Conference president Arthur G. Daniells, the professor stood taller than most other leaders in the church because he was blessed with a profusion of the "rarest gifts" any Adventist leader possessed.[2] What were these gifts?

Prescott possessed an exceptionally sharp intellect and a prodigious memory. His abilities of analysis and synthesis were extraordinary, his judgment of human nature unusually accurate and perceptive. These qualities, enhanced by the even more important attributes of a keen spirituality and moral sensitivity, had been carefully nurtured in a tradition of culture and refinement at some of New England's best schools. Not only was he a sincere, devout Christian, colleagues observed; he was also a gentleman in the first degree. He had large executive ability and at the same time was a powerful and dynamic preacher whose polished use of the English language and of the language of Scripture inspired congregations wherever he went. Although he was not a genius in the sense of an Einstein, a creative inventor of completely novel, radical ideas, he nevertheless had the gift of seeing things in fresh new ways, and in new relationships; and he was very widely read in scholarly literature. These attributes made him a power of the first order. Well-known radio evangelist H.M.S. Richards, for example, regarded him as "the most overpowering personality" he had ever met.[3]

At times, however, Prescott could also be an irritation of the first order. Prescott's dogmatism and his potential for becoming obsessively preoccupied with a particular theme on occasion prevented him from seeing the larger picture. Furthermore, the assertiveness with which he pushed his viewpoint could sometimes seem aggressive. Barriers were sometimes created by other traits of his personality. For example, melancholy and depression were sometimes his companions, although he struggled to distance himself from them. Perhaps unaware of his inner battles, a few contemporaries such as Arthur W. Spalding saw him as aloof, imperious, or just too "British."[4]

Some of the professor's apparent aloofness arose from the fact that he was in many ways a private person. We know almost nothing about the inner relationships of his family life. Nothing of his correspondence with his first wife and son or with his extended family has apparently survived. His second wife, frightened by the harshness and suspicion that some of his later opponents manifested toward him, seems to have destroyed all private family letters. Also, Prescott's breadth of learning and large intellect frequently gave him a perspective on life and truth that not many of his contemporaries shared. He was not by any means clairvoyant in the common way, but he could see beyond the present in the sense that he often grappled with solutions to problems before others were even aware there might be a problem. In this respect he was often ahead of his time, a factor that sometimes contributed to his being misunderstood by those of lesser stature. This combination of rare gifts, in spite of their associated weaknesses, set him apart from his fellows.

In the view of most of those who really mattered in church affairs, however, Prescott's theological insights gave fresh credence to Adventist teaching. LeRoy Edwin Froom, for example, noted that during the 1920s Prescott's "lofty concepts" emphasizing the Christological focus of Adventist doctrines were "like a great breath of fresh air." In his view they were just what was needed to stir the church out of its theological doldrums. Although the farsighted, troublesome professor had been trumpeting such concepts for more than 30 years, according to Froom they were still "ahead of his time—many years ahead."[5]

Prescott's name was and still is closely linked with that of Ellen G. White. In his early career he worked alongside her in hammering out a workable educational program for the denomination's colleges. He became an aggressive advocate of her educational ideas and, later (at some personal cost), her administrative reforms. At various times he was also involved in the preparation of her manuscripts for publication. The relationship between the two leaders was from the first more a warm and trusting friendship than a formal working relationship. The professor was her preferred candidate for the General Conference presidency in 1897. In later years, though, as Ellen White became more frail, the relationship on her side became decidedly cool and distant, a result of Prescott's outspokenness and of his falling out with some of her older, more traditionally oriented first-generation "pioneering" colleagues. Rumor and misrepresentation became confused with facts in the complex conflicts that consequently arose between Washington, D.C., and California. This caused considerable emotional turmoil for the professor and distressed such longtime colleagues as W. C. White, who certainly had no sympathy for the "harsh and misguided" men "ploughing up and down" on the professor's back.[6]

Although badly hurt by the turn of events, Prescott never wavered from his firm belief in the uniqueness of Ellen White's prophetic gift and the blessing that her writings had been to the church. His insider's perspective on the way in which Ellen White and her helpers worked enabled him to articulate a more factual understanding of inspiration. This aspect of Prescott's life, therefore, has great value for the unique insights it provides into the dynamics and the interactions that existed between Ellen White in the exercise of her charismatic prophetic gift and those in her circle of associates called to exercise the gift of administration. Such a study has particular contemporary relevance. This is another of the many reasons that Prescott's biography is a "must read" for church leaders.[7]

The primary purpose of this biographical study is to understand the life and work of William Warren Prescott and to analyze and evaluate his contribution to the reshaping of the Adventist Church for the second generation of believers. Its secondary purpose is to shed light on the professor's complex and fascinating personality and to answer the question "What kind of person was Professor W. W. Prescott?"

I have followed a basic chronological approach in trying to understand Prescott's life, though distinct stages mark his career. Within these stages, however, it has been more helpful at times to discuss the professor's activities and accomplishments in a more thematic fashion. While this creates a little overlap in some places, it has not posed a serious difficulty in terms of interrupting the overall flow of the biography.

This present volume represents the recasting on an earlier publication, *The Shaping of Adventism: The Case of W. W. Prescott,* published by Andrews University Press in 1992. The revised edition incorporates much more reference material and footnoting than was possible in the first work. It has also provided opportunity to expand the discussion of Prescott's role in the church's theological development in the area of Christology and the doctrine of the Trinity. I have been able to include extensive referencing to more recent studies and understandings of the church's development in these areas. The interpretations adopted continue to be valid. Recent studies have clarified some points and have enabled the adding of greater detail.

As an author I continue to acknowledge a heavy debt to George Knight, who provided guidance and friendship in the development of my passion for understanding the church and its development. His valuable counsel helped develop the needed research skills in my doctoral study, and his own prolific writing both challenged and inspired me later to present the material for a wider readership. I am also indebted to the help of my good friends Richard Stone and Adrian Bell, both of whom helped in reading the manuscript and whose expert "feel" for the English language saved me from numerous blunders in rhetoric and logic. Appreciation is also owed to Bernard and Alyna Taylor, of Loma Linda, for the quiet haven they provided for the work that needed to be done on the revisions. I would like to express my thanks for the helpful assistance of Janice Little and her colleagues at the Loma Linda University Library and White Estate Branch Office. I have also appreciated the help of my secretary, Sheila Fanwar, for her coordination skills; Winyou Silipachan for his help with photographs; and Tran Thi Thuy Tram and Dzidzornya Dzuali for their help with some of the technical aspects of the preparation of the manuscript. Thanks are also due Gerald Wheeler and Jeannette Johnson for their encouragement and editorial assistance and to my administrative colleagues at Mission College for providing financial support and time for undertaking the research and revisions.

My hope is that this study will help a new generation of readers not only to understand William Prescott but also to gain a richer understanding and appreciation of both the church and the Lord that he loved and served with such energy and devotion.

—Gilbert M. Valentine

---

[1] W. G. Johnsson, "The Best From the Press in '92," *Adventist Review*, Dec. 10, 1992, pp. 12, 13.

[2] A. G. Daniells to W. C. White, June 25, 1908.

[3] H.M.S. Richards to author, May 21, 1981.

[4] A. W. Spalding to P. T. Magan, Nov. 23, 1920.

[5] L. E. Froom, *Movement of Destiny* (Washington, D.C.: Review and Herald Pub. Assn., 1971), pp. 348, 377, 379, 380.

[6] W. C. White to W. W. Prescott, May 7, 1915.

[7] Johnsson, p. 13.

FOREWORD

W. W. PRESCOTT: *Forgotten Giant of Adventism's Second Generation* follows Gerald Wheeler's *James White: Innovator and Overcomer* (2003) and my own *Joseph Bates: The Real Founder of Seventh-day Adventism* (2004) as the third volume in a groundbreaking project in Adventist biography. Future volumes are scheduled to present such personalities as J. N. Andrews as Adventism's earliest scholar and first missionary; W. C. White as his mother's assistant and a man at the center of action; Ellen White as a woman in a man's world and Adventism's prophetic voice; and Ellet J. Waggoner as a leader in the revival of righteousness by faith. Each biography will focus on the individual's major contribution to the church and will be written by a person well versed in his or her topic.

William Warren Prescott was a towering figure in Adventism's second generation. He not only directed the denomination's educational program and served as the editor of the *Review and Herald* and other periodicals, but was also the denomination's first vice president and one of the foremost Adventist thought leaders for nearly four decades.

As might be expected, given Prescott's many-faceted career, he did not manage to avoid controversy. To the contrary, it surrounded him for much of his career and even dogged him into old age. Early in his Adventist journey he aligned himself with A. T. Jones and E. J. Waggoner and became one of the foremost preachers of righteousness by faith during the 1890s. But the new century saw Prescott split from Jones and Waggoner as they sided with J. H. Kellogg in a controversy that took all three out of the denomination.

For his part during those divisive years, Prescott stood with Arthur G. Daniells over against his one-time colleagues as the new General Conference president sought to bring stability to the growing church. Other controversies would include Prescott's ongoing battle with S. N. Haskell over the daily of Daniel 8 and his enthusiasm to set forth

Trinitarian concepts that were in harmony with both the New Testament and *The Desire of Ages*.

Gilbert Valentine's telling of Prescott's life and contributions to the Seventh-day Adventist Church is a fast-paced account that makes for a good read. *W. W. Prescott: Forgotten Giant of Adventism's Second Generation* is based upon Valentine's much more extensive Ph.D. dissertation entitled "William Warren Prescott: Seventh-day Adventist Educator" (1982). Much of the material also appears in his earlier work, *The Shaping of Adventism: The Case of W. W. Prescott* (Andrews University Press, 1992).

The present biography is a "warts and all" approach that outlines the life of a major contributor to the development of Adventism but does not avoid its subject's shortcomings. I highly recommend *W. W. Prescott: Forgotten Giant of Adventism's Second Generation* to those who have an interest in Adventist history, in biography, or in nineteenth- and early-twentieth-century American Protestantism.

GEORGE R. KNIGHT
CONSULTING EDITOR
ANDREWS UNIVERSITY

W. W. Prescott

CHAPTER Î

A NEW ENGLAND HERITAGE

THE CONGREGATION shifted uneasily. It was already difficult to hear the speaker in the huge crowded tent. The May shower that announced its arrival with a musical tattoo on the taut canvas was unwelcome. But within minutes the playful splatterings had become a thunderous downpour. Long slivers of water penetrated the splices, and the listeners shuffled restively to avoid getting wet.

The shallow-chested preacher of the hour, already half cowed by the task of reaching the distant ears of his listeners in the back rows, strained to outshout the drumming rain. These were the days before the invention of microphones and loudspeakers, and his words vanished almost without a trace. Even the front benches sat looking blank. Irritation in the audience quickly swelled to an ominous murmur. These delegates had come a long way to attend the 1913 General Conference session being held in Washington, D.C., but what good was it if they could not hear the preacher?

Then rising above the hubbub, urgent voices from scattered quarters of the tent began to echo each other with the cry "Prescott! Prescott! Where's Prescott!" Responding to the cries, a dignified-looking gentleman emerged from the front rows. Of medium height and solid build, the bald middle-aged professor quickly strode to the pulpit to stand beside the hapless preacher. There, in booming but polished New England accents, he translated and amplified the rest of the sermon above the sound of the rain until the cloudburst had passed.

🐾 🐾 🐾

Who was this barrel-voiced Prescott who could be heard at a General Conference session even above the tumult of a thunderstorm? Professor William Prescott was a household name in Adventism. For 20 years he had served the church in a variety of positions: president of Battle Creek College; educational secretary for the General Conference; Foreign Mission Board secretary; conference president; editor of the church's leading journal, the *Review and Herald;* and vice president of the General Conference. His words and ideas had already helped to shape the church's educational system. In a marked way they had also reshaped the theology and the policies of the church. They would continue to do so for another quarter of a century. His prominent positions in the church enabled this powerful writer and preacher to exert an unusually large influence during some of the church's most critical developments.

No one present at William's birth in the quiet New Hampshire hamlet of Alton could possibly have foreseen such a future for him. No one, except perhaps his mother, who first heard his insistent voice on a crisp September day in 1855.

The descendant of hardy and devout New England farmers, Prescott could trace his lineage back eight generations. Almost 200 years previously the first Prescott on American soil, a young James, migrated from Derby in England. The adventurer had settled in central New Hampshire, married, and quickly established himself as an influential landowner.

During the ensuing two centuries William's forebears participated actively in civic and community affairs. The Prescott family took pride in its links with early America and its involvement in the development of the young republic. Some of the family saw service in the 1755 war with France and others in the Revolutionary War with England 20 years later. A prominent relative, Col. William Prescott, had commanded the opening revolutionary military encounter at the famous battle of Bunker Hill. Another, Dr. Samuel Prescott, accompanied Paul Revere on the desperate midnight ride on April 18, 1775, a ride that became an American legend.[1]

At the time of William's birth, political tensions were building again in America. Within the life span of a single generation the emergent American nation was again to be locked in bloody conflict. This time it would be brother against brother; the Civil War was less than six years away. William's parents—James and Harriet Prescott, of Alton, New Hampshire—saw these dark clouds as signs of the soon-coming Jesus. James was 5 when his father, Amos, took him outside to witness the spectacular meteor shower that so startled New England on the night of

November 13, 1833. The scene left an indelible impression upon James. Five years later he was baptized and joined the Freewill Baptists, the church of his farmer parents.[2]

In 1842 the Prescott family had become further convicted of additional light with which to interpret the times in which they lived. In nearby Concord, New Hampshire, James and his father went to hear Millerite preacher Joshua V. Himes preach on the Advent. Persuaded by the forcefulness of Himes's arguments and their own experience of 1833, the whole family cast their lot with the Advent cause. Hope that the physical reappearance of Christ in the heavens would occur in 1843 led to disappointment, but James and his mother were present at the Exeter camp meeting, where another Millerite evangelist, Samuel S. Snow, explained his "seventh month" idea and the new date of October 22, 1844. This time, certain of the great consummation, they left their grain unharvested and their potatoes to rot in the ground (in later years the family often pointed out the field to young William). Now in his midteens, James keenly felt the bitterness of this second disappointment, but neither he nor his parents were ready to surrender their hope.

Shortly afterward, James left the farm and took up an apprenticeship as a shoemaker. Two and a half years later, at the age of 19, he married 16-year-old Harriet Tripp, a girl of similar spiritual convictions. Harriet's forebears had descended from the Scottish Covenanters and had been active in the Congregational Church.[3]

Upon completing his cobbling apprenticeship, James and his new wife moved from town to town in central New Hampshire. It was the ministry, however, rather than the pursuit of business that seems to have provided the reason for the frequent moves. James had established himself as a self-supporting preacher. He was often called upon to minister to the scattered Advent believers in this area who were later to comprise the Advent Christian denomination. James had become very involved with this particular group, which continued to adjust the reckoning of the prophetic time periods.

They advocated 1854 as the next date set for the return of Christ, but not until their projections had failed again in 1857 did the group abandon the idea of time setting altogether. Not long after this, James ceased his itinerant ministry to concentrate on business. Only after his retirement, 30 years later, did he again take up part-time ministry. Recipients of his part-time pastoral care remembered him as a kindly, devout, and deeply spiritual man who firmly believed in spiritual healing of the sick. His was a simple and direct faith; he believed that ailments as assorted as sprained ankles, peritonitis, and tumors had been cured through prayer alone.

William was only 3 years old when his parents encountered the teaching of the seventh-day Sabbath in 1858. Father James had stayed with a Sabbath-observing family while traveling in Vermont. Upon acquainting himself with the scriptural arguments for the Sabbath, he became convinced of their veracity, promptly joined the movement, and kept the very next Sabbath. Harriet joined him, and grandparents Amos and Lydia Prescott soon followed.[4]

The home that James and Harriet provided for William and his eight brothers and sisters placed a high value on truth. Although the social stigma resulting from their failed end-of-the-world predictions eventually diminished, the family's adoption of the seventh-day Sabbath ensured that they remained identified with an unpopular minority group within the community. The Prescotts, however, had long since shown that they were more concerned with the integrity of their consciences and their standing before God than with their standing in the community. Quietly instilled in William during childhood, these values of independent thought and loyalty were tested during his teenage years when he became the only Sabbathkeeping student at Dartmouth College. The preparedness to think for himself and to be guided by his conscience subsequently became characteristic of his later life and ministry.

The intensely eschatological nature of Adventist belief shaped the Prescott home. Their sense of the imminence of Christ's return placed great importance on industry, time, and accountability. These values, and the home environment in which they were shaped, significantly influenced William's character. They fitted him for the contribution he was later to make during 52 years of service to the Seventh-day Adventist denomination.

SCHOOL DAYS

William spent his early childhood in a number of small New England towns, including the hamlets of Barnstead and Penacook in New

Hampshire, and Wells on the Maine coast Eventually, in 1864, when William was 9, the family settled more or less permanently in North Berwick, a town close to the state line between Maine and New Hampshire. Here William's father found the chance to develop his entrepreneurial talents. Hard financial times forced James to drop his shoe-finishing contract for a Massachusetts marketing company and branch out into other business areas. Engaged at first as a salesman for a stove polish company, he eventually purchased the company when its owners experienced difficulties following the stock market collapse of 1869. Prescott Universal, the stove polish that William's father produced in the barn at the back of their house, soon became a household word throughout New England. William, with his five brothers and sisters, shared in the manufacturing tasks. William's responsibility was transporting the raw materials by wheelbarrow from the local railway station to their home. He then had a return trip with the finished product.[5]

The business grew rapidly, and within a decade several new lines were added. Later relocated in New Jersey, the Prescott business still survives and presently employs a large workforce. Father James came to be known in the community as "a man of strict integrity, scrupulously honest, and upright in all his dealings," and as one who "contributed liberally to the needy and to benevolent enterprises."[6] William's early informal education in this family business not only taught him industry, but bred in him a sense of sound business management, good judgment, and a fine moral sensibility. These qualities would later enable him to be successful in his own business and as a senior administrator within the Adventist denomination.

Not everything young William experienced at this time was so simple. As the business was still getting under way the 14-year-old learned sobering lessons about the frailty of life. Within the space of two weeks in early December 1869 three of his younger brothers (aged 6, 3, and 1) died—all victims of a particularly virulent epidemic. It remained the saddest Christmas of William's life.

Four years later, during William's first year at college, another family funeral reopened the old griefs. His 3-year-old brother, Fred, had succumbed to a childhood disease. In later years William would recall these sorrows and write, "I have looked upon the faces of my beloved dead, and have seen their lifeless forms consigned to their resting places in the city of the dead, and I have turned away with a biting grief in my heart which refused to be soothed."[7]

His early acquaintance with grief contributed much to the sensitivity of Prescott's nature and made him keenly sympathetic to others' feelings. Prescott had witnessed the tears of a brokenhearted mother and had sensed in his own life the awesome emptiness the death of a loved one leaves in its wake. Bitter and painful experiences such as these gave depth to his later ministry. Congregations responded warmly to his preaching. He was more than just a rich, resonant voice; because of his own personal struggles he had something meaningful to say about life.

We know little of William's elementary schooling except that it must have been thorough. Before he had completed high school he was able to teach classes in Latin and Greek. More information survives about his secondary education and, in view of his significant role later on in the shaping and development of Adventist education, it is useful to note his schooling in some detail. The high school William attended, South Berwick Academy, was known at the time as one of the oldest and most prestigious schools in all of Maine. It would seem that the family chose this school rather than institutions closer to home because of its emphasis on "piety, religion, and morality."[8] It offered boarding accommodations and private rooms for pupils who did not live in the immediate township of South Berwick. These "school homes," the catalog pointed out, were not military-type barracks. They were "homes" where "kind and discreet guardians" would give careful attention to "health, manners, and deportment." Already the foundations were being laid for Prescott's plan of "school homes" that he was later to introduce as president of Battle Creek College.[9]

The South Berwick Academy's catalog announced that the entire institution was fundamentally religious. "This school is established upon the Bible as its basis. . . . Appropriate religious exercises, so essential to moral training, . . . are daily observed." Instruction was given in biblical geography and antiquities, and attendance was required at Sunday worship services. Students, however, could attend the church of their preference. A trust set up by one of the school's founders provided for a Bible to be presented to each student with the stipulation that a chapter was to be read each evening and morning—a requirement honored more in the breach than in the observance, according to one former pupil.[10]

Of the two courses offered at South Berwick, science and classical, it appeared that Prescott took the latter. Later he was to major in the study of ancient languages. By the time he started college he was thoroughly familiar with such authors as Virgil, Xenophon, Sallust, Cicero, and Homer. William, however, completed only three years of studies at South Berwick, changing schools in the autumn of 1872 to complete his "finishing" year at Penacook Academy. Although a school with a religious orientation very similar to that of South Berwick and offering similar courses, Penacook was of more recent origin and less prestigious.[11] We are left to surmise as to the reason for this sudden change in schools.

In the summer of 1872 William attended the Massachusetts Adventist camp meeting, where General Conference president George I. Butler and the young denomination's most well-known scholar, J. N. Andrews, were the leading speakers. Although, as Butler reported to *Review* readers at the time, the Massachusetts meeting was hardly as "spiritual and profitable" as others during the season, for William it was a very meaningful event. It was here that he made a personal commitment to Christ and was baptized by Andrews.[12] William was 17 years old.

Perhaps it was this decision that precipitated the change of schools to Penacook. On the other hand, the change may have been more because of a matter of the heart. At Penacook attractive 16-year-old Sabbathkeeping Sarah Sanders was a student. According to the school records, she was, for a time, enrolled in Prescott's classes in Latin and Greek. While we can only presume that mutual interest embraced more than books at this stage, the subsequent romance and marriage is a persuasive bit of evidence.

With high school behind him and a good academic record to his credit, William set his sights on Dartmouth College, a highly reputable school. Sarah's older brother, Charles, was just completing his engineering studies there. So, in the autumn of 1873, along with 80 other freshmen, Prescott gained admission to Dartmouth. He was the only Seventh-day Adventist enrolled. His new commitment to Christ and the Sabbath was about to be rigorously tested.

---

[1] William Prescott, *The Prescott Memorial; or a Genealogical Memoir of the Prescott Families in America* (Boston: Henry W. Dutton and Sons, 1870), p. 229. See also *A Story of American Enterprise, Being a Brief History of the Founding of the J. L. Prescott Co., Together*

With an Account of Its Growth, 1870-1945 (privately printed for the J. L. Prescott Co., 1945), p. 3.

[2] *RH,* Jan. 11, 1898, p. 31; *RH,* Jan. 9, 1908, p. 5; WWP to WCW, Apr. 6, 1915.

[3] George L. Randall, *Tripp Genealogy; Descendants of James, Son of John Tripp* (New Bedford, Mass.: n.p., 1924); Epsom, N.H., church records.

[4] *RH,* Jan. 9, 1908, p. 5; "James L. Prescott Memoir," GCAr.

[5] *J. L. Prescott Co.,* p. 2.

[6] Clayton C. Woodford, *History of York County, Maine* (Philadelphia: Everts and Peck, 1880), p. 311.

[7] W. W. Prescott, *The Saviour of the World* (Washington, D.C.: Review and Herald Pub. Assn., 1929), p. 63; see also "James L. Prescott Memoir."

[8] Sarah Orne Jewett, "The Old Town of Berwick," *New England Magazine,* July 1894, p. 598.

[9] *Catalogue of Berwick Academy,* 1857.

[10] Cited in Marie Donahue, "Maine's Oldest Private Academy," *Down East: The Magazine of Maine,* October 1966, p. 27.

[11] "Academy Records," *Catalogue of Officers and Students of Penacook Academy* (1870).

[12] *RH,* Sept. 17, 1872, p. 6; WWP, "Morning Bible Study," 1936.

CHAPTER II

COLLEGE DAYS

"THERE WAS A STRONG religious sentiment pervading the institution," recalled Prescott of his time at Dartmouth College in the 1870s.[1] But that and rigorous academic standards were exactly what the trustees intended. With more than a century of educating New England youth already behind it in 1873, the school enjoyed the best of reputations. The president was a clergyman, and the school expected students to attend religious services seven days a week. Classes each Monday morning began with a lecture on the Greek New Testament, something that Prescott heartily approved of.

Tuition at Dartmouth was expensive. The Prescotts paid more than three times as much for William's education as students paid at the Seventh-day Adventists' own fledgling college at Battle Creek. Because Dartmouth was out of the financial reach of many, students came almost exclusively from the more prominent and highly placed New England families. But the Prescott family's prosperous new business venture in North Berwick eased any financial burden that William might otherwise have felt.

Apart from his unique religious background, William differed little from any other eager young New England student. His classmates nicknamed him "Billy." He was to spend four years at Dartmouth gaining an education regarded as among the best that America could offer. Leadership qualities that characterized his later life emerged and received opportunity to mature and expand. His intellectual and social horizons broadened as he mingled with the flower of New England's offspring. Dartmouth gave him a training in scholastics that equipped him to make a lasting contribution to his church. But here also he imbibed a philosophy of education that only years of trial, a personal encounter with Ellen White, and a revolution in his own spiritual experiences would erase.

An explanation of his religious principles in an early nerve-racking interview with the college president secured for William an exemption from Sabbath classes for the duration of his studies.[2] One Roman Catholic classmate jokingly recalled that Prescott was so conscientious that he would not even snore on Sabbath. With no Adventist church nearby, he must have spent many lonely Sabbaths quietly by himself. His faithfulness, however, and his cheerful Christian sincerity won him the respect and admiration of his classmates. They would later vote him into class leadership.

Dartmouth offered many opportunities for the development of Prescott's interests and abilities. He sang in the Handel Society, which gave performances in town and the surrounding district. Also he participated in the campus debating societies. Throughout his life he was never one short of words.

William also enjoyed considerable success in the school sports program. During the late decades of the nineteenth century Dartmouth placed increasing emphasis on sports as a way of counteracting the traditional unruleliness of student behavior. Intense class rivalry led to repeated "rushes"—disruption of each other's class sports events. During Prescott's time at Dartmouth such "rushes" resulted in extensive damage to college property and interruption of the school program. Whether Prescott was involved is not known. But school authorities had endeavored to correct the trend by building a gymnasium five years before he became a student. In his second year the college formed an athletic association and organized field days. Because of his strength and agility Prescott gained firsts in the hammer throw and the 440-yard and 100-yard sprints. At succeeding meets he also achieved firsts in the shot put.[3]

William's classmates recognized his personal charisma and leadership qualities when he served as president and vice president of his class during his last two years. His duties involved considerable responsibility in organizing speech nights, debates, and other activities. In his senior year he also served as an editor of the student weekly magazine, during which he developed a taste for journalism. Later in his career he would spend 20 years in editing or publishing of one kind or another.

Academics, however, were the major reason that Prescott had gone to Dartmouth. Bypassing the science, engineering, and recently established agricultural departments, he chose what had been his interest in high school: classical studies. It would appear that teaching had been a long-term goal. In his first two years William studied nothing but Greek, Latin, and mathematics, except for a dash of French and mechanics toward the end of his second year. Greek and Latin continued as the main core of his third-year studies, with classes in logic, physics, astronomy, and rhetoric added during the second term. In his fourth year his studies broadened to include classes in English literature, psychology, geology, political economy, Christian evidences, and morals.

Prescott's academic performance indicates both a keen intellect and an aptitude for study. School records reveal that he ranked among the top six in his class. In his last year only .02 percentage points separated the top six contenders for first place. As a recognition of his academic achievement the school invited him to deliver one of the orations at the graduation exercises.[4]

Practical experience, however, balanced William's study of the classics. Twice during his coursework he took time out to teach in nearby district schools. By the end of his college studies he had had a full year of classroom teaching experience to his credit. Apparently, however, he was not above using the extended "teaching" leave to his own advantage. A rare faculty record dealing with school discipline during Prescott's senior year noted, with a sense of irritation, that Prescott was absent from the college "but was not engaged in teaching." The faculty voted to write him "for an explanation."[5]

The late nineteenth century was an exciting time for the nation's educators. Winds of change were blowing through the halls of American academia. While Prescott wrestled with his Latin conjugations, debate about educational philosophy swirled over the campus. Dartmouth's president, a Presbyterian clergyman, Asa Dodge Smith, firmly opposed "electives" and any move away from the classics. He sided publicly with Princeton's James McCosh in his dislike of the idea of a "restaurant system" infiltrating the American college curriculum.[6] As a college student in the 1870s Prescott could hardly have been unaware of the controversies. Manual labor and agricultural training—so central to Adventist educational philosophy—were also hot reform issues in his college days. At Dartmouth, alumni and parents expressed considerable disquiet about the quality of the agricultural program that the college had introduced a decade earlier. Their fellows deemed the students involved in agricultural studies as second-class citizens.

During Prescott's third year the school magazine boldly criticized the agricultural department, asserting that its admission standards were abysmal and its requirements for graduation "beneath contempt."[7] The issue stirred the campus. The faculty had forbidden the magazine to publish the offending article and now demanded an apology from the editors as well as an acknowledgment in the next issue that the faculty had a right to censor student publications. The student editors complied. They had the last word, however, by refusing to publish any further issues that year as a protest against such censorship.[8]

Prescott became an editor when the publication resumed the following year. He could not have been ignorant of the issues. The censorship episode may help to explain his apparent sympathy toward the expression of student opinion on school affairs later when he was president at Battle Creek College. (In 1889 the school's trustees closed down the loss-making manual labor department, partly as the result of a student debate.)[9]

Four years passed quickly. On the last weekend in June 1877 William, along with 59 others who survived from his freshman class of 80, received his bachelor's degree in arts. On the basis of academic merit he was awarded the coveted honor of giving one of the commencement orations. His six-minute speech summarized the task he saw before the class. The subject, "The Office of the Thinker," was almost prophetic. William was ready now to step onto the stage of life and demonstrate what a "Dartmouth man" could do.[10] "Billy" had come to adulthood.

According to college policy, William could have requested his master's degree three years later in 1880. The institution awarded the degree, not on the basis of further classes or the presentation of a thesis, but in recognition of the professional application of earlier study. Although the degree was highly esteemed, Prescott did not feel the need to seek it until he was asked to be Battle Creek College president in 1885. His Dartmouth education had put him academically well in advance of his fellow church members. Everett Dick, Union College historian, commented that for 31 years after Prescott's presidency at Union College, none of the eight succeeding presidents held a master's degree.[11]

In later years Prescott acknowledged his debt to Dartmouth for the expertise he gained in scholarship, leadership, and rhetoric, skills achieved in spite of the narrowness of the curriculum. He maintained contact with his alma mater through the alumni association, and the alumni journal continued to report news of his activities. Inasmuch as the Adventist denomination benefited from Prescott's skills most of all, it too stands in Dartmouth's debt.

EARLY CAREER

Prescott spent the first eight years of his career after graduation in education and publishing. In a real sense they served as an apprenticeship for his later lifework. In total, 31 of his 52 years of service in the church involved either college administration and teaching or writing and publishing.

Soon after graduation Prescott found a post as principal of a school in Northfield, Vermont, 12 miles from the state capital. A sleepy town of almost 3,000, Northfield lay in the heart of one of Vermont's richest dairying areas. With an enrollment of 330, the school boasted a stately, brand-new, two-story building replacing a structure that had burned down 18 months previously. The year of practice teaching during his college studies now stood the fledgling teacher in good stead. Twenty-two-year-old Prescott was responsible for teaching the high school grades as well as supervising the conduct of the entire school, pocketing $24 a week for his efforts.[12] (The annual income for most people during this period was $300-$500.)

Two years later Prescott moved into the very heart of the state capital to take up the principal's post at Montpelier's leading school—the combined Washington County Grammar and Montpelier Union School. A more prestigious post, the new position offered a 20 percent increase in Prescott's monthly pay packet. Modern teachers would consider the pay hard-won. The average class size for Prescott and his seven teaching colleagues was 44.[13]

The Montpelier school had developed an excellent reputation throughout the state. Many graduates went on to such prestigious schools as Yale, Harvard, Dartmouth, Amherst, and Williams. It was also a good training ground for Prescott. Citizens in the state capital held high expectations for their school and for its principal. The job description was detailed, and his superiors closely monitored the required monthly reports.

Prescott's duties no doubt brought him into contact with many of Vermont's prominent citizens and legislators.[14] But the years 1879-1880 did not represent hard work only. His relationship with Sadie Sanders began to deepen, and it is evident that the year was spiced with courtship and romance for the young bachelor.

After completing her studies at Penacook Academy, Sarah apparently pursued some short-term summer studies in the women's division at Harvard University. Her father, Jacob Sanders, an astute businessman of German ancestry, had prospered in his retail business. The family owned quite a stretch of commercial buildings on Main Street, and they occupied a large, graceful, Romanesque home on a hill commanding an excellent view of Penacook.[15] It was in this home that on July 8, 1880, William and Sarah were married. She was 22 years old and he 24.

He had chosen well. Sarah was refined and gracious, with an intellect matching her husband's. More important, though, her natural cheerfulness provided the counterpoint for his tendency toward melancholy. Having been baptized sometime during her seventeenth year, Sarah retained a spiritual sensitivity. Taking a keen interest in William's work, she, as a constant and valued helper, shared his burden for the church. Her judgment and counsel was appreciated by not only her husband, but also other church leaders who at times sought her advice. She would remain at his side for the most important and productive years of his ministry until her death from cancer in 1910, at the age of 54, after 30 years of marriage.

But marriage was not the only thing on Prescott's mind in the summer of 1880. While preparations were under way for the wedding, a change in career was also on the horizon. Although the school committee in Montpelier hoped to retain William as principal, a proposal for him to join his younger brother Charles in a publishing venture attracted him more. Charles Prescott had just completed law school in Boston and been admitted to the York County Bar, but he had not found the profession to his liking. Together in mid-July, aided no doubt by some of their father's capital, the two brothers launched into journalism with the purchase of their home county newspaper, the Biddeford *Union and Journal,* based in Biddeford on the coast of Maine. William and Sarah had little time for honeymooning. The first issue of their paper was due one week after their wedding.

[1] L. B. Richardson, *History of Dartmouth College* (Hanover, N.H.: Dartmouth College Publications, 1932), p. 540.

[2] "Student Secures W. W. Prescott's Life Story," *SM*, Oct. 27, 1932, p. 3.

[3] "Comstock Scrapbook," ADBML; "Faculty Records," Dartmouth College, Apr. 11, 1875; Sept. 7, 1876.

[4] "Comstock Scrapbook," ADBML.

[5] "Faculty Records," Dartmouth College, Jan. 15, 1877, ADBML.

[6] J. F. Chase, *A History of Dartmouth College and the Town of Hanover, New Hampshire*, ed. John K. Lord (Cambridge, Mass.: Wilson and Son, 1891-1913), vol. 1, p. 546. Asa Smith was a graduate of Andover Theological Seminary. He retired from his 14 years as Dartmouth president in the same year that Prescott graduated.

[7] *The Dartmouth*, April 1875, ADBML.

[8] *Ibid.*

[9] CWI, "The Divine Remedy for Our Educational Ills," *RH*, July 12, 1923, p 10.

[10] "Comstock Scrapbook," ADBML.

[11] E. D. Dick, *Union: College of the Golden Cords* (Lincoln, Nebr.: Union College Press, 1967), p. 345.

[12] Julia W. McIntire, *Green Mountain Heritage: The Chronicle of Northfield, Vermont* (Canaan, N.H.: Phoenix Publishers, 1974), pp. 241-244, 482.

[13] "School Committee Report [1879]," Montpelier Union School Records 1860-1880, VHSL.

[14] Hamilton Child, *Gazeteer of Washington County 1783-1889* (Syracuse, N.Y.: Syracuse Journal Co., 1889), pp. 338-340, 412.

[15] David Arthur Brown, *History of Penacook, New Hampshire* (Concord, N.H.: Rumford Press, 1902), pp. 106, 291, 292.

CHAPTER III

INKY THUMBS AND PARTY POLITICS

THE PRESCOTT BROTHERS launched their new enterprise with obvious enjoyment and vigor. In their first issue the paper sported a new name: the Biddeford *Weekly Journal.* It also showed a marked change in style. Previously bland and matter-of-fact, the tone of the four-sheet broadside was lightheartedly provocative and saucy under William and Charles. Welcoming the new editors, a neighboring newspaper commented, "As the new proprietors . . . are quite young men, we expect to see the fire fly." The Prescotts' rejoinder: "Spare our blushes, Watson. We'll try not to burn anyone."[1]

Republican politics was the primary focus of the *Journal,* although temperance and education also figured prominently. Published each Friday morning, the newspaper's columns also reflected the Prescotts' religious interests. A story with some moral, along with some display advertisements, usually occupied the front page. Local news, politics, and editorials commanded the center spread, while the back page carried a temperance column, poetry, and miscellaneous items. The Prescott editorials carried on a vigorous discussion of current issues and engaged in good-natured banter with opposition papers.

It may not have been the brothers' intention to burn anyone, but on some issues feelings certainly ran hot. Vandals smashed windows of the newspaper office after an electoral win by a Republican candidate that the Prescott brothers had vigorously supported. Undeterred, the young editors assured their readers that the paper would continue to be "lively without being sensational, aggressive without being coarse, and . . . strive to be fearless and independent in the championship of right."[2] Politically, William and Charles declared themselves so unbiased that they would "fearlessly denounce the shortcomings" of their own party if necessary.[3]

None of the editorials or articles were signed. Evidence indicates, though, that William did much of the writing. The same wit and spicy provocative style is also evident in a later paper he owned.

Under William and Charles the *Weekly Journal* prospered. The brothers succeeded both in increasing its size and in enlarging its circulation. Advertising space was in high demand, and the ledgers showed a sizable profit. Two years into the partnership, however, found William deciding to strike out on his own.

Whether difficulties had developed between the two brothers, or whether William simply deemed it an appropriate time to expand his publishing interests, is not clear. By the time of the break, though, Charles was no longer a Seventh-day Adventist. After buying William out, he reverted to a six-day workweek, opening the office for business on Saturday. The editorial tone of the paper became more subdued. It introduced a serialized detective story and focused more narrowly on politics. Charles stayed on in Biddeford, and shortly after William's departure he founded another daily newspaper that eventually became the town's largest and longest-surviving publication. Over time Charles became quite prominent in Maine's business and political life. He became president of two banks and a railroad company and served as a director for numerous other enterprises. For a number of years he was a member of the state legislature and received appointment to a number of other public offices. In 1904 he ran unsuccessfully for the governorship.[4] Such family ties kept William well informed on Republican Party politics.

April 1882 found William and Sarah moving back to Montpelier in the Green Mountain State, where they had purchased the *Vermont Watchman and State Journal.* Vermont's oldest and most influential Republican newspaper was no small undertaking for a 26-year-old. A leading advocate for the Republican cause, it had retained its reputation as a strict party journal under its previous owners and was widely read, even outside the state. But William was ready for a challenge. Two weekly church newspapers and a well-established publishing company went with the paper. It was one of the largest business enterprises in the state capital.

His predecessor in the editorial chair introduced William to his readers as one who was "in the early prime of manhood, of liberal education and culture, and with the advantages of several years' experience as an educator and journalist." He further identified him as a person governed by thorough Christian principles and convictions and as an outspoken supporter of the temperance cause.[5]

Prescott's "Christian principles" attracted early attention. In a rather revolutionary move for Vermont, Prescott determined to close the publishing office from sunset Friday to sunset Saturday as well as on Sunday. Despite warnings and protests from his employees about financial disaster, he remained adamant and hung a notice of intention in the window during the first week. Though most considered a five-day week at this time economic madness, the business prospered nonetheless. The same Christian principles led William to reject the offer of free passes from railway companies who simply requested favorable mention of their political candidate in return. While his predecessors had followed the practice, Prescott would have none of it. The stand lost him some friends and some business, but such friends he could do without. The enterprise seemed to prosper well enough without them.[6]

Although William also owned two church newspapers, he seems to have had little to do with them. The *New Hampshire Journal* served the Congregationalists in New Hampshire, while the *Vermont Chronicle* had as its readership those in Vermont. Each paper had its own clergyman editor. Prescott's relationship with the editors seems to have been very cordial. His Seventh-day Adventism does not appear to have raised any problems.

William focused his energy on the main paper, the *Watchman*. In his first editorial he declared his intention to continue to make the paper "a true exponent of Republican principles" and a "friend of temperance, education, and all true reforms."[7] He should have been experienced enough now to know that to befriend reform of any sort was to invite controversy and criticism. And he was not to be disappointed.

One of his earliest editorials argued that the quickest way to upgrade the educational system was to improve the caliber of teachers, and that meant licensing only those who were qualified. He boldly asserted that superintendents who failed to do their duty in this matter should be removed. In strident tones he lambasted the Vermont Teachers' Association for the "slumberous character" of its meetings. Some remedy was quickly needed to redeem it from being "a sort of fossilized mutual admiration society." Prescott's public criticism brought a storm of protest from other newspapers. However, one correspondent defended his call for reform: "I believe the influence of your editorial will be felt in the cause of education long after the bitter and vindictive strictures upon your position will be overlooked and forgotten."[8] At least people were reading Prescott.

Other educational issues he discussed in his columns included the need to enlarge the public school curriculum to make room for industrial education, and the value of the summer educational institutes proposed by John Heyl Vincent, the cofounder of the Chautauqua movement. Public school education was "mischievously inadequate," he argued, because it did not make room for industrial education.[9]

His stinging attack on the teachers, however, did not cause him to be ostracized. The city of Montpelier invited him to become a trustee of the school he had formerly headed as principal. He also served as a member of the district education committee.

Labor unions, railway regulations, and civil service election reform were all subjects for Prescott's editorials. But it was his viewpoint on politics that drew the most severe criticisms. His support for an alternative Republican candidate in the elections of 1884 apparently gave rise to party factionalism and branded him as something of a maverick. Prescott's exposure of shady behind-the-scenes plotting at the convention did nothing to help his cause. In the eyes of the party loyalists, at least, he was not a "true exponent" of Republicanism. Other correspondents defended him, alleging that the kind of "party fealty" other newspapers adopted and expected did not represent the principles of true Republicanism anyway.[10]

A year later, with controversy still swirling in Republican circles, Prescott announced on July 8, 1885, that he was selling out. In spite of his explanation that his appointment to the presidency of a denominational college in Michigan was the only reason behind his decision, rival papers quickly pounced on the announcement to make capital for their cause. They alleged that his poor management and his unpopular stands had caused the paper to lose money. The fact that the buyer was his chief journalistic antagonist apparently clouded the question further. Prescott asserted in the next issue that there was "absolutely no ground for such statements." In fact, both the circulation and size of the *Watchman* had increased, and advertising revenues were up. Moreover, he had upgraded the office plant with new equipment and bought out two other smaller papers, incorporating their subscription lists into that of the *Watchman*. Prescott's contention that the prospects of his paper were "never brighter" than at the time he made the contract to sell seems to be accurate.[11]

The departing publisher took pride in his paper's accomplishments in the area of education and social reform. He acknowledged that he had pursued such issues with "a zeal and an enthusiasm that not infrequently have drawn fervor and endurance from the obstacles, natural and artificial, which have sometimes encumbered the way."[12] But in spite of opposition he felt that he had been able to contribute significantly to change. Even in these early years it was clear that Prescott was a natural reformer and shaper of ideas and opinions. The skills he had honed as newspaper editor he later found useful in his vigorous and articulate advocacy of new theological and educational ideas in the denomination now seeking his services.

Criticism alleging disloyalty to the Republican Party seemed to sting Prescott the most. In his last issue he offered an extensive defense of his course. Still lively, assertive, and convinced of the correctness of his position, Prescott nevertheless seemed somewhat chastened and mellowed. Decrying the current form of Republicanism that required "stolid straightness of party alignment" without regard to convictions of fundamental right and wrong, he wrote rather introspectively, "We leave the editorial chair cherishing only feelings of good will for those with whom we have differed or whom we have opposed. Our conduct may at times have been somewhat impetuous, but it has been imbued with a feeling of genuine respect for an open and manly antagonist, as it has quite uniformly been characterized by candor and frankness in the treatment of disingenuous opponents. After the fight we have been ready to shake hands with those whom we have encountered in the lists."[13]

Prescott acknowledged that he had received an important political trust from his predecessor and that the *Watchman* had been a leading voice in shaping the national Republican Party. But he claimed that he had not betrayed that trust. Rather, he had sought to educate readers regarding all sides of political questions. His purpose had been to try to lead public opinion, not follow it. Acknowledging that he had probably been more frank and candid than some other "ardent journals which have been visiting maledictions on our head," he firmly asserted that he had not been "wanting in loyalty to the Republican Party."[14]

Ignoring Prescott's explanations, his successor asserted in his first issue that he would endeavor to give the *Watchman* "stability" in its political character akin to that established by veteran pre-Prescott editors. As far as the new owner was concerned, William was an unfortunate parenthesis.[15] Just three years later, however, a group of local businessmen purchased the paper from its radical right-wing owner and appointed Prescott's former chief editor as manager, apparently vindicating William's more moderate political stance.

His lengthy defense indicates the degree of hostility he had aroused. It also illustrates his sensitivity to criticism—a problem he would have to face with pain and some frequency in later life.

If it was true that Prescott's astute and aggressive management had made the paper prosperous (and the evidence is conclusive), then why did he accept the invitation to become the president of a small, struggling, and financially strapped denominational college in the Midwest? It was not a sudden decision. In fact, for some time prior to the summer of 1884 Prescott had been more and more impressed that God was calling him to take a more active part in church activities. Perhaps the preaching of Ellen White and George Butler at the 1883 Montpelier camp meeting had been the catalyst for his thoughts. At the 1884 Vermont camp meeting at nearby Burlington he took the opportunity to approach Uriah Smith regarding his burden to serve the church. Smith had encouraged him to believe that the Lord would open the way, and the professor later recalled that he had greatly appreciated the editor's kindly expressions of interest and sympathy at this "turning point" in his life.[16] For a year Prescott waited, but nothing happened.

Meanwhile, at Battle Creek, the denomination's first college floundered. Reopened in 1883 after a year's recess because of student discipline problems and a schism between the faculty and the board of trustees, the college was being managed temporarily by W. H. Littlejohn, an elderly blind pastor. Denominational leaders had made unsuccessful attempts to lure former principal Sidney Brownsberger back to the school or to secure Professor W. C. Grainger of Healdsburg as president. According to W. C. White, the trustees were "in a box on the manual labor business" and thought that either of the men from California would help them get started. But neither was willing.[17]

Frustrated by the refusal of the two men, church leaders decided to elect young "Will" Prescott. In early June 1885 they asked him to meet with them to talk over the proposition. He agreed that if his business would sell he would accept the position. In less than a month the sale of the business in Montpelier was wound up, and Prescott notified the trustees that he was coming "to take charge" of the college.

Just approaching the age of 30, Prescott had enjoyed an enriching variety of work experiences. With confident aggressiveness he had taken on important responsibilities and carried them well. He had worked among and learned from the leading citizens of three major New England towns. Prescott's move to Battle Creek, though, was more than simply a transfer from one state to another. It brought him into the limelight of a church organization through which the sphere of his influence would include the whole world.

---

[1] *Biddeford Weekly Journal,* July 23, 1880.

[2] Biddeford *Weekly Journal,* Dec. 30, 1880.

[3] Biddeford *Weekly Journal,* Jan. 6, 1887.

[4] Biddeford *Daily Journal,* Dec. 19, 1923; *Maine: A History, Biographical, Centennial Edition* (New York: American Historical Society, 1919), p. 281.

[5] *Watchman,* Mar. 29, 1882.

[6] "Student Secures W. W. Prescott's Life Story," *SM,* Oct. 27, 1932, p. 3.

[7] *Watchman,* Apr. 5, 1882.

[8] *Watchman,* Aug. 16, 1882; Sept. 20, 1882.

[9] *Watchman,* July 25, 1885.

[10] *Watchman,* Aug. 16, 1882; Sept. 20, 1882.

[11] *Watchman,* July 8, 1885.

[12] *Watchman,* July 22, 1885.

[13] *Ibid.*

[14] *Ibid.*

[15] *Watchman,* July 29, 1885.

[16] *RH,* Sept. 16, 1884, p. 8; WWP, in *RH,* Mar. 10, 1903, p. 7.

[17] CW to SNH, July 3, 1885; BCCBdMin, June 17, 1885; BCCBdMin, July 12, 1885.

CHAPTER IV

COLLEGE PRESIDENT

GIVING UP A PROMISING career in publishing in order to work for the church was not a step Prescott took lightly. His income dropped substantially. At Battle Creek College his $700 annual salary was little more than half of the $1,200 he had earned six years earlier as an unmarried principal fresh out of college. But Prescott had not come to Battle Creek to become rich. Rather, he had a deep spiritual conviction that he should be more directly involved in advancing the Advent cause.

His arrival at church headquarters in late summer of 1885 marked the commencement of a nine-year term as college president and a 52-year career of service to the church. George McCready Price, a student at Battle Creek College at the time, reported that Prescott "presented a handsome appearance." He was a little above medium height, and his carefully groomed chestnut hair, "parted in the middle," matched his dark-red "square-cut" beard.[1] Dressed immaculately with his erect bearing and booming deep-toned voice, he exuded confidence—inspiring awe in both students and staff. His impressive natural gifts combined with his training and experience made him an imposing, almost overpowering, personality.

Local newspapers reported the new note of optimism and confidence on campus. "The college under the efficient management of its new president, Prof. W. W. Prescott, is in a flourishing condition. The professor evidently understands his business, and by his presence and timely remarks . . . gives a new impetus to the college work."[2]

Church leaders and trustees felt they had found their man. At last the college was on stable ground. So relieved were the stockholders at the end of Prescott's first year that they took the unusual step of formally voting their "full confidence" in the young professor and thanking God for the "marked prosperity" experienced under his management. Twelve months later board members were still on a high. Chairman George I. Butler announced in his annual report that while there had been "difficulty in the past in finding a suitable principal," now, under Prescott, the school was definitely in "good standing."[3] Within four years Prescott's reputation for effective management had become a byword. With calculated understatement the General Conference secretary, Dan T. Jones, commented to Butler, "You know what Professor Prescott takes hold of generally comes out about right."[4] Prescott was making his mark. But not without hard work.

Founded in 1874, Battle Creek College had experienced a checkered decade before Prescott's arrival. As already noted, two years previously the institution had closed down for 12 months after open conflict had erupted between staff and students, with one senior staff member being physically assaulted. Conflicting expectations over standards of conduct and confusion about the school's purpose quickly produced a crisis of identity. Was the college supposed to be like the state degree-granting institutions producing public school teachers? Hastily installed President Alexander McLearn, a recently converted former Baptist, had tried to make it so. Students eagerly espoused his permissive approach. Other longtime staff, however, felt it should focus specifically on training people for denominational employment. And so did the board. A year with the classrooms empty allowed the dust to settle, and then the school again made a timid start with a "safe" but lackluster interim president, W. H. Littlejohn. The atmosphere was still heavy with apprehension. Prescott readily endorsed the objectives expressed by the trustees. The primary purpose of the school was to train ministers, teachers, and others for "the cause."[5] For the professor, that meant tighter discipline and a higher, not lower, standard of work. His first challenge was to make the school truly denominational—and what it claimed to be: a college.

Adamantly opposed to schools advertising themselves as something they were not ("inflated," he called them), Prescott set about "remodelling" courses and upgrading standards. It took three years. At first he tried to separate the elementary grades from the "college" and shuffle them off to the care of the local Battle Creek church. The congregation was not interested. Frustrated in that direction, he turned to the top end. He would recruit older students and better-qualified faculty members to teach them. Prescott sought students of "suitable age" and "ability." He ardently believed the denomination needed a "more thoroughly trained" class of employees. Along the way, numerous "animated" discussions about "higher education" and "degrees" spiced board meetings, but by the end of 1889 Prescott was eventually able to persuade his trustees to approve the reintroduction of "the usual degrees."[6]

Buildings, as well as academics, received his attention. At the beginning of his presidency the institution consisted of two buildings: a three-story, 300-desk classroom building and a small hostel. By the end of his nine years in office the classroom building tripled its classroom capacity and the school had built a large four-story residence hall and cafeteria building, a power house, and a manual arts workshop. More than 10 percent of the cost came from Prescott's own generous pocket.[7]

Burgeoning school enrollments necessitated the expansion. As a result of increasing interest in secondary and college education throughout North America, many schools were expanding rapidly.[8] But at Battle Creek College Prescott himself generated much of the increase. Deeply burdened about the need for young people to receive educations and by the desperate need for staffing for a growing church, Prescott embarked on a vigorous recruitment campaign. He made his pitch at Sabbath school institutes, churches throughout New England and the Midwest, and camp meetings.[9] Camp meeting appointments became a regular feature on his summer calendar. His constant theme was that Battle Creek College was different from other schools; the cause urgently needed rightly trained personnel; and (most important of all) Battle Creek College was the place for such education. Robert M. Kilgore reported that Prescott's efforts were "highly prized" and would be "felt all over the state." Others wished that more than just those attending the camp meetings could have heard his "burning words of truth."[10] Prescott himself had become the best advertisement the college had. And if people could not actually hear his talks, at least they read him in the *Review,* which carried many articles from his pen.

Enrollments climbed from 400 to 450, where they hovered through the late 1880s before reaching a peak of about 720 during Prescott's last two years. Including students attending the special General Conference Bible school hosted annually by Battle Creek College, overall attendance in the last three years of his presidency averaged around 850. One year the combined enrollment exceeded 1,000. The increase was remarkable considering that Prescott had also helped establish three other major new schools in different parts of the country during this same period.

The growth did not come without some misunderstandings and differences of opinion. For example, to alleviate the overcrowding at the college in December 1891 (worship rooms, the reception room, and the library were all being used for classes), the trustees approved a second classroom extension. They had plans drawn up, voted funds, and signed contracts. By the end of March 1893 work was well under way. Not long after construction had started on the building, however, both John Harvey Kellogg and Prescott received letters from Ellen G. White (who was in Australia) suggesting that Mount Vernon Sanitarium in Ohio be turned into a school to alleviate the overcrowding instead of putting up the addition. When the college had erected its first residence hall in 1884, she had lamented that it was not a fourth large enough.[11] Now she saw other priorities. But church officers had already decided to convert Mount Vernon into a school, and, apparently feeling that it would not substantially reduce the enrollment problem at Battle Creek, they went ahead with the proposed extension. Keenly sensitive to the lack of church funds in Australia, Ellen White protested strongly in a letter mailed in September. She felt "pained" over the matter. Perplexed, the apologetic Prescott replied, "My mind is greatly exercised by what you write, and I hardly know what my duty is in the matter. . . . I certainly regret that we have used any means in building up the work here, which ought to have gone to other fields."[12] But by September it was too late. The building had been finished. Nevertheless, Prescott had learned something. In future years he would take care to counsel with Ellen White before erecting anything that she might question the need for.

The building program was expensive. Capital investment totaled $49,000. As a result, college debt, which was $19,000 upon his arrival, rose to almost $49,000 by the end of his nine years in office. Some have suggested that "financial discernment" was not one of Prescott's talents.[13] To the contrary, however, it is a tribute to the man's financial astuteness that he accomplished so much development without creating a much larger debt. And in later years Union College specifically invited Prescott as its president to help it out of its financial problems. But as Everett Dick, noted historian of Adventist education, has observed, twentieth-century church administrators came only slowly to the conviction that it was "impossible to support a college on tuition alone."[14] In the 1890s they had not yet learned this lesson. Offsetting the debt by raising the modest tuition charges was impractical. Students could scarcely manage to pay the fees as they were. Yet the denomination expected Prescott to operate entirely from his fee revenue. A modest $3,000 annual subsidy from the General Conference easily would have kept the school in the black.

As business manager the professor kept a close rein on financial matters, but that did not stop him from being sympathetic to students in need. He repeatedly assisted them with fees and clothing from his private resources. Although it was a practice he continued all his life, at Battle Creek it was easier to do. He had voluntarily chosen to live with his students in the newly erected residence building called West Hall.

SCHOOL HOMES

Discipline problems during the early 1880s at Battle Creek College had largely resulted from the lack of residence facilities. Students boarded themselves around the town or in the homes of church members. The construction of a hostel in late 1884 combined with a sustained dose of Prescott's discipline in 1885 obviated much of the problem, but the professor still sensed a lack. The school at least required another larger dormitory. He eventually concluded in mid-1886 that what Battle Creek College needed was a "school home." How better to nurture culture and refinement of manners than to have faculty live in the residence with the students, dine with them, and generally act in loco parentis.

An old English plan recognized for its academic and cultural benefits, the idea was uncommon in America and almost unknown to Adventism apart from a minor attempt to implement the concept at Healdsburg in 1883. Prescott saw the possibility of giving the approach a unique Christian setting. The idea could be utilized even more for its spiritual benefits than for just its academic advantages.

During the construction of the new residence hall, Prescott, his wife, Sadie, and the college matron, Effie Rankin, arranged a visit to various schools in the Northeast that operated student housing. The tour included Holyoke Women's Seminary, Wellesley College, Hampton Institute, and Oberlin College. The trustees studied Prescott's written report together with Ellen White's counsels, and a new plan evolved. It would eventually characterize Adventist institutions around the world as Prescott protéges from Battle Creek took the idea to new schools and colleges.[15]

The chapel and dining room constituted the dual focus of Prescott's new approach. At the dining table the president and his gracious wife modeled refinement and correct manners. The school assigned students to tables at which a male and female host from their own particular group waited on them. Table company changed at monthly intervals. Only the personal permission of President Prescott granted the rare exception. Occasionally he augmented the example of the presidential couple by him reading from his "don't book" on dining room etiquette. The system highly prized punctuality and regularity. Four years after the inauguration of the plan Prescott could boast that the time of the meal had been known only once to vary five minutes from the established program.[16]

Prescott demanded order and quiet in the corridors and expected neatness of dress. Contemporary photographs of the campus reveal carefully kept lawns, and students later recalled bright, attractive flower beds. Prescott's outdoor campus matched the ideals he tried to uphold indoors.

CHAPEL

As president, Prescott did not have time for classroom teaching. Besides the dining room, therefore, the daily 9:30 a.m. chapel period became the chief focus for his new approach to making education at Battle Creek thoroughly Christian. It was not that he undervalued academics, but that he considered the spiritual welfare of his students of first importance. As a pastor-president he stood squarely in the tradition of Thomas Arnold of Rugby.[17]

Whenever he was on campus (in later years he was often away), he took the chapel period. His talk usually centered on the theme of character development, or else he would present an extract from some biography he had just completed reading. A voracious reader and talented speaker, Prescott's chapels were rarely dull. Wallace Newton recalled that some students still tried to use the time for study and earned themselves the professor's stern rebuke.[18] Prescott also used Sabbath afternoon social meetings, Friday vespers, and Thursday evening missionary society meetings to foster the spiritual interests of his charges. Sadie loyally assisted him, occasionally conducting the evening worship services and chatting with students in their rooms.[19]

Prescott attempted to secure the best Bible teachers available. But with a board of trustees that included such traditionalists as Uriah Smith, however, he was not always successful. For example, just prior to the historic Minneapolis conference of 1888 some had sought the young and innovative Alonzo T. Jones as a teacher to assist Smith. The board, under Smith's influence, declined to act on the request. Jones's later aggressive performance at Minneapolis disqualified him even further in the eyes of some trustees. Instead, the board nominated the quite ordinary and "safe" F. D. Starr as Bible teacher. To resolve the issue required an extraordinary joint session of the board and the full General Conference Committee. Jones eventually joined the faculty but not without first being forced, after a long interview with a Smith-dominated subcommittee, to comply with the "creedal" resolution that some of the church leadership had unsuccessfully tried to pass at the General Conference session.[20] The requirement incensed Ellen White. She had vehemently opposed the introduction of any regulation that would forbid teachers from presenting anything other than what the denomination had already taught.[21] Prescott, soon a convert to the new theological emphasis emanating from Minneapolis, found ways to get around the restriction, thus effectively unleashing Jones. Shortly afterward he also arranged for E. J. Waggoner to lecture at the school. But the tensions remained for some time.

Religious revivals were not quite as frequent as the theological stirrings at Battle Creek, but Prescott actively fostered those that did occur. The year 1890 witnessed one such revival. More notable, though, was the great revival of 1892.

In the late 1880s Sunday law agitation by the Protestant National Reform Association alarmed Adventists. They saw Reform leader William Blair's success in having Sunday legislation bills considered in Congress as a direct threat to religious liberty, and it intensified the already heightened eschatological expectations of church members. Many interpreted the events as a sure sign of the end of time, and it gave great urgency to a new emphasis on righteousness by faith that had started at the 1888 General Conference session.

Elaborating on the connection between the two developments, Ellen

White declared in the November 22, 1892, *Review* that the long-hoped-
for time of the "loud cry" had begun. The article had an immediate impact. Five days later, in Prescott's absence, a revival broke out on the
college campus, precipitated by a disciplinary situation involving the president's nephew. Two couples had gone sleigh riding together without
either permission or a chaperon. In an effort to be redemptive, the faculty
had dealt with the miscreants rather leniently. Its response surprised the
student body. The day after the faculty's decision, a letter from Ellen
White arrived and was read to the school during chapel period. Some
phrases seemed to powerfully encapsulate the gospel. The Christian, she
had written, was one "content to receive without deserving." God's eternal love was a "free, everlasting gift."[22] The response, especially in the context of the recent disciplinary action, was electric. The offenders gave
public confessions, producing a profound impression on the student
body. The school canceled classes, and chapel continued for four hours.

For the next two weeks the revival, with its extended prayer and
praise meetings, disrupted the regular program. Prescott did not seem at
all perturbed when he returned on December 15 in time to conduct previously scheduled prayer meetings. At the end of the week, the last day of
the school term, another letter from Ellen White arrived. Prescott presented it at chapel. Breaking into tears as he read, the conscientious
Prescott frankly confessed his past diffidence in responding to the "new
light" of righteousness by faith. Again the student body was stirred.
Chapel continued until 6:00 p.m. with a short break for supper and then
on until 10:15 p.m. During the Christmas leave that followed, the students scattered everywhere, enthusiastically sharing their new experience.

Motivated by a strong sense of the end of time and keenly aware of
the disunity and alienation among church leaders, Prescott spent day
after day during the next two months striving to effect reconciliation
among his colleagues. He achieved commendable success. Some, however, such as *Review* editor Smith, saw the whole movement as nothing
more than an "excitement," but the editor earned Ellen White's rebuke
for his skepticism.[23]

The episode reveals not only Prescott's sense of priorities but also
his spiritual sensitivity. In spite of his concern for academic quality and
integrity, he was prepared to override his faculty and dispense with the

necessary routine of class schedules in order to maintain an openness to the unexpected initiatives of the Holy Spirit. Such openness, however, could also prove to be a liability, as shown in his too-ready acceptance of Anna Phillips' visions and his overenthusiastic, uncritical endorsement of some of Waggoner's strained ideas on sanctification in the 1890s. (We discuss both episodes in more detail in later chapters.) At the same time, however, it enabled him to respond to counsel, acknowledge his error, and take steps to rectify it. Some more stolid types, such as Stephen N. Haskell, would subsequently regard him as an "unsafe" leader. But it was this very characteristic that enabled Prescott to become such a strong and influential voice in a movement still heavily dependent on charismatic leaders.

DISCIPLINARIAN AND SPORTSMAN

If Prescott was flexible and open in spiritual matters, on matters of behavior he was extremely firm. Lack of discipline had brought the college to its knees in 1881. Recognizing this, he realized that diligence in the area must be one of his primary objectives.

Reflecting the Victorian standards of his day, Prescott outlawed courtship and curtailed entertainment. But, like his predecessors, Prescott soon found himself at cross-purposes with parents and the general church membership. In early 1888, exasperated by lack of parental support, he provoked vigorous discussion on the topic with two sermons in the Battle Creek Tabernacle. He did not mince matters. Protesting the criticism of school rules and the indifference to standards he had faced from parents from the beginning, he cited a number of lax practices and complained: "What has become of the good old-fashioned way that we followed in New England?"[24] Raising the issue in public enabled Prescott to obtain a commitment from parents—at least in the short-term.

At first, public rebuke constituted Prescott's usual way of dealing with errant students. Although normally affectionate and gentle, the professor could be severe when stirred. As a result he received repeated, kindly expressed counsels from Ellen White. A deeper understanding of the redemptive aspects of discipline in the post-1888 years also helped to soften his approach.[25]

Another way Prescott coped with the youthful energy of his students was to involve them in sports and gymnastics. Its need became more acute after he had phased out the industrial labor program in 1889 because of economic pressures and lack of student interest.

Not only did he encourage the setting up of gymnastic equipment, but he also personally demonstrated to admiring students skills and techniques he had learned in his Dartmouth days. But not many were enthusiastic about routine calisthenics. Students much preferred the outdoor games permitted on the college lawn between 2:45 p.m. and 3:45 p.m. each day. Such recreation periods quickly developed into highly competitive football and baseball games that, at the time, were also becoming the fad on campuses across the country.[26]

The Sunday afternoon games drew large crowds of spectators to the college grounds, creating both a security and an image problem. In mid-1891 Prescott found himself forced to discontinue them—at least temporarily. But with student interest in them so strong, the college had a hard time enforcing the prohibition. After all, games had been popular even in Prescott's first year when Ellen White's own son, Edson White, had captained a team that competed with those from the local community.[27] But by 1893 football matches between the college and the teams of local industries had commenced again and had become so popular that they were making headlines in the newspapers. A student apparently sent one such headline to his very strict anti-football mother in Napier, New Zealand, just when Ellen White happened to be visiting the home.

Mrs. Caro, a dentist, had, at great expense, sent her two sons and a promising young Maori chieftain to Battle Creek for schooling. The young Maori had struggled to give up rugby football when he first became an Adventist in New Zealand.[28] The game had become a preoccupation of many New Zealanders. For Adventist young people it usually involved Sabbath problems. Dr. Caro was horrified that she should now find such activities approved at the church's headquarters. It mortified her to think that the church's college was "no better" than the New Zealand "public schools" (in the British system, actually private schools), to which she could have sent her boys. Confronted with the situation, Ellen White was highly embarrassed. A stiff testimony found its way to Prescott's office.[29]

In reply, Prescott apologized, explaining that he had already begun to take corrective measures and would certainly do more. "Greatly grieved" that what had happened on his campus had made problems elsewhere, he nevertheless tried delicately to explain to Ellen White that perhaps Mrs. Caro had not received "the best view of matters here." Prescott had already discovered that the Caro boys were not the easiest to help and stated that the older son "blames the college for results which he and we together ought to have cooperated to prevent."[30] Nevertheless, the troublesome football stopped forthwith.

Prescott would have substituted an industrial program for the sports if he had known how to make it work. He had tried for four years to conduct such a project and was firmly committed to the ideal. How to make it instructional and yet financially viable at the same time seemed an insoluble dilemma. Most students were short-term and much more interested in getting their money's worth in the classroom than at the workbench from which most of them had previously come. Parents did not support the concept either.

Although Prescott had visited other institutions to see how their work-study programs functioned, the insights gained, if there were any, did not seem to help Battle Creek. Eventually in 1889, after a student debate on the topic and in the face of continuing losses, the trustees voted to scuttle the idea. In its place the college required all students to work one or two hours each day in domestic labor. It was not a lack of conviction on the part of the president, as some writers have thought. Nor was it apathy on the part of the trustees that lay at the base of the failure of the program. How to make it economical and get students to participate was the hurdle. Not until Prescott's last year did the school again try industrial education.

ADMINISTRATOR

Administration and organization were unquestionably Prescott's strong points. A detail person with an extraordinary capacity for work, it helped him maintain close contact with both staff and students in his early years as president. After 1888, though, church leaders pressed him to take on added responsibilities, such as the office of General Conference education secretary, a duty that often took him away from the campus. As the load grew he found it more necessary to delegate minor details of management to his staff. Hiring a private secretary and bookkeeper also helped (the General Conference apparently shared in carrying the added expense).[31] In his first years as president the school could not afford such luxuries. In addition, he began to lean much more heavily on the standing committees he had instituted to care for academic affairs, discipline, religious activities, and social life.

In 1889, as the college began to expand and as the president became increasingly absent from the campus (between 1890 and 1893 he missed more than a third of his faculty meetings), he appointed a principal to care for the day-to-day routine. But keeping principals or even his better staff for any length of time proved difficult. Critical personnel shortages occurred as Prescott fostered the rapidly expanding network of church colleges. Thus it was not always easy to run a quality program. Prescott was humanly unable to make a success of everything he put his hand to. Likewise, it was difficult to keep up with all the reforms being urged. Yet one of the features of his administration was his emphasis on the enrichment and professional development of his faculty. He encouraged faculty colloquiums and the presentations of serious thought papers at faculty meetings.[32]

Prescott's style of administration was charismatic rather than autocratic. Preferring consultation and consensus to commands and orders enabled him to foster happy and meaningful working relationships with his staff. But in the 1890s, when responding to pressure and clamor for reform in Adventist education, he found himself in difficulty. Then, as we note in a later chapter, he had to resort to calling on the support of his trustees to push through changes in the face of opposition from a recalcitrant faculty. Fortunately, he always seemed to be able to count on his trustees. Though necessary, given the circumstances, it was not an approach that would win him friends. The seeds of alienation that later led to his appointment to a "Siberian exile" in the British mission were probably sown at this time.

In some areas of reform Prescott moved slowly. For example, during the 1891-1892 school year, when the college debated the question of a meatless diet in the college dining room, the school family divided sharply. One faction, encouraged by staff members E. A. Sutherland and P. T. Magan, felt that it was wrong to serve meat. The other argued that the college was already too strict and should not judge in matters of meat and drink. Inclined to think that the move was too extreme, perhaps fanatical, Prescott tried to take a median position and ended up discouraging the reformers. The vegetarians claimed that at least they should have equal opportunity. Surely the college could provide some vegetarian options on the menu. It was finally agreed that the dining room would serve some of the soups without meat. Prescott's resistance may have been more a reaction to the overzealousness of the leading reformer (John H. Kellogg) and the methods adopted (staff member E. A. Sutherland had organized a petition signed by 150 students) than to the idea itself.[33]

Both Prescott and J. H. Kellogg, superintendent of the sanitarium across the street, were gifted, forceful leaders with strong convictions. Both ran large enterprises, and although they shared the same beliefs and ideals, clashes were inevitable as their programs interacted. Storm clouds first appeared on the horizon of their relationship in 1890 over plans for summer school courses. According to General Conference secretary Dan T. Jones, Kellogg got "a pretty correct idea of the professor's feelings," and the result "was something like an irresistible force meeting an immovable substance."[34] Further thunderstorms developed when Prescott, supported by his faculty, complained to the General Conference Committee about Kellogg's poaching of students from the college before they had finished their courses. He complained also about the sanitarium curriculum, alleging that technical medical training was eclipsing the missionary part of the program.[35]

Lack of cooperation was still apparent when, in January 1892, college board member Kellogg once again raised the question of the college diet. He had been listening to complaints from dissatisfied students who had begun boycotting the dining hall. Prescott reacted stiffly to the proposal that an external investigation be conducted into the "bill of fare." (Kellogg was not arguing for elimination of all meat but rather for slow changes that would include dispensing with pickles and vinegar.)[36] The resulting discussion degenerated into a petty argument over what constituted "fried carrots." Prescott asserted that he knew what fried carrots were and that his dining room did not serve them. Kellogg replied that carrots cooked in oil or butter were "fried" and that they appeared regularly on the menu. An oversensitive Prescott reacted sharply to the criticism.

In a written report to General Conference president O. A. Olsen, Kellogg conceded that his own belligerence may not have helped the situation. Unrepentant, however, he declared that it was time something was done and that he was "ready for war" on the issue if necessary. Subsequent discussions failed to effect a compromise, leaving Kellogg complaining that he had been offended by Prescott's and Jones's ungentlemanly "taunts and guffaws."[37]

Two years later Kellogg campaigned again about the meat soups and gravies, sour bread and too much butter, and the once-a-week serving of meat. He acknowledged this time, however, that the problem was not Prescott, who by now seemed to have been converted on the topic.

Reports of the unsatisfactory menu reached Olsen and Ellen White by way of New Zealand's Dr. Caro, providing the occasion for some strong criticism of the college diet. Prescott explained that he had been trying to implement changes for some time by employing cooks specially trained at the sanitarium and personally recommended by Kellogg. Three had proved a failure and left, leaving his wife, Sadie, to fill the gap until the college could find new cooks.[38] Whether she was a "meatless" cook we do not know.

In spite of the friction and, at times, vigorous disagreements, both leaders managed to achieve a reasonable working relationship and continued to consult each other on common concerns. But both administrators were strong-minded and shared a tendency to grossly overwork, thus creating a potential for larger conflict. In this light, the traumatic schism in the church that involved the two men during the early 1900s becomes more understandable.

As already noted, Prescott had an enormous capacity for work. He found it difficult to say no to requests from others. Committee leadership naturally came his way, and during Olsen's long absences overseas, Prescott was frequently assigned, or assumed, added burdens. For example, it often fell to him to follow up many administrative details for the General Conference, such as implementing committee decisions or informing people of committee actions. A type A overachiever, he found it difficult to follow the repeated counsel from Ellen White that he should lighten his workload for the sake of his health. Others urged him to hire assistants to help him, but that was easier said than done, given the budgetary constraints. Highly conscientious, he found it difficult to leave duties unattended.[39]

Although considerably worn, the still energetic 39-year-old professor should have enjoyed a sense of personal satisfaction as he handed over the president's office in 1894 to his successor, George W. Caviness. Battle

Creek College was a much stronger, healthier, and more stable institution than the one he had taken over nine years before. No doubt he felt a sense of relief, frustrated as he had been at the slow pace of educational reform. But he looked forward to hastening the educational process in the church-at-large without the encumbrance of his presidential duties. By mid-1894 the demands of the overall education program of the church had grown so much that church leaders eventually recognized that someone needed to give their full attention to it. Prescott seemed the obvious choice. He had already served part-time in the capacity of general educational secretary for the past six years.

---

[1] George McCready Price, "Memories of Battle Creek." AUHR.

[2] Battle Creek *Daily Journal,* Oct. 24, 1885.

[3] *GC Bulletin,* Nov. 18, 1887.

[4] DTJ to GIB, Nov. 26, 1889.

[5] "SDAES 11th Annual Meeting," *RH,* Dec. 22, 1885, p. 12.

[6] BCCBdMin, Nov. 21, 1889.

[7] According to W. C. White, Ellen White felt sorry to see Prescott rapidly disposing of what he had accumulated by hard labor and urged him to not give such large amounts. By being more frugal he would later be able to help more people with smaller donations. WCW to AGD, Jan. 3, 1911.

[8] H. G. Good and J. D. Teller, *A History of American Education,* 3rd ed. (New York: Macmillan, 1973), pp. 221, 237.

[9] *RH,* Aug. 30, 1887, p. 8; July 5, 1887, p. 11.

[10] *RH,* Aug. 31, 1886, p. 13; July 5, 1887, p. 11; Aug. 30, 1887, p. 8.

[11] "SDAES 10th Annual Meeting, 1884," *SDA Yearbook* (1885), p. 52.

[12] EGW to WWP, Sept. 5, 1893; EGW to JHK, Feb. 19, 1893; WWP to EGW, Mar. 23, 1893.

[13] E. K. Vande Vere, "W. W. Prescott: Administrator," p. 3.

[14] E. D. Dick, *Union,* pp. 89, 97.

[15] *RH,* May 10, 1887, p. 16; Mary E. Lamson, "Evolution of the School Home in the SDA Educational System," pp. 6-8. AUHR.

[16] Ruth Haskell Hayton, in *RH,* Aug. 1, 1929, p. 23; *GC Bulletin,* Oct. 22, 1889.

[17] Arnold Whitridge, *Dr. Arnold of Rugby* (London: Constable and Co., Ltd., 1928), pp. 89-111.

[18] Cited in E. K. Vande Vere, "The Wisdom Seekers," p. 13. MS, AUHR.

[19] Hayton, p. 23.

[20] GCCMin, Apr. 5, 1888; BCCBdMin, Nov. 22, 25, 1888; Nov. 21, 1889.

[21] EGW, "The Discernment of Truth," MS 16, 1889. For a more extensive discussion of this episode, Ellen White's reaction to it and the implications for ministerial training and

inappropriate ways of achieving orthodoxy, see my article "A Slice of History: The Difficulties of Imposing Orthodoxy," *Ministry,* February 2003, pp. 5-9.

[22] EGW to OAO, Oct. 26, 1892. In the absence of both Prescott and Olsen, the president's wife, Mrs. Sarah Prescott, read the letter at chapel.

[23] EGW to US, Nov. 30, 1893.

[24] *RH,* Jan. 17, 1888, p. 1; Jan. 24, 1888, p. 5.

[25] EGW to WWP, Sept. 10, 1888; BCCFacMin, Mar. 19, 1893.

[26] Rebecca Brooks Gruver, *An American History,* 2nd ed. (Reading, Mass.: Addison-Wesley, 1976), p. 654.

[27] Battle Creek *Daily Journal,* Aug. 2, 1886.

[28] Sir Maui Pomare went on to study medicine through Kellogg's medical school in Chicago and became the first Maori to complete a medical degree. Misunderstandings with sponsors and church leaders in Australia occurred, and when he returned to New Zealand in 1901 he was no longer a practicing Adventist. He later became a prominent politician in New Zealand and was knighted by King George V of England for his long services to government. For a fuller study of Pomare's work and his relationship to the church, see Gilbert M. Valentine, "An Alumnus of Distinction: Sir Maui Pomare, K.B.E, C.M.G.," *Adventist Heritage* 11, no. 1 (Spring 1986): 40-45, and "Maui Pomare and the Adventist Connection," in *In and Out of the World,* ed. Peter H. Ballis (Palmerston North, New Zealand: Dunmore Press, 1985).

[29] EGW to WWP, Oct. 2, 1893.

[30] WWP to EGW, Oct. 5, 1893. See also EGW to WWP, Oct. 25 1893; WWP to [College Principals], Aug. 1, 1895.

[31] BCCBdMin, Feb. 8, 1889; Sept. 8, 1889.

[32] BCCFacMin, Sept. 5, 1890; Sept. 28, 1890; Oct. 25, 1891; Dec. 20, 1891.

[33] BCCFacMin, Dec. 1, 1891; Warren S. Ashworth, "Edward Alexander Sutherland: His Life, Work, and Philosophy" (1978). AUHR. Kellogg was urging a totally nonmeat menu in the Battle Creek Sanitarium at the same time. DTJ to RSD, Jan. 5, 1891.

[34] DTJ to LCC, Sept. 23, 1890.

[35] *Ibid.*

[36] JHK to WWP, Jan. 7, 1892; JHK to OAO, Jan. 8, 1892.

[37] JHK to OAO, Jan. 10, 1892.

[38] JHK to OAO, May 6, 1893; WWP to EGW, Oct. 5, 1893; OAO to WWP, Sept. 7, 1893.

[39] EGW to WWP, Oct. 25, 1893; WWP to OAO, July 15, 1894.

CHAPTER V

EDUCATION DIRECTOR
AND PRESIDENT-AT-LARGE

"I WAS ALL WRAPPED UP in raising chickens, and I went to camp meeting with my head full of chickens," reported David Paulson of his experience at the South Dakota camp meeting of 1889. "But when I saw that man [Prescott] walk across the ground," he went on, "he put a hunger in my life for something that I did not have, and I never could get rid of that hunger till I went to school."[1] Paulson later became the founder of the Hinsdale Sanitarium and Hospital in Chicago and frequently related the story of his encounter with Prescott. He was typical of many. In fact, the dignified, educated Prescott engendered the hunger for something better in a whole generation of Adventist youth, and, as a result, the denomination's schools began to burst at the seams.

The growth in Adventist education eventually led to the appointment of a full-time General Conference educational secretary. Prescott thought the denominational leadership had been slow in recognizing the need. As early as 1889 he had become convinced that the position required a full-time person.[2] Carrying both the presidency of Battle Creek College and supervision of the General Conference educational program as a part-time director put him under great pressure. He, therefore, had asked church leaders to release him from the college presidency. But because of the lack of qualified educational personnel and funds the General Conference asked him to continue doing both jobs as best as he could.

The initiative for the creation of a position of secretary for education had come from W. C. White at the General Conference session in 1887. As the church grew, extra responsibilities piled up on the shoulders of General Conference president G. I. Butler. A worried W. C. White took the opportunity before a vote was called on the Nominating Committee's report to argue that the session appoint three additional officials. He believed that the General Conference should set up home missions, foreign missions, and education as separate functions. (White did not yet have in mind the full-fledged departments of later years.) But he had difficulty persuading his fellow delegates to amend the constitution to allow for the new offices. Some felt the church was top-heavy enough already. But Ellen White vigorously supported the move and threatened that she would refuse to vote for Butler's reelection as president unless the denomination provided the extra help. When the Nominating Committee brought back its final report, it included the changes. Prescott's appointment to the education office was one of the last actions of the session.[3]

With eight schools, a total student body of 1,155, and a combined teaching force of around 50, the educational program in 1887 was modest. But as W. C. White pointed out to the delegates, the denomination needed many more schools, and the existing schools as they jealously guarded their own interests prevented the development of new institutions. He had in mind the negative attitude of school officials in Healdsburg who opposed the adding of new schools in the relatively nearby Los Angeles. Sectionalism, White explained, would best be overcome by the appointment of a general supervisor. Such a person would be in a better position to care for the recruitment of teachers and general supervision of the curriculum.

In private correspondence to Prescott (who did not attend the session), White added some things he did not feel brave enough to state on the floor of the conference. For instance, he felt that the ministry had a great need for "better educated workers." Many "lacked judgment" and "discretion" in their work and were unable to meet their more highly educated opponents. Many conferences, White alleged, had an entrenched "indifference" (if not outright "resistance") on the part of presidents and committees toward having their ministers better educated. Such a state of affairs must be overcome, he said.[4]

With these few suggestions from his mentor, Prescott launched into his new duties. He had little else to guide him. The first job description (delightfully vague) required him "to carry out the duties pertaining to the office." He would have to fill in the specifics as he went along. The denomination, though, had taken a significant step in its development.

Events soon initiated Prescott into his new role. The 4-year-old

South Lancaster Academy in Massachusetts had become antagonistic toward Battle Creek College because of the latter's recruitment of students from its "territory." It began to develop a market of its own outside the church. In the opinion of church leaders it was starting to "drift away" from the religious and spiritual purposes for which the church had established it. Prescott visited the school in May 1888 to counsel with key school officials. Board meetings and committees followed. After conducting a series of sermons emphasizing the vital relationship of religion to education in a church school, he reported to *Review* readers that the "drift" had been corrected. Prescott had set himself a pattern for much of his later work.[5]

But the new education secretary did not confine himself to school campuses. His new position also gave him added influence in the church as a whole. In fact, the most effective preaching and counseling of this polished, dynamic advocate of Christian education occurred on the camp meeting circuit. His stirring addresses and personal example captured the hearts of multitudes of youth and inspired them with a vision of Christian service and the need for education. Schools began to multiply.

SHAPING AN EDUCATIONAL POLICY

Prior to 1887 schools started haphazardly with little or no coordination between them. Prescott recognized the need for orderly development, for maintaining acceptable standards, and for unity in the educational program of the church. Five months after his appointment he was ready to make several recommendations to the General Conference Committee. He had framed the beginning of an educational policy. It called for the South Lancaster and Healdsburg schools to drop their "advanced" college courses. Only Battle Creek would offer them. Schools other than Battle Creek should confine themselves, at least initially, to the "grammar grades" (high school). Furthermore, the schools should use the same textbooks and include systematic Bible study in the curricula.

Some, no doubt, thought that Prescott had vested interests in Battle Creek College, and perhaps he did. But his concern for maintaining an "honest" academic standard of work and avoiding uneconomical duplication of programs was above reproach. His policy also sought to make it easier for students to transfer from one institution to another.[6]

Understandably, school boards were reluctant to comply with the new requirement. Prescott had to reiterate the policy repeatedly.

Another feature of his program—that of exchanging faculty among the various schools—had as its primary objective eliminating sectional jealousy and the parochial mentality of local school boards. It soon became obvious that all educational work was to be conducted under the supervision of the General Conference Committee. By mid-1890 Prescott could report to his president, O. A. Olsen, that there seemed to be a "disposition on the part of all those who have to do with local management of our schools to act in harmony with, and place the general supervision of the work in the hands of the educational secretary."[7] One exception was the school in California.

Prescott first visited Healdsburg in May 1890. Board chair W. C. White had hoped that Principal W. C. Grainger might profit from Prescott's suggestions. White also indicated his hopes to fellow board member S. N. Haskell that Prescott would feel "free to speak plainly, criticizing that which is faulty and advising as to how we can make improvement."[8] As it turned out, the educational secretary was too "free" and spoke too "plainly." He did not get much of a hearing as a result. Shocked at the Western permissiveness and lack of culture at Healdsburg, he had asked just what kind of a school it was where "boys ran in and out of the dormitory in their boots" and where "anybody and everybody invaded the privacy of the presidential sanctum at will."[9] Grainger and his staff did not appreciate such questions. Who was to say that the "Yankees'" way of doing things was the only right one?

Upon returning home, Prescott observed to W. C. White that "Californians had a good opinion of their own ability to manage their affairs without special suggestions from outside."[10] He subsequently found excuses not to visit Healdsburg for another four years. Eventually, though, responding to pressure by the General Conference to confront the renegades again in 1894, the formal "Eastern establishment" Prescott finally effected sweeping changes in the administration and brought Healdsburg into line with other schools. According to the new principal, F. W. Howe, the Westerners did not appreciate Prescott's "high and lordly way."[11] Normally sensitive about such criticism, Prescott realized he had to learn to live with it if he was to accomplish his objectives.

The centralization of educational effort proved to be sound policy. It negated sectional interests, gave cohesion to the program as a whole, ensured higher academic standards, and provided a solid base for later developments.

EDUCATING EDUCATORS

One of the first tasks Prescott set for himself as educational secretary was to develop a list of Adventist teachers. He came up with nearly 200 not already employed in Adventist schools. Not too many, however, received job offers. Prescott preferred to employ those already "qualified" in denominational schools. Even they he felt needed further training.

In order to provide it, Prescott early on adopted the strategy of conducting teachers' institutes, finding it a helpful way to develop a greater sense of unity in the school system. His first program was a five-day seminar conducted for 30 participants in the summer of 1888. The themes, typical of Prescott's later emphasis, involved integrating religion into the curriculum and the teaching of Bible. The meeting concluded by recommending that the denomination give increased importance to educating the clergy and by affirming the need for new schools to be established under general denominational supervision rather than by local churches.

Although an enthusiastic Prescott planned to conduct four other institutes, only two actually materialized. Both of the meetings, however, played a highly significant part in the shaping of the educational program of the church. The 1891 convention at Harbor Springs in Michigan was the most important. It involved nearly 100 participants (including teachers and clergy). In the opinion of many contemporaries it marked the "definite beginnings" of a "reformatory movement" in Adventist education.[12] The institute focused on making Adventist curricula more Bible-centered and produced for the very first time a college curriculum specifically designed for ministerial training (after Battle Creek College had been educating ministers for 15 years). The four-year Biblical Studies course for ministers was a major breakthrough for Prescott.[13]

According to delegate F. W. Howe, the 1894 convention grappled once again with the question "How can our educational institutions be made of the most value to the work of the denomination?"[14] Prescott needed no prompting for an answer. Simply make the study of the Bible central to the Adventist school program. He and A. T. Jones then turned words into action by planning a detailed four-year Bible syllabus for college students other than ministers. The adoption of their plan by the convention represented a major accomplishment.[15]

Professional development for the teacher was also a theme that figured prominently at the 1894 convention. As a result, it developed some surprisingly forward-looking (but grandiose for the time) plans for a denominational graduate school. The session nominated Prescott as president, established course requirements for master's degrees and doctorates, and selected a faculty. The scheme, fostered eagerly by Howe, was to have been recommended to the General Conference. However, the idea seems to have embarrassed Prescott, and we have no record that the General Conference ever discussed it. It was an idea born out of time. Not until 60 years later was the church ready for such an ambitious undertaking.

A project that Prescott pushed hard at the 1894 convention was the need for an educational journal. Such a publication, he hoped, would unify the educational program and provide a vehicle for expounding the developing Adventist philosophy of education. As secretary for education, Prescott would naturally be the editor. Later the same year he vigorously promoted the concept in the General Conference Committee, but the inertia was too great. The leadership took no action. At the 1895 General Conference session Prescott again promoted the idea, but jittery conference presidents and partisan Review and Herald stockholders feared that it would compete with the Review. The idea lapsed. Not until 1897 did an educational journal get off the ground. Prescott's enthusiasm never waned, but hands other than his would edit its pages.[16]

SUPERVISING EXPANSION

Without doubt the aggressive promotion of education by the Battle Creek College president gave great impetus to the expansion of the educational program of the church during the 1890s. As General Conference education secretary, Prescott was in a key position to shape that growth. And shape it he did. Both Union College in Nebraska and Walla Walla College in the Pacific Northwest stand as enduring monuments to his foresight and vision as an educational leader.

UNION COLLEGE

It took only a short time in office to convince Prescott that the church's existing policy of "schools in many different localities" was not viable. Chief among the difficulties was the inability of individual conferences to bear the heavy expense, as well as a lack of competent teachers. The establishment of small schools in both Minnesota and Kansas during the late 1880s had stretched the denomination's resources to the limit. Parents in other conferences clamored loudly for schools in their own local areas, but Minnesota and Kansas strenuously objected for fear they would lose some of their support.

In April 1889, while officiating at the closing exercises for the Minnesota school, Prescott broached the idea that it would be more efficient if several conferences combined their efforts to establish and maintain a school. Having learned a little more about diplomacy, he allowed time for the idea to germinate. He waited a month before convening a formal council to consider the proposal. At that historic meeting at Owatonna, Minnesota, church leaders from Minnesota, Iowa, Wisconsin, and the Dakotas agreed to unite. In response, a delighted Prescott immediately headed south to the Kansas camp meeting to persuade church leaders there also to abandon plans for their own local school and join in a union scheme. The local newspaper, the Topeka *Daily Capital,* reported the history-making discussions in great detail.

Kansas leaders first responded to Prescott's suggestion of a combined school by proposing to link up with yet another group of conferences further to the south to inaugurate a second combined school. He had to talk hard and fast to persuade them to pool resources for one central institution for the whole Midwest. Simply "renting a few rooms in a town" to start a school was not the way to go, Prescott argued. Echoing Benjamin Franklin's Poor Richard, he insisted that "a poor school was a poor investment . . . cheap all through." "Religious training should be a prominent feature," and the most effective way to ensure that was by having a "school home" with good faculty. The needs of South Lancaster and Minneapolis had already depleted Battle Creek College of good staff members. "Where else can your help come from if you start [more] schools?" the persistent professor asked. Individuals "'qualified' to teach might be plentiful, but good 'spiritually minded' faculty were rare . . . ; few could be sent out whom he could safely recommend, even from Battle Creek," he asserted.[17]

Ellen White was also at the Kansas camp meeting. Along with A. T. Jones she was fighting vigorously to stem the tide of prejudice, opposition, and disunity that had spilled over at the Minneapolis General Conference session five months previously. Lending her support to the new plan, she recalled the difficulties of Battle Creek College in the early 1880s when a shortage of the right kind of teachers had led to a collapse of standards. To have many smaller schools would make it very difficult for a "moral and religious influence" to prevail in them. The arguments were persuasive. The camp meeting concluded with a consensus stating that Kansas would support the idea of one central Midwestern school for all nine conferences between the Mississippi and the Rockies. Four months later the General Conference appointed a location committee and a board of management for the proposed institution. Prescott served on both. By January 28, 1890, after a monthlong inspection tour of seven possible sites, church leaders signed papers to secure a large property at Lincoln, Nebraska.[18]

Sectional feelings ran higher still for a while after the choice of Nebraska. General Conference president O. A. Olsen counseled Prescott that in a "cautious and prudent way" he should make it clear "from the very beginning" that "the institution was not a Nebraska Conference college" but a General Conference institution. Even politician Prescott, who had coined the name "Union College," had a hard time placating the disappointed conferences. But disillusionments turned into enthusiasm during the next 18 months as "mammoth buildings" rose on the site. Impressed local newspaper editors asserted that the school would be the largest college in the West.

Opened on Thursday, September 25, 1891, this newest vessel in the Adventist fleet of educational institutions was also commanded by Prescott as president, now wearing his third cap. No one seems to have thought the professor to be on an ego trip. The shortage of qualified personnel was genuine. In his opening address, "Christian Education," the new president elaborated on the objectives of the school. To bring students to the knowledge of God as revealed in Jesus Christ, he asserted, was its ultimate raison d'être.[19]

Five days later 70 students began classes. More were on the way. "We are extremely busy," Prescott wrote. No one who knew him was going to doubt it. (Two weeks earlier he had already started Battle Creek College on its way for the year.) Makeshift planks on boxes had to make do for desks and chairs because a railroad accident had smashed the school furniture en route. But such calamities were no excuse for lack of decorum. Californians might not think it important, but Prescott determined to prove that one could still maintain culture and refinement as far from the Eastern states as the Midwest! Even the heavy rains that created a sea of mud during opening week did not deter him. The fastidious Easterner courteously greeted students at the door and reminded them to take off their "rubbers" or to clean their shoes before entering. The "rubber rack" quickly became an institution in its own right.[20]

A funeral for faculty member John Hobbs, who died on what was meant to be the first day of school, resulted in cancellation of classes for that day. Understandably, his death cast a pall upon opening week. The administration had to reassign classes and rearrange class schedules. But the program quickly fell into full stride. Chapels began, and Prescott established that all-important dining-room pattern. Although the professor had J. W. Loughhead, who enjoyed Prescott's full confidence, appointed as principal, he nevertheless stayed on for several weeks to ensure that the enterprise received the right stamp from the outset. Prescott continued as president of the institution for the next two years. He was much more than just a figurehead. Repeatedly he made the 24-hour rail trip from Battle Creek to College View to keep in touch and maintain firm control over affairs. The Prescott mold gave permanent shape to the school. It remains an enduring legacy.

WALLA WALLA COLLEGE

Adventist education in the Pacific Northwest in 1890 confronted similar problems to those faced earlier by the Midwestern conferences. Two small conference schools, apart from having Adventist teachers and a daily chapel, had little else to qualify them as distinctly religious institutions. Intense rivalry polarized the two conferences as well as the schools. Prescott's suggestion about uniting, made during camp meeting that year, met with opposition and stolid inaction. But the people who really mattered did approve the proposal. O. A. Olsen and Ellen White lent their support with pen and voice. As a result, a committee formed to investigate possible sites. Meanwhile, Prescott, troubled by the two schools' continual "striking at each other," made repeated visits to try to reconcile the factions.[21]

Further visits and inspections by Prescott during early 1891 led to a decision by the General Conference in March to build on a 40-acre site at Walla Walla, much to the mortification of the Milton, Oregon, school supporters, who had hoped the new college would come to their site. Again feelings ran high. The local conference president, D. T. Jones, pleaded with Olsen to send Prescott back to the upcoming camp meetings. He is "the man and the only man that will fill the bill at the present time" and who can "turn the tide in favor of our school," he wrote.[22] Pacified by Prescott's diplomatic efforts and encouraged by his account of developments in Nebraska, conference delegates finally voted to accept the General Conference recommendations and merge the two institutions.

During the months that followed, Prescott coordinated the work of architect W. C. Sisley and Review and Herald financier A. R. Henry as they made decisions about campus layout and building designs. Further visits during the next year kept a check on construction progress. Finally, the committee set plans to open the school on December 7, 1892, even though buildings were not fully completed and the heating plant had yet to be installed. Fifty-six students attended the opening ceremonies conducted by Prescott, who now held the office of college president at three institutions. This time his presidency was much more of a figurehead role, partly because of the greater distance of Walla Walla from Battle Creek and, no doubt, partly because of the greater demands on his time by duties closer to home. Principal Edward Sutherland received free rein. He had served a number of years at Battle Creek College, anyway, and knew the Prescott formula well. Even so, he insisted that Prescott be present during the first few weeks of school to ensure a successful beginning. Olsen concurred with the plan, noting that it was more important that Prescott "help shape the policy of the school at its opening than to come in later to try and do it."[23]

An economic downturn during 1893 created a rocky start for Walla Walla. Within a year it had acquired $12,000 in debt. Prescott and Henry had to intervene to keep the college solvent. But the crisis passed, and enrollment soon increased.

Despite the fact that Prescott was able to visit the school only occasionally, the principal kept him informed by frequent correspondence. After two years the professor relinquished the presidency to Sutherland, as he was more than satisfied that the principal was making the school all he would have wished had he been there himself.[24]

FOSTERING THEOLOGICAL EDUCATION

The need to provide adequate training for the ministry of the denomination became the passionate concern of Prescott's later life. None of the contemporary Adventist schools offered anything in the way of systematic theological study. Up until 1888, for example, the only Bible study offerings scheduled at Battle Creek College consisted of a ninth- and tenth-grade class in Old and New Testament history, and a two-term, twice-weekly lecture by Uriah Smith on church doctrines. Attendance was purely voluntary. The college had held a three-week extension of Smith's lectures during previous winters for church employees in the immediate area of Battle Creek, but Prescott did not consider this good enough. The bitter results of the theological confrontation at Minneapolis in 1888 reinforced his convictions.

The feud that erupted between Butler, Smith, and others and Waggoner and Jones began in 1886. By November 1888 it had split the ministry of the church and was fast destroying any fraternal spirit that had existed. Threatened by Waggoner's new interpretation of Galatians 3:24, the old-timers felt he was ruthlessly chipping away a "foundation stone" that had stood the "test of forty years." The strong emphasis of the latter pair on justification by faith sounded like "cheap grace" that would undermine the importance of God's law. According to W. C. White, the "old guard" was obsessed with "a craze for orthodoxy." On the other hand, A. T. Jones's arrogance and cocky attitude did not earn a favorable hearing for his new views. He should not be blamed, he said, simply because he knew more about prophecy than did Smith, who had not done his homework. Prescott became convinced that ministers needed better theological education to broaden their minds. Only a right understanding of the gospel would soften and renew hearts.

In early 1889 he devised a plan that called for a five-month-long Bible school, especially for ministers, to be conducted on the Battle Creek campus but under the auspices of the General Conference, "entirely separate from the college." Enthusiastic about the proposal, the General Conference officers expressed the opinion that the plan would "prove of inestimable value to the cause" and predictably appointed him as the principal, assigning him the task of drawing up the curriculum. Prescott responded by designing a 20-week intensive course of studies modeled on William Rainey Harper's "Chautauqua plan." The program endeavored to avoid the problem of "long courses" that Ellen White had said were not necessary when the church so urgently needed personnel in the field.[25]

The curriculum, akin to Prescott's own Dartmouth studies (minus the classics), featured courses in Christian evidences, church history, Greek, Hebrew, church government, logic, civics, biblical studies, and Bible doctrines. The advertising brochure explained that the courses sought to develop "mental power" and not just to provide facts. The program attracted a surprising 157 ministerial students.[26] Classes commenced on October 31, 1889, with Smith, Prescott, and E. J. Waggoner as instructors. Waggoner was the star attraction.

Prescott's endeavor to have the church commit itself to theological education for its ministry had a number of problems to overcome. Although it established a pattern for the future, the venture began in an atmosphere of highly charged controversy. The appointment of Smith and Waggoner to the teaching staff proved an incendiary mix. Denominational leaders soon found themselves embroiled in bitter conflict over whether they should permit Waggoner to teach his new concepts about the two covenants in class. Prescott and Olsen favored the idea, but Smith and D. T. Jones, the General Conference secretary, violently opposed it. Smith published a provocative disclaimer in the *Review* about any responsibility for Waggoner's new "teaching" appearing in the current Sabbath school lesson quarterly, while Jones handed in a pompous resignation as Sabbath school teacher in the Battle Creek Tabernacle over the issue. His "worrying and fretting" over the matter had hurt him "more than half a year's work," he complained.[27]

Horrified by the extent of the animosity, Ellen White joined a series of early-morning Prescott-sponsored dialogues between the protagonists. The professor hoped that the meetings would help find a way through the theological minefield. Waggoner's opponents eventually became convinced that there was no conspiracy to promote the new views and conceded that wrong attitudes were a greater problem than the particular biblical interpretations involved. A truce enabled classes to conclude on a quieter note.[28]

But the truce would prove short-lived, for despite Prescott's best efforts to maintain peace, the fires of controversy flared again at the school the following year. Having agreed this time to assign Waggoner his teaching area rather than allowing him to choose his own, Prescott decided to conduct the sensitive class on the book of Galatians himself.[29] But if he had assumed that such a move would quench the controversy, he had to think again. What he taught in the Galatians class got reported just as far and wide and analyzed just as closely for heresy as if Waggoner had given the course himself. As a result, the professor came under attack for presenting Waggoner's new position. "Great Scott, has it come to this that such things [as Waggoner's "absurd position"] are to be indoctrinated into the minds of our young people . . . ?" fumed ex-GC president Butler in a letter from Florida to Dan T. Jones.[30] Denominational leaders, however, remained firmly committed to the program and were not prepared to let such objections deter them. The ministerial Bible schools continued until 1896, by which time, under Prescott's prodding, the colleges had adopted a full-scale biblical studies curriculum for theological education into their regular programs.

Prescott left his duties as educational secretary in 1897 when the denomination assigned him as superintendent of the British Field. He could look back on his decade of educational leadership with some satisfaction. It had established strong schools, brought order and harmony to the development of the educational system, and standardized the academic programs throughout the colleges, resulting in both stability and quality. The professor had done much to shape the future of Adventist education. Furthermore, his establishment of the Bible schools and fostering of much more adequate ministerial training courses were of paramount importance for a young church that intended to reach all classes of people with its message. His pioneering efforts to develop syllabi for systematic biblical study classes not only broke new ground but helped shape the theological training of the ministry for years to come. In a significant measure he helped lay the foundations for refocusing the theological understandings undergirding the denomination.

The professor left his office at the General Conference, however, with deep frustrations as well. He was disappointed that he had not accomplished more in curriculum reform in the colleges. Despite vigorous agitation on the issue, the classics still dominated college offerings. Also, he felt frustrated in not having been able to get schools to incorporate vocational training in their curriculum, and he believed that much more needed to be done to integrate religion and education. Although he had long advocated changes in these areas, he had seemed unable to accomplish anything substantial.

One of the obvious reasons was that teachers resisted change. But there was another problem, something more fundamental, something arising from his own personality: his choice of unpopular issues and his style in agitating them. Sometimes he created the impression of an extremist by overstating his case and by keeping up agitation after he had made his point, such as in the discussion on the role of the Bible as a textbook during the late 1890s. In advocating reform he appeared to be swinging the pendulum too far in the direction of change. It cost him the support of many denominational teachers and detracted from his effectiveness as an educational leader. Ironically, when Prescott moved off the scene, the task of continuing educational reform fell to the younger and even more radical E. A. Sutherland.

During the decade of his educational leadership at the General Conference much more than just education had occupied Prescott's time. The professor was a man of many talents and interests and had made a substantial contribution to the church in other areas. We will examine them in the following chapter.

---

[1] See *RH,* Nov. 16, 1916, p. 16.

[2] GCCMin, Mar. 25, 1889.

[3] *GC Bulletin,* Nov. 28, 1887, p. 4; Oct. 23, 1889.

[4] WCW to WWP, Feb. 8, 1888.

[5] *RH,* May 22, 1888, p. 9; Feb. 12, 1889, pp. 12, 13.

[6] GCCMin, Apr. 5, 1888; Mar. 25, 1889.

[7] WWP to OAO, June 30, 1890.

[8] WCW to WCG, May 16, 1890; WCW to JNL, Apr. 16, 1890.

[9] Walter C. Utt, *A Mountain, A Pick Axe, A College: A History of Pacific Union College* (Angwin, Calif.: Alumni Association, Pacific Union College, 1968), p. 26.

[10] WWP to WCW, Aug. 10, 1893.

[11] FWH to OAO, Oct 25, 1896.

[12] *RH,* Aug. 6, 1901, p. 10.

[13] *GC Bulletin,* Feb. 23, 1893, p. 350.

[14] "FWH, "Proceedings of the Third Teacher's Institute . . .," July 22-Aug. 6, 1894, pp. 17, 18.

[15] *GC Bulletin,* Feb. 23, 1893, p. 350.

[16] GCCMin, Oct. 17, 1894; *GC Bulletin,* Feb. 20, 1895, p. 249; Feb. 26, 1895, p. 358; Feb. 27, 1895, p. 371.

[17] Topeka *Daily Capital,* May 26, 28, 1889. OAO to WWP, Jan. 31, 1890.

[18] *Nebraska State Journal,* Jan. 30, 1890, p. 4; Feb. 7, 1890, p. 6; Lincoln *Call,* Feb. 7, 1890, p. 4.

[19] DTJ to OAO, Sept 19, 1890.

[20] WWP to OAO, Sept. 29, 1891; *RH,* Oct. 6, 1891, p. 614.

[21] OAO to WWP, Sept. 19, 1890; WWP to OAO, Sept. 25, 1890; DTJ to RAU, Jan. 5, 1891. See also *Sixty Years of Progress: The Anniversary History of Walla Walla College* (College Place, Wash.: Walla Walla College Press, 1952), p. 83.

[22] DTJ to OAO, Apr. 16, 1891.

[23] OAO to WWP, Nov. 2, 1892.

[24] *GC Bulletin,* Feb. 23, 1893, p. 353.

[25] *GC Bulletin,* Oct. 21, 1889, p. 30.

[26] "Announcement for 1889-1890 Bible School for Ministers," p. 8, AUHR.

[27] *RH,* Jan. 28, 1890, p. 16; DTJ to GIB, Feb. 13, 1890.

[28] DTJ to RMK, Mar. 16, 1890; DTJ to CHC, May 7, 1890; EGW MS 22, 1889.

[29] DTJ to RCP, Oct. 23, 1890.

[30] GIB to DTJ, Feb. 16, 1891.

CHAPTER VI

MORE THAN A PRESIDENT

GEORGE BUTLER BELIEVED that he could recognize a leader when he saw one. Had not his grandfather once been governor of Vermont? And had not he himself been General Conference president for nine years? Surely that was qualification enough to make him a reliable judge. So he did not doubt the leadership qualities he saw in the young ex-publisher whom he called to Battle Creek in 1885. Prescott was destined to be more than just a school president. Of that Butler was sure. Prescott could "fill a very useful position in different branches of the work,"[1] he reported to readers of the *Review*.

Church members did not have to wait long to find out what Butler had foreseen. In a remarkably short time the charismatic professor became involved in major church leadership positions well beyond his college campus. It was an astonishingly rapid rise to prominence for one so "young"—a tribute as much to the perspicacity of Butler and other church leaders as to Prescott's own talents or forceful personality. In this chapter we will see how Prescott's other activities provide important insights into the man's spiritual dimensions.

As already mentioned, in 1887, at age 32, Prescott had been appointed to the newly created office of General Conference education secretary. The following year the General Conference session asked him to serve on the influential book committee, and at the same session he fell just one vote short of being elected to the General Conference Executive Committee.[2] Three years later the church elected him to the prestigious five-man General Conference Committee. All this was in addition to his duties as president of two (soon to be three) colleges and as principal of the Minister's Bible School. Each General Conference session during the 1890s added more responsibility to his shoulders until in 1894, his last year as Battle Creek College president, he carried 10 other official positions.

The conscientious Prescott was not one just to occupy an office. For example, in 1892 he attended more than 20 meetings of the book committee besides the large amount of scholarly labor required outside of committee to read and evaluate manuscripts for publication. In addition, the committee made him chair of the subcommittee on doctrinal works—an appointment that probably helped in his early recognition by the church as an authority in such matters. Surviving book committee records include numerous lengthy manuscript evaluations. They reveal a probing mind, thorough and systematic and at times hypercritical. Prescott was particularly sensitive about weak arguments used by denominational writers in their doctrinal polemics. His passion for accuracy in citing authorities served as a helpful check in preserving the church's credibility and reputation on more than one occasion.[3] Fortuitously, his role on the book committee also enabled him to be a discrete advocate for the new (and suspect) ideas of Jones and Waggoner. He also undertook the writing of tracts himself, some of which became so popular as to achieve a circulation of almost a quarter of a million.[4]

If Prescott thought his book committee responsibilities demanded much time, he found that his membership on the church's highest executive committee required even more. During General Conference president O. A. Olsen's lengthy overseas travels the committee conscripted Prescott to serve as its interim chair. Olsen clearly valued Prescott's able judgment and depended on it. "The positions you have taken in regard to various matters are very satisfactory to me," he wrote in 1894. On another occasion Olsen urged Prescott to travel all the way to the West Coast to meet him on his return from an overseas journey. They would spend the three-day journey back to Battle Creek consulting together about church affairs. Many times the professor found himself with the extra burden of being the only committee member present in Battle Creek. It required lengthy correspondence to keep Olsen informed about happenings at headquarters. "I miss Elder Olsen very much, and his absence makes work much heavier," he complained to Ellen White in 1893. "We are often weighed down by the care and perplexities connected with the work."[5]

Prescott's drive and decisiveness evidently kept many committees moving. His clear, analytical thinking proved helpful in summarizing discussions and clarifying alternatives. Committee records reveal that more often than not Prescott was the one to initiate the actual framing of a resolution or to move the adoption of a motion.[6] Nor did he like the tendency to fritter away time on "matters of ordinary detail." Major policy issues "underlying the work," he argued, should be the committee's major concern.[7] His compulsion to keep things moving and not waste time often led him to take on more subcommittee assignments than he could afford to. But who could be more efficient at getting things done than himself? Planning a World Fair display or a convention for denominational booksellers, outfitting the mission ship *Pitcairn,* organizing a new conference, or investigating an embezzler—all crowded themselves into his schedule.

Why did Prescott allow himself to become so preoccupied with off-campus duties? For one thing, the denomination had few qualified leaders and Prescott was willing and able to take on the many responsibilities. For another, and no doubt more important, being on the executive committee and involved prominently with church activities allowed him more influence in fostering the interests of education so close to his heart. The extensive administrative and pastoral capabilities he demonstrated during this period led to his being considered as a logical choice for General Conference president to follow O. A. Olsen in 1897.[8]

PASTORING AND PREACHING

The congregation at Battle Creek, accustomed to Uriah Smith's dry and labored sermons, did not take long to develop an appreciation for the dynamism of William Prescott's preaching. The professor's ability in the pulpit was extraordinary. Almost without exception congregations found themselves profoundly impressed with his richly resonant eloquence. If General Conference secretary D. T. Jones read the popular sentiment aright, Prescott was the best speaker the church had. In 1887 his Tabernacle preaching led to the inauguration of a new column in the *Review* entitled "The Tabernacle Pulpit." It sought to give its readers the benefit of the denomination's "most able speakers."[9] The *Review* made frequent favorable reports on his preaching, and the denomination transcribed and published many of his sermons as tracts.

At the 1889 General Conference session delegates formally moved to recognize Prescott's pastoral and preaching gifts by voting to ordain him to the ministry. But Prescott was surprisingly reluctant. When the licenses and credentials committee first brought its recommendation to the session, Prescott himself referred his name back. Apparently he felt personally unworthy for what he saw as a high and holy office. He considered his primary duties to be educational and administrative rather than pastoral. A month of prayerful reflection (which included a personal interview with Ellen White in which she counseled him to follow the dictates of his own conscience) eventually led him to change his mind. Subsequently on November 9 he was "set apart" at a special service in the Tabernacle.[10]

Whether Prescott's ordination to the gospel ministry heightened his pastoral concern or whether the peculiar circumstances prevailing at the end of 1889 increased it is not clear. What is obvious, though, is that his pastoral labors during this period contributed in a major way to the moderating of the highly charged atmosphere at church headquarters. That was important, since tensions and ill-feeling following the debates at the Minneapolis meeting still remained unresolved.

Apart from presenting his educational report, Prescott had not participated in the divisive discussions at the stormy Minneapolis meeting. It was the first session he attended as an official delegate. According to W. C. White, Alonzo Jones's provocative and "uncouth" style of speaking had bothered him, but on the questions in dispute he tried to maintain a neutral stance. His natural loyalties lay with Butler and Smith, to whom in many respects he felt he owed his position. Thus he found himself uncomfortably awash in the turbulent wake that followed the session.

On the first Sabbath morning following the Minneapolis conference, Prescott, along with two other Tabernacle elders, under Smith's prejudiced direction, visited Ellen White. They planned to caution her about what she should say in her sermon that morning from the pulpit. But were they acting advisedly? Was she not indisputably the "mouthpiece of the Lord"? Would she tolerate such interference with the Spirit's leading? Their visit greatly disturbed her.

As an elder, Prescott was also (however willing or unwilling) a party to the ploy to prevent Jones himself from preaching in Battle Creek after the conference. Such "bigotry" "greatly stirred" the ire of Ellen White. It reminded her of the similar treatment meted out to her own family in

Portland, Maine, during the 1844 movement. Despairingly she noted in her diary the possibility of real schism. Given such attitudes, she fretted, perhaps it might be necessary for another denomination to emerge.[11]

But Prescott was not hardened in his attitudes. Rather, he seems to have felt torn in three directions: a sense of loyalty to his seniors, a revulsion to Jones's unrefined manner, and the appeal of the new ideas. During the annual Week of Prayer, 13 months later, he rose to give a testimony but was overcome with conviction and emotion. According to Ellen White, who was conducting the meeting, he stood, weeping and unable to speak, for five minutes, finally concluding with an acknowledgment that he was glad he was a Christian. During the post-Minneapolis years William and Sarah repeatedly visited with Ellen White. Such times of "precious talk" reassured her of the couple's genuine spirituality. "Professor Prescott and his wife are glad in the Lord," she commented in her diary. The new Christological emphasis that, for Prescott, constituted the essence of the "Minneapolis Message" appealed to him more and more. A year later Ellen White again played host to the Prescotts, who came to seek counsel and exchange views on education and the spiritual welfare of their students.[12]

By mid-1890 there was still no sign of any letup in the hostilities over the new theological interpretations. Prescott, who had managed to pour oil on troubled waters earlier in the year during the Minister's Bible School through a series of early-morning meetings, felt that further dialogue might develop the needed friendship and harmony. Accordingly, he planned for a consultation for the "leading teachers of theology" at the Chautauqua center in New York. Church leaders enthusiastically gave the plan their blessing. Keen for Prescott to succeed, W. C. White wrote to Ellet Waggoner and his employer C. H. Jones, encouraging them and suggesting that "the trouble of the past two years would never have been" if such meetings had occurred previously. Worried at the "terrible loss" if Prescott's planning for the conference fell through, and urging the reluctant Waggoner to attend, W. C. White explained, "I presume you both know, that Professor Prescott has been a peacemaker from the start . . . and is intensely anxious to see the breach between the leading teachers and writers healed. Whenever he has been with us in book [committee] where controverted points were up, he has been able to help much by laboring for an understanding."[13]

Eventually only 18 scholars participated in the meeting. The turnout disappointed Prescott. Hostilities were so deep that the chief protagonists, Waggoner and Smith, stubbornly refused the invitation and found excuses for not participating.[14]

By year-end a powerful testimony came from Ellen White regarding the continuing rift. Because it arrived too late in Battle Creek to be included in the last regular *Review* for the year, the magazine published it as an *Extra*. Prescott, who could be considered a nineteenth-century equivalent of a public-address system because of his vocal powers, was asked to read it in the Tabernacle. Rebuking those who "cast contempt" on the "Minneapolis Message" and thought it "dangerous," the *Extra* declared that the theme of Christ's righteousness was so vital it should "swallow up" all other subjects.[15]

Feeling increasingly guilty even as he read, Prescott had difficulty continuing and paused often to weep. (In spite of his personal efforts at conciliation he saw himself rebuked in the testimony.) At the conclusion he confessed to the crowded church that at the Minneapolis meeting his feelings had not been right. He asked forgiveness of Jones and Waggoner. According to Ellen White's report, the effect was profound. Going down into the congregation, he took the arm of the elderly Uriah Smith, and both proceeded to the rostrum together. But still Smith dragged his feet. Why should it be only he who needed to change his attitude? Prescott made one more pastoral call the following week. Smith continued to hedge.[16]

What troubled the obstinate Smith was not the specific theology of Jones and Waggoner so much as Ellen White's role in supporting it. The venerable editor had understood her to have condemned Waggoner's position on the basis of a vision back in 1856 when Waggoner's father had advocated the same idea—i.e., that the law referred to in Galatians 3:24 was the Decalogue. It perplexed Smith that Ellen White could now apparently do an about-face and endorse what she formerly opposed. He was sure that there had to be a conspiracy afoot.[17]

For her part, Ellen White could not remember the particulars of the 1856 testimony, nor could she find a copy of it. She insisted that the church should judge Waggoner's new view on its own merit. In agony of spirit over Smith's stubbornness, her erstwhile ally and friend, Ellen White sent what she intended to be a final letter of appeal for him to change his negative attitude to her and her fellow workers. At last he relented, confessed his wrong attitude, and apologized to Ellen White. Rejoicing, she declared that Smith had finally "fallen on the Rock" and been "broken."[18] But his response had its qualifications.

The editor's confession related strictly to his attitude to Ellen White, not to the theological issue. Just a year before his death he stated that he had never altered his view on the law in Galatians. He continued to oppose Waggoner's interpretation and the emphasis that went with it. Smith's attitudes generally were slow in changing. Thus, despite his public confession, deep-rooted alienation continued into 1891, and on more than one occasion Prescott found himself engaged in a kind of shuttle diplomacy between the two camps.[19]

By the end of 1892, when a revival swept the college campus in Battle Creek, resulting in the baptism of 30, suspicion and opposition still poisoned the atmosphere. Smith labeled the revival a mere "excitement," his quoted remarks effectively chilling the movement, much to the distress of the spiritually sensitive and now-exasperated Prescott. The professor reported to Olsen, who at the time was visiting Australia, that he had awakened at an unusual hour one Saturday night not long afterward with his mind "deeply exercised." He saw "in a very clear way" that something needed to be done "at once" to try finally to clear up the whole messy business.

The following afternoon, in the company of A. T. Jones, he visited W. H. Littlejohn, Battle Creek church pastor, and Uriah Smith, who still served as senior elder of the congregation. They arranged a series of meetings with about 20 prominent leaders. In them Prescott unburdened himself with "very plain talk" about the "estrangement" that existed between the leaders, "the lack of cooperation between the institutions," and "the need for earnestly seeking God."[20]

His shock tactics seemed to work. He held "plain talk" sessions with many, including Kellogg. Both men discussed "in the plainest way" the "whole ground" covered since the Minneapolis meeting. More pastoral visits ensued until Prescott had spent the better part of a month at it and was exhausted. He complained to Olsen that he had not had regular sleep in a long time, but he detected at last that there was a "new spirit" in church affairs and "a drawing nearer together" among the leadership. Prescott hoped that the new attitude manifested by editor Smith would at least result in a change in the tone of the *Review*. "I believe that Brother Smith will have a new spirit in the work," he wrote to Olsen.[21] Six weeks later, warmer relations between Jones and Smith and Kellogg and Prescott permitted another attempt at "consultation" on the semantics of "righteousness by faith" and "faith and works." The meeting led to a consensus that there was really no basis for disagreement. But the resolution agreed upon seems to have come more from an overwhelming desire for unity than from any clearer theological understanding.[22] O. A. Olsen, looking back a few years later, felt that the period was "remarkable" because the "opposition to righteousness by faith gave away" and church members and the ministry "generally fell in with that truth."[23]

In reality, though, opposition to the themes sounded at Minneapolis continued for decades afterward. For instance, A. G. Daniells reported in 1902 that he was encountering opposition on the issue of righteousness by faith, and that young ministers in Midwestern conferences faced attacks when they preached on it. As late as 1908 R. A. Underwood was still attempting to publish leaflets urging a return to pre-1888 interpretations.[24]

Prescott's hope that Smith's new spirit would manifest itself in a more lively *Review* was an empty one. From the professor's perspective, too much "dead matter" cluttered the pages, and the magazine was "losing its hold on people." Readers shared his attitude, he charged, citing criticism voiced in the field. The figures spoke for themselves. In spite of increasing church membership, *Review* circulation not only was declining; it was being overtaken by the *Home Missionary,* a more lively alternative church journal.[25]

By October 1893, even though chairman Olsen was absent (Smith also "happened" to be out of town), Prescott was concerned enough to call a joint meeting of the General Conference Committee and the Review and Herald board to discuss the wilting paper and its lifeless editor. Review officials at first were piqued that Prescott should interfere in Smith's business, but the one-time journalist and editor so pressed his point that they reluctantly conceded that something did need to be done. He was vindicated a few days later when, at the last minute and at considerable expense, the publishing house had to retrieve an issue of the *Youth's Instructor* from post office mailbags being loaded at the railway station because it had included an offensive article. Smith had authorized the piece.

Unfortunately, nothing decisive came from the meeting. Although publishing house officials affirmed Prescott's concerns, they felt it would be impolitic to effect any radical changes at that time. Meanwhile, Prescott continued to encourage the *Review* to present more about the "living issues" of the new Christological emphasis. The paper remained indifferent.

EVANGELIST

During the 1890s Prescott let no opportunity slip to preach on the theme of the righteousness of Christ. Whenever it was announced he would have the pulpit, people crowded the Tabernacle. As a featured speaker he also delivered lengthy series at the General Conference sessions of 1891, 1893, and 1895. The college even adjusted its schedule to enable students to hear their president at the GC sessions.

Although already overcommitted in late 1892, Prescott felt burdened to conduct an evangelistic series for the citizens of Battle Creek. A powerful sense of the imminence of the Advent motivated him to go beyond the call of duty. According to W. A. Spicer, foreign mission secretary, the concept of public outreach in the headquarters town was "new territory" for the institution-oriented Battle Creek congregation. Prescott secured the use of a centrally located independent Congregational church for three months. Here the college president would hold the meetings and more besides. How the musical Prescott found time to organize and lead a choir is a marvel, but he did. The local press gave the meetings highly favorable coverage.[26]

Ever the educator, Prescott hoped that the series would serve as a model for others, particularly the fresh "gospel-centered" approach he adopted in presenting the doctrines. He had done a lot of thinking since Minneapolis. The public responded warmly. According to Spicer, one prominent citizen commented that "they had heard more gospel here" than they had "for many years."[27] Transferred later to the larger and more neutral Opera House, the meetings continued to attract the public. The local clergy decided that this would not do, so they urged their members to stay away from Prescott and called in a well-known temperance evangelist by the name of Tracy as a counterattraction. Not interested in engaging in argument with the visitor, Prescott, with his usual magnanimity, visited the evangelist and even assisted him at his meetings with his "West-End singers." Disillusioned with the local clergy and with his small audiences, Tracy stayed only a short time. Prescott kept preaching.[28]

But not all the professor's endeavors were as successful as his evange-listic campaign and his encounter with Tracy. A few months later his judgment—usually so valued by Olsen—let him down badly.

THE PITFALLS OF ZEALOUSNESS

During this period the professor knew he was overworking. Although not one to talk about his ailments, he did, nevertheless, speak a number of times to his colleagues of excessive weariness. More than once Ellen White cautioned him not to overdo things by taking on more responsi-bility than he could successfully carry, advice that Prescott found difficult to follow. Olsen also urged him to employ one or two men "whom you can rely on" to lighten the load. But for whatever reason, whether lack of a budget, lack of satisfactory personnel, or Prescott's own unwillingness to delegate, he continued to push himself. Partly as a result of this and partly as a result of what might be termed his hyperspirituality, he made two blunders in quick succession. Both incidents illustrate a weakness in Prescott's personality. They certainly tarnished his reputation as a leader.

In late 1893 Ellen White wrote a series of strongly worded warnings to church leaders about "crowding" too many "interests" together at Battle Creek. On October 14 A. T. Jones discussed them in his Tabernacle ser-mon and urged church members to spread out to other locations. In a later personal letter to Prescott, Ellen White warned that if people did not move, God would send a "scourge" to drive them out.[29] Prescott knew what a "scourge" was. When he was a teenager, three of his brothers had died within a few days of each other as the result of one. In the context of the Sunday law agitation and the intense atmosphere of revival, the warning carried strong eschatological overtones. In the light of Ellen White's much-heralded statement of just a few months earlier that the end-time "loud cry" had already commenced, the effect of the warning would be dramatic.

Prescott and A. T. Jones, taking Ellen White literally, organized a group of believers willing to leave almost immediately. More than 100 re-sponded. The men held meetings to train the would-be missionaries. In a masterstroke of semantic subtlety, Prescott reported to Olsen, "our pur-pose is to keep up this agitation, . . . we are not trying to drive anyone but are presenting before them their privilege."[30] The new General Conference secretary, L. T. Nicola, supported the development. "There are a great many people here who could make as good living some other place, and who might at the same time do more good," he wrote to his predecessor.[31] For A. T. Jones, preaching that the "selling time" (when believers should dispose of their possessions) had arrived was no mere lip service. He sold his own property.

Alerted in Australia to what was happening, Ellen White became alarmed at the prospect of a stampede and wrote hastily to warn them against any rash moves. After all, one needed to consider the financial setback to the church and its members if real estate values collapsed. Would-be missionaries also needed to make sure that good business prospects existed at their intended new locations. Ellen White was aware that on occasion she could state things too strongly, but, on the other hand, she also lamented that people such as Prescott and Jones tended at times to "hear things with such a strong spirit." Lack of judgment in practical matters, she warned them, was a "weakness" in their leadership. She advised them strongly to proceed with caution. Read to the leadership of the Battle Creek church in late January 1894, her caution eased the "pressure" and helped to mitigate the excess of the "exodus movement."[32] Chastened, Prescott retired to lick his wounds.

But yet another trap awaited the professor. During this period of what some have labeled as the "loud-cry" movement, Prescott publicly endorsed the so-called testimonies of Anna Phillips (sometimes called Anna Rice). It was a humiliating mistake.

During the latter part of 1892 and in 1893 Anna Phillips, a woman in her late 20s, experienced what she thought were genuine visions. On the basis of them, she sent letters of spiritual counsel both to individuals and to the church as a whole. With uncritical spontaneity, Prescott quoted the letters in his Tabernacle sermons and urged that church members could "hear the voice" of God in them for themselves. Many in the denomination, including the leadership, regarded the letters as a further fulfillment of the promise of Joel 2 that the Holy Spirit would more widely bestow the gift of prophecy on the church. J. H. Durland, Bible teacher at the college, began making copies of the letters available to his students, and soon the Phillips writings circulated throughout the church. But no one, apparently, had thought to consult with Ellen White about the new "prophet."

In faraway Australia, where she was struggling to help establish the denomination, Ellen White grew alarmed as news reached her of the new excitement being fanned by Prescott and Jones. She became more troubled when a Melbourne newspaper published an embarrassing report from a New York correspondent about a stupendous offering—including such things as furs, jewelry, and real estate—that people had given in a revival meeting at the Battle Creek Tabernacle. The total amount was $21,347.[33] Prescott himself donated $5,000, which, according to one General Conference officer, was all he had in the world. According to the newspaper reports, Adventists had linked Ellen White's writings with those of the new prophet, Anna Phillips, and it had helped spark the "enthusiasm." The whole tenor of the articles indicated that the religious fervor in Battle Creek had begun to border on the extreme. But the excitement stopped abruptly in mid-February 1894. Jones had received a letter from Ellen White telling him plainly that he had been wrong in supporting Miss Phillips.

Prescott was at Walla Walla College when someone rushed a copy of the letter to him. He had firmly intended, even in the face of opposition from S. N. Haskell, to read some of Miss Phillips' letters to the student body (Haskell did not dispute the validity of Miss Phillips' experience, but questioned the public use being made of the "visions").[34]

The word from Ellen White, however, quickly settled the matter for Prescott. Revising his plans, he commented to Haskell, "Now I will take some of the same medicine that I have given to other people."[35] It was a bitter elixir. Other church leaders also felt bad about the error and sympathized with the professor. F. M. Wilcox, for example, acknowledged that had he been "in the same position," he probably would have made "just as great a mistake." He appreciated the careful way Prescott endeavored to redress the damage by trying to stop the circulation of the Phillips letters while at the same time taking pains not to make matters worse.[36]

Prescott's suffering was intense. The fact that some of his colleagues, such as E. W. Farnsworth and J. H. Durland, were just as mistaken was small consolation. Olsen found the professor feeling like a "whipped dog" and "greatly discouraged" when the General Conference president returned from Australia shortly after the affair. It disturbed him, knowing as he did that the anti-Jones faction quietly gloated over the turn of events and that Smith had expressed himself as being glad that Ellen White had given Prescott and Jones a good "whack on the snout." Olsen feared that the two might never regain the confidence of denominational leadership.[37]

He need not have worried. Time would heal the wound. Three months later Olsen could report to Ellen White that the matter was "not so serious" as he "feared it might be." But the situation had developed in the church, he reflected, because too many had placed Prescott and Jones on a pedestal. If they just uttered a word, "that was the end of all disputes." It is a "terrible thing . . . when a man gets into the place where people look to him and not to God." But Olsen was sure of both Jones's and Prescott's integrity. They had the best of intentions.[38]

Prescott's and Jones's ready public acknowledgment of their failing helped to restore the confidence of denominational leadership in them. Ellen White herself also helped facilitate the healing process. In a June 1894 letter to Haskell also circulated to other church officials (Haskell had been rather harsh in his judgment of the two men) she recognized that the two leaders had been too ardent and had carried things "in too strong a manner."[39] Nevertheless, the church needed such "ardent elements" because it was indeed involved in "an aggressive work." She had more confidence in the men after the experience than before and regarded them with the most "tender feelings." Rebuking those who would triumph over their mistake, she added that she was glad the trial had come to "men who truly loved and feared God" and not to those who had been the opposition at Minneapolis.[40]

As time continued its healing work, the incident faded into the background, although the scars remained. In later years and in future conflicts, Prescott's foes in the church would continue to use the mistake as ammunition to destroy his credibility and reputation.

How Sarah coped with these crises and the continual activity generated by her husband's extensive activities is not known. Prescott rarely talked of his wife in his correspondence. He had precious little time for his family, which had expanded with the addition of a baby son, Lewis, in October 1891. Residing in West Hall with the students must have been like living in a goldfish bowl and meant that they were constantly on duty. The annual summer visit to his parents' home in North Berwick, Maine, no doubt provided some relaxation and a chance to recuperate in the cool summer weather of New England. But even that time he usually spent writing articles for church publications or in catching up on editorial work on Ellen White's education manuscripts or other projects for the book committee. Attempts to lighten his workload remained unsuccessful. Olsen, however, could empathize with Prescott. "I know what a desire you and I have to make reforms in the way of our working. But the difficulty in carrying it out is greater than anyone can appreciate."[41]

Overwork was a problem the professor faced repeatedly. Strain and pressure sometimes combined with his overwrought religious sensitivity and enthusiasm to skew his judgment, as in the Anna Phillips affair. But despite his vulnerability, we can have little doubt that the overall contribution made by Prescott outside his officially required duties as college president greatly enriched the church.

---

[1] *RH,* July 28, 1885, p. 8.

[2] His name was replaced at the last minute with that of G. I. Butler in a 40-39 vote as a result of the political turmoil arising from the replacement of Butler as General Conference president (*GC Bulletin,* Nov. 2, 1888, p. 2).

[3] Book Committee minutes, Mar. 4, May 1, Aug. 10, Oct. 3, 1892.

[4] WWP to OAO, Nov. 1, 1893; WWP to Book Committee, Oct. 28, 1894; WWP to FDS, Dec. 2, 1894.

[5] GCCMin, July-August 1891; July 10, 1893; WWP to EGW, Oct. 5, 1893; Dec. 3, 1893.

[6] For example, see GCCMin, Mar. 16, 1895, in which he moved six of the eight actions.

[7] WWP to OAO, Nov. 1, 1893; GCCMin, Apr. 10, 1894.

[8] WCW to OAO, June 2, 1896.

[9] *RH,* Apr. 12, 1887, p. 5; DTJ to GIB, Feb. 18, 1891.

[10] *RH,* Nov. 12, 1889, p. 16.

[11] EGW MS 30, 1889; MS 16, 1889.

[12] EGW MS 25, 1888; MS 17, 1889; MS 24, 1889.

[13] WCW to CHJ, June 17, 1890.

[14] WCW to OAO, Aug. 18, 1890; WWP to OAO, June 20, 1890.

[15] *RH Extra,* Dec. 23, 1890.

[16] DTJ to RAU, Jan. 10, 1891; EGW MS 54, 1890.

[17] US to EGW, Feb. 17, 1890.

[18] EGW MS 3, 1891; EGW to JSW, Jan. 8, 1891.

[19] US to LFT, Feb. 11, 1902; DTJ to GIB, Jan. 26, 1891; OAO to EGW, Oct. 4, 1892.

[20] WWP to OAO, Jan. 4, 1893.

[21] WWP to OAO, Jan. 5, 1893.

[22] "Report of Righteousness by Faith Committee," Feb. 18, 1893.

[23] OAO to WWP, Aug. 30, 1896.

[24] AGD to WCW, May 12, 1902; WWP to AGD, Aug. 7, 1908.

[25] WWP to OAO, Nov. 1, 1893.

[26] WWP to EGW, Dec. 28, 1892.

[27] WAS to WCW, Jan. 4, 1893.

[28] GCCMin, Jan. 20, 1893; WAS to WCW, June 26, 1893; WWP to EGW, Jan. 24, 1893.

[29] *RH*, Oct. 17, 1893, p. 16; EGW to WWP, Oct. 2, 1893.

[30] WWP to OAO, Nov. 1, 1893.

[31] LTN to DTJ, Dec. 28, 1893; LTN to WEC, Feb. 13, 1894.

[32] EGW to WWP, Dec. 22, 1893.

[33] A ministerial annual salary in 1894 was under $1,000. The offering was equivalent to 22 or 23 years of salary for an individual minister.

[34] FMW to NZT, May 4, 1894.

[35] SNH to EGW, Mar. 9, 1894.

[36] FMW to DAR, Mar. 8, 1894.

[37] OAO to EGW, Mar. 29, 1894.

[38] OAO to EGW, Apr. 26, 1894.

[39] Haskell had written a two-part series in the *Review* to try to correct things using theological arguments of dubious quality (*RH*, Apr. 3, 1894, p. 10; Apr. 10, 1894, p. 9).

[40] EGW to SNH, June 1, 1894.

[41] OAO to WWP, July 1, 1894.

CHAPTER VII

EDUCATIONAL PHILOSOPHER
AND REFORMER

THE "COLLEGE IS DEAD," declared angry Battle Creek College professor C. S. Hartwell. In his mind the reforms that Prescott was trying to force upon the school would surely kill it. Students would stop coming. Members of the board of trustees listened in awkward silence to the impassioned outburst. On the other side, Prescott was more temperate but just as adamant. The reforms he advocated were, in fact, absolutely necessary to keep the school alive as a truly Adventist educational institution.

The dispute was typical of a number of episodes during his last years as president of Battle Creek College—conflicts that resulted from his responses to the writings of Ellen White and his attempt to introduce reform in the educational system. Like her, William Prescott was not satisfied with the status quo.

Although an energetic organizer and industrious committee member who focused discussions and facilitated decisions, Prescott had another side to his personality. He enjoyed reading and found it essential to have time alone to think. He was introspective, reflective, and at times almost melancholic.

In his 1877 graduation class speech Prescott had spoken at length on the topic "The Office of the Thinker." Now in the 1880s and 1890s, unwittingly or not, he found himself fulfilling that role through his educational leadership in the Adventist Church. He did not discover it an easy one. To think is to raise questions, to unsettle the status quo, to be in front leading the way, and thus to invite opposition and criticism.

Prescott often found the task intensely frustrating. Not only was his own understanding of the issues still developing, but he also seemed unable to enunciate clearly in practical terms, for himself or for his staff, exactly how to implement the concepts about which he felt so strongly.

Parents and students, slow to see wisdom in his ideas, resisted the changes he considered necessary. But Prescott still made remarkable progress in clarifying, reshaping, and developing his own, and thus the church's, educational philosophy during the decade of his educational leadership. It was a highly significant contribution.

Some earlier students of Adventist education have seen Prescott as an antireform classicist who tried to impress on Battle Creek College a New England style of education. However, a careful study of the evidence suggests quite otherwise. In this chapter we recount the development and shaping of the professor's philosophy of education and his attempts to implement the new focus at Battle Creek. It is an intriguing story that needs to be told.

As we noticed earlier, Prescott was undoubtedly aware of some of the basic issues in educational reform, even while a student at Dartmouth. His eight years in teaching and publishing in Maine and Vermont gave him firsthand exposure through debates and discussions on the need for transforming standards of teaching and education. Clearly he was very familiar with the ideas of such writers as Pestalozzi, Herbart, Froebel, and Spencer and cited them as the "most advanced scientific educators of the age" when he defended the manual labor program at Battle Creek in 1888.[1]

Prescott also kept himself abreast of developments in the educational field by occasionally attending meetings of the National Education Association and by examining experimental schools. He also encouraged his staff to keep up to date by having them visit other schools around Battle Creek to learn new methods. Among the schools Prescott himself took time to inspect were General Armstrong's Hampton Institute in Virginia (noted for its emphasis on manual education) and the famed Cook County (Illinois) Normal School operated by Colonel Francis Parker. He also visited Buffalo Teachers College to talk with the noted follower of J. F. Herbart, Frank McMurry. The latter visit resulted in Prescott's being offered a number of scholarships for his staff, some of whom, such as Frederick Griggs, he sent to study under McMurry. Others studied under Parker.[2]

Unquestionably, however, the writings of Ellen White were the most influential source of Prescott's emerging philosophy of education. At the time of his arrival at Battle Creek in 1885 he was already familiar with her counsel. During his first year as president he published a pamphlet containing her early articles on the topic of education. Furthermore, the professor and his wife spent many an hour during the late 1880s in personal conversation with Ellen White on educational matters ("precious seasons of communion together," Ellen White called them). Their recurring preoccupation centered on how to combine the study of religion with secular subjects. It appears that the discussions were mutually beneficial in clarifying what needed to be done. Ellen White wrote in her diary after one such visit, "We cannot go back upon this important subject of keeping the education of every faculty equal."[3]

Prescott continued to collect her writings on education, some of which came to him as personal correspondence and some of which she published in various periodicals. He also continued to wrestle with the problems of how to implement the ideas they contained. In 1892 he suggested that a book specifically on the topic of education might help church members better understand the basic principles. Surely, he reasoned, a more informed constituency would be more receptive and willing to cooperate in pointing the college in a new direction. As so often happens, the enthusiastic advocate received the task of compiling and editing the book himself. Completed by October the following year, it was published as the 251-page *Christian Education* (1893).

With Ellen White away in Australia at the time, Prescott did the editing as best he knew without her direct supervision. Uncertain as to how much liberty he should exercise in altering the prophet's words, he made only "such changes as seemed to be necessary for clearness." However, later involvement with her editorial staff during 1895-1896 and observation of their work in the preparation of *The Desire of Ages* convinced him that he had been too cautious, so he subsequently advised that the book be revised with "a more careful editing of the matter."[4] Again in 1897 he assembled and edited a third collection of Ellen White's articles that he had received during the mid-1890s, this time under the title *Special Testimonies on Education.*

Prescott's lengthy stay with the Whites in Australia during 1895-1896 gave him the opportunity for many further talks on education with Ellen White. He was eager to discover how to implement the philosophy, how to make it work. The 70-year-old Ellen White clearly enjoyed the discussions. Prescott "drew me out" just as her husband used to do, she reported, thus helping her to clarify her own thinking and enabling her to say things she "otherwise might not have spoken." "We could see some matters in a clearer light," she remarked after one visit.[5]

The two-way dialogue evidently helped to inform Ellen White on practical educational matters and, in turn, also helped mold and shape Prescott's own thinking on education. For example, he explained to her the significance of college degrees, a subject, he reported, that she knew little about. She then offered light on their place in the school system. Prescott was glad to have such exchanges, for he had learned from experience that success in his educational plans had come "as we have endeavored to follow the light."[6]

In Prescott's view, preparing "workers" for the Advent cause was the basic reason for the existence of Seventh-day Adventist schools. "The first principle in planning the work to be done in our schools," the professor noted, is that "first place should be given to those studies that will bear most directly upon the work of the third angel's message."[7] If some suggested that it was too narrow a goal, Prescott would respond that actually a "preparation to labor in this message is the best preparation for life."[8] Christianity had a twin task: proclaiming salvation to the unconverted and readying the already converted for participation in the coming kingdom of God. Both tasks constituted the distinctive thrust of the Adventist message. Thus it followed that Adventist education should focus on the same goals.

Such an understanding seems to have been Prescott's basic rationale right from his first day at Battle Creek College. To have "a religious element in our schools" has been our "general purpose," he explained to General Conference delegates in 1893—thus his emphasis on a strong religious atmosphere on the campus, the importance of chapel periods, and good "school homes."[9] But around 1889 the professor had begun to feel that more needed to be done.

As a result, his ideas began to undergo a marked development. Shortly after the Minneapolis session in 1888 Prescott became persuaded that the study of Scripture needed to be much more central to the curriculum. The conviction grew out of his new theological insights and his involvement in the successful implementation of the two General Conference Bible schools for ministers in the years following Minneapolis.

The only way for ministers and other church personnel to become more Christ-centered, he decided, was for them to become more "Word"-centered, and the classrooms had to help make that happen.

During the next two years the conviction deepened. Not only should the Bible be more fundamental and taught more systematically on an equal footing with other subjects, he reasoned, but it should be "the foundation of every other study." In true education Bible study and secular study needed to be thoroughly integrated and treated as one comprehensive activity that led to the knowledge of God. Isaiah's utterance "They shall be all taught of God" became his favorite expression, proclaiming the essence of his burden.

Closely related to this core theme was the idea that each human being was an indivisible "whole" and that education should develop all their faculties: physical, mental, and spiritual. Prescott protested against the commonly held view that it was the duty of one class of people to do the thinking and the other to do the drudgery. "It is just as honorable . . . to dig in the dirt as to dig into books." God did not make people in separate "pieces," he declared. "The mind can do its best work only when the body has been developed equally well."[10]

By the mid-1890s Prescott had established his basic philosophy of education. True, he continued to participate in the sometimes heated discussions about "the Bible as a textbook" that dominated later General Conference sessions, but they largely represented debates about the practical application of the philosophy rather than the theory itself. Espousing the concepts enunciated by Ellen White was not so difficult. What was challenging—for Prescott and other Adventist educators during the late 1890s—was how to put theory into practice. It was in the area of resolving Ellen White's teachings into a practical system that Prescott made a significant contribution.

EDUCATIONAL REFORMER

"It is very much easier to run a school from the floor of the conference than in the school itself," Prescott retorted during one of the heated arguments at the 1899 General Conference session. "It is a very different thing to meet a school day after day, year after year, and apply these principles, so that the students shall study and be benefited."[11] Ex-president of the college by now, Prescott spoke from painful experience. In trying to implement reforms in the curriculum he had encountered resistance from skeptical students, doubting parents, and an uncooperative faculty. Some regarded him as a "dreamy idealist," and he knew it. It frustrated him that many of his teachers dismissed his ideas as all theory that would not work in practice. Prescott himself may not have known how to translate all his reforms into everyday experience, but at least he was willing to experiment. The existing system, however, with its exclusive focus on the classics, was deeply entrenched. His faculty, tied as they were to the traditional subjects, feared that anything else would cheapen the educational program. Other schools around the country might have caved in to "popularist" educational notions, but the faculty at Battle Creek would stand for quality.

Informing Olsen in 1896 about the unwillingness of teachers to try new approaches, Prescott complained: "It is much easier [for them] to follow the old ruts with textbooks all prepared for the work rather than to enter upon a line of work that requires original thinking and planning and for which there are few textbooks at hand adapted for use."[12] The conviction slowly settled on him that progress in implementing reforms would result only through removing the uncooperative faculty. But even that he found difficult to accomplish.

Prescott first began to agitate for "radical" curriculum changes in 1890. The success of the "systematic" Bible study component of the 1889 Bible School for Ministers persuaded him that it should become part of the regular college program. At the commencement of the next school year he stimulated discussion on the topic in faculty meeting by requesting his principal, Eli Miller, to present a faculty colloquium paper on the Bible in the college curriculum. Then Prescott himself gave the response. The dialogue resulted in at least a start on some specific curriculum improvements.[13] D. T. Jones reported to S. N. Haskell a few weeks later that "Professor Prescott is planning to bring more Bible and missionary work into the schools under his charge as Educational Secretary. Lincoln College will open next September, and will contain a more thorough Bible Department than any school which has yet been established among our people. Battle Creek College will also have a more thorough Bible course next year than it has ever had."[14]

Continuing the dialogue into early 1891, Prescott told a faculty meeting that he had been "mulling over" the question for some time. Just how adaptable are "the present courses of study in the college to the purpose for which the college is established?" he asked.[15] But Eli Miller pointed out that the faculty faced a practical difficulty. Teachers and students were already complaining that courses were too full. The college was expecting too much of them. Adding extra Bible classes to the study load would only compound the problem. Miller wondered what adjustments or substitutions the administration could make. Prescott recognized the difficulty. He felt convinced, nevertheless, that action was needed and dared to suggest that the school should drop some of the classes in the (pagan) "classics." Only then could the faculty bring biblical teaching into "more intimate connection" with the other subjects.

But it was not just the teachers who required persuading. The constituency had to see the light as well. Prescott seized his chance at the 1891 General Conference session, expounding at length on the importance of Bible study. His purpose? To cultivate a readiness for change. To the General Conference Committee he was more simple and forthright. The "time had come," he declared, "for quite a radical change to be made in the curriculum."[16]

Within the college itself Prescott set up a faculty committee to incorporate the changes. It made adjustments in the academic requirements to allow for a three-term sequence of church history in all courses and for advanced Bible subjects offered as "options" in the upper levels of the B.A. program. Just how "radical" the proposed changes were may be gauged from the report of the Michigan State Board of Visitors, who inspected the school a month or two later. "Some may suspect that the college was trying to bring the Theological School down into the college and preparatory grades," they said, but they preferred to see the changes as an "experiment" on "moral education." The educational inspectors applauded it warmly.[17]

In spite of the rhetoric, though, the steps taken were not great enough. Not until later in 1891 did the school make truly major strides down the reform path. They occurred at a historic meeting in northern Michigan.

THE HISTORIC HARBOR SPRINGS CONVENTION

It was in March of 1891 that Prescott had suggested to the General

Conference Committee the idea of a second educational convention. He felt it could serve as a workshop to lay practical plans that would give substance to his dream of religion classes for every college student. The committee endorsed the idea and asked him to serve as convener. Prescott planned for a small select working group of 15 or 20—"those who have rather a molding influence"—and scheduled six weeks of meetings to begin July 15. Too many attending might defeat the purpose of the event. Eventually, however, the conclave held at picturesque Harbor Springs, a balmy lakeside resort near Petoskey in northern Michigan, attracted close to 100.[18]

Initially reluctant, Ellen White attended the meeting only at Prescott's repeated urging. She, along with Jones, Prescott, and Kellogg, led the presentations. Sermons, Bible studies, discussions, and workshop sessions filled the days. The topics discussed included Bible teaching, a redemptive approach to school discipline, the elimination of pagan authors, and the teaching of physiology and health. Permeating the whole program and inspiring the delegates in a new way was the 1888 theme of the centrality of Christ. According to a delighted Prescott, many delegates experienced spiritual renewal and began to appreciate the real purpose of our schoolwork "as never before."[19]

In practical terms, the convention produced three major initiatives: a four-year "biblical course" (for ministerial training, parallel to the classic course), a four-year sequence of history subjects to be taught from a biblical perspective, and a series of college-level Bible subjects. Prescott was particularly happy with the latter initiative because it represented a major shift toward incorporating the new theological emphasis into the curriculum. The new approach, he explained later, would study "the Bible as a whole" "as the gospel of Christ from first to last." Furthermore, it would present the church's doctrines as growing out of "a belief in Jesus Christ as a living, personal Savior." They were "simply the gospel of Christ rightly understood." Prescott had grasped the heart of the 1888 emphasis and placed it squarely where it belonged—in the classroom.[20]

Looking back a decade later, Percy Magan saw the 1891 convention as the birthplace of genuine "Christian education" in Adventism. The meeting, he wrote, was "remarkable." The "definite beginnings of the work of an educational reformatory movement owe their birth to this gathering."[21]

Implementation of the changes commenced at Battle Creek College immediately. The trustees formally adopted the new biblical studies course. In a revolutionary measure—that proved far easier to vote for than to put into actual practice—they also took action to drop the two major classics-oriented degree courses. They intended that the latter action would become effective two years later, in 1893.

The administration appointed another faculty subcommittee to plan for the incorporation of the new Bible subjects. Clearly apprehensive about the possibility of lowering standards, the faculty instructed the subcommittee to ensure "uniformity." The new classes should be at the same level of difficulty as the old.

It is important to note that at this initial stage the new Bible subjects were still not required studies. Rather, the college offered them as optional courses. Students had to petition the faculty to take them instead of required classes. The college permitted the substitution of Bible for Latin and Greek only in the less-prestigious "English" course, not in the superior "academical" (classical studies) program.[22]

A year passed, but still the faculty made no move to drop the Greek and Latin authors. Prescott was able to rearrange the schedules and the curriculum to "permit" students to take the Bible study options more easily, but his faculty was having difficulty swallowing the new diet.[23] To them, such an à la carte approach to study, allowing students to choose for themselves, was "cheap" and far too permissive. Even the idea of teaching Greek or Latin from medical literature and Christian writers was unpalatable. The faculty just could not see beyond Homer, Plato, and Seneca.

Prescott seemed to have an easier time at Union College. After careful explanation, he managed to persuade its trustees and faculty to adopt the new courses. Other schools and colleges slowly followed the tentative lead given by Battle Creek. By 1893 Prescott could report that most Adventist schools had benefited from the changes. But, still sensing the need to educate the constituency, he continued to busy himself writing on the themes of Bible-centered Christian education in the *Review*.

Other reforms followed in the wake of the 1891 convention. Vegetarianism became an issue in early 1892. Then later the same year the college dropped the issuing of grades to students in an attempt to counteract student rivalry and competition that had become very intense.

Faculty kept their own records, but simply notified students whether they had passed or failed.

REACTION

For Prescott, it seemed that the progress of reform was snail-paced. But near the end of 1893 when he began to press for further changes, he sparked a major faculty rebellion. The episode offers important and fascinating insights into the fierce curriculum struggles that beset early Adventist education. An interesting train of events led to the showdown.

During early 1893 Prescott had been exceptionally busy off campus attempting to remedy the post-1888 alienation that still plagued church leadership. A seven-week stint visiting other denominational schools followed. Prescott was becoming an absentee president and losing touch with his faculty. Some teachers had also reacted skeptically to a religious revival in Battle Creek that had occurred the previous winter, leading to tensions among the faculty. The resultant breaches of loyalty and unity spread in turn to the student body. It seemed, Prescott later related to Ellen White, "more like the old spirit which came in years ago and resulted in the closing of the college, than like anything I have known of since I have been here."[24] He lamented that he did not at the time take firmer action on the matter. At first he had allowed events to continue with little interference, although he did talk with board chair O. A. Olsen about it.

About the same time, Prescott received two letters on education from Ellen White. Addressed to his teachers as well, the first called for higher standards and made a marked impression—at least on some. Prescott's own reaction was to determine to work for "a different order of things" the next year. The second letter contained a strong protest against the new building extension at the school. Discouraged, the spiritually sensitive Prescott resolved that if the college could not "more nearly meet the purpose of God" during the following year, he would resign and go into the pastorate.[25]

The 1893 academic year started inauspiciously in August. An eager batch of freshmen had trodden up the neatly groomed paths to register as usual in the imposing gray sandstone building. Returning students had noted with pleasure the fresh beds of late summer flowers as they renewed acquaintances and scanned the class schedules for changes. Everything looked the same. The school had taken no action to implement the board's intention to phase out the classical courses. Impetus for reform, it seemed, had withered away. While the administration had given scant attention to revitalizing the manual labor program, Prescott had allowed sports and gymnastics to flourish in its place with football becoming a major attraction. It seemed that the college had shelved curriculum reforms.

Ironically, as the academic year got under way the professor was industriously studying and editing manuscripts for Ellen White's *Christian Education*. He had hardly finished when a new batch of letters arrived, including one that contained a sharp reprimand about the playing of football. Prescott quickly took steps to curb the game after he had read the letter to both staff and students. A month later two more very strong letters arrived from Australia. This time Prescott was stunned. "On my first reading of them, there seemed to be nothing but the severest rebuke."[26]

Some matters in the letters continued to puzzle the conscientious president even after repeated reading and much prayer. But they stimulated him to make his own study of the Old Testament "schools of the prophets"—a theme referred to in the letters. In so doing he became more convinced than ever of the need for implementing further reforms. During the following two weeks he convened six faculty meetings to plan for change. Probably remembering the program his trustees had approved two years previously, Prescott decided the time had finally come to cut the cherished classics. "I have become fully convinced," he informed Ellen White in New Zealand, "that there ought to be radical changes in our plans of work and that some of the subjects which have been occupying a prominent place and taken much time, ought to be either entirely omitted or relegated to a secondary place."[27]

"You know," he reminded Olsen in another letter written the same day, "that it has seemed to me for some time that we ought to give more attention to our own work. . . . Some studies," he went on, "notably the classics and higher mathematics, as well as some lines in philosophy, . . . ought to be entirely omitted or be put on a different basis."[28]

With the cooling showers of midautumn, the effect of the September testimonies also dissipated, being replaced with mounting opposition. In the view of some faculty, Prescott had declared war. If Battle Creek was to become a battleground again, so let it be. They would see to it that his demolition of "liberal education" would not come without a fight.

E. D. Kirby, C. S. Hartwell, and W. E. Sanderson were three professors who reacted strongly, protesting that Prescott would "cheapen" the college as well as kill "liberal education." In a letter that the beleaguered president went out of the way to type himself rather than dictate to his secretary, Prescott named the men, informed Olsen of the volatile situation, and expressed his anxiety that the resistance was also spreading quietly among the students. He was fearful of "losing ground." Waiting "ever since the Harbor Springs Institute" and hoping for the time when all would "see alike" to make reforms on a united front, Prescott now feared that the opposition was stronger than ever. But rather than postponing it any longer—even for a reply from Olsen—he resolved to take up the matter with his trustees.

He invited additional experienced church leaders to provide wider counsel for the board as it met to review the recently received testimonies with Prescott, who then presented to his trustees "exactly the same plan" he had given his faculty. It involved reorganizing the core of the main college course to make English language, history, and Bible the main required subjects. Classical language study, mathematics, and science would thenceforth only be offered as electives. The point of the reform was to remove the emphasis on the classics and put into effect the Harbor Springs recommendations.

After some discussion the trustees approved the plan with the recommendation that Prescott should explain to the students the rationale behind the change in a series of chapel talks. Students who wanted to continue the old program for the remainder of the year could do so if they wished. Thus united, the board had just one obstacle to overcome—the faculty. Prescott summoned the latter to a joint meeting with the board of trustees.

Tensions ran high at it. The board presented its decision first. Then, in response, Professor Hartwell threw down the gauntlet, creating a major stir with his short emotional speech in which he fumed that "the college is dead, . . . liberal education is dead, . . . religious liberty is dead." How could the board "require" students to study the Bible? Where was the religious liberty in that? The board members listened, embarrassed as the last angry words disappeared among the rafters. Then they responded vigorously, persuasively defending the plan and indicating clearly that they had thought the matter through carefully. Chagrined and outmaneuvered by the board's determination, the opposition—for the moment, at least—was squelched.[29]

But now the school had to sell the students on the change. As one can imagine, the effect on the student body of such a major shift was traumatic. What disturbed them so deeply was not that the administration had clumsily made it in midterm after they had already registered for the year, but that it was evident that the change was not intended only for Battle Creek. Prescott intended a fundamental transformation in the focus of education throughout the church. Wilmotte Poole, a student at Battle Creek at the time, explained the far-reaching change to his parents: "Many of the Classical scholars are all broken up about the decision the faculty have come to in regard to the languages. Many have spent years of diligent study in this line supposing that they would be called to teach in our other schools. But now this study is set at naught. In the meeting [a social meeting held in the chapel on the evening of December 15] several told of their struggle but declared their resignation to the will of God."[30]

Prescott was succeeding in bringing about change, but its specific nature and the fumbled timing of its implementation angered and alarmed many. But what was he to do? He could not bear another "heavy" testimony from Australia like the ones he had already received. It seemed that misunderstandings on both sides of the debate were inevitable.

Struggling to understand the moves on the basis of Prescott's brief, hastily written correspondence, even the usually supportive Olsen was disturbed. Neither he nor Ellen White, with whom he discussed the matter, could understand the professor's full intent. They wondered if he really was "cheapening" the educational program. "We cannot think for a moment to lower the grade of our work in the least," Olsen wrote. "We have none too high a standard as it is." The "regular lines of study" must not be undercut, Ellen White added, but at the same time the Bible was to be made "paramount."[31] Trying to resolve that tension in a practical way in the structuring of a curriculum was the very difficulty Prescott was trying to overcome. It is a concern that still haunts many Adventist schools to this day.

Fearing that Prescott had overreacted to her perhaps-too-strongly-worded letters, Ellen White regretted that she could not make herself more clear. Anxious lest "errors should be committed through misunderstanding of my words addressed to you," she wrote again in January 1894. She hoped Prescott would not misinterpret her. Later, however, after he had time to explain his efforts more clearly, it allayed her fears. She affirmed and endorsed Prescott's reforms, although rather awkwardly: "I cannot discern that your ideas [on education] are incorrect."[32]

Because of misunderstanding on one hand and faculty resistance on the other, reconstruction of the curriculum did not progress nearly as far as Prescott would have liked. Then Olsen's return from Australia provided the professor opportunity to elaborate on his views. Now aware of the true state of affairs, the General Conference president jettisoned his caution and strongly supported Prescott's attempt to call the controversial E. J. Waggoner from England to take charge of the Bible department and implement the new approach. Olsen acknowledged to a surprised W. C. White that it might sound like a desperate move to bring Waggoner in, but he was now willing to agree that something desperate needed to be done to maintain the progress of reform. Unfortunately, the plan did not work, disappointing both Prescott and Olsen.

The eventual outcome of the upheaval of the winter of 1893-1894 was the adoption of a much-watered-down package of reforms. Implementing the new curriculum was fraught with complexities. Thus, instead of displacing the classical subjects, the college simply added Bible subjects to the existing curriculum. With the courses lengthened by a year, students carried an extra class, and classes began to meet six days a week instead of five. According to Prescott, both faculty and students seemed reasonably happy with the compromise, but he was far from satisfied. Nor was Ellen White, who wrote yet again, emphasizing now the need for shorter programs.

In his annual report to school principals in 1895 (one year after he had vacated the president's chair at Battle Creek College) Prescott reflected on the state of affairs in Adventist education. Noting the limited progress that had been made, he asserted that there still existed a number of areas of study that should be eliminated to make the schools of more value to the denomination. "My own idea," he explained, "would be to construct a course in which the needs of those preparing for our own work would receive first consideration." Only studies that would support such a goal should occupy first place. Asserting that Adventist schools should teach languages from Scripture or Christian writers, he concluded that "I can only continue to enter my protest against teaching the languages from pagan authors."[33] If one could recognize little change in his last Battle Creek College bulletin, it was certainly not for his want of trying.

THE STRUGGLE CONTINUES

Although bruised and discouraged, Prescott harbored no grudge. Nor did he blame or criticize his faculty. As he told Olsen, they were "simply following the plans according to which they were educated and which are standard among the educators of the day."[34] On the other hand, neither did the persistent professor give up his attempt to reform the system. With Olsen's support, he planned another institute for the summer of 1894 to again emphasize the place of the Bible in the school. This time only principals and Bible teachers attended. The meetings resulted in further progress toward developing the four-year sequence of studies for college-level students.

The strong undercurrent of resistance and opposition continued to hamper progress. As a supporter and advocate of the ideas of A. T. Jones, who was the main speaker at the institute, Prescott had difficulty establishing his credibility with some. The skeptical L. T. Nicola, for example, reported to Olsen, "Of course Professor Prescott acted precisely as on all former occasions when Elder Jones was prescribing—he took the dose just as directed." Commenting further on the suggested curricula reforms, Nicola remarked, "Of course you know what line Professor Prescott has been pulling on for some time. He has not changed of late." According to Nicola, the teachers were aware of Ellen White's letter to Prescott questioning the wisdom of his 1893 stands. They were thus still convinced that his innovations at Battle Creek College were "calculated to lower the standing of the school." As far as they were concerned, he was reaching after "something in the dim distance."[35] Unfortunately, the faculty did not know about the subsequent letter Ellen White had sent to Prescott responding to his explanations, removing her objections, and in effect endorsing his initiatives. Public knowledge of it would have helped clear the air. If the principals thought he was lowering the standard with his proposals in 1894, they would have been astounded at the radical program Ellen White vigorously supported later, both at Cooranbong and at Emmanuel Missionary College.

Prescott found it difficult to articulate his educational ideas in a way that his audience could grasp. But part of the problem also lay in the prejudiced minds of his hearers, steeped as they were in traditional concepts in education. Much of what Prescott said had to do with creating a vision. He wanted teachers to be willing to experiment and cooperate with him in venturing out to develop new materials and new ways. Unfortunately, they found such a thing difficult.

After the institute Prescott continued to agitate for reform in ministerial and teacher training progress. He succeeded in having the General Conference appoint a committee to draw up further plans. Whether the committee accomplished much is not clear, but the topic of educational reform was high on the agenda of the 1895 General Conference session. His position as educational secretary gave Prescott the necessary platform to voice his concerns, which he did repeatedly with all the eloquence at his command. As well as defending his reforms, he addressed the objections raised by students. Some complained, he said, that Bible study did not provide them with the necessary mental cultivation. They felt they needed mathematics and other studies first, and then, if they had any time left, they could "crowd in the Bible. . . . This order ought to be reversed," thundered the determined Prescott.[36]

While the 1895 session adopted the resolutions submitted by Prescott's subcommittee, the exercise was largely a rhetorical one. Nothing really happened. Inertia in the colleges continued to prove an obstacle to actual reform. At Battle Creek College the issue festered during the next two years, until at the 1897 stockholders' meeting open conflict again broke out between the faculty and the board. In the interim Prescott spent much of his time visiting Australia, where he counseled at length with Ellen White and found deep satisfaction in participating in the founding of the Avondale School for Christian Workers.

If Olsen thought that with Prescott out of the country the tensions over educational reform would subside, he was mistaken. Board members of the Battle Creek school, increasingly dissatisfied with the deteriorating situation, continued to press for reform. Wearied from the struggle, Prescott enjoyed a refreshing respite from criticism and opposition out in Australia. At the same time he kept himself informed of the developing crisis through letters from his friends. With stiffened resolve he prepared to make yet one more attempt to improve Adventist education, but that would come after his Australian experience.

---

[1] *SDA Yearbook,* 1888, p. 81.

[2] Jessie B. Osborne, "A Teacher Education in the Early Days," *Journal of True Education,* June 1953, p. 11.

[3] EGW MS 62, 1889; MS 23, 1889. *Selections From the Testimonies Concerning the Subject of Education* (Battle Creek, Mich.: College Printing Department, 1886).

[4] WWP to EGW, July 30, 1896. In 1930 W. C. White reported to T. G. Bunch, "I wish to say with all truthfulness and emphasis that Professor Prescott had nothing to do with the preparation of her manuscripts for the printer" (WCW to TGB, Sept. 21, 1930). His comment to Bunch did not take into account Prescott's involvement at this time (1896) nor his role when at times as *Review* editor in 1907 he corrected a manuscript before he sent it to press. It appears to be an overstatement if taken as a general principle. Perhaps he may have been referring to the specific question as to whether it was Prescott who introduced the American Revised Version into Ellen White's manuscripts. W. A. Spicer, on the other hand, considered that too much had been made of the emphasis by her "bookmakers" that all the work had been done "under observation" and that this therefore guaranteed "correct work" (WAS to LRC, Nov. 30, 1914).

[5] EGW to JEW and ELW, Feb. 16, 1896; EGW MS 62, 1896.

[6] WWP to EAS, Apr. 29, 1896; WWP to EGW, Dec. 27 1892.

[7] *GC Bulletin,* Feb. 23, 1893, p. 357; Feb. 15, 1895, p. 157.

[8] *GC Bulletin,* Feb. 23, 1893, p. 357.

[9] *Ibid.,* p. 350.

[10] *GC Bulletin,* Feb. 15, 1895, pp. 156, 157.

[11] *GC Bulletin,* Feb. 19, 1899, p. 31.

[12] WWP to OAO, Feb. 20, 1896.

[13] BCCFacMin, Nov. 9, 1890.

[14] DTJ to SNH, Dec. 18, 1890.

[15] BCCFacMin, Mar. 23, 1891; Mar. 28, 1891.

[16] GCCMin, Mar. 28, 1891.

[17] Fifty-sixth Report of the Superintendent, p. 335.

[18] WWP to OAO, June 26, 1891.

[19] *GC Bulletin,* Feb. 23, 1893, p. 350.

[20] *Ibid.*

[21] *RH,* Aug. 6, 1901, p. 10.

[22] BCCFacMin, Aug. 26, 1891; Sept. 7, 1891; Sept. 9, 1891; Sept. 13, 1891.

[23] BCCFacMin, Dec. 18, 1892.

[24] WWP to EGW, Mar. 23, 1893; July 4, 1893; WWP to WCW, June 26, 1893.

[25] WWP to WCW, June 26, 1893; WWP to EGW, Sept. 7, 1893.

[26] WWP to EGW, Nov. 8, 1893.

[27] *Ibid.*

[28] WWP to OAO, Nov. 8, 1893.

[29] *Ibid.*

[30] Wilmotte Poole to Parents, Dec. 16, 1893.

[31] OAO to WWP, Dec. 20, 1893.

[32] EGW to WWP, Jan. 18, 1894; OAO to WWP, Dec. 20, 1893; EGW to WWP, Apr.10, 1894.

[33] WWP to Dear Brother, Apr. 10, 1894.

[34] WWP to OAO, Feb. 10, 1896.

[35] LTN to OAO, Aug. 23, 1894.

[36] *GC Bulletin,* Feb. 15, 1895, p. 157.

ChAPTER VIII

REFORMERS IN REFUGE DOWN UNDER

T HE LONGER I STAY, the better I like the place," Prescott wrote to the *Review* nine months after his arrival in Australia in 1895. Ellen White, who had already been there six years and eventually made the country her home for nine, shared his sentiments. Both of them found "down under" was much less stressful than Battle Creek.[1]

Ellen White may not have been "transported" to Australia the way the continent's first convict settlers had been, but she did feel as though she had been exiled. Church leaders in America, she was convinced, wanted her out of the way because of her outspokenness. "I dare not mention the state of things in the office presented to me, for I am then sure they would firmly conclude I must go," she confided to her diary when the trip to Australia was still just a suggestion.[2] Eventually she dutifully complied with the request. But she was decidedly unhappy about having to go. Then, after her arrival in the strange land, her sense of exile, the culture shock, ill health, and crippling financial circumstances compounded her unhappiness. But the longer she stayed, the better she liked it. At least the mood of suspicion, hostility, and prejudice that she had felt in Battle Creek was noticeably absent. Eventually she came to believe that God had overruled in the situation. He could use her in Australia.[3]

During the latter part of the decade Ellen White steadfastly refused to return to the United States despite the pleas of General Conference presidents. The painful memory of how the "jealousy" and "evil surmising" of the "hard-hearted" leadership in Battle Creek had almost killed W. C. White remained too fresh. "The terrible siege I had there for two years, with so few to help me, remains with me as a warning," she replied to Olsen. Besides, she argued, she had learned that she could accomplish tenfold more by her pen in Australia than by her actual presence in America. She preferred to remain in her haven in the "far-off country."[4]

Prescott also found Australia to be a refuge during his extended visit with the Whites. A series of problems had marred his final year at Battle Creek College. The rash endorsement he gave Anna Phillips and his intemperate fostering of the Battle Creek "exodus" had resulted in embarrassment and humiliation. His support of some of the extreme religious liberty ideas of A. T. Jones had further weakened his credibility and fostered the perception that he was an uncritical Jones disciple. Finally, the negative reaction to his attempt to respond to pressure from Ellen White and implement educational reforms had left him frustrated. He felt isolated and misunderstood. Some of his teachers, he knew, would be quite satisfied to see his stay "prolonged" for some time in the "region beyond."[5] On the other hand, in Australia he found himself among friends—friends who responded enthusiastically to his preaching and who were even more eager than he to implement educational reforms. As with Ellen White, Prescott would return to America only reluctantly.

Simply providing Prescott with an escape was not exactly what church leaders had in mind when they had urged the professor to undertake the overseas tour. The denomination actually had serious needs abroad. Its educational program required fostering outside America. W. C. White, in particular, hoped that Prescott would be able to persuade Australian Adventists of the necessity for a first-class training school, just as he had done with Union College and Walla Walla. White, who felt quite out of his depth in such matters, eagerly anticipated Prescott's practical advice on both curriculum and campus layout for the proposed "new permanent school." In addition to these benefits, Olsen suggested, a tour around the world via Australia would be "a most excellent thing" for the "enlargement" of Prescott's own experience.[6] The plan called for him to visit South Africa and Europe for three months each on his way back from Australia. The General Conference president also hoped that, in dialogue with Ellen White, Prescott might get a better grasp on educational ideas. And if Battle Creek could sense the peace of a truce by separating the chief 1888 theological protagonists for a while, well, that would be a bonus.

Fortunately, Prescott had decided to take his wife and son with him on his first overseas trip. Even while the professor was en route, W. C.

White was negotiating with the General Conference to extend the three-month Australian sector of the itinerary. The denominational program there desperately needed "a shot in the arm," he argued. Three months would not be long enough for the medicine to take effect. Isolated from the currents of change, according to White, Australia was becoming dry and barren. If America did not want its revivalist preachers, the continent down under would happily receive them. Prescott also quickly became convinced that three months would be too short a stay. His first inspection of the new school at Cooranbong revealed nothing more than "an industrial department" with a mere 25 students. Much still had to be done. The professor would remain in Australia almost a year.[7]

EVANGELIST TO THE ANTIPODES

The extended sojourn enabled Prescott to do much more than develop the school program. Arriving in the midst of an evangelistic campaign in Sydney in August 1895, he found himself pressed into doing most of the preaching. His Christ-centered sermons, proclaimed in a rich American accent, made an immediate impact on colonial ears accustomed to the raucous call of currawongs and kookaburras. Eventually he helped conduct public evangelistic meetings in all five of the eastern colonies, enabling him to model effective new patterns of evangelism. At the same time, he used his writing and editorial expertise in producing new tracts and pamphlets for evangelistic activities. Ellen White also utilized his editorial help in working through some difficult sections of *The Desire of Ages*.

As we have noticed previously, Prescott's theological emphasis had changed radically since 1888. Events following Minneapolis had led him into a new religious experience that centered on a "personal relationship with Christ." As a result, he now saw the doctrines of the church from a quite different perspective. As he explained years later to delegates at the 1919 Bible Conference, the change had come to him "almost like a personal revelation, like a person speaking to me." When he first "started out" in denominational service, he thought, "the thing to do was to prove the doctrines. . . . As I had observed and heard," he added. (He had not had the benefit of any special homiletics training in a Bible institute or seminary.) Most Adventists considered the preacher's task "simply to demonstrate the truthfulness" of church teachings. Since his "new vision," however, he had "cast the whole thing aside and started in the simplest way presenting Christ."[8] Church doctrines, he now believed, should be presented as "simply the gospel of Christ rightly understood." They should "grow out of a belief in Jesus Christ as a living personal Saviour."[9]

It was not some artificial additive or some sugarcoating that Prescott considered necessary to give Adventists a superficial gospel flavor. Rather, it was a genuine, total reorientation of his belief structure. A spiritual and theological paradigm shift. As a result, it set the pattern for the rest of his ministry. To bring other Adventist preachers to the same conviction and perspective became his lifelong burden. "That ye might know him whom to know is life eternal" became his hallmark text of Scripture, remembered by generations of his students.[10] According to noted radio speaker H.M.S. Richards, who attended some of the professor's later ministerial institutes, Prescott's "legacy to Adventist preachers" was that "Christ must be the center of every sermon."[11] Australia in the 1890s was still largely untouched by the gospel message of 1888. Prescott's emphasis stirred not only the minds but the hearts of the people.

The story of the camp meeting at Armadale, in Melbourne, in late 1895 illustrates well the kind of impact produced by the new perspective in Prescott's preaching. Pitched in the center of a prominent middle-class suburb, not far from the city center, in full view of a major city railway line, the 65-tent encampment presented a striking novelty for the community. As the meetings progressed, an inquisitive public augmented the regular congregation of 200 church members during evenings and weekends. Evangelist John Corliss and Ellen White shared in the preaching, but it was Prescott who dominated the meetings not only by the frequency of his preaching but also with his charisma. Undoubtedly, the professor's legendary voice attracted some of the colonials, but, according to those present, it was the Christ-centered content of his sermons that pulled in the crowds in ever-increasing numbers.

The public interest astonished the church workers, particularly in light of the widespread prejudice against Adventists that had developed in the community. Colporteurs had widely distributed Uriah Smith's *Thoughts on Daniel and Revelation,* and its Arian slant on the preexistence of Christ caused many to view Adventists as a heretical, sub-Christian sect that denied the divinity of Christ. Prescott responded to the criticism by preaching sound Christian doctrine. "His theme from first to last and always is Christ," reported an ecstatic W. C. White. "Preaching Jesus as Professor Prescott has done," added local conference president Arthur G. Daniells, "seems to have completely disarmed the people of prejudice." He felt that the professor had "completely revolutionized" the public image of Adventists.[12] But it was not just the public perception of Adventism that had altered. Adventism itself was changing. The Armadale meetings, as we shall note later in this chapter, led to profound shifts in Adventist thinking and understanding on Christology. A quiet revolution was truly under way.

Prescott even managed to turn the traditional Adventist Saturday-Sunday polemic into a remarkable gospel presentation. Several weeks after the presentation on the Sabbath doctrine the seasoned but awed W. C. White was still marveling at what the professor had done. Prescott had preached "with a clearness and power that exceeds anything I have ever heard in my life," he reported. He said that Prescott had presented Adventist teaching "with a freshness and a brightness" never seen in it before. White recalled that he had not even once heard the professor preach "what we are accustomed to call a doctrinal sermon" on "the old lines." "The old lines of work" of creating an "interest" by "presenting the prophecies" must "be abandoned," he asserted. "The whole thing" must receive "a new setting." He longed to see "every one" of the ministers emulate Prescott in "preaching Christ and Him crucified."[13]

Ellen White too was ecstatic over Prescott's sermons and the quality of the people attracted by his exaltation of Jesus. They represented "the very best class" of society. "Unbelievers turn pale and say, that man is inspired," she reported to her son Edson.[14] She saw in Prescott's Christ-centered evangelism a pattern for the whole church. Testimonies went out encouraging others to follow the professor's example. Clearly Ellen White applauded his refocusing of the denomination on Jesus in this fresh new way. It took a long time, however, before others caught the same vision. Prescott in this, as in other things, was ahead of his time.

The new strategy of having secretaries take down the sermon in shorthand and transcribing it for printing and distribution to the homes of the people during the following week also proved highly successful. It provided the Australian field with much-needed tracts and booklets for evangelism. Australia was "years behind" in that regard, according to W. C.

White. Others back home in Battle Creek, while applauding the progress, would have preferred it to have come from the hand of someone other than Prescott. Their negative reaction highlights the continuing tension over the "new theology" in the church at the time.

One pamphlet, entitled "The Law in Christ," reproduced what Prescott considered one of his best Armadale sermons. Approved by the Australian book committee, it later evolved into a series of six articles in the *Bible Echo,* the Australian church publication. During October 1895 Prescott sent the manuscript to the Battle Creek publishing house, hoping that it would receive wider circulation. A Christocentric presentation of the law and justification by faith, the manuscript incorporated Prescott's new understanding of the law in Galatians. Two months later the Battle Creek committee informed Prescott that they would not publish the pamphlet. It contained "fundamental errors," they said, an assessment that "greatly surprised" Prescott's Australian friends.[15]

Prescott replied to the announcement with studied understatement by saying that he found the refusal a "trifle peculiar." Almost amused, he ventured to ask for an explanation. But Ellen White saw no humor in the situation. Absolutely indignant at the book committee, she stated plainly that she had no confidence in them. They were not adhering to the principle of "the Bible only" as the "rule of doctrine," she said, and rebuked them for "restricting" the circulation of the gospel. Several months later, still bristling at the memory of the episode, she wrote one of her sharpest testimonies ever to the General Conference and set out some important principles about the church being open to developing understandings of truth. Boldly she declared that the committee had been "following in the paths of Rome." Taking up cudgels in defense of the Minneapolis reform preachers, she declared it was not for the men on the committee to "condemn or control" the productions of those whom God was using as "light-bearers to the world." She repeated her charge that the committee had been acting like the Papacy.[16]

Some months later—when Ellen White wrote to S. N. Haskell in South Africa just before Prescott was about to leave Australia to visit him—she again alluded to the incident. Mindful of Haskell's suspicion of the professor because of the Anna Phillips episode and fearful that he might still react negatively to the zealous reformer, she urged him to receive Prescott with confidence. "The truth" was "in his heart," she said, "as well as on his lips." The church needed every ray of light that heaven shed. Haskell should beware of becoming like the unbelieving people of Nazareth, she admonished, noting that such unbelief prevented Jesus from doing mighty works among them. Waxing even stronger in Prescott's defense, she pointed out that "men in authority" in the church were "not always to be obeyed." In fact, "God . . . sometimes commissions men to teach that which is regarded as contrary to established doctrines," and no "priest or ruler" has a right to prevent them giving "publicity" to their opinions. Just to make sure that the conservative Haskell would not miss her point, she lamented that "the spirit which ran riot at Minneapolis" was still alive in the church. Adventists were "in danger of closing their eyes to truth" simply because it contradicted something they had previously accepted.[17]

Australian Conference president A. G. Daniells did not require such apologetics. In fact, he was doing his best to persuade the General Conference officers to allow Prescott to stay on in Australia in order to put a "permanent mold" on the work. But his efforts were unsuccessful.

But Prescott did put his impress on Daniells himself. During the Armadale meetings the two ministers developed a respect for each other that blossomed into genuine friendship. Prescott's Christian experience and the time he spent in Bible study and prayer greatly impressed the future General Conference president. He had been amiss in this respect himself. In turn, Prescott rejoiced that Daniells had "turned a new leaf" and declared that he could help him renew his Christian experience. "He hardly seems to me like the same man now," Prescott reported to W. C. White afterward.[18] He was sure the change would be of much benefit to the church. The professor conceded to Olsen that giving attention to the spiritual and personal side of the work had taken much time, and thus he had given less to administrative aspects. But the pastorally sensitive Prescott recognized that it was a work "which had to be done at a certain time or not at all." It had to take place when people were experiencing spiritual need.[19] Six years later the mutual respect and friendship would bear fruit. After Daniells' election to the leadership of the General Conference he would insist that the General Conference Committee appoint Prescott to serve as his lieutenant.

REORGANIZING A SCHOOL OF THE PROPHETS

If Prescott's stamp on Australian evangelism was considered valuable, his work in plotting a course for the educational program received equal favor. The denomination had already secured land for the school at Cooranbong a year before he had arrived. Students had enrolled and a principal had come from America, but the institution had not yet erected any buildings. According to Prescott, the term *school* was a euphemism. In reality, all that existed was a "manual labor department." Things were in a "chaotic state," as W. C. White willingly acknowledged. Thus the ever-practical professor spent the final six months of his stay in Australia getting the new school "shaped up."

Prescott had serious misgivings about the site at Cooranbong despite the fact that Ellen White had urged the purchase of the property in 1894. His first visit to the drab-brown, drought-stricken property a year later did nothing to change his opinion. It was, indeed, a far cry from the rich and fertile loams of the corn belt surrounding Union College or the lush green valleys around Walla Walla. But by the time the wearied evangelist returned to Cooranbong in January 1896 the drought had broken, the vegetation looked refreshingly green, and the fruit trees were bearing their first harvest. Prescott found the quiet isolation of Cooranbong therapeutic, and his opinion about the place began to change. Appointed chair of the board of the new school soon after his arrival in Australia, he also became chair of the education committee at the union conference session. W. C. White, who engineered his selection, wanted to ensure that Prescott would be in a position to give "the full strength of his influence."

Under Prescott's influence the education committee came up with three recommendations for the school. First, that it should discontinue the "Industrial Department" (a move designed to get the curriculum correctly focused). Second, the name should change from Avondale College to Avondale School for Christian Workers (a modification intended to clearly express the purpose of the institution and the nature of its nontraditional curriculum). Third, "the highest priority" of the school should be the preparation of people for denominational positions. The last two recommendations typified the educational reform emphasis Prescott had been pushing for during the previous three years.[20] Through it he determined to achieve what he had been unable to accomplish "in the schools in America for lack of proper cooperation among the teachers."[21]

Scheduled to open in March 1896, the school soon ran into snags. Legal wrangling over the title deeds for the property frustrated any hope that it could quickly erect buildings. Then the new principal, L. J. Rousseau, fell ill and returned to America. Leaders postponed the start of school 12 months while Prescott struggled to contain his disappointment.[22] In place of the school, Australian Adventists quickly organized a Ministers' and Teachers' Bible Institute, as church leadership was concerned not to lose Prescott's influence. During the month of April a delegation of 40— including ministers, church officials, and teachers for the intended school—tented at Cooranbong for a seminar on Christian education. Once again the denomination transcribed and circulated Prescott's lectures in order to provide a charter handbook on "the courses of study, and the best methods of teaching" for those who would conduct the school.[23]

During his stay in Australia the professor had been able to spend many hours in personal conversation with Ellen White. They had talked long about the practical details of subjects and timetables for the kind of educational program that Avondale would offer. According to Ellen White, both had seen things in a clearer light.

At the institute Prescott seemed able at last to get his listeners to understand what he was trying to do. One reporter wrote in the *Bible Echo* that Ellen White's counsel was "now . . . being given serious attention" and was being "resolved into a system."[24] School planners also found Prescott's expertise helpful in laying out the Avondale campus. The institute determined sites for the major buildings. Although the school had not started by the time he left Australia, Prescott felt that he had been able to set the future work of the school "upon a proper basis."[25]

REFORMING A DOCTRINE

Prescott's 1896 Cooranbong Bible Institute is noteworthy not just for the charter it produced for the development of Avondale. It is significant also because it proved to be a kind of crucible for the profound new developments emerging in Adventist theology represented by the approach that Prescott had demonstrated in Melbourne. Jerry Moon assesses them as "an irreversible paradigm shift."[26] How this came about illustrates the

extent of Prescott's influence in refocusing the theological emphasis of
the church.

Prior to his journey to Australia the church had commissioned the
professor to write a one-year Sabbath school lesson series for 1896-1897
on the Gospel of John. He considered it "no small task." Thus while riding the swells across the Pacific en route to Sydney he took time for an intensive study of the Gospel. After his arrival the early-morning
kookaburras stirred him to further study and to work on his manuscript.
W. C. White, with whom Prescott shared it, was impressed. The lessons
were "more appropriate" than former ones, he thought, and he urged the
Battle Creek Sabbath School Association to accept it. As we might expect,
the fourth Gospel also provided the basis for much of Prescott's preaching during this time.

One of the questions that grew out of his study involved the preexistence and eternal deity of Christ and its implications for the church's generally accepted teaching on the Godhead. Many Adventists at the time
associated the doctrine of the Trinity with Catholicism. But was that necessarily a valid linkage? Prescott had visited a secondhand bookstore
shortly after first landing in Sydney in August and bought himself a copy
of Augustus Neander's classic, Lectures on the History of Christian
Dogmas. The book, now in the Andrews University Library, contains extensive underlining by Prescott's editorial blue pencil. The chapters that he
has marked are those that deal with the Christological controversies of the
early centuries. Clearly he was intently studying the specific issues of the
Trinity, and the divinity of Christ had obviously occupied his close attention.[27] As noted earlier, the widespread prejudice against Adventists in
Melbourne arising from the circulation of Uriah Smith's Thoughts on Daniel
and Revelation also bothered the professor. Its strongly Arian slant on the
preexistence of Christ no longer seemed adequate in the light of his new
study of the fourth Gospel with its strong emphasis on the divinity of
Christ. He felt that the fact that the public viewed Adventists as a heretical,
sub-Christian sect denying the divinity of Christ was most unfortunate.

Prescott's three months at Cooranbong was, in effect, a research-and-
study leave. For six months he had been constantly involved in intense
evangelism and counseling regarding church administration and was
rather exhausted. He planned his return to Cooranbong, with explicit

General Conference consent and local leadership support, as a retreat. His purpose was to write out the materials he had been using in preaching, complete his Sabbath school lesson series on John, spend time with Ellen White and, at her specific request, assist in the editorial work on her life of Christ project.

As a result of his continued studies in the Gospel of John, Prescott's preaching at the Cooranbong institute specifically emphasized the full eternal sonship of Christ and the need for Adventist teaching to have a clear Christological focus. He preached a series on the great "I Am" statements of the Gospel of John, and talked of Jesus being the Jehovah of the Old Testament.[28]

Daniells, with his renewed spiritual experience, had begun to adopt the same approach and was also preaching the same theme.[29] Following the Armadale meetings and prior to the Cooranbong institute, denominational personnel in Melbourne under his leadership had followed up the interest stimulated by Prescott and had been studying the doctrine of the Holy Spirit in their daily staff meeting. As a guide to their study of Scripture on the subject Daniells used a book by Anglican theologian Andrew Murray, *The Spirit of Christ.* Soon the ministers were actively discussing the work and the person of the Holy Spirit.[30] At the Cooranbong institute Daniells gave presentations on the same theme during the evening meetings.[31] Ellen White, who attended the meetings along with her literary assistants, highly lauded both themes. W. C. White commented shortly afterward that while the institute "was a big interruption" of Ellen White's editorial work on the life of Christ, nevertheless it was a "grand success," and "it has been a blessing to all her household and especially her literary helpers." She was thankful at this time for "the best set of workers she has ever had."[32] As already noted, Ellen White and her team were focused on the manuscript that eventually became *The Desire of Ages.* She had solicited Prescott's help in critically reading her material from literary, biblical, and theological perspectives.[33] Why? She sought help in organizing the material. And, it seems clear, it was important that the new book properly present the new emphasis Prescott was giving.

According to H. Camden Lacey, W. C. White's brother-in-law and one of the young Avondale teachers at the time, Marian Davis, Ellen White's leading book editor, was struggling with the arrangement of material for the first few chapters of *The Desire of Ages*. She found the professor's help invaluable. His assistance and emphasis, Lacey reported, brought about a clearer and more decided presentation of Christ's deity in the book. "Professor Prescott's interest in the 'Eternity of the Son' and the great 'I Am's' coupled with the constant help he gave Sr. Davis in her preparation of the 'Desire of Ages' may serve to explain the inclusions of the above-named teachings in that wonderful book."[34] As Jerry Moon observes, the majority of the new scriptural passages Ellen White drew attention to in the new emphasis came from the Gospel of John.[35]

Lacey had been at the Armadale meetings and the later Melbourne sessions with Daniells. His particular responsibility at Armadale had involved the nurture of the new believers.[36] He reports that his own interest at the time had been in emphasizing "the personality of the Holy Spirit" and that the subject had also been an important part of the doctrinal and theological agitations at the time.[37] Although Lacey wrote his memories down in the 1940s, they are consistent with the primary source documentation available from the period. He does not seem to have overstated his case, nor did he see Prescott's help as undercutting Ellen White's claim to inspiration.[38]

M. L. Andreasen, a leading denominational Bible teacher in the 1930s and 1940s, also recalled how the new emphasis in *The Desire of Ages* made a large impact on the church. "I remembered how astonished we were," he wrote, "for it contained things that we considered unbelievable: among others the doctrine of the Trinity."[39] Most Adventists considered such statements about Christ's life being "original, unborrowed, underived" as almost revolutionary.[40] Many decades would pass before the church would develop any unanimity of conviction on the eternal deity of Christ and its implications for the doctrine of the Trinity, but Prescott left Australia having solidly helped set the church on a path toward that end.

VISIT TO SOUTH AFRICA

The three-and-a-half-week voyage from Melbourne to South Africa through the stormy southern Indian Ocean gave Prescott less leisure than he had hoped for to complete his Sabbath school lessons. But the storms did not prevent the travelers from arriving in time for the mid-year committee meetings at church headquarters in Cape Town. In spite of the fact that he was six months late, the local believers enthusiastically welcomed the professor.

Immediately following the meetings, a five-week tour of the colonies in the company of Stephen N. Haskell and the local president, Asa T. Robinson, enabled Prescott to acquaint himself with the conditions of local Adventists and the challenges they faced. Did the opportunity for Prescott and Haskell to travel together help generate any warmth in their relationship? Later developments suggest not. In education, outlook, and experience they were too different. As the years passed, Haskell became increasingly antagonistic to anything associated with the "unsafe" Prescott. On the other hand, the professor considered Haskell too narrow and legalistic in outlook. In fact, Prescott believed that legalism had infected the entire denominational staff in South Africa and that, as a result, it hampered their success in evangelism. Add to this other culture-related problems, and it is easy to understand why Prescott's evangelistic series in the center of Cape Town (combined with a three-month Bible institute for the ministers and other workers) met with only a fraction of the success he had enjoyed in Australia.

The professor also found little readiness in South Africa for the acceptance of his educational ideas. He believed that in his presentation he had been able to "shape up these principles in a clearer light" than he had even at the Cooranbong institute. But the concepts he advocated were "squarely contrary" to the thoroughly traditional approach followed at Claremont, the South African denominational school. He was successful, however, in having church leaders agree to a change of educational leadership. As a result, he would send out a more reform-minded principal from Battle Creek to help the school adopt a more enlightened approach.[41]

In August, urged by local church leaders and probably lured by a sense of adventure, Prescott toyed with the idea of extending his itinerary to include an eight-month overland expedition through the wild African interior that would also comprise part of his journey home. He figured that the trip would benefit the church and thus ventured to suggest it to his superiors.

O. A. Olsen, however, had other things in mind. He had determined to retire from the General Conference presidency at the next session and wait for another appointment elsewhere. The thought that Prescott should think of missing the session brought him almost to the point of panic. Far more important than any expedition to view lions and hyenas, the professor should plan to be back to face the opposition at home. The meetings would be crucial. In fact, Olsen told him, he needed to arrive six weeks before the session so that the two of them could adequately counsel together. Prescott dutifully complied and exchanged Africa's sunburned velds for the snowdrifts of a Michigan winter. He reached home in time to preach the Christmas sermon at the Tabernacle.[42]

BACK TO THE FRAY

Besides the forthcoming elections for the General Conference presidency, Olsen had other reasons for wanting the educational secretary back in his office. Headquarters found itself in trouble. Battle Creek College was getting almost out of hand. In late 1895 a group of traditionally minded faculty had lobbied to have four of their own number elected to the board of trustees. The ploy, if successful, would have given the faculty a clear majority of the resident members of the board. As Prescott saw it, "the running of things" would then fall "wholly into their hands." But the move backfired. None of the faculty got elected. In the tussle, however, tension between the progressives and the conservatives had heightened to flashpoint.

From his safe haven in Australia Prescott had followed the struggle with interest. But by mid-1896 Olsen felt it was time for him to be home. Later that same year agitation started again, this time from the progressives. Moves began to remove the traditionally minded college president, George Caviness. Caviness had been resisting the implementation of a manual training program, and Kellogg had threatened to start up his own industrial school if an immediate change did not happen. Pressure was mounting to bring in the young Edward A. Sutherland of Walla Walla to clean the place up.

Olsen was distressed, as was Prescott, who worried that his own "hard work of years" was rapidly being thrown away. The "present administration," he agreed, was a "sore disappointment," and there would be "no general improvement" until the board found someone else "to take charge of the institution." Other faculty also needed moving. But it was too soon for Sutherland. He was still too young. Remembering his own bitter experiences, Prescott stated emphatically to Olsen: "I am utterly opposed to sacrificing any promising young man by putting him into that combination."

The General Conference president did not need convincing. Conditions at Battle Creek, he was sure, would not give Sutherland a "free hand." He would be "hampered and bound up, discouraged and criticized to such an extent that he could not do justice to himself nor the school," a comment that illustrates the conditions Prescott himself had confronted earlier.[43]

The success of E. A. Sutherland's curriculum experiments at Walla Walla College had encouraged both Olsen and Prescott. The latter was particularly glad, although he felt a little piqued as well. Recalling Olsen's previous ambivalence on educational reform, he defensively pointed out to the president that Sutherland's plans were really "nothing different" from what Prescott himself had advocated repeatedly at Battle Creek. Unfortunately, his faculty "had not been prepared to give them a fair trial." Both men, however, felt it important to have Sutherland stay at Walla Walla to consolidate his program there.

Prescott was convinced, though, that some in the ranks at Battle Creek College needed purging. On his way to Africa he had written Ellen White: "I am now prepared to take strong ground on this matter and to insist that our school work shall be conducted strictly in harmony with the light which God has given and I am fully ready to dispense with the services of any or all teachers who are not willing to follow this light. We have been held back all too long by those who preferred the plans of the world. . . . I want to see a change without further waste of time."[44] On his arrival back in America in December 1896 he was ready for action.

Within two weeks of his return he had counseled with his colleagues in the General Conference and called meetings of both faculty and trustees. Board members requested him to present a strategy for the reformation of the school and appointed a subcommittee of three (J. H. Kellogg, G. C. Tenney, and himself) to work on plans to implement it. Eight days later Prescott's subcommittee presented its report to the board. First, it called for a two-year "evangelistic course" concentrating on the English Bible, missions, hygiene, practical evangelism, methods, and science, and second, recommended a one-year teacher's course. Also, it urged the appointment of "appropriate" faculty.[45]

The board responded enthusiastically about the new approach. And who better to implement it than Prescott himself? To the professor's evident discomfort, the trustees determined that he should be the new man at the helm. They commissioned the board's standing subcommittee on staffing "to make arrangements" and also to select "cooperative" teachers. During the week that followed, however, the trustees had second thoughts. Sweeping changes in administration and faculty in the midst of a school term might just be too hasty. Besides, the college stockholders' meeting and the General Conference session were less than a month away. Precipitate action now would preempt any actions those bodies might wish to take. Olsen and Prescott also seem to have quietly resigned themselves to the idea that Sutherland might be the best man after all. They prevailed upon the board to delay formal action.

The plan to have Prescott at the college, it seems, may have disturbed what Olsen had in mind for the professor, but at this stage he was in no position to show his cards. Prescott also seems to have felt decidedly uncomfortable with the prospect. He did not want to be tied up in Battle Creek.

Furthermore, just after his departure from Australia, both Ellen White and W. C. White had intimated strongly to him that he would probably be the next General Conference president. It was a suggestion he resisted, being not at all enamored with the idea.[46] But it certainly would have not been prudent to divulge any of this information to the college board. As events turned out, Prescott was too much of a political hot potato ever to get elected as president. The session passed him by.

The 1897 General Conference session, held at Union College, was stormy, to say the least. Stephen Haskell had anticipated a crisis and with Ellen White had elected to stay away.[47] Prescott could not. Heated debate over organizational structure and session protocol snarled the progress of the meetings for days, delaying the acceptance of the Nominating Committee's report until the last two days of the 14-day-long session. In the early stages of the meeting, Prescott had been too forceful in his attempt to effect some of the organizational reforms that Ellen White had called for. (She had sent him a great many manuscripts on the topic and had urged him to be at the meeting.) He was misunderstood, his approach alienated others, and his political liabilities increased.

Debates on education at the session also gave rise to some "delicate" moments as Prescott diplomatically reported to Ellen White later. Someone even suggested putting Prescott at Union College and making it the "central school" of the denomination and a center of educational reform. The Battle Creek school would have then become a medical school connected with the sanitarium.[48] That concept failed to win support, and the end of the conference found Prescott dropped from all his previous positions. He had been appointed—"exiled"—to Great Britain to head the mission there. As we will have occasion to notice again later, the reassignment had come not from the Nominating Committee but from the floor of the conference on the very last day.[49]

Not so easily disposed of were Prescott's cherished educational reforms. Contentious debate on the subject spilled over into the college stockholders' meeting that followed the session, finally resulting in a new resolve to implement the reforms without delay. According to George A. Irwin, the new General Conference president, the incumbent George Caviness "kindly resigned." The euphemistic expression[50] disguised the fact that the leadership had forced Caviness out of office. He was decidedly unhappy about his "banishment" to Mexico for translation work. In his place the young Sutherland received the task of "Prescottizing" the institution. The irregular midyear change caused chaos on both campuses, but as Irwin explained to the union president in the northwest, "unless the victory gained" at Battle Creek was followed up and "crystallized into something permanent" immediately, "the battle would have to be fought over again later on," and it would be much harder then to bring things to a focus. Even so, it was extremely hard going for Sutherland.[51] For another 12 months the struggle continued at the college, with Professor Aul—an antireform classicist troublemaker—still attempting to accumulate proxy votes in order to get traditionalist faculty elected to the board. At first, he was partially successful. Then a constitutional revision reversed his gains and finally thwarted the antireform protesters.[52]

Languishing in the imperial fogs of London, Prescott was glad that he was out of the firing line in Battle Creek, although, of course, he faced problems of a new kind in his current field of labor. But Australia had given him a taste for evangelism, and, considering the circumstances, he now really preferred to be somewhere away from America. He continued to follow the fortunes of educational reforms with interest, but for the next several decades education would become a secondary matter. His major work would be in evangelism and administration—first in a local field and then again at headquarters.

[1] *RH,* May 26, 1896, p. 8.

[2] EGW MS 29, 1891.

[3] *RH,* Apr. 1, 1892, p. 7. See also W. P. Bradley, "When God Overrules," *RH,* Apr. 1, 1982, pp. 7-9.

[4] EGW to JEW, May 6, 1896; EGW to OAO, May 25, 1896.

[5] WWP to OAO, Nov. 20, 1895.

[6] OAO to WCW, Apr. 18, 1895; May 25, 1895.

[7] WCW to OAO, Aug. 5, 1895; Sept. 29, 1895; Oct 24, 1895.

[8] "1919 Bible Conference Transcript," July 13, 1919.

[9] *GC Bulletin,* Feb. 23, 1893, p. 350.

[10] Interview with George S. Hutches, Feb. 11, 1981.

[11] HMSR to GMV, May 21, 1981. In Richards' view, Prescott "knew how to use the English language, not pedantically, but in its glorious strength and beauty."

[12] WCW to Brethren, Nov. 21, 1895; AGD to OAO, Nov. 22, 1895.

[13] WCW to SMcC, Nov. 5, 1895; WCW to AJB, Nov. 22, 1895.

[14] EGW to SNH, Nov. 6, 1895; EGW to JEW, Nov. 1895.

[15] Book Committee minutes, Nov. 13, 1895; WWP to FDS, Jan. 16, 1896. The problem in the manuscript that the committee had difficulty with was clearly his interpretation of the law in Galatians. This section of the manuscript (p. 7) in the book committee's files is marked with a question mark and three other Scripture references in handwriting that appears to be that of Uriah Smith.

[16] EGW to OAO, May 22, 1896; EGW to Book Committee, Oct. 26, [1896]. (Internal evidence suggests that this letter was written in 1896, not 1898, as indicated on the document. See my dissertation, vol. 1, pp. 212, 213.) The members of the committee were G. C. Tenney, U. Smith, M. G. Kellogg, G. W. Caviness, J. Kolvoord, F. M. Wilcox, and F. D. Starr.

[17] EGW to SNH, May 30, 1896. For a more extensive discussion of this episode and its implications concerning the need for openness to further theological development and understanding, see my article "Developing Truth and Changing Perspectives," *Ministry,* April 2003, pp. 24-29.

[18] WWP to WCW, June 5, 1896; Sept. 5, 1896.

[19] WWP to OAO, Dec. 19, 1895.

[20] AUCSM, Nov. 11, 1895. The resolution is almost exactly the same as the one Prescott presented at the 1894 convention and the 1895 General Conference session.

[21] WWP to OAO, Nov. 20, 1895.

[22] Prescott felt it to be a mistake that school planners had used up donations in getting ready to start and had nothing left to construct buildings. WWP to OAO, Oct. 13, 1895.

[23] AGD, "Our School," *Gleaner,* January 1897, p. 1. The transcribed manuscript no longer exists.

[24] *RH,* June 16, 1896, p. 10.

[25] WWP to OAO, Nov. 20, 1895; Dec. 19, 1895; *RH,* Dec. 24, 1895, p. 826.

[26] Jerry Moon speaks of the changes that occurred at this time as a "continental divide" in Adventist Christology (*The Trinity* [Hagerstown, Md.: Review and Herald Pub. Assn., 2002], pp. 196-198). The book is coauthored by Woodrow Whidden, Jerry Moon, and John W. Reeve. Jerry Moon's two chapters on the historical background of this area of Adventist theological development seem not fully aware of the extent of the focused biblical and theological discussions that took place in Australia at this time or of the extent of Prescott's involvement in them.

[27] In spite of the anticreedal origins of Adventism Prescott felt it was of value to understand how the early church had interpreted the biblical materials and how it expressed its convictions. There is some irony to this.

[28] By February Prescott had completed the manuscript for the second quarter of lessons on John and had been reading volume 1 of the "Life of Christ," which at that time was almost complete. WWP to OAO, Feb. 10, 1896.

[29] Daniells relates in detail to Prescott how he found the new Christological understanding to be helpful and effective in his evangelistic preaching of the Sabbath. His letter clearly indicates that he was relating to Prescott as a mentor. AGD to WWP, Mar. 3, 1896.

[30] Daniells had found the little book in a secondhand bookstore and had been impressed with its teaching. He reported to Prescott that it had been a blessing to himself and his workers. AGD to WWP, Mar. 3, 1896; HCL to AWS, June 2, 1947.

[31] "The Cooranbong Institute," *RH,* June 16, 1896, p. 10.

[32] WCW to OAO, May 1, 1896.

[33] It was Ellen White's pattern to seek such assistance. She had earlier sought the help of Jones and Waggoner in editing a manuscript from a biblical and theological perspective. If they detected "any passages that are still obscure, or anything that is apparently contradictory, or conflicting with the Scripture," they were to let Ellen White's editorial staff know. WCW to CHJ, May 18, 1887.

[34] HCL to LEF, Aug. 30, 1947. See also WWP to OAO, Feb. 10, 1896; EGW MS 62, 1896; MS 64, 1896. The "Life of Christ" manuscript was actually reworked and not published for another two years.

[35] *The Trinity,* p 198. The passages from John are John 1:1; 8:57, 58; 10:30; 11:25; 16:8; 14:16-18, 26; 16:8, 12-14. Other scriptures included Col. 2:9; Heb. 1:3; Matt. 28:19, 20; Prov. 8:30; Rom. 8:16; and 1 Cor. 2:11, 12.

[36] AGD to WWP, Mar. 3, 1896; HCL to AWS, June 2, 1945.

[37] Interestingly, when Daniells reported to Prescott about the helpfulness of Andrew Murray's book in his Armadale workers' meetings, he still refers to the Holy Spirit by the impersonal pronoun: ". . .we studied about the Holy Spirit and prayed for *its* indwelling presence, we felt assured that *it* came to us and truly blessed us" (AGD to WWP, Mar. 3, 1896). The usage may simply indicate that Daniells was unconsciously locked into his usual language or that the issue of the personality of the Spirit came up in the later meetings at Cooranbong rather than in Melbourne. Lacey's correspondence with Froom implies the latter (LEF to HCL, Aug. 8, 1945).

[38] Lacey's letter to LeRoy Froom came as response to a request from Froom specifically

inquiring about any "agitation or discussion" of any sort occurring in Australia at the time the much clearer statements on the eternal deity of Christ appeared in *The Desire of Ages*. M. L. Andreasen had been suggesting there had not been (LEF to HCL, Aug. 8, 1947). But Froom took the view that "the spirit of prophecy was never the instrument to initiate doctrine, or other truths among us" (LEF to HCL, Sept. 26, 1947). Lacey, connected to Ellen White's extended family circle through marriage, was, in a sense, part of the "inner circle" as it were and is thus an important witness. The two families were closely connected. Lacey's aged parents, who had moved to Cooranbong from Tasmania to be with their children. In his response to an earlier inquiry from Spalding on the same issue, Lacey cited some of the changes Adventists had adopted in the lyrics of certain of the "outstanding hymns of the Christian Church" to avoid overt references to the Trinity and the personality of the Holy Spirit (as well as some allusions to righteousness by faith). The changes to the wording had bothered his Anglican church-musician mother when she became an Adventist. Lacey was glad that the 1941 *Church Hymnal* had reverted to the original wordings—although the compilers still could not bring themselves to include the verse to the hymn "Holy, Holy, Holy" that referred to the Trinity.

[39] MLA, unpublished chapel talk, Nov. 30, 1948. EGW, *The Desire of Ages*, p. 530. See also Russell Holt, "The Doctrine of the Trinity in the Seventh-day Adventist Denomination: Its Rejection and Acceptance" (unpublished paper, Andrews University, 1969), AUHR, and Jerry Moon et al., *The Trinity*, pp. 196-198, for further historical background.

[40] The statement paraphrases one from a devotional commentary by John Coming entitled *Sabbath Evening Readings on the New Testament: St. John* (London: Arthur Hall, Virtue and Company, 1857), p. 6. It is probably not without significance in the context of the central theme of the Australian Bible institute to note that commentary was on the Gospel of John.

[41] WWP to SNH, Nov. 4, 1896; WWP to EGW, Aug. 9, 1896.

[42] OAO to WWP, Aug. 31, 1896; WWP to EGW, Nov. 10, 1896.

[42] WWP to OAO, Feb. 10, 1896; OAO to WWP, Mar. 27, 1896.

[44] WWP to OAO, May 4, 1896; WWP to EGW, July 3, 1896.

[45] BCCFacMin, Jan. 4, 1897; BCCBdMin, Jan. 5, 1897.

[46] WWP to EGW, July 16, 1896; Nov. 15, 1897; *GC Bulletin*, 1897, p. 143.

[47] WWP to WCW, Sept. 5, 1896.

[48] *Nebraska State Journal*, Mar. 1, 1897, p. 8.

[49] GC Recording Secretary, Mar. 4, 1897.

[50] GAI to RSD, Mar. 26, 1897; ERP to AGD, Jan. 16, 1903.

[51] GAI to RSD, Mar. 26, 1897; *GC Bulletin*, Feb. 20, 1899, p. 34.

[52] GAI to WWP, Apr. 8. 1898.

CHAPTER IX

FRUSTRATED ADMINISTRATOR

WHAT HAD GONE WRONG? The news of Prescott's transfer to Great Britain astounded Ellen White. She had quite expected that the 1897 General Conference session would have elected the professor-evangelist as president. But she was not the only one startled. As we have seen, the outcome of the meetings surprised Prescott as well. But then the 1897 session was not a normal one. According to the journalist who reported the session in detail in the *Nebraska State Journal,* the respected local newspaper, the meetings were more like war. At the height of the "hostilities" there was a "freedom of speech" and "expression of opinions" that was "quite out of harmony" with the "decorum usually witnessed" in business sessions of the denomination. It had been a meeting Prescott would never forget.[1]

According to the *General Conference Bulletin* editor, the session saw less business transacted than "any previous meeting for years."[2] Many, including Ellen White, who had hoped that the session would accomplish major reforms, found themselves deeply disappointed. It introduced only one significant organizational change: the approval of the experimental Australian and European union conference idea. The obstacle that held up the business of the session was what should have been a simple matter— the election of officers. The lack of consensus and ill feeling over it created barriers that prevented the adoption of other reforms. Not until just two days before the assembly dispersed and only after numerous heated exchanges did the delegates finally resolve the issue of the elections.

Several months prior to the meeting, and after a number of straightforward letters from Ellen White, O. A. Olsen had informed her of his decision to step down from the presidency. "It seems very clear to me that the Lord does not want me to occupy my present position after the next

General Conference."[3] After months of repeated stern rebukes and warnings from Cooranbong he felt almost a total failure. Overwhelmed by the
continual perplexities and pressures of laboring with strong-minded individuals and overworked and wearied beyond measure, he acknowledged
his "inadequacy" to implement the required reforms. He suggested to both
W. C. White and his mother that her son be the one to replace him. "I
cannot think of anyone so well fitted . . . , knowing your intense anxiety
for the work," he had written to W. C. White.[4] But having recently become aware of her son's lack of management expertise and the difficulties
he had fallen into as president of the Australian Conference, she strongly
rejected the idea. Instead, once they had heard the news from Olsen, both
she and W. C. White had nominated Prescott as the favored candidate. At
an earlier General Conference session W. C. White reminded Olsen that
Ellen White had remarked that it would be good for Prescott and Olsen
to work together. Ever since that time, he suggested, he had been sure that
Prescott was the one "the Lord was preparing to take the presidency"
whenever the time came for Olsen to "have a season of release."[5] The
prospect of such a thing, when the professor learned of it, filled him with
dread. He preferred to be "away from America," not "caught up again" in
boards and committees. "I feel that I cannot go back to the old regime and
bind myself up with the same management any longer," he responded.[6]
Ellen White gently assured him that he would know his duty when the
occasion came and that times of necessity were God's opportunities.

What frightened Prescott so much about the prospect of becoming
president was the recent string of stinging testimonies from Ellen White
about the faults of church administrators. While he was in Australia she had
personally unburdened herself to him a number of times, mentioning things
she would not even talk about to her son. She knew that he could not do
anything to change the situation, and to discuss the problems with him only
made him depressed. Ellen White had steadfastly refused to attend the upcoming session herself, but sent Prescott a letter after urging upon him the
responsibility of trying to effect a change. "What can I do?" he had asked
helplessly.[7] The eschatological "shaking time," he was convinced, had come.
Nevertheless, he came up with some constructive suggestions about reorganization and election procedures and wrote them to Ellen White, who
seemed to regard them with favor and elaborated on them in reply.[8]

Referring to one of Ellen White's sharpest statements, he commented to W. C. White, "It is a terrible thing to me when the Lord tells us that his voice is no longer heard through the . . . General Conference." But he assured Ellen White that when the time came for action he would exercise "whatever influence" he might have.[9]

But Prescott apparently miscalculated the time for action or had lost whatever influence he had once had. His intervention was a disaster. Seeing problems right at the outset of the meeting, he "protested earnestly." He particularly objected to the fact that the previous General Conference Committee continued to exercise executive authority even during the conference when the conference in session ought to have been acting for itself. He also bristled at the practice that allowed the incumbent president to select the personnel for the subcommittees of the conference before the session began. Such practices, he argued, would naturally tend to preserve the status quo. There was no way that the much-needed reforms (or any new approach at all) could be achieved if such practices continued. And he said so plainly. The role of the Executive Committee, he asserted, should be limited simply to calling the conference together at session time and planning for the physical details.[10] The session would then organize itself and appoint its own committees (a reform not adopted until the dramatic beginning of the 1901 conference when Ellen White and A. G. Daniells finally broke with tradition).[11] According to the local journalist who covered the session, when someone questioned the "almost unlimited authority a certain office conferred upon its holder," the reply came back that it was expected that "only converted people" would occupy the position, "and they would not misuse the power."[12] Whether Prescott's protest was either ill-timed or ill-expressed or perhaps both, the result was the same. It backfired. According to his own account, delegates somehow assumed that he was seeking Olsen's place. But if Prescott is to be believed, he could have thought of nothing worse.

Not until 11 days after the session began did the Nominating Committee bring in its first partial report. The list did not include Prescott's name (apparently because it was intended that he should go to Union College as president). A two-hour discussion ensued, studded by a "crossfire" of "testy speeches" and "tart replies" that, according to the local newspaper, "betokened considerable feeling." The delegates subsequently referred the report back to the committee, effectively blocking "the wheels of all other business."[13] The following day the nominating report listed Prescott as president of the new European Union Conference. The report itself turned the delegates "from prayer to scrapping," according to the sensationalistic newspaper headline. The debate lasted the whole day. During the free-for-all some attempted to bypass the Nominating Committee by calling the conference to vote by ballot from the floor for the election of its officers. The voice vote was so close that the chair called for a count. The motion lost by 46 to 57. Not willing to accept the verdict, one reform advocate and Prescott supporter attempted a motion from the floor anyway. In the provocative action, J. E. Graham of Melbourne, captain of the mission ship *Pitcairn,* proposed that Prescott's name be substituted for G. A. Irwin as president of the General Conference. It lapsed for want of a second. That was the nearest Prescott got to the presidency. Subsequently, the session even dropped him from being named president of the European Union Conference, because, some told him, he lacked the right foreign languages.

Toward the end of the day's contentious proceedings another motion from the floor sponsored by E. J. Waggoner proposed that Prescott go to England. It carried. Jubilant that the "deadlock" had finally broken, the entire assembly broke out in singing the doxology. But even then the delegates subsequently voted only four of the names in the Nominating Committee's report that day. The rest passed without objection on Sunday, the last day of the conference. It was certainly not the usual way for the church to conduct its business.[14]

After all the harsh things Ellen White had said about General Conference boards and committees, Prescott found comfort in the fact that he had been sent to England "without any recommendation from any committee but under what seemed to be the special guidance of the Spirit of the Lord by the direct action of the full conference."[15] Although some, dismayed at the state of church politics, might have felt that the denominational leadership had sent him to "Siberia," the professor chose to look at the move more positively. He reported to Ellen White that he had "never felt of better faith and courage in the Lord's work."[16] It was just as well. His sojourn in England would call for all the courage he could muster.

During most of the two decades Adventists had worked in Great Britain, progress had been slow. When Prescott arrived to superintend the region in late 1897, membership stood at 590. Only five ordained ministers, six licentiates, and a few Bible instructors and door-to-door booksellers constituted his worker force. Worst of all, the budget assigned was only $3,000, having been reduced from the previous year's $10,000. "Crippled on every side," Prescott joked with Ellen White, adding that he felt like appealing to the (poverty-stricken) Australian field for help.[17]

But budget or no budget, he still had work to get done. One of his first major moves was to give some formal structure to the church. Less than 12 months after arriving he called a monthlong general meeting at Bath. Before its close on August 27, 1898, delegates voted to form the British Union Conference of Seventh-day Adventists. Prescott was now more than a superintendent. He could call himself president.

True to his contention that he preferred evangelism to being locked up in boards and committees, Prescott threw himself into evangelistic activities. His first series in a London suburb with Waggoner yielded a few young women converts, but he hankered after larger results. Forsaking the usual tent-meeting style of campaign, he headed to the beach during the summer with some of his staff, rented a private schoolhouse, and attempted to run a street mission with open-air preaching. His ruse was to attract a crowd with music (a portable organ, impromptu quartets, and his own expertise on the cornet) and then conduct a short preaching service. It worked. The mission attracted large crowds and produced "excellent interests." Prescott felt the approach differed from that employed by the Salvation Army, although it is not clear in what way.[18] But it appears that the initial success did not last. By the end of the year the professor had returned to the usual tent-meeting approach despite England's inclement weather.

Other campaigns followed in cities around the country, but progress was glacial. Membership inched up to 800 by 1899, but did not cross the 900 mark until after 1900. Considering the effort expended, Prescott regarded the results as minimal at best. With E. J. Waggoner's *Present Truth* magazine increasing its circulation to 16,000 per week and with the addition of a health outreach by Drs. Daniel and Lauretta Kress, he had hopes of realizing more baptisms. But it was not to be. Growth remained disappointing.

In spite of his busy evangelistic schedule, Prescott seems to have found plenty of opportunity for study in England. Living in a duplex right next door to E. J. Waggoner provided many occasions for theological dialogue. The professor also continued his long-established custom of frequenting secondhand bookstores, doubtless keeping Waggoner up-to-date on his latest finds. The dialogue had its effect. Prescott felt that Waggoner helped him gain "enlarged" views of the gospel.

Other ministers in Britain, however, were not sure that the Waggoner-Prescott theology was altogether "kosher." For example, E. E. Andross, a fellow American working in Birmingham, complained to Haskell about the "extreme" ideas on sanctification the two men were developing. Their enthusiastic emphasis on "what, when, and how to eat"—possibly encouraged by the Drs. Kress, who also tended to extremes on health—and their suggestion that in some sense every meal was a sacrament in which believers ate the body and drank the blood of Christ concerned him. It sounded fanciful. (In fact, Waggoner pushed his emphasis to the point in which he believed that if church members lived strictly according to his "new gospel of health," they should expect never to get sick again.)[19]

Andross and another old-time minister, J. N. Loughborough, talked with the two leaders, who subsequently modified their health emphasis. But then, according to Andross, a new theological issue, "the daily" of Daniel 8:13, caught the attention of the pair, and what they did with it perplexed him just as much. This issue would trouble not just Andross but much of the church for several decades in the early part of the twentieth century. It would result in some seriously questioning of Prescott's orthodoxy and cause a good deal of personal anguish for the professor. (A later chapter discusses this problem in detail.)

Sensing that Waggoner might be running into difficulty, Ellen White tried to lure him to Australia with an invitation to work alongside her. He declined, preferring to think that England needed him more. That decision, in hindsight, may have set a pattern of resistance to her counsel. Thus it was not until 1901, when the General Conference elected Prescott as field secretary of the Foreign Mission Board, that the two kindred spirits went their separate ways. In the meantime the "strained" views on sanctification that the pair debated between them and proclaimed as a "gospel of health" (to some it sounded suspiciously similar to pantheism) were enough to "taint" the professor in the eyes of church conservatives for the rest of his days, as we note in a later chapter.

Daniells, the new General Conference president in 1901, felt glad that Prescott was at last away from Waggoner. Prescott "works intensely," he wrote, "and if allowed to let his mind run on a single topic or on a narrow range, he is in danger of taking an extreme position, or at least it looks extreme. He needs a greater variety and a broader range for balance."[20]

TROUBLESOME INSTITUTIONS

If the meager results of his evangelistic efforts in England frustrated Prescott, the failure that met his efforts to establish stable church institutions bothered him more so. The only institution owned by the church when Prescott arrived in England was the small London publishing house. In spite of his vigorous efforts to establish a college, a hospital, and a food factory, the publishing house would still be the only denominational entity in England when he left four years later.

Prescott tried his hand at the health program first. Shortly after arriving in England he acquired property on which to establish a sanitarium and a food factory. He also launched a health magazine. The sanitarium accommodated only eight patients (euphemistically called "friends" because the Kresses were not legally able to practice in Britain). But it was a start. Six months after the health project was under way, however, fire completely destroyed the factory plant. Insurance covered only a fraction of the loss, an oversight that hurt Prescott keenly, as he had invested thousands of dollars of his own money in the project. Not long afterward ill health forced the Kresses to return to America. Their loss proved fatal. As a result, the small sanitarium closed, and the health magazine promptly ceased publication.[21]

Astounded at the rapid rate that his carefully crafted health program was "going to pieces," Prescott turned philosophical. Perhaps, he mused, he had devoted too much of his time "to the business side of the work." Preoccupation with "financial burdens and perplexities" had prevented him from spending as much time as he should have in evangelism and pastoral work. He would endeavor to learn from the lesson.

Establishing an educational program proved equally frustrating. It was financial limitations, not the lack of trying, that blocked a permanent school. The enthusiastic educator made two attempts to get one started. One was an evening school in London, and the other a school in Redhill, Surrey. Both were designed as a follow-up to evangelistic campaigns to train workers for the church, but neither lasted for more than three or four months. Although disappointed, Prescott was thankful for the chance to try out his curriculum ideas. The Bible had served as his principal textbook. "I am sure that I should not have been able to work these things out in any of the large schools in America," he commented acidly to Ellen White.[22]

Despite such failures Prescott refused to give up the idea of a denominational school. He eventually selected a place in the country 60 miles from London and explored the idea of establishing a shoe factory as a source of student income. But obstacles abounded. Not even the usually supportive Ellen White encouraged him. Any spare church funds at headquarters were being channeled to the South Pacific. As W. C. White explained it, his mother viewed Australia as having more pressing needs at the time. "While Australia is very small compared with the dimensions which our work in Great Britain will soon attain—it is our duty to develop the work here rapidly just now." Whether we should view his statement as a prediction or just a W. C. White hope, it never materialized in Prescott's time or later.[23]

Not one to give up easily, Prescott continued his endeavor to generate interest and raise funds locally or from any source he could think of, including his own. But he found himself blocked at every turn.[24] Finally, at the last annual conference he presided over in 1900, he managed to persuade his constituency of the need for a school. They voted to commence a full-fledged "missionary training school." But further problems delayed progress, and by the time it finally opened in January 1902, Prescott had already returned to America. He had not been able to see the fulfillment of his dream, but he found satisfaction in laying the groundwork for what today is Newbold College.

His struggles with the health and educational programs were nothing compared to his anguish over Britain's infant publishing house. First set up in Grimsby in 1884 as the International Tract Society Limited, the office later moved to London. The plant possessed a bare minimum of machinery, and Prescott felt it served more as a distribution depot for the American publishing houses than anything else. A short time after his arrival in the country he had been appointed chair of the board, but when he saw what he had inherited he wished he did not have the responsibility. The affairs of the publishing office were fearfully tangled.

With no operating capital, management talent, or effective sales agents, and bound by complex interchurch financial arrangements that prevented it from having an independent management, circumstances had driven the institution to the point of bankruptcy. The complex financial structure made it exceedingly difficult to collect from its interchurch creditors, the largest of which was the Echo Publishing Company in Australia managed by W. C. White. The Australians owed the British plant a large amount of money, and the British house could not persuade them to pay it. Prescott thought it grossly unfair that the Echo Publishing House should embark on an extensive expansion program using his capital. The affair exasperated him and strained relationships with other church leaders.[25]

Repeated unsuccessful efforts to straighten things out led him to threaten the so-called board of directors with his resignation. He did not wish to "remain in a false position any longer."[26] Visits from General Conference officials and emergency sessions of the board resulted in changes that promised to give the English management more independence. They requested Prescott, with his expertise in publishing, to give the problem his personal attention. The professor complied, but six months later, convinced that it was "impossible to straighten things out in the office" or to get W. C. White to pay his bill, he handed in his resignation. He would get back to looking after his ministers and promoting evangelism—"the legitimate work of the conference." The American overseers could look out for the publishing house themselves. Not until after Prescott had left Great Britain did the denominational leadership finally resolve the publishing house tangle. In mid-1902 it eventually became fully independent under the direct supervision of the British Union Conference.[27]

Prescott found the publishing house perplexities particularly painful because of the business attitudes of his colleagues. An officious letter from W. C. White in 1899 and Prescott's biting 13-page reply led to an exchange of correspondence that illustrates well the intense aggravation the professor experienced at this time. It also offers insight into Prescott's relationship to White.[28] White's first letter stunned him. In fact, he read it "several times to make sure" he "understood it correctly" and waited several weeks before undertaking a reply. It seemed clear to the professor that White was being sharp and mercenary, introducing a "new order of things" into the publishing program. Prescott explained, therefore, with considerable understatement, that he would be "a little more frank" in reply. Though clearly angry, he was still gentleman enough to make sure that his quarrel with White would remain private. He took the trouble to type the reply himself, "so that it should not be put through any stenographer's mind."[29]

Prescott had a string of objections to White's proposals. It extremely annoyed him that White should think he could unilaterally usurp valuable sections of the sales territory of the London publishing house. Furthermore, the prices White requested for printing plates and the royalties he demanded were "beyond all reason." He also felt that White's intention to use certain illustrations in denominational publications without permission or payment was an unethical infringement of copyright laws. "You have no more legal right to use them in Australia than we have in England, but we must leave that with you to consider."[30] But more than anything it was the spirit in the work that seemed to the professor to be wrong. White's assertion that "we control and are now willing to receive offers from you" with regard to sales territories seemed foreign to Prescott's concept of Christian business relationships. "You state with all frankness what is so evident all the time," he charged; "your purpose [is] to bring the London house to terms quickly." Why should institutions and "brethren" have to "haggle" and "badger" each other about how much to pay each other to "compensate . . . for the privilege of spreading the message in the different parts of the world?" It wearied Prescott. He was not interested in running a church business just as a commercial undertaking. If commerce and profits were all that important, he would not have left his own business so many years previously.

W. C. White's connection with his mother did not seem to intimidate the professor. If Prescott felt that there was "hard dealing and overcharging," then it needed to be put right, even if it involved the son of the prophet. He was well aware, however, that he had spoken bluntly. As a result, he offered an apology for anything he might have said that may have been "calculated to wound" White's feelings. The whole business was "a sore trial." White, in a conciliatory response, acknowledged that he had written "with much emphasis" upon "financial features." But he assured the professor "with all candor and frankness" that he did not "cherish such feelings" toward Prescott's work as the professor might have thought from reading his letter.[31]

The professor's quarrel with White actually reflected deeper concerns, ones that he would voice again at the 1901 General Conference session. He was intensely frustrated with the perilous state of church organization in general. One of the major reasons for the slow progress of the denomination in Britain was that it received so little financial help from outside. He felt that the General Conference had been starving the church in England. "Officialism" stood "between the people and the work," he claimed. "Every effort to do anything" in England had been "hampered," and he was sure that a change was needed at Battle Creek headquarters before the denomination could conduct anything "advantageously."[32]

Having been on the receiving end of the overcentralized and out-of-touch General Conference bureaucracy, Prescott felt he understood more about Ellen White's complaints, protests, and calls for reform during the late 1890s. Just prior to the 1899 conference she lamented that it had been some years since she had considered the General Conference to be "the voice of God."[33] But how to bring about any change?

At the 1899 General Conference session in South Lancaster, Massachusetts, Prescott tried again. For a second time he protested the power of the chairman to appoint the session's committees and the continuing executive function of the General Conference Committee during the session. Such practices resulted in the conference being "stage managed" or "rigged" like a political convention. His speeches became more strident than ever. Reforms, he argued, could never happen with the session locked up so tight before it even started. He also advocated other ways of decentralizing authority in the denomination. But his pleas for a more open approach to church organization fell once more on deaf ears. To the current leadership, his ideas sounded like an invitation to "anarchy" and "disorganization." The professor fumed that the church was nearer to "papacy" than to "anarchy."[34]

In another debate he dared to expose publicly the misappropriation of mission field funds by the General Conference treasury. (Treasury officials had secretly credited private donations sent directly to Ellen White in Australia to church books and then subtracted the amount from "official" general appropriations to Australia.) But the speech only created further hostility. His superiors felt he was simply being disruptive and hard to get along with. Prescott knew he was being misunderstood, but felt helpless as to how to change things. "The brethren think I am in favor of disorganizing the work; but so far as I am personally concerned, this does not worry me. . . . If the brethren understood me, they would not think so."[35]

The combative advocate of reform had taken a tumble once again. In a way, it was inevitable. In his defense one can say that Prescott was able to see solutions before his colleagues even recognized the problems. They then often viewed his approach to solving problems as the problem itself. At the 1899 conference Prescott continued to be associated with the incautious A. T. Jones. His apparent unqualified endorsement of Jones' overstated ideas created barriers in the minds of Prescott's hearers. As a result, the conference session passed by without any major changes being accomplished. Prescott went back to England further discouraged, while defensive General Conference officials laid secret plans to make sure the professor would not have as much to say at the next General Conference session.[36]

But the church structure would not always remain resistant to restructuring. Nor would the conspiracy to silence Prescott be effective. Although no major breakthroughs occurred in 1899, the airing of specific problems and wrongs and Prescott's articulate explanation of the constitutional and procedural reforms needed undoubtedly paved the way and prepared minds for what happened two year later.[37]

The 1901 General Conference adopted Prescott's long-advocated reform right at the start. With the arrival of Ellen White and A. G. Daniells on the scene, the momentum at last became sufficient to roll over any objectors. Those who advocated change cast precedent aside in a couplike maneuver, and the very first meeting undertook a series of bold moves that enabled the session itself to set up its own working committees and an agenda for reform. As a result, changes came thick and fast, and they included Prescott's own role within the church. When it was over, he found himself appointed back to Battle Creek headquarters. As secretary of the Foreign Mission Board he occupied one of the most important positions in the denomination. A. G. Daniells, the new General Conference president, relied on him as his "lieutenant." And before the next General Conference session, Prescott would receive further important duties that would place him in a position to exercise a dominating role in church affairs for the next decade.

---

[1] *Nebraska State Journal,* Mar. 3, 1897, p. 3.

[2] *GC Bulletin,* Mar. 8, 1897, p. 320.

[3] OAO to EGW, Apr. 24, 1896.

[4] OAO to WCW, Apr. 23, 1896.

[5] WCW to OAO, June 2, 1896. Ellen White's remarks apparently occurred at the 1891 General Conference session. W. C. White recalled that it was the last GC session he had attended before moving to Australia.

[6] WCW to WWP, June 2, 1896; WWP to EGW, July 16, 1896; Aug. 9, 1896.

[7] WWP to WCW, Sept. 5, 1896; WWP to EGW, Oct. 6, 1896.

[8] WWP to EGW, Nov. 10, 1896; WWP to WCW, July 30, 1896; WWP to EGW, July 30, 1896; Aug. 9, 1896; EGW to WWP, Sept. 1, 1896.

[9] WWP to WCW, Sept. 5, 1896; WWP to EGW, Oct. 6, 1896.

[10] See Prescott's recollection two years later, *GC Bulletin,* Feb. 27, 1899, pp. 90, 91.

[11] For further discussion of how the systemic conflict of interest created difficulties for the reforming of church organization, see Gilbert M. Valentine, "Conflict of Interest: An Impediment to Reform, 1897-1901," *Adventist Professional* 3, no. 3 (September 1991): 7-10.

[12] *Nebraska State Journal,* Mar. 1, 1897, p. 8.

[13] *Nebraska State Journal,* Mar. 8, 1897, p. 3.

[14] *GC Bulletin,* Mar. 8, 1897.

[15] WWP to EGW, Aug. 4, 1897.

[16] WWP to WCW, Nov. 15, 1897.

[17] WWP to EGW, Nov. 15, 1897; *RH,* Sept. 13, 1898. See also Nigel Barhum, "The Progress of the Seventh-day Adventist Church in Great Britain, 1898-1974" (Ph.D. dissertation, University of Michigan, 1976).

[18] WWP to EGW, Feb. 21, 1898; Sept. 12, 1898.

[19] EEA to SNH, Nov. 12, 1900.

[20] AGD to WCW, July 1, 1901.

[21] WWP to WCW, Mar. 30, 1900; *GC Bulletin,* Apr. 22, 1901, p. 395.

[22] WWP to EGW, Feb. 21, 1898.

[23] WCW to WWP, Aug. 22, 1899.

[24] *GC Bulletin,* Apr. 22, 1901, p. 395.

[25] WWP to WCW, Oct. 16, 1899; Dec. 28, 1899.

[26] WWP to WCW, Mar. 16, 1900.

[27] AGD to WWP, June 8, 1902.

[28] WCW to WWP, Aug. 22, 1899; WWP to WCW, Oct. 26, 1899.

[29] WCW to WWP, Oct. 22, 1899; WWP to WCW, Oct. 26, 1899; WCW to WWP, Jan. 15, 1900; WWP to WCW, Dec. 28, 1899; Mar. 16, 1900. Letters crossing in the mails did not help things.

[30] WWP to WCW, Mar. 16, 1900. This letter Prescott also typed without the aid of a stenographer in order to keep it confidential and protect W. C. White's reputation.

[31] WCW to WWP, Jan. 15, 1900.

[32] WWP to EJW, June 15, 1902.

[33] Cited in *GC Bulletin,* Feb. 24, 1899, p. 74, but apparently written Aug. 26, 1898.

[34] *GC Bulletin,* Feb. 23, 1899, p. 61.

[35] *GC Bulletin,* Feb. 26, 1899.

[36] WWP to EJW, June 15, 1902.

[37] A. J. Breeds' speech indicates that Prescott was being heard. *GC Bulletin,* Feb. 27, 1899, p. 94.

CHAPTER X
GENERAL CONFERENCE ADMINISTRATOR

THE DENOMINATION WILL break up, and there will be a new coming out," Prescott declared to W. C. White as the twentieth century crept over the horizon. He could see schism directly ahead unless the church made certain reforms. The upcoming 1901 General Conference session would undoubtedly "mark a crisis," because both the organizational structure and the attitudes of the leadership had become so "hardened." "There must be a change," he warned.[1]

The 1901 session was scheduled to be held in California in mid-February, but Prescott doubted that "he could do any good" by attending. He had failed miserably in trying to bring about change at the previous two sessions. The delegates had misunderstood his efforts and misrepresented his ideas, and he knew that the American leadership regarded his work in England with "much suspicion." What was the worth of going? Discouraged and feeling discredited in the eyes of church administration, he felt sorely tempted to stay at home.

A visit from A. G. Daniells in mid-1900 helped encourage the despondent professor. The Australian Union Conference president, on his way back to the United States, had stopped in England to spend time with Prescott and to speak at camp meetings. The visit gave opportunity for the two to compare their experiences and vent their frustrations. They also, no doubt, discussed what changes they saw needed in church organization and what strategies they might employ to accomplish them. Both local presidents had been on the receiving end of a church organization that was no longer adequate for the needs of a rapidly expanding denomination. Daniells was as adamant as Prescott in his opinion that the situation simply could not continue as before. Things had reached the breaking point. "It will be a great calamity to have this conference go through as the last one did," he told W. C. White after he had visited Prescott.[2] When Prescott sailed for America in early March, he was glad that this time other strong voices would be advocating reform. As it happened, neither president was disappointed. Not only did the 1901 General Conference session effect major changes in church structure; it brought both men to center stage in denominational affairs.

For Prescott, the 1901 session spelled a remarkable reversal of fortune. Recalled from England at Daniells' insistence, the professor found himself appointed by the delegates to direct the overseas mission program of the church as secretary of the Foreign Mission Board. Once back in Battle Creek, however, he found himself quickly involved again in the medical, educational, and publishing interests of the church as well as that of foreign missions. For the next eight years he would be second in command in church affairs, working closely with Daniells in guiding the church through one of the most turbulent and important decades in its history. Later chapters examine his editorial work and his involvement in the Kellogg crisis that occurred in this period, but here we look at Prescott's role in General Conference administration until 1909.

The history-making 1901 session eventually convened, not in Oakland, California, but in Battle Creek on April 2. Prior to the official start of the meetings, a large number of delegates met with Ellen White in the Battle Creek College library. Many shared the sentiments of Prescott and Daniells about the utter seriousness of the situation facing the church. They were eager for change. For one and a half hours that warm spring evening the 73-year-old Ellen White preached revolution. She called for immediate and far-reaching changes. Denominational leadership, she argued, needed to have wider representation from the church as a whole. There should be no "kings," and the denomination should blend its evangelistic and medical elements. Picking up on a strategy that Prescott had fruitlessly urged at the two previous sessions, she asserted in her "epoch-making" address that delegates needed to grasp the nettle and change things right from the outset. "Do not wait until the conference is over and then gather up the forces to see what can be done," she declared.[3]

The following day Ellen White made the same point in her address to delegates at the official opening of the conference. She did not know how the reorganization should be done nor what changes would be best—she simply knew that things must change. The gauntlet had been flung down. Directly after her speech Daniells strode to the front and asked for the floor. He recounted the meeting of the previous night. Then in a lightning stroke that looked suspiciously like a strategy that Prescott may have suggested, or that they had both planned, Daniells quickly moved that "the usual rules and precedents for arranging and transacting the business of the conference be suspended."[4] The motion was seconded and voted before a protest could surface, overcoming the first hurdle. Instead of the usual standing committees named by the incumbent president (and thus stacked by favorite status-quo yes people), the delegates appointed one large committee of 25 members as a working group. Named as a "committee on counsel," the group would serve as a general steering committee, and it received the task of reorganization as well as preparing an agenda for the delegates. Kellogg's separate sanitarium organization had directly appointed six of its members. The pattern of the past had been shattered in one fell blow. Prescott was thrilled.

The "committee on counsel" eventually expanded to include 75 delegates. It set up its own subcommittees and assigned them set tasks while the rest of the delegates listened to sermons and reports. Before the meeting was over, it had approved three major changes that changed the face of the denominational organization. It created union conferences throughout North America in order to localize administrative control; it made the General Conference Executive Committee more representative by enlarging it to 25; and it decided to bring the various independent church agencies—such as the Sabbath School Association, the Tract Society, and the publishing and educational societies—directly under the control of the central committee. Previously they had been completely autonomous organizations with their own governing boards, committees, and constituencies. Further refinements to these basic structural changes occurred in 1903 and 1905, but the new shape of the church produced by the 1901 session remained basically the same.

Prescott's role at the meeting seemed to be much less public than in previous sessions. Apart from one major evening sermon and a report on the denomination's activities in England, his public appearances were limited to short statements clarifying issues on behalf of the "committee on counsel" or urging the adoption of some particular reform. He had lost not an ounce of his reforming zeal, though he appeared to be less confrontational. But even then he still managed to nettle a few fellow delegates with some forthright statements. For example, in his evening sermon of April 15 he drew a parallel between Israel's rejection of Christ and the church's persistent resistance to "the message" that had come at Minneapolis. "How far has that truth been received . . . ? Not far, I can tell you." According to the professor, many had "turned against" it, and many were "rejecting it and turning from it" still. Prescott's continued agitation on the topic of righteousness by faith did not endear him to the delegates, but he could not help himself. "I am not speaking . . . simply to fill the hour," he explained. "My soul is distressed over this thing."[5]

On another occasion Prescott's audacity in publicly rebuking a number of conference presidents who failed to show up for the constituency meeting of Kellogg's Medical Association was not appreciated. He even bothered some of his close colleagues by his dogged insistence in committee that the "old ring" of former administrators, such as G. A. Irwin and I. H. Evans, be completely dropped from elective positions. Only after a lot of persuasion did he soften his stance.[6] Other sensitive reform themes that he publicly urged at the conference included the need to restore a balance between the size of the medical and ministerial programs, the urgent need for unity of action between church organizations in sending out missionaries, and the need for a more equitable distribution of money and personnel around the various mission fields. But those he did not press. He was enough of a realist to know that not everything could be transformed overnight. Already there had been changes enough. Implementing the reforms voted and stopping up loopholes would keep leadership busy for months. Ellen White was delighted. "I was never more astonished in my life than at the turn things have taken at this meeting," she commented to the delegates.[7]

FOREIGN MISSION BOARD SECRETARY, 1901-1903

Prescott's 1901 appointment as secretary of the Foreign Mission Board ranked him, in actual practice, second in authority to Daniells, who served as "chairman" of the General Conference. The 1901 session had directed that the Foreign Mission Board, though still existing in name, should work toward delegating its role to the General Conference

Committee. It was also to enlarge its scope to include North American missions as well as foreign outreach. Previously the board had functioned as an autonomous agency, and since 1897 it had even had its office geographically separated from the General Conference—an arrangement that Prescott had opposed vigorously when proposed and had clashed with W. C. White in repeated attempts to block the move. The East Coast location had never worked satisfactorily. Although the board was not formally and legally subsumed under the General Conference Committee until 1903, in practice, under Prescott's leadership, the board was the General Conference Committee.[8] In his role as board secretary Prescott often served as Daniells' personal envoy, as illustrated by his first assignment supervising the restructuring of the church organization in Europe. In late 1901 he spent several weeks implementing the new reforms in what became known as the "European General Conference."[9]

The professor found that his appointment to the Foreign Mission Board also put him back into editing and publishing—work that he had not done since he had sold his own newspaper business 16 years earlier. He took up his editor's pen again with great enthusiasm. The *Missionary Magazine* was a popular journal published by the board. Prescott immediately set about revamping it, adding new features and adopting a new format with the June 1901 issue. Circulation began to increase. Three months after he took over, the magazine absorbed the smaller *Medical Missionary* and *Gospel of Health,* and before the end of the year circulation of the paper rivaled that of the *Review.*

An immediate by-product of Prescott's enthusiastic promotion of foreign missions was an increase in those who offered themselves for overseas service. During the two years Prescott directed the foreign mission program the board sent 183 missionaries abroad. He also sought for new and innovative ways to sustain the increase. One approach called for local conferences to assume financial responsibility for denominational employees who came from their territory. Prescott had raised the idea with Ellen White back in 1896 as a way of providing larger support and because it appealed as a means of keeping the homelands directly in touch with the mission field. Under the arrangement, the General Conference simply served as a clearinghouse for assignments and as an agency for forwarding payments.[10]

One of the reasons Daniells had urged the committee to appoint Prescott as his associate was his recognition that the task of reorganizing would take special skills and creative thinking. He found the professor particularly helpful in the months that followed the General Conference session. Daniells reported to W. C. White that he enjoyed and appreciated the professor's enthusiasm and the "lively interest" he had taken in all aspects of denominational activities. Prescott's counsel "regarding intricate, complicated matters" had also been beneficial. "It has been such a help to have him for a counselor as we have traveled around and have been obliged to give counsel to our brethren," the president commented. He was especially glad of Prescott's acquaintance with the field and his familiarity with the particular problems faced by the state conferences. "He forms a quick, accurate judgment, and has a lot of courage." [11]

Friendship between the two men flourished, their relationship extending beyond the office and beyond working hours. Each took a personal interest in the other's family affairs. The frequent correspondence between the two evidences a warm collegiality, even if at times it still required formality. "My Dear Brother" was their common literary form of address.

VICE PRESIDENT, 1902-1905

Should a church have a president as its chief executive? Discussions about the question occupied a good deal of time among church leaders at the turn of the century. What was the nature of the office and what terminology should the denomination use for it? Both Prescott and A. T. Jones had quite strong views on the matter. Ellen White had raised the danger of having one individual as president, and they interpreted her very literally. They understood that the term itself gave the wrong idea of church governance. The church was best governed by committee or some sort of triumvirate that shared and rotated leadership responsibility. In deference to these firmly held ideas concerning what Ellen White had intended (and she apparently did not offer any alternative interpretation), the 1901 session took care not to designate any one person as president. Daniells simply served as "chairman" of the Executive Committee.

But he soon found that the practical demands of the business world and legal formalities required something more than a chairman. He had difficulty having his signature accepted as "chairman" of a General

Conference that was not technically a conference unless it was in session. Railway companies, for example, would not accept his signature. Both Prescott and Daniells wrestled with alternatives, but none seemed workable. *President* was a term the business world understood. Confronted by pragmatics, Prescott gave up his objections and found another way to interpret Ellen White's statement. When Daniells assumed the title of president, the task of explaining the change to the committee fell in Prescott's lap. After all, it was he that had done the about-face. The idea had never really troubled Daniells.[12]

If Prescott had any idea that a shift in the General Conference leader's title would mean a change for him as well he did not say. But it seemed obvious to the committee that if the church needed a president, then it also needed a vice president. In the reshuffle of responsibilities on February 22, 1902—and whether Prescott felt comfortable with it or not—he found himself named as vice president of the denomination. He was the first person ever to serve officially in that capacity.[13]

The three years Prescott served at headquarters as vice president of the denomination were troubled ones, and he often wished he were elsewhere. As he joked to W. A. Spicer on one occasion, he would have welcomed "a ticket to some foreign land" to escape the unending pressure. But there was no escape. Work still had to be done and problems sorted out in spite of the pressure and the tension at Battle Creek. Daniells appreciated Prescott's readiness to stand by his side through thick and thin. As he commented later, the professor's "good judgment and strength at the helm" during "the most serious and perilous crisis this cause has ever had" was of immense value.[14]

But what created so many difficulties? One source was the response to the organizational reforms. The medical branch in particular reacted negatively to the moves toward more centralized control of church institutions by the General Conference. Another reason was the clash that developed between the medical leadership and the General Conference administration. The disagreement between Daniells and Kellogg became a bitter power struggle complicated by personality differences.

The first signs of an open split between the two men appeared just a few months after Prescott's appointment as vice president in 1902. Daniells' insistence on a no-debt policy thwarted Kellogg in his attempt to build a new sanitarium in England, infuriating the doctor. About the same time, and without any collusion between the two GC leaders, Prescott's detection of "pantheistic sentiments" in Kellogg's *Living Temple* stymied the physician's main fund-raising drive for his rebuilding program in Battle Creek. Kellogg felt that the two were ganging up on him. Tensions heightened. During late 1902, as the conflict festered, Prescott found that "saying nuffin to nobody" was the safest course. Yet he feared that if nothing happened to "settle the atmosphere . . . one tremendous crash" would occur. And he was right. Before 1902 had ended, the conflict had erupted publicly.[15]

The Annual Council at Battle Creek in October witnessed a head-on confrontation between Kellogg and Daniells. They exchanged charges and countercharges in lengthy public sessions, with each leader explaining and attempting to justify his position. As Daniells had hoped and confidently expected, the General Conference Committee supported the positions that both he and Prescott had taken. The result, however, did nothing to mollify the Kellogg forces, who promptly began to lay plans for a coup d'état. They intended to replace Daniells with A. T. Jones. At the next General Conference session—in four months—they expected to unseat him. But the plan failed—Kellogg's side lacked the numbers.[16]

As a result of the tension, the March 1903 General Conference session held at Oakland, California, proved an extremely trying time for both Daniells and Prescott. The fact that Prescott suffered from a badly infected tooth and was ill for some time did not help matters. The inclusion of a president in the list of officers submitted by the Nominating Committee brought a storm of protest from the Kellogg faction. But Daniells and Prescott, supported strongly by Ellen White, won the day. Mrs. White, recognizing the pressure the two men were under, repeatedly called for them privately and advised them on how to meet the onslaught.[17]

Prescott, in spite of his indisposition, was happy also that his campaign to democratize the business sessions now made further progress. He was successful in reaffirming the principle that the session should organize itself. The first action taken by the delegates was to appoint a nominating committee that then established the standing committees. Another important change involved a modification to the constitution to provide for the election of General Conference officers by the session delegates rather than by the Executive Committee. But the serious divisions in the church made it difficult to correct other weaknesses in the organizational structure—weaknesses that had become apparent since the 1901 initiatives.

Nevertheless, the conference completed important reforms initiated two years earlier. For example, it made formal provision for departments in the General Conference, and it phased out the Foreign Mission Board, passing its function to the General Conference Committee. But the latter made Prescott's position as secretary redundant.[18]

The slate of officers elected in 1903 made provision for two vice presidents, one (Louis Conradi) to care for the European field, the other the North American field. Daniells did not yet feel secure enough to have anyone replace Prescott. Even though the professor had picked up heavy publishing responsibilities in the meantime (as editor of the *Review*), the session reappointed him as vice president to work with the union conferences in North America. Daniells anticipated that his own next term would be rocky, and desperately needed someone he could rely on.

Probably the most far-reaching decision of the 1903 General Conference session, however, was the vote to transfer both the church headquarters and the publishing house from Battle Creek. It was a major undertaking involving complicated legal and administrative difficulties and the dislocation of scores of employees. The decision resulted in a huge stir among the highly polarized membership in Battle Creek, creating a vigorous and heated opposition. Prescott, in his dual role of editor and vice president, found himself saddled with much of the burden of persuading the Battle Creek congregation of the wisdom of the move. It was not easy, and he was only partially successful. In the meantime the denomination had also asked him to assume the presidency of the new Review and Herald Publishing Association that it would establish in Washington, D.C. Overseeing the transition, in addition to his already heavy work load, would stretch him to the breaking point. The first issue of the Review published at the new location was dated August 20, 1903.

Remarkably, in spite of his overloaded schedule, Prescott still found time for preaching. Ellen White had never forgotten the powerful influence of his sermons in Australia. In 1902 she urged him not to allow his administrative and editorial duties to quench his gift for preaching the Word. "Your testimony is greatly needed in our large gatherings," she wrote. "Brother Prescott, the Lord has a message for you to give His people in regard to the preparation that must be made for the coming of the Lord." She did not want him to miss the camp meeting circuit.[19]

Prescott responded positively to the counsel, regularly spending several weeks each year visiting camp meetings and union conference sessions. He also became a popular Week of Prayer speaker at colleges. His burden during this period was the "plain truths" of "this message."[20] His hidden agenda involved protecting the church against the inroads of "Kelloggism." Somehow he even found time for public evangelism as well. Shortly after his arrival in Washington he linked up with Luther Warren to run a large evangelistic outreach in the capital.

It was clear, though, that the professor was overworking. How long could he continue to carry the responsibility of two or three men? And how long could he continue to cope with the pressures created by the ongoing struggle with the Kellogg faction? He would have to neglect something. As it happened, he found that he had to lay aside much of the administrative details for North America simply to keep up with the immediate needs of reestablishing the General Conference office and the publishing house in their new location. The denomination planned new buildings for both enterprises, and the demands of his work seemed almost overwhelming. As 1905 approached, Prescott realized that he could not do justice to all that the church had asked him to do. Consequently, after consultation with his colleagues, he decided to let go of the vice presidency and focus his energies on the *Review* and establishing the new publishing house. The 1905 General Conference session a few months later elected G. A. Irwin vice president in the professor's place.[21]

EDUCATOR

Although assigned to carry general church administrative duties, Prescott continued to have a keen interest in its educational program. He was still an educator at heart. And he did not have to wait long to have his interest satisfied. In late 1901 the General Conference had asked him to serve as a member of the restructured Education Department. Here he again became an outspoken proponent of reform. During the first year the professor either moved or seconded the majority of actions taken by the department. The same year he also eagerly supported a summer school at

Berrien Springs, Michigan, in order to foster educational reform. The following year, in addition to being the general vice president, he also served as chair of the Education Department. In this role he finally achieved his long-cherished goal of having the Battle Creek congregation establish its own elementary school—an accomplishment made easier by the prospect of the imminent closure of Battle Creek College and its transfer to a rural location in southwestern Michigan.[22]

Prescott's involvement with the relocation of Battle Creek College to Berrien Springs was not a success story. His lack of confidence in the school administration led, unfortunately, to misunderstandings with the faculty, and that in turn resulted in decades of soured relationships with key educational personnel. The story provides some interesting insights into Prescott's personal relationships. It also casts light on the political dimensions of a conflict that became a significant crossroads in the educational history of the Adventist Church.

According to Percy Magan, one of the leaders of the educational reform movement at Battle Creek, the proposal to close Battle Creek College and reopen it in a rural area first began to circulate in late 1900.[23] But Ellen White, not sure the time was right, vetoed the idea. It surfaced again at the 1901 General Conference session and this time met with general approval. Things moved quickly after that. On April 12 the stockholders voted to relocate, and the legal body for Kellogg's sanitarium voted to acquire the old college property four days later. The denomination purchased the new site at Berrien Springs on July 16.[24]

A nostalgic closing ceremony for the old school took place in May. Then in June the college held a summer school for the teachers in its new location. Prescott took a leading part in both. Sometime in August or September of that year he was elected as a trustee of the new institution and shortly afterward installed as chair of the board.[25] It was a position he assumed most reluctantly and with very mixed feelings. "You doubtless know," Prescott commented to Daniells almost a year later, "that I have not felt altogether free in this position from the first."[26]

Why did the professor have such mixed feelings? Why did he feel so reluctant about what should have been an interesting challenge? For one thing, he was already carrying heavy responsibilities. And for another, it seems that his confidence in the capabilities of the school president, E. A.

Sutherland, had diminished. He was also aware that Daniells and General Conference secretary W. A. Spicer were even more apprehensive about the competence of Sutherland and his associate, P. T. Magan, than he was. Apparently none of the General Conference administrators thought that the educators were able or broad-minded enough to run the new institution successfully. Prescott's colleagues seem to have urged his involvement in an attempt to provide balance to the youthfulness and zeal of Sutherland and Magan. At any rate, they apparently put considerable pressure on him to take the reins of the school into his hands.

In October 1901, just days prior to the start of the first term of the new institution, both Daniells and Spicer tried to suggest the change. Could he not try a repeat of the 1890s Walla Walla arrangement with himself as president and Sutherland as principal? Prescott was not interested.

According to a disillusioned Percy Magan, who complained of the matter to Ellen White, the "leading brethren" felt that Prescott's "age, experience, and general bearing . . . would help bring Emmanuel College into favor more than anything that might be done by Brother Sutherland or myself." Magan was not sure how Prescott himself felt about the idea, but he assumed that he went along with it "to a greater or lesser extent."[27] When Daniells presented the idea to the board, however, it met strong resistance from the other trustees, particularly Kellogg. The General Conference president immediately dropped the motion without even bringing it to a vote. It was a maneuver that did nothing to help the self-confidence of either Sutherland or Magan, and it achieved even less in improving relationships between the General Conference and the young college administrators. Nor did it help Daniells' relationship with Kellogg. In the doctor's version of events the incident marked the beginnings of his bitter clash with the General Conference president.[28]

Despite the faltering start, the trustees laid plans to have Prescott teach a Bible class during the first term. Everyone thought that his name would be a good draw card for the new enterprise. Ellen White heartily applauded the notion. "This first term must be a success." But as it happened, the professor got caught up with more urgent work, and Ellen White's letter arrived after the term had already commenced. Thus the school year started and finished without him.[29]

It was inevitable, however, that Prescott, as board chair, would become involved in other ways in the affairs of the fledgling school. During the first half of 1902, for example, he led in formulating plans for the campus layout, including decisions on the kind of facilities needed and the location of the principal buildings at the new site.[30] He also delivered the commencement address at the end of the first academic year. But by mid-1902 relationships between the board chair and the school administration had deteriorated rapidly. Before the year ended, Prescott had resigned, triggered by a conflict about the appointment of E. J. Waggoner as a Bible teacher. What led up to it is an interesting story.

As we have noticed previously, some of his college staff had regarded him as an extremist in the early 1880s. A number of the reforms he had advocated at Battle Creek College seemed far out. He acknowledged that some of his ideas were radical. But he insisted that they seemed that way only because what he was trying to change was so far from the ideal. By 1900 things had improved considerably. Reform now needed to be more steady and incremental. The curriculum plans of Sutherland and Magan, however, worried Prescott. He was certain he saw unwarranted and unreasonable extremes in them and, as he explained to Daniells, he felt "uneasy a good deal of the time" about his role as board chair. His disquiet and uncertainty had evidently communicated itself to the two sensitive men. Magan complained to Daniells not long after Prescott became chair that the professor had failed by not giving their work the "hearty and enthusiastic support" that a board chair should. Rather, he had created the impression that he had limited confidence in their "ability to make the thing win." "I should judge he felt we were good, well-meaning boys, who wanted to bring about certain reforms which he himself believes are good," Magan continued, "but that we do not have sufficient grasp of the educational problems to carry them through on solid and right lines." Sutherland and Magan clearly felt insecure.[31]

At the same time that he complained to Daniells, Magan also reported his concerns to Ellen White. He was careful to point out that Prescott's fault was not his lack of warmth, for he had been "kind and brotherly" to them. Neither had he done anything "to make their work hard." Rather, he simply did not have enough confidence in them. Thus tension developed that soon became exacerbated on both sides by indifferent health and grossly overloaded work schedules. A clash seemed almost inevitable. It did not take long to happen.[32]

While visiting London in May 1902, Daniells had talked with E. J. Waggoner about the possibility of his being invited to go to Berrien Springs to teach Bible. The General Conference president had participated in the previous board discussions about the requirement for a good Bible teacher. "How many times," he reminded both Prescott and Sutherland, "we have talked over our great pressing need for a good Bible teacher . . . and . . . wound up with a wish that we might have Dr. Waggoner." They had dropped the idea, however, because they thought it "altogether impossible." To Daniells' surprise, Waggoner was now quite interested in going to teach on the banks of the St. Joseph, and he promptly gave him a formal invitation. "I know of no man in the denomination who is better prepared to . . . conduct a model Bible training school," the excited president reported to Prescott and his fellow trustees.

Daniells had not forgotten to seek counsel from Ellen White on the matter. She too responded favorably. Such an appointment, she thought, would be a "vindication" for Waggoner. According to her son, she felt that "some of our people were well pleased to have him removed from the work at Battle Creek by his appointment to work in England." Ellen White had been shown, however, that the talented minister "would be brought back again to assist as a teacher at the heart of our work."[33]

Following the interview with Daniells, Waggoner wrote an enthusiastic response to Prescott. In it he talked of the need to "establish a new order of things." There had "never yet" been, he exaggerated, a real Bible school in the denomination. He would like to conduct an institute for the teachers to share his vision before the school opened.[34] According to Daniells, Waggoner had dashed off the letter late at night after a hard day's work and had never intended for anyone to take it as an exact statement of his ideas. Nor did he mean it as a formal discussion of the conditions under which he would come to the school. It was no more than an excited response to the proposal and an "off the top of the head" discussion of what might be possible. But to Magan, the letter sounded entirely different. He was not all that keen on having Waggoner on the faculty anyway and, apparently unbeknown to the others, had been quietly lobbying (unsuccessfully) to have S. N. Haskell join the faculty.[35] In his thinking, Waggoner's letter sounded like a manifesto: "I'm coming, and yes, I'll take charge."

Upon receiving the letter, Prescott had immediately telephoned Sutherland and indicated that Waggoner would be willing to accept a call. From his conversation he understood Sutherland to be agreeable to the proposal. He therefore proceeded to formalize the invitation to Waggoner and at the same time confirmed in writing to Sutherland what he had done, including with his letter a copy of the relevant parts of Waggoner's letter.

The take-charge tone of Waggoner's letter offended Sutherland and Magan, even though Prescott had carefully explained in his accompanying note that he did not think that Waggoner planned any "independent course that would not recommend itself to the rest of us."[36] Insecure, Sutherland and Magan felt almost insulted. How could Waggoner intimate that they did not know "how to reform"? It seemed to them that Waggoner clearly wanted to assume control of the school, and they began to suspect that a coup d'état was in process. Quietly they waited their chance to respond. It came a few days later.

On June 19 Prescott presided at a board meeting at Berrien Springs. The agenda was so long that the session skipped the lunch break. But Prescott adjourned the meeting early enough in the afternoon to enable him to catch the 4:20 p.m. train back to Battle Creek.

Surprisingly, the agenda did not mention Waggoner, nor did the board members discuss his appointment. That evening, however, after supper Sutherland called the remaining members together to discuss the Waggoner matter. The two school leaders expressed their opposition to his suggestions. As far as they were concerned, the letter was an unfounded expression of a lack of confidence in their leadership. They rejected the "unfair insinuations" that they were not reforming properly. Persuaded, the board members voted that Waggoner's ideas were too radical for them to accept.

Furthermore, their action stated that they considered what they had already done was quite satisfactory enough! But they would seek advice from Ellen White.[37]

When he received his copy of the minutes several days later, Prescott was astonished and irate. How could the board meet without the presence or even the knowledge of the chair? And why would they pass such a "very silly" resolution? He remarked later to Waggoner, "Their action comes nearest to the famous resolution: 'Resolved, that the saints will inherit the earth. Resolved, that we are the saints.'"

Magan reported to Prescott that it was the sentiment of all present at the rump board that if Waggoner's letter meant what it said, it would only be fair that he should be appointed as college president. It was clear that he had no confidence in Sutherland's leadership. Spicer interpreted the incident as that the two inexperienced men had simply become panic-stricken.[38]

Magan was the one assigned to lay the case before Ellen White. Having lived for some time in her home, he knew her best. Surely she would understand his position. He sent her a copy and asked her to read it "as carefully as you can," suggesting that if the letter meant what it said, he did not favor Waggoner's coming.[39]

Ellen White, however, had already seen Waggoner's letter, A. T. Jones having forwarded her a copy. But she was not aware of the discussions between Waggoner and Daniells both before and after Waggoner had written his letter and that clearly qualified its contents. Thus Ellen White also concluded that perhaps Waggoner might be desirous of displacing Sutherland. She passed word back through W. C. White, indicating that if Waggoner should come "to take a leading part in the Bible instruction," it should be "for steady earnest work for a couple of years" and not just for a "limited period." She did not say that he should not come, but she did offer a caution about placing people in charge who would make a "great showing" for a short time "and then depart leaving everybody in discouragement."[40]

Sensing that difficulties might be developing at Berrien Springs, Ellen White wrote to Prescott, admonishing him to encourage Sutherland and Magan. He should realize that schools could be successfully managed "by [those] who are not the most advanced in years and experience." Sutherland and Magan were "working on right lines" and should be allowed to continue. She had evidently heard of Daniells' plan the previous year to have Prescott appointed president of the school. This was not to be. The professor was not to confine himself to any one school "as a manager or teacher." He was "greatly needed" in the "large gatherings."[41]

As a result of the controversy, Waggoner did not go to Berrien Springs at all, disappointing both Daniells and Prescott.[42] Daniells, who was in

W. W. PRESCOTT'S
WORLD

William Warren Prescott,
president of Battle Creek College, circa 1892.

Editorial staff of The
Dartmouth (1877).
Prescott is third from
left in the back row.

William Warren Prescott, graduation
picture, Dartmouth College (1877).

James J. and
Harriet M. Prescott,
circa 1880.

Northfield Elementary and High School building. Immediately after graduation at age 22, Prescott took his first job here as principal of the school and teacher of the high school grades.

Above: Penacook Academy building in Penacook, New Hampshire. Prescott took his last year of high school studies here and taught Greek and Latin classes to the senior students.

Jacob P. Sanders' home in Penacook, New Hampshire. Prescott's marriage to Sarah Sanders took place here in 1880.

Sarah J. Prescott and son Lewis (1892).

Above: Battle Creek College campus (1891). Sanitarium buildings are in the upper right corner of the picture.

Right: Battle Creek College main building (1885).

Right: West Hall -
Prescott's "school
home" (1894).

Below: Union College
campus, circa 1891.

W. W. Prescott's turn-of-the-century home in
Battle Creek. The house was owned originally
by Review and Herald treasurer Harmon Lindsay.

W. W. Prescott's home on Blair Road, Washington, D.C.

Daisy Orndorff and William Prescott two
or three years after their 1911 marriage.

W. W. Prescott, field secretary of the General Conference (1915).

Editorial convention (1919). Picture shows many of Prescott's colleagues. Prescott is at left, in front row, in white shoes.

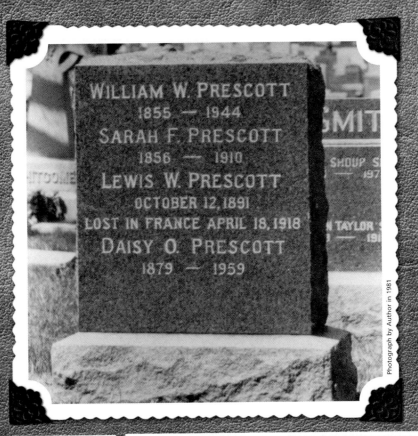

Photograph by Author in 1981

WILLIAM W. PRESCOTT
1855 — 1944
SARAH F. PRESCOTT
1856 — 1910
LEWIS W. PRESCOTT
OCTOBER 12, 1891
LOST IN FRANCE APRIL 18, 1918
DAISY O. PRESCOTT
1879 — 1959

Above: W. W. Prescott family tombstone in Rock Creek Cemetery, Washington, D.C.

Right: Prescott at age 86 at work in his library at home in November 1941.

Courtesy T. K. Martin

London with Waggoner during the whole episode, was angry that those in Berrien Springs had "entirely misunderstood" Waggoner's "position and motives." Defending Waggoner's plans to W. C. White, he explained that the doctor had simply wanted to get the faculty together for a few weeks before school opened, just as Daniells himself had done at Avondale a decade earlier. Waggoner had not once hinted that he had no confidence in Sutherland. As for Magan, Daniells was disgusted at his letter reporting the board's action. It was an "ungracious . . . cruel attack" on Waggoner, and he had refused to let the doctor read it. He did not want to make Magan's own tattered standing any worse in the eyes of church leadership.[43]

Prescott too was "thoroughly disgusted" at the deceitful way the Berrien Springs leaders had acted. "I do not consider it a fair thing that you should have a meeting of the board of trustees, of which I am chair, and that such an action be taken and recorded as an action of the trustees." He would not be chair of a body that did its work in this way. The improper meeting should be redressed. But if the members were going to stand by their action without any further "consideration," he threatened Magan, he would know what his "duty" was.[44]

Prescott evidently held little hope that there would be any change, because two weeks later he informed Daniells of his intention to resign. "I think the brethren . . . will be relieved if I should withdraw from this position." Five months later, on November 17, at the next meeting of the board, he followed through on his promise. In October he had talked over the "Waggoner episode" with Sutherland and Magan in a free exchange of opinions. Tempers had cooled, and Prescott insisted that he maintained "the utmost good feeling toward all members of the board." The diplomatic reason given for his resignation was that his work load had increased. So it had. But the truth was that Prescott had lost interest in the school. Furthermore, he did not want to continue that unnecessary tension.[45] Unfortunately, the alienation from the GC leaders provided an opportunity for Kellogg to gain the sympathy of Magan and Sutherland.

Daniells also lost interest in Emmanuel Missionary College as a result of the incident. Initially he had intended using all the weight of his office to make the Berrien Springs school the leading Bible school in the denomination. But now, he explained, trying to hide his feelings, he had come to realize that other schools in the denomination also needed his attention. EMC would have to compete on an equal footing with its siblings.

Although he severed his relationship with EMC, Prescott did not abandon his interest in education as such. He participated in the conventions of 1903 and 1906, served as a charter member of the board of trustees of the new college in Washington, D.C., and occasionally taught classes there. In 1907 some considered appointing him as president of the Washington college, and three years later church leaders asked him to head Union College. But he chose to stay away from formal education until late 1921, when he went to Avondale College in Australia as president. For the greater part of the next 20 years Prescott would remain unusually busy in general church administration and editorial work.

WORLD TRIP, 1906-1907

The tension and stress that resulted from prolonged overwork undoubtedly contributed to some of the suspicions and mistrust that characterized the Waggoner episode. The two Berrien Springs educators were under great pressure trying to start a new school with meager resources and in less than ideal conditions. Prescott also was carrying too many responsibilities for his own good. Besides his Foreign Mission Board responsibilities, the vice presidency of the General Conference, and the chair of the General Conference Education Department, he was also editor of the *Review*. And Sutherland and Magan were not the only unhappy ones. G. I. Butler was upset because he felt the new administration was not giving enough attention to the Southern states. According to Prescott, Butler suggested it was time for "a new Moses" (Butler himself) to rescue the people from the "new pharaohs" (Daniells and Prescott).[46]

Kellogg was unhappy. The Battle Creek Sanitarium had recently burned down, and relationships with the doctor had become much more complicated. Prescott felt the stress.

With Daniells away from headquarters much of the time during the first years of his administration, a great deal of the work involved in the transfer from Battle Creek to Washington, D.C., fell upon Prescott. Although he relinquished the General Conference vice presidency in 1905, that was only because he needed to spend more time in establishing the new publishing association. It seemed to Prescott, and even more so to his family, that he was forever at work.[47] By 1906 he was increasingly unable to cope with the load, and a serious nervous breakdown threatened. The professor needed a nightly massage and hydrotherapy treatments to help him sleep. Clearly he needed a vacation, even if it was a working one.

An extended overseas trip with long periods of time spent in relaxing sea voyages seemed the perfect answer. Denominational employees in China, Korea, and Japan had repeatedly requested a visit from a General Conference officer. Why not send Prescott? Besides, a General Conference meeting would convene in Gland, Switzerland, in mid-1907. Could not the two trips be combined? The leadership soon had an itinerary worked out and temporary replacements appointed to care for Prescott's editorial duties, and the professor was on his way with a prayer that the changes of labor and pace would work wonders on his health.

The three-week voyage from Vancouver to Japan provided plenty of time for reading and rest, but, according to the professor's report, it was not sufficient to make any "marked change in a case of nervous trouble." But further voyages lay beyond Japan. In fact, the five-month itinerary eventually took him through Hong Kong, Singapore, Penang, Ceylon, Bombay, and then through the Suez to Naples and finally on to Gland via Rome. He would certainly have lots to see and ample time for rest.

Prescott, however, was too conscientious to allow his first visit to Asia to become merely a pleasure trip. If he had known anything about travel in the East, he need not have worried. As it was, he resolved to learn as he went and to provide assistance to the church's workers wherever he could. His experience of the rigors of travel and his exposure to the harshness of the conditions that pioneering missionaries endured deepened his admiration for their courage and commitment. It also highlighted for him the immense needs of the mission field. The record of his journey, his reflections along the way, and some of the highlights of his experience appeared in the *Review* as a series of 21 editorial letters. They still make fascinating reading.[48]

Prescott's overwhelming impression of the East was of people—vast numbers of them. "I shall . . . never be able to shut out from my mind the impression of the almost uncounted millions of the Far East." He now carried a burden he had never known before—to proclaim the gospel to such teeming multitudes. "I have left the East," he wrote on his way to Europe, "but the East is still with me."[49]

However, not all was seriousness. Prescott found plenty of experiences that he could laugh at. *Review* readers enjoyed his "roadside inn" experiences, such as the one in Japan. The only hotel room his missionary host, F. W. Field, could find in Kyoto was one that opened directly on to the main street. Sliding screens served as walls. Prescott and Field had just gotten up the following morning when the cheerful Japanese maid removed the screens without warning. Prescott's naked fellow traveler ("decidedly dishabille" was Prescott's delicate expression) found himself suddenly exposed to a busy streetful of people highly amused to see much more of a foreigner than usual.

Another unforgettable hotel-inn was a one-window room in rural China the professor shared with four other missionaries, two national evangelists, and two donkey-team drivers. Beds consisted of mats laid on top of "two or three armfuls of potato vines." Sleep would have been easier if it had not been for the donkeys that occupied the same room, but that were denied the comfort of the sleeping mats. Prescott and his traveling party were exceedingly amused when they rose at 4:00 a.m. to find that three members of the innkeeper's family had also somehow found space on the floor.

Daniells, who at first had been concerned about how his "staid, dignified" professor friend would handle the "rough-and-tumble" of travel, need not have worried. Prescott's sense of humor was sufficient for most occasions. He became used to being stared at in his "foreign dress," and he agreed with the view that the most comfortable way to ride in the Korean sedan chair was to get out and walk. In his estimation the same principle applied in general to the Chinese cart.

The General Conference president appreciated Prescott's well-thought-through written reports. "I felt more grateful than I could express to see the grasp obtained of the situation there," he responded. "Few of our men who have visited mission fields have given the conditions such close study and systematized the results . . . as you have done."[50]

Eager to ensure that her husband was fully recovered before he returned to Washington, D.C., Sarah Prescott sailed to Europe to meet him. She had resolved that she would keep him in Europe longer if he was still "in the run-down physical condition that he was in when he left." Apparently she found him with still a way to go. Denominational leaders asked him to stay in Europe for the remainder of the summer, visiting camp meetings and conference sessions. He also found time to visit secondhand bookstores, collect materials from the British Museum, and do some library research on the side. Finally, in July 1907, he returned to Washington, much improved after an eight-and-a-half month absence.

After only a few weeks Prescott began to feel he was "back into the old swing and under the old pressure," although he did his best to avoid getting locked into his previous overloaded routine. Within 18 months or so, however, Prescott's health would again be in tatters. This time a family crisis caused the breakdown. But if other clouds were yet to appear on Prescott's horizon, at least some of the present ones were fading away. By late 1907 the problems arising from the protracted Kellogg crisis had begun to abate. During the previous half decade church administrators had hardly had time to think about anything else.

------

[1] WWP to WCW, Aug. 24, 1900.

[2] AGD to WCW, Aug. 23, 1900.

[3] EGW, "Verbatim Report" (library meeting), 1901. Three versions of this speech still exist, each recorded by a different stenographer.

[4] *GC Bulletin,* Apr. 3, 1901, pp. 24-27.

[5] *GC Bulletin,* Apr. 17, 1901, p. 302; Apr. 18, 1901, pp. 320-322.

[6] AGD to WCW, July 1, 1901.

[7] *GC Bulletin,* Apr. 25, 1901, p. 464.

[8] *GC Bulletin,* Mar. 2, 1897, pp. 213, 215; Mar. 3, 1897, p. 230; Apr. 12, 1901, p. 201; *Missionary Magazine,* June 1901, p. 244; *GC Bulletin,* Apr. 14, 1903, p. 195.

[9] AGD to WWP, June 24, 1901; *GC Bulletin,* Third Quarter 1901, pp. 515-519.

[10] WWP to EGW, July 30, 1896.

[11] AGD to WCW, July 1, 1901.

[12] *GC Bulletin,* Apr. 10, 1903, pp. 159, 160; AGD to WCW, July 1, 1901.

[13] *GC Bulletin,* First Quarter 1902, pp. 590, 591.

[14] AGD to WCW, Feb. 15, 1932.

[15] WWP to AGD, May 19, 1902; Oct. 13, 1902.

[16] WWP to AGD, Jan. 25, 1903.

[17] AGD to WCW, Feb. 15, 1932; *RH,* Apr. 28, 1903, pp. 12, 13.

[18] *RH,* Apr. 28, 1903, pp. 12, 13; *GC Bulletin,* Apr. 10, 1903.

[19] EGW to WWP, July 7, 1902.

[20] WWP to AGD, May 19, 1903; ERP to WAS, June 1, 1903; WCW to Mrs. WWP, June 12, 1903; *RH,* Feb. 17, 1903, p. 18; Aug. 18, 1904, p. 24.

[21] *RH,* Aug. 3, 1905, p. 5; WCW to WWP, Apr. 12, 1905; *RH,* May 25, 1905, p. 23.

[22] *RH,* June 17, 1902, p. 24.

[23] Magan's remarks are stenographically reported in EMCBdMin, July 12, 1901. Moving the college had actually been considered as early as 1895, when room was needed for a new medical school. OAO to WCW, Nov. 30, 1895.

[24] *GC Bulletin,* Apr. 18, 1901, p. 313.

[25] His election may have occurred at the thirteenth meeting of the trustees held on the morning of September 24, the minutes of which no longer exist. He was not a trustee at the earlier twelfth meeting (July 12), and at the fourteenth meeting on the afternoon of September 24 the minutes note him as simply occupying the chair.

[26] WWP to AGD, July 16, 1902.

[27] PTM to AGD, June 23, 1902; PTM to SNH, Aug. 6, 1901.

[28] JHK to SNH, Apr. 5, 1904.

[29] EGW to PTM and EAS, Nov. 5, 1901. The letter (if the date is correct) was written six days after the term had already commenced. AGD to WWP and EAS, May 15, 1902.

[30] EMCBdMin, Jan. 29, Apr. 23, May 28, 1902. Prescott suggested a change to the original design for the campus to avoid using the lowest ground for the principal buildings.

[31] WWP to AGD, July 3, 1902; PTM to AGD, June 23, 1902.

[32] PTM to EGW, June 23, 1902.

[33] WCW to AGD, May 30, 1902.

[34] EJW to WWP, June 11, 1902.

[35] PTM to SNH, Aug. 6, 1901.

[36] WWP to EJW, July 3, 1902.

[37] EMCBdMin, June 19, 1902; PTM to EGW, June 23, 1902; PTM to WWP, cited in WWP to EJW, July 3, 1902.

[38] PTM to WWP, cited in WWP to EJW, July 3, 1902; WWP to AGD, July 30, 1902.

[39] PTM to EGW, June 23, 1902.

[40] WCW to AGD, July 3, 1902.

[41] EGW to WWP, June 30, 1902; July 7, 1902.

[42] E. K. Vande Vere assumed incorrectly that Waggoner's appointment as Bible teacher actually materialized (*The Wisdom Seekers* [Nashville: Southern Pub. Assn., 1972], p. 114).

[43] AGD to WCW, Aug. 22, 1902.

[44] WWP to PTM, July 3, 1902.

[45] WWP to AGD, Oct. 13, 1902.

[46] WWP to AGD, Mar. 12, 1902; Apr. 3, 1902; May 19, 1902.

[47] AGD to WCW, Dec. 25, 1904.

[48] *RH,* Jan. 24-July 25, 1907.

[49] *RH,* June 13, 1907, p. 4.

[50] AGD to WWP, June 24, 1907.

CHAPTER XI

THE KELLOGG CRISIS

PRESCOTT IS THE "wildest and most unsafe man that has ever undertaken to pose as a leader of this denomination," fumed Kellogg at the height of the doctor's struggle with the church. On the other hand, A. G. Daniells held exactly the opposite opinion. The professor had uncommonly "good judgment," and his "strength at the helm" was just what the church needed during the crisis.[1] Opinion is still sometimes divided over the helpfulness or otherwise of Prescott's role in the conflict. But no one can dispute that next to the General Conference president he was the most prominent figure in the schism. It was to be the most traumatic event ever to seize the denomination and cost it heavily in losses of membership and property.

Most church conflicts involve more than just a single issue, and the Kellogg one was no exception. Differences in theology, differences in understanding the mission of the church, and differences over administrative policy fueled the flames of conflict. But primarily the issue was political. It was a power struggle and a personality clash between two similar and extremely strong-minded men. As Percy Magan caustically remarked: "No kingdom can have two kings at one time."[2]

The political issues in the dispute clearly manifested themselves at the first open clash between the two leaders in October 1902. The General Conference would not allow the building of further medical facilities on borrowed capital. Furthermore, Daniells would not tolerate the medical employees bullying the General Conference Committee. Committee members would be allowed to think and decide for themselves. Related to these two issues was the fund-raising campaign based on Kellogg's *Living Temple* with its questionable theology. All three of the issues, however, revolved around one major administrative problem: Kellogg's refusal to bring the Battle Creek Sanitarium and its related agencies under the control of the General Conference.[3]

Prescott's major concern at first was the doctrinal question. But as vice president of the denomination, editor of its leading periodical, and staunch friend of Daniells', he inevitably found himself drawn into the political struggle. In this chapter we look closely at his overall role in the conflict. It provides valuable insights into the professor's personality and his theology. And it also provides important background information for understanding the future development of his career.

BACKGROUND

Like both Daniells and Kellogg, Prescott was an extremely strong-willed person. Earlier clashes had occurred between the doctor and the professor. In 1891 they had quarreled over the recruiting of students for their respective institutions, and Prescott had appealed to the General Conference Committee about the problem. A year later it was Kellogg's turn to ask for help from the General Conference. Prescott, he alleged, was opposing his educational efforts at the sanitarium. On this occasion O. A. Olsen felt inclined to sympathize with Kellogg. "I have sometimes wished that Prof. Prescott could better appreciate the needs of the sanitarium . . . that he might be more thoroughly interested." Olsen even wondered if some prodding from Ellen White would help. "If your mind should be led out to write anything on this question," he wrote to her, "it would be a blessing to the work." But as it happened, Ellen White apparently had nothing to say. She chose not to intervene.[4]

The sharpest conflict that occurred between the two Battle Creek leaders during the 1890s involved the issue of vegetarianism. Prescott's slowness in adopting "hygienic" principles (a vegetarian regimen) in the college dining room frustrated Kellogg. Even the college board of trustees (of which Kellogg was a member) would not move on the question, leading him to charge that the body was "scarcely more than a figurehead" anyway. Prescott was a dictator who ran the school just as he liked.[5]

Kellogg never did succeed in converting Prescott to vegetarianism. It was Dr. Daniel Kress who did that in England in 1899. Kress, who at the time tended to be an extremist himself on "health reform," convinced both Waggoner and Prescott to stop eating meat completely. The two became eager disciples and for a time were even more conscientious than Kress himself. As Kellogg later reported it, "in straightening up, they bent over backwards" and in their "enthusiasm" caused problems for their English converts. They "taught the people stricter doctrines than they were prepared to receive."[6]

Health reform finally made sense to Prescott when he saw it theologically related to the gospel. The new "gospel context" at last helped him also to see a strong theological basis for the unity of both the medical and the ministerial interests of the church.[7] Fired up by his new insights, he enthusiastically endeavored to share the light with fellow delegates at the 1901 General Conference session and worked hard to build unity between the two branches. The effort led to a campaign known as "The Forward Movement."

At Prescott's urging, the General Conference Committee, at its October 1901 meeting, approved a plan for a special six-month educational effort "on behalf of the gospel of health." The session named Prescott chair of the working committee. It called for church publications to print articles on the topic, special-purpose study materials developed for use in local churches, and state committees formed to foster the program. The committee requested Kellogg to prepare the study materials in a 26-lesson format. The materials would also eventually appear in a denominationally produced book to be entitled *The Living Temple*.[8]

With the program scheduled to start January 1902, preparation of materials proceeded at full speed. Circulars went to conference presidents and all church elders, and articles appeared in the *Review*. "The time has come for a genuine revival . . . in that phase of gospel truth which relates to the body as the temple of the living God," Prescott wrote. Spelling out the practical implications, he conceded that in the past "antagonism" had existed between the "evangelical and the medical" wings of the church. But this would be corrected. The Forward Movement would unite the "various phases of this message." Prescott was building bridges again.[9]

Ellen White also waxed enthusiastic about the program, and the new-year issue of the *Review* carried her endorsement. "We want to unite with Dr. Kellogg. . . . He knows what he is talking about."[10] Thus 1902 began with high expectations and the best of intentions. Before the year stretched out to its close, however, the thin fabric of unity, so carefully woven, ruptured from a series of calamities that left evangelical and medical personnel more divided than ever.

1902—A YEAR OF DISASTERS

On February 18, 1902, the soot and ash of a massive fire that burned the two main sanitarium buildings to the ground blackened and muddied Battle Creek's winter whiteness. The disaster stunned church members, as it did Kellogg, who was out of town at the time, but not for long. Before he had even reached home to survey the damage he was busy "making plans for a new and better structure."[11]

Daniells, who was down in Kansas at the time, knew Kellogg well enough by now to anticipate the doctor's response to the calamity. As soon as the General Conference president received word of the disaster he wrote to Prescott urging him to convey to Kellogg the need for restraint in any rebuilding program. The professor communicated Daniells' concern privately to the doctor, and he also raised the matter with the sanitarium board at its first meeting after the event. Kellogg assured Prescott that the planned new building would be no bigger than what the sanitarium could pay for "in cash." The money would come from insurance and donations. He apparently already had in mind offers of support from prominent Battle Creek citizens. The city council and businesspeople worried about the possible disastrous impact on Battle Creek's economy should the denomination use the opportunity to rebuild the hospital elsewhere. The city quickly set up a citizens' committee to see that such a thing did not happen. Kellogg assured them that if the local residents contributed and met certain other requirements, his management would erect a sanitarium "far surpassing the structures destroyed by fire." In capacity, design, convenience, and beauty it would be better. Kellogg was already ignoring Daniells' desire for a more moderate building, but the General Conference president was still out of town. Prescott, who could see that things were getting quickly out of hand, met again with Kellogg and urged him to keep close to the "organized work." The sanitarium's success would be in staying "as a definite part of this general Advent movement," he argued.[12] Did Kellogg sense that somehow he would have to outflank the General Conference administrators to get his way? He called in "representative brethren"—union and local conference presidents—to meet with his board. On the basis of his assurances of restraint the board voted to give him the go-ahead. The doctor quickly had plans drawn up and estimates obtained. But to those most closely concerned it was evident that he was saying different things to different people. Widely different expectations circulated about the project, and the doctor's laborious statement in the *Review* that he was not building bigger and better but only in harmony with the counsel of church leaders was just so much obfuscation that convinced neither the editor nor the other GC Executive Committee members. In spite of the misgivings worrying the General Conference leaders, relationships still remained cordial. Only months later, in the midst of a heated conversation with Daniells, did Kellogg reveal his real plans. He boasted that he had actively schemed to bring the Battle Creek citizens to their knees by "pretending" to consider moving the sanitarium from the city. The doctor also admitted that even though he had asked the General Conference Committee to pray and counsel over the question of moving, he really had not the slightest intention of actually leaving Battle Creek. The admission, Daniells reported later, destroyed any confidence that he might have had left that Kellogg was an honest man.[13]

Just a few days after the sanitarium disaster the General Conference Committee, in a gesture of goodwill and financial support, had taken an action authorizing the use of Kellogg's forthcoming book for the Forward Movement program as a fund-raiser for the rebuilding program. Kellogg would donate the manuscript to the church, and the General Conference would endorse its sale. Daniells had thought the idea a splendid one, because the doctor's books had always been good sellers. But he nonetheless offered Kellogg a word of caution about the book's content. He had heard some people remark that in some of his talks Kellogg had been "grazing about very close to pantheism." In order for the book to sell well among the church membership, the General Conference leader asserted, it should be "entirely free from any just criticism." He was glad Prescott would critically review the manuscript, because what would "pass his reading" would "stand with the people."[14]

Although suspicions may have been lurking in the background, outwardly, at least, relationships between the three leaders were still friendly when in midyear Kellogg and Daniells attended meetings in London. Before the doctor left for Britain, Prescott had taken several opportunities to talk with him about his manuscript. Both had agreed on a delay because the field was not yet ready for the book's promotion (a development Prescott thought most fortuitous).[15] He had sensed trouble just from his first cursory reading. As he pointed out to Kellogg, he worried that readers might misunderstand some parts of the book. He informed Daniells about his concern and later sent a written copy of his criticisms to both Kellogg and Daniells in London.[16]

Prescott's objections to the manuscript concerned such statements as "God Himself enters into our bodies in the taking of food" and "There is a tree-maker in the tree, a flower-maker in the flower." He thought Kellogg had misinterpreted some Bible texts and that his discussion of the will, consciousness, and the soul didn't seem altogether orthodox. The professor explained to the doctor that he was not against the consideration of new ideas. But they should not appear in a book designed for mass circulation. It would be best to delete the problem areas.

Kellogg's visit to London was not a pleasant one. He had been pained at the fresh reminder during his meetings with his ministerial colleagues that many of them were still not vegetarians despite all their talk about the Forward Movement. On top of that he had clashed with Daniells about plans for financing the proposed new sanitarium for England. The General Conference president refused to allow the sanitarium to use borrowed funds. In Kellogg's view, Daniells was stubborn, unreasonable, and not really committed to the health program. On the other hand, from the latter's perspective, Kellogg was a bulldozer using the General Conference simply for his own ends. According to Daniells, the doctor "entirely broke" with him after the two "had had a very plain, clear-cut, stiff argument."[17]

Back in Battle Creek the quarrel between the two men simmered away all summer until November when it erupted publicly at the Annual Council. Both parties exchanged viewpoints freely in three extended sessions, but Daniells, who had in the meantime had his position reinforced by Ellen White, refused to give any ground. The major issue involved financial and administrative policy. Who was in control? Daniells, supported by the council, held tenaciously to the principle that the money raised for the sanitarium in England should be spent only "under the direction of the British Conference." Kellogg and his independent Benevolent Association should not control the new sanitarium.[18]

The General Conference also made it known that it would not be responsible without their approval for the increasing debt from the rebuilding of the Battle Creek Sanitarium. Daniells clearly felt that the doctor needed to be held in check. Kellogg learned just how serious the General Conference was when he found out that Prescott, as the head of the publishing house, had assisted Daniells by persuading the Review and Herald board to refuse further credit to the sanitarium. Also, the professor had refused to publish advertisements for sanitarium bonds in the *Review*. The actions left Kellogg livid. "Prof. Prescott seems to have lost his head completely . . . ; [he] appears to me to be in an unbalanced state of mind," he exploded to W. C. White. Within days the whole of America knew of the quarrel. Nationwide newspaper headlines proclaimed that Kellogg was being "driven out of the denomination."[19]

Kellogg's *Living Temple* had been another source of tension at the 1902 Annual Council. When he had indicated a willingness to make changes, the denomination set up a four-member panel: Prescott, Kellogg, A. T. Jones, and a young sanitarium doctor, David Paulson. From Prescott's point of view, the panel was a disaster. After a week of discussions Kellogg, Jones, and Paulson concluded that the manuscript had nothing at all objectionable in it. Prescott's only recourse was to submit a minority report elaborating at considerable length on the criticisms he had previously raised. (A second, much closer reading of the manuscript had convinced him that it was fatally flawed.) The three members of the panel's majority were stunned when the General Conference Committee accepted Prescott's minority report. The General Conference then withdrew its support for the book and promptly canceled the promotional campaign.

The doctor, however, refused to allow himself to be so easily forced into a corner. He defiantly ordered a personal printing of 5,000 copies from the Review and Herald. Before the publishing house could fill the order, however, its plant burned to the ground in a suspicious fire—the second disaster to strike the church that year. But even a fire would not stop the determined Kellogg. He simply had it printed elsewhere. Five months later copies went on sale.[20]

A YEAR OF CRISES, 1903

For Prescott, 1903 seemed to be a succession of crises. Daniells had been out of town at the time of the December 30, 1902, Review and Herald fire, and the professor found himself once again trying to bring order out of chaos. Finding temporary quarters for his editorial office and alternative printers so that the *Review* could be kept coming out on time was a nightmare. The burden of reading several letters to church members and publishing house employees from Ellen White fell on his shoulders. They stated clearly that the recent fires were a sign of God's judgment on the church. Talk consequently turned to the possibility of moving the institutions out of Battle Creek—a development that made Kellogg even more irate. By now the sanitarium was already partially rebuilt.

Among Kellogg's supporters, talk soon turned to sedition, and rumors flew around the sanitarium. It was time, many felt, to turn Daniells out of his position. As we have already noticed, the mutinous sentiments toward the president provided a tense background to the 1903 General Conference session three months later in California. The Kellogg conflict dominated the proceedings of the session. But since Daniells and Prescott clearly had the support of Ellen White, the mutiny eventually ran out of steam. Not so with Kellogg himself.

The director of the sanitarium declared vehemently that he would not be "bound." The session had taken action incorporating denominational medical institutions into the church structure. Kellogg would simply ignore it. He refused to let the General Conference control him. What did ministers know about running sanitariums? Before the end of the session A. T. Jones, in an attempt to mediate the dispute, had papered together a reconciliation between the two leaders. But it was tissue-thin—within weeks the war resumed. As Daniells saw it, Kellogg's actions showed that he was in "competition" with the church. He ardently hoped that Ellen White would "sound a ringing note" of warning about the danger from Kellogg. Prescott concurred. To him, it also seemed that the doctor was making a "set and determined effort to make the medical work an independent movement" and was misusing Ellen White's writings as the basis for his position.[21]

What convinced Daniells and Prescott that Kellogg desired independence was the doctor's provocative attempt to reopen the old Battle Creek College. After strongly supporting its relocation in Berrien Springs, Kellogg now made an about-face and decided that a college was necessary in Battle Creek after all. The change in attitude had resulted from pressure by educational authorities who were questioning whether to continue accreditation of his medical school in Chicago. Some church officials thought Kellogg had a good case with strong arguments in his favor. But Prescott and Daniells concluded otherwise, and they interpreted the doctor's action quite differently. In Daniells' view it was "a deep-laid scheme to get control of the education of our young people." Reopening the college would be a trap to "force" all young people interested in the medical profession "to go through the mill at Battle Creek." Ungraciously he suggested, "There is nothing Dr. Kellogg desires more than to inoculate the young . . . of this denomination with his new philosophy."[22]

Through the pages of the *Review* Prescott publicly opposed Kellogg's "ill-advised" venture, even though it "greatly stirred" the doctor. But the professor could see that the move to revive a college in Battle Creek would seriously damage the Berrien Springs school and would only "bring confusion." Again, with Ellen White's support, he and Daniells succeeded in blocking the attempt, but the episode further polarized the two factions.

What troubled Prescott even more than the school episode, however, was Kellogg's defiant circulation of his book. The "real crisis," the professor suggested, was "now drawing on." "We might as well face the fact," he wrote to Daniells in September 1903, "that we have started in now for a campaign which will not end until these things have been fully and openly considered."[23] Would Daniells approve a series of articles to correct and expose the theology of the book? Yes, he would.

Two months later the theological issue came to a head at the October council of the General Conference in Washington, D.C. A strong representation of medical personnel led by David Paulson persuasively argued the doctor's case and almost swayed the delegates in favor of accepting the ideas in *The Living Temple*. Only the timely arrival of explicit testimonies from Ellen White during the session turned the tide. Although she had received a copy of the book earlier in the year, she had not gotten around to glancing through it until September 23. Kellogg's embarrassing claim that the book was "in perfect harmony" with her own writings prompted her to look at it. Then she immediately saw its dangers. Prescott felt vindicated.[24]

Faced now with Ellen White's clear nonendorsement and her warnings concerning its theology, Kellogg publicly agreed to eliminate all the-

ological references. Evidently, in an attempt to demonstrate his orthodoxy, he also engaged in several friendly but unconvincing theological
discussions with Daniells and Prescott. If Daniells' account is reliable, the
doctor now asserted that he had changed his views on the Trinity. He now
believed that "it was God the Holy Ghost, and not God the Father, that
filled all space and every living thing." It did not impress the General
Conference president. He was certain that Kellogg neither understood
himself "nor the character of his teaching."[25]

Magan, a Kellogg sympathizer, felt that the doctor had made a heroic
effort to work cordially with Daniells and Prescott. But the two General
Conference leaders continued to have deep suspicions. Kellogg's willingness to change the book, they suspected, was simply a shift in tactics.
They did not detect any new willingness to yield up his cherished independence. It had, in fact, come to their ears that the doctor was eager to
have the General Conference "fix up" the book and make it orthodox only
so he could solve his financial problems at the sanitarium. He had
planned a campaign to sell a total of 500,000 of them and hopefully
100,000 before Christmas.

For his part, Prescott had lost interest in helping correct the book. He
stubbornly resisted the idea of going through it simply to "cut out" the
problem statements. Under pressure from Kellogg, however, he eventually
consented to at least give the book another careful examination and then
"write the doctor his decision." Obviously he was just buying time. From
his previous review he had conscientiously come to the view that the
manuscript's theology was misleading. Ellen White's letters had simply
confirmed his assessment. It was almost pointless to look at the book again.

Daniells concurred with the professor. In fact, he was certain it was
not worth it for Prescott to waste any more time on the manuscript. But
at Kellogg's insistence, and in an effort not to appear close-minded,
Prescott gave one more full day to the task. It "thoroughly convinced" him
that the book was impossible to revise. How much his judgment rested on
the contents of the book itself as opposed to his fears of Kellogg's devious
efforts to still maintain his independence is not clear. The professor was
in no mood to compromise, and the door of opportunity for reconciliation clanged shut. He wrote Kellogg of his decision.[26] Unfortunately, the
letter arrived too late.

The doctor's associates, anticipating a favorable decision, had preemptively sent announcements out to all the churches that the General Conference Committee was revising the book and that it would be ready in three weeks. Apparently they acted independently and without the knowledge of Kellogg, but Prescott and Daniells would not know that till later. The premature move infuriated them and confirmed their worst suspicions. The doctor was manipulating them. Kellogg had not changed at all.

Did Ellen White understand what was happening? Could W. C. White see through the doctor as they could? At first Daniells and Prescott were not sure. As the controversy developed, the General Conference president took pains to keep W. C. White informed. If any other "ruptures break out," Daniells wrote in late 1903, "I . . . want you to know just where we stand." But just what was W. C. White's position? "So much depends, humanly speaking, upon the general attitude W. C. [White] takes in regard to the whole situation," Prescott perceptively observed to the General Conference president when the controversy first broke into the open.[27]

After the General Conference leadership had declined to approve or modify *The Living Temple,* Kellogg cut out a few of the problem pages and circulated it himself, claiming that W. C. White had consented and "could see no objection to it." Nor, the doctor claimed, had Ellen White objected to the idea when approached. Prescott felt betrayed. "For over a year now we have tried to stand against this thing and you know something of the experience through which we have passed . . . ," he wrote to W. C. White. If it was true that Ellen White's son had supported the circulation of the book, Prescott stated bluntly, he was no more "excusable" than the doctor. Kellogg had succeeded in "hiding behind you and your mother," he protested angrily to White. "You can perhaps imagine how we feel over the matter. I hardly need to attempt to put it into words." What Prescott thought was better left unsaid.[28]

The lack of solidarity seriously worried Daniells and Prescott. More than a few had reported that Ellen White was really backing Kellogg. Percy Magan, who claimed private access to her, had been widely reporting a conversation in which she allegedly stated that "Daniells and Prescott were trying to knife Kellogg."[29] The doctor himself had also let it be known that Sara McEnterfer, a nurse who was one of Ellen White's close assistants, was a "friend at court."[30] Further evidence of the personal stresses emerged years after the conflict had passed. J. S. Washburn, a noted opponent of Daniells, quoted him as saying "we had all we could do to keep Sister White from going with Dr. Kellogg when the conflict was on." The statement, even if authentic, was undoubtedly a hyperbole, but it reflects something of the torment of torn loyalties that church schism inevitably brings.[31]

Like Prescott, Daniells had been so worried about being left out on a limb politically that he had also protested to Ellen White that people were "trading on her influence" and claiming a "private walk" to her residence. Comments that she reportedly made in private seemed to conflict with what she had said in her written testimonies to Daniells. Perhaps it was time to publish her letters in order to vindicate his position. Could he have permission to do so?[32]

The protests produced results. W. C. White decided it was time to visit Washington. He arrived in early 1904, and Ellen White followed a short time later. "From some of the things which he has said," Prescott informed an inquirer soon afterward, "I feel quite certain that a view of the situation as it now is, has been presented to his mother."[33] For the moment he felt relieved, but he suspected that the problem would probably get worse before it got better.

OPPORTUNITIES FOR RECONCILIATION SPURNED: 1904

Scheduled for the spring of 1904 at Berrien Springs, the Lake Union Conference session held promise that the warm rains of confession and repentance would allow reconciliation to blossom. Ellen White was hopeful that peace would prevail. Most leading figures in the denomination planned to attend. The meeting, however, only further polarized the two parties. The wispy possibility of harmony and light sputtered out in a cold fog of ill-feeling and bitter recriminations that blanketed the gathering. For Prescott, who figured more prominently than he had intended, it was a particularly chilling experience.

Ellen White's first address at the session on Wednesday, May 18, brought the theological issues into the open. (The session's conveners had asked her to conduct the early-morning devotional series.) Directly addressing the problem of pantheism in *The Living Temple,* she related how that when she had eventually given close attention to the book in

September she recognized the problem and then compared the ideas to those she had encountered in the 1840s. The sermon strongly warned the church not to accept the concepts.

Prescott had also planned to address the topic of pantheism in his major Friday evening address. Ellen White, whom he had consulted on the topic, advised him to go ahead. But later, on second thought, she changed her mind, fearing that some in the audience might feel called to defend the doctor. She passed a short note to W. C. White and asked him to deliver it to Prescott. It never got there. For some reason, her son deliberately chose to keep the note in his pocket until after the professor had delivered the talk. If Kellogg is to be believed, White actually advised Prescott, who by Friday morning was beginning himself to have doubts about the idea, to go ahead with the topic. It was a fateful decision.

The meeting produced exactly the reaction Ellen White had feared. For example, the doctor walked out after five minutes. He afterward described the presentation as "too disgusting to be endured."[34] Other Kellogg supporters, however, stayed and publicly challenged the professor. Prescott had quoted from some book other than *The Living Temple* to illustrate his point about pantheism, and some in the audience received the impression that he had inferred that Kellogg had actually made the statements. Greatly upset, some challenged the professor. At the conclusion of his talk Prescott allegedly cast the book to the floor in a "dramatic flourish."[35]

Did he deliberately mislead his audience? That hardly seems likely. The evidence for his integrity and his basic honesty is too strong. Besides, the risk of exposure by such a hypercritical and sensitive audience would have been too weighty a deterrent to try deceit. Nonetheless, in the highly charged atmosphere that characterized the meeting, some misunderstanding seems to have occurred.

Feelings against both Daniells and Prescott ran hot the next few days. On Sabbath delegates attended the funeral of Percy Magan's wife—one of the first casualties of the conflict. Late in 1903 the rumor mill had reported that Ellen White had finally turned against Percy Magan, one of her "sons." When the rumor reached his wife, it resulted in her suffering a mental breakdown. She languished for a few months and finally died on Thursday, May 19, the day of Prescott's evening talk. Ellen White's comments in her Friday morning meeting about Mrs. Magan's death resulting from "unsanctified tongues" caused further misunderstanding. Many delegates had attributed the spreading of the reports to Daniells and Prescott. In fact, they had originated among an anti-Magan faction based in Battle Creek. But the rumors had done their evil work, and feelings became exceedingly hostile to the General Conference leaders. Before the meeting closed, Ellen White wrote a letter to be publicly read to the delegates to correct the wrong impression, but even mature individuals such as Haskell and Butler chose not to read it. W. C. White presented it himself.[36]

Monday, May 23, proved to be the bleakest day of the session for Prescott. It began at 5:45 a.m. when A. T. Jones, after a brief devotional, launched into a spirited two-hour reply to the professor's Friday night talk. Over the weekend Jones had spent his time surveying recent issues of the *Review* and collecting extracts that purported to demonstrate that Prescott was as much a pantheist as the doctor. Kellogg jumped into the fray as well by alleging from the floor of the meeting that the quotations cited by Jones showed clearly that the professor himself was the source of many of the ideas in *The Living Temple*. The charge produced a spirited rejoinder from Prescott's supporters. The delegates forgot their breakfast as charge followed countercharge, with Sutherland and Magan adding to the confusion in the midst of it all by submitting their resignations from the college. Not until 1:00 p.m. did delegates finally adjourn to satisfy their hunger.

The session concluded with Kellogg and his supporters exulting in the show of strength they had been able to muster. The rush of individuals to defend the doctor distressed Ellen White. She was convinced that the meeting would have reconciled him permanently to the church had his followers helped him to see that "he had sinned and needed to repent" instead of gratifying him.[37]

Kellogg followed up his spring "victory" with conciliatory requests for further discussions on the theological issues. Would the church appoint a panel of experienced church leaders? The General Conference declined the request. Why rehash the conflict? Instead it assigned Prescott to meet personally with Kellogg. He traveled to Battle Creek for an interview that extended into the early-morning hours. But it was a fruitless endeavor, producing no change in Kellogg. A follow-up all-night session between W. C. White and the doctor also occurred, during which Kellogg proposed further theological discussions. Prescott's reaction was that he would be ready to buy himself "a ticket to Europe" if such a thing were to be done. (Spicer's stenographer commented that Spicer was glad he already had his purchased.) Prescott and Kellogg parted, with the professor consenting at least to avoid what others might construe as attacks on the doctor in the *Review*.[38]

If other church leaders felt inclined to respond favorably to Kellogg's pressure for further theological discussion, they soon had reason to think otherwise. Ellen White strenuously advised against it. Many leaders were so blind, she stated in July 1904, that they did not yet themselves discern the misleading character of the doctor's sentiments. Any dialogue with him would be futile and dangerous.[39]

Finally Kellogg himself revised the troublesome book and reissued it under a different title, *The Miracle of Life*. In Prescott's view the leopard had not in the least lost its spots. "Although it protests against pantheism," he wrote to the doctor after he had reviewed the new version, "there is a general tendency . . . to represent God as a universal presence" or an "all-pervading intelligence." But the professor was not surprised. Had not Kellogg told him his opinions had not changed in the least since he had written the first draft?

The fact was that Kellogg had not needed to touch on theological issues at all in his book for the Forward Movement. A general book on the value of healthful living and Christians' obligation to care for their bodies in the setting of end-time events would have been sufficient. Others had done it. For example, a comparison of a volume by F. M. Rossiter, also written in 1902, reveals a similar discussion of physiology and the need for healthful living. The book had an almost identical title. Rossiter's *The Story of the Living Temple* was entirely free of the theological and philosophical statements that characterized Kellogg's book.[40]

PRESCOTT—A PANTHEIST?

Had Prescott himself taught pantheism and then suddenly changed in November 1902, as A. T. Jones strongly contended at Berrien Springs? It was a question he would have to face repeatedly to the end of his life. Jones's arguments sounded persuasive, at least to those who already had other reasons to be unhappy with the professor. For example, Butler and Haskell appeared to have been convinced.[41]

On the other hand, Daniells felt that Jones was far from proving his point. He recounted to an associate five weeks after the memorable Monday morning meeting how I. H. Evans, a longtime Review and Herald official, had stood up and destroyed Jones's argument by asking one single question. How could Prescott's editorials in the *Review* possibly be the source of the ideas in Kellogg's book when the professor had written them six months after Kellogg had authored his book? If Daniells' account is correct, Jones simply "looked into blank space and said nothing," while Kellogg ventured that "perhaps there had been a mistake on this point."[42] The doctor thought, however, that the professor had perhaps earlier presented something similar at the sanitarium. What then did Prescott actually teach? Not pantheism!

Unquestionably, he had, for a brief time at the turn of the century, advocated some "strained" and "extreme" ideas. But they were on the theme of sanctification, not the nature of God. And they grew out of the greatly heightened sense of the end time that characterized the thinking of most in the church during the closing years of the nineteenth century. Prescott, for example, had balked in 1897 at the requirement of his real estate agent in London to sign a three-year lease on his rented house. The Lord would surely have come before it expired. In this intense eschatological context, a number of preachers began to argue that if the believers lived faithfully in accordance with health reform principles they would not see death but become increasingly perfect physically and spiritually (just like Daniel, who at the end of his 10-day trial was fairer and fatter in flesh). Even gray hair, asserted Waggoner, would regain its original color. Such "physical righteousness" would enable believers to be translated, as Ellen White had pointed out in her comments on the translation of Enoch in one of her pamphlets. The prophetic books of Daniel and Revelation were the focus of this new study. "I feel as though I had a new revelation of truth for us in the books of Daniel and Revelation," Prescott confided to Ellen White in 1900. He felt that the teaching provided an excellent basis for uniting the "evangelical" and the medical programs of the church.[43]

Haskell was not at all sure about the gray hair nor, probably, the total emphasis. He wrote to W. C. White and his mother seeking advice. W. C. White replied that he could see nothing wrong with the basic idea. The children of Israel "could have been translated and made immortal during the time of their existence, if they had faithfully kept God's commandments," he replied. But apparently after Andross and Loughborough had raised the matter with the professor he had let the issue die, even "as a hobby."[44]

Neither Haskell nor Prescott could see any merit, however, in the way some expanded the idea. They argued that if we could see God at work restoring human beings, we could also observe Him transforming the natural world back into its original state. Thus we should respect all life because it belonged to God. We should not even kills mosquitoes and other insects—an emphasis that some of Sutherland's colleagues promoted in his organic farming program at Berrien Springs.

Prescott's distinctive emphasis was the "gospel of health," and he advocated it enthusiastically at the 1901 General Conference session. Some of the overwrought language and expressions both he and Waggoner used apparently alarmed Ellen White, and she responded to the situation in her own talks. Without making it obvious or raising any specific statement as a public issue, she took opportunity in her own public addresses to speak in a way to balance the picture and counteract the more extreme positions. What "overdrawn expressions" she had in mind she did not say when she recalled the incident and commented on it to Daniells two and a half years later; but they were to be shunned and feared. She did not, however, point this out personally to the men at the time. It is an important point to notice, especially since in later years Prescott's critics created the impression that somehow her warning was public, and they used her later explanation to Daniells as ammunition in their ad hominem attack on Prescott. The professor was unaware of her feelings at the time. And she apparently felt that her own corrective statements were adequate. Instead, she wrote Prescott a number of letters encouraging him in his gospel emphasis. It was just the preaching, she said, that the church needed.[45]

According to Prescott, if "an apparent likeness" existed to Kellogg's concept of God in nature there was, nevertheless, "an immeasurable difference between the two views."[46] What did he mean? Some at least had a hard time seeing any difference. Was the professor simply trying to extract himself from an embarrassing situation?

A statement that may serve to illustrate his point is one that he presented on a number of occasions: "God Himself enters our bodies in the taking of food." The context in which he made it indicates that his meaning was that the Christian has a heightened appreciation for God's provision of life's bounties in Christ. Christians should view even eating sacramentally. Prescott did not intend the expression to be taken as an ontological statement about the nature of God any more than Jesus Himself did when He declared, "I am the bread." The difference between Prescott and Kellogg was that when Kellogg used such expressions he was speaking ontologically about the nature of God's being. Prescott was not.

In Prescott's first hurried critique of *The Living Temple* in May 1902 he pointed out that readers would misunderstand some expressions unless Kellogg "qualified and further developed" them. Some of the expressions were similar to the professor's own. Had he begun to see how they might give a meaning different from that which he had intended? His November 1902 confrontation with the reading panel over the acceptability of Kellogg's manuscript indicated even more clearly that, though the words might be the same, the meaning could be quite different. Subsequently, Prescott began avoiding such expressions.

Prescott consistently maintained this explanation. In 1904 he reminded his old friend Waggoner how in England they had seen things "in about the same light" until the latter began to present some views with which he could not agree. "It seemed to me," he went on, "that your view that every man was a temple of God without regard to his character involved conclusions I could not admit." He reminded Waggoner that he had written to him about the problem after he had found the same idea taught in America.[47]

Later Prescott reviewed Kellogg's book and felt compelled to oppose it "as subversive of the truth of the Gospel." When he fully expected Waggoner to do the same, the stark difference between them then became apparent. "I did not have the least idea that in your teaching about the revelation of God in nature you intended to set forth the same things as are set forth in that book. When therefore both you and Brother Jones sided with Dr. Kellogg in the controversy over that teaching and openly sustained the book, I was terribly shaken up." He would have opposed Waggoner more strongly earlier had he fully understood what his friend had in mind. "I certainly did not include such interpretations of scripture and such views of God in my teaching," Prescott declared. If people derived such ideas from the expressions he used, he would repudiate them.[48]

Some have suggested that his denials and explanations were simply a face-saving way of repudiating a teaching that had become an embarrassing political liability. Was it a way of extricating himself without his having to admit he had been in error? The evidence suggests that his clarifications were bona fide. Careless he may have been, but a pantheist he was not.

Prescott argued that the difference between his teaching and that promulgated by Kellogg in *The Living Temple* was profound. One could summarize Kellogg's errors simply. The doctor taught (1) "a wrong view of God and His dwelling place"; (2) a religion "which set aside any need of atonement and the work of Christ as our high priest in the sanctuary above"; and (3) "a breaking down of the distinction between the sinner and the Christian by teaching that every man is a temple of God regardless of his faith in Christ."[49]

According to Prescott, the chief heresy in Kellogg's teaching was that it negated the objective nature of Christ's atonement. If human beings could become like the divine simply by conforming to divine and natural law, they had no need for divine power to help. Neither did they require Christ's substitutionary death. Though popular at the time in the Western religious world, in Prescott's mind such a subjective view of the atonement denied the very essence of Christianity. The best response to it was to emphasize the mediation of Christ and the teaching of the book of Hebrews.

Prescott's own preaching would typically emphasize the *indwelling* Christ. In the same sermon, however, he would distinguish between this and God as an essence pervading all nature. Often he would cite Ellen White to support the distinction he was making. If God dwells in all human beings, then "man has only to develop that which lies within him" to attain holiness. "These theories do away with the necessity of the atonement."[50] Adventist preaching and teaching, he argued, should be thoroughly Christocentric. The theme became Prescott's lifelong consuming passion.

Though invalid, Jones's 1904 criticism of Prescott received periodic resurrections and recycling. In response the professor became quite sensitive on the matter. For example, he encountered it at the 1919 Bible conference in Washington when he was preaching a series on the mediation of Christ. His emphasis on the indwelling Christ was so strong that some thought they heard pantheism. Responding to the accusation, Prescott recounted his 1904 experience. "I was accused of having held exactly the same views as Dr. Kellogg had, and yet it fell to my lot to fight him face to face . . . and through the *Review*." How could that be if we were just the same? he asked. The vital difference, he still maintained, was that Kellogg made no room for Christ as mediator. For Kellogg, God was "immediately" in each human being. For Prescott, God was "mediated" to humanity through Christ. But such distinctions, vital to Prescott, were lost on many of the conference delegates, some of whom already had axes to grind with the professor on other issues.[51]

The insinuation in 1919 that Prescott was not a reliable guide because he was "just the same as Dr. Kellogg and Wagner [sic]" hurt the professor. On this occasion his critics were bold enough to allege publicly that Prescott "brought it over from England" and was really "in the mess" himself. The charge touched a raw nerve. Losing patience, he fumed that he would very much "rather get out among the heathen" (he had just returned from an extended sojourn in China). They had never charged him with pantheism in his work for them, he countered. Overcome by emotion, he refused to continue his talk, and Daniells had to intercede. After some apologies the meetings proceeded.[52]

Later opponents of Prescott, such as evangelist Judson S. Washburn, also circulated the allegations of Prescott's pantheism in a pamphlet war during the early 1930s. (He also disagreed with the professor over other theological issues.) But nothing Prescott could say to such individuals would make any difference. They had already made their minds up.

Kellogg himself also vigorously denied the charge that he was tainted with pantheism. He asserted that he still believed in a "personal God . . . sitting upon a throne." But Prescott could not equate the claim with other statements Kellogg had made, such as "nature is simply a philosophical name for God," or "sunshine is the true Shekinah, the real presence," or "God is not behind nature, nor above nature, He is nature." The real reason the General Conference banned his book, Kellogg continued to argue, was not heresy but politics. They had wanted "to dodge the responsibility" of raising funds for the sanitarium. The campaign against him was "nothing more than a struggle for supremacy," dignified by making it appear as "a battle for truth."[53]

While Kellogg's claim did have its points, it was not the whole truth. As was his custom, he was overstating his case.

There was, in fact, a substantive theological dispute. As Bert Haloviak has astutely observed, however, the church might well have resolved the theological issues much more easily and amicably had its leadership not been so politically divided. If Kellogg had not been so determined upon independence for his medical program, the tendencies to pantheistic expression would probably have faded out with time.[54] It was true that the membership losses the denomination sustained as a result of the conflict did not result from disputed doctrine but administrative differences. Given the intense polarization, however, the church still had to deal with the theological aspects. Prescott may have made the issue bigger than it was or perhaps should have been, but it was, nevertheless, a substantive issue. His role in the resolution of the conflict helped maintain the dominance of the objective view of the doctrine of the atonement in the denomination—a significant contribution to the theological shape of the church.

THE OMEGA OF APOSTASY, 1905-1907

It was almost as if the events of 1904 had exhausted the chief contenders. For several months a lull settled over the dispute. In the interim, Prescott pleaded with his former colleagues, Jones and Waggoner, to reconsider their position, but it was too late. By October 1904 the denomination had finally transferred the medical institutions to conference organizations, and Daniells felt that "the danger line" had passed. Although urged by Ellen White to find ways of helping Kellogg, Daniells and Prescott felt that there was nothing else they could do. They were determined, though, that the conflict would not spoil the forthcoming 1905 General Conference session. The dispute had dominated the previous two sessions. In no way would they allow controversial issues—theological or otherwise—to trouble the next meeting. The church had had enough of theological brouhahas. (From that perspective, Albion F. Ballenger's "new light" on the sanctuary could not have been more ill-timed.)

Early in 1905 the church's quarrel with Kellogg turned to property. A. T. Jones, as president of the Sanitarium Association, "swindled" the church by refusing to transfer the Mexican Sanitarium at Guadalajara to the conference. A legal battle then ensued over ownership of the Sanitarium Association. When the General Conference finally assumed control, the "San" was $80,000 in debt and soon went bankrupt. At that

point Kellogg became totally intransigent, and the General Conference re-
sorted to dealing with him only through attorneys. According to Daniells,
even here the church lost heavily when one of the lawyers charged the
church excess fees. Relationships turned exceedingly sour. And the end
was not yet.

In early 1906 both Daniells and Prescott visited Battle Creek to arrange for the final withdrawal of the remaining operations of the Review
and Herald. During their visit the local congregation disfellowshipped a
number of members, and a call was made for members to leave the city.
The General Conference, having given up on trying to regain control of
sanitarium affairs, now sought to isolate Kellogg. In retaliation, Jones or-
chestrated a public attack on the church leaders and vowed to wrest control of the Battle Creek Tabernacle from the organization. The General
Conference president feared that he was "in for the bitterest struggle this
cause has witnessed."[55]

In such last bitter moves Ellen White recognized the "omega" of an
apostasy that she had seen with prophetic vision when the troubles first
broke out five years previously. As it happened, the church retained possession of the Tabernacle building, although it lost much of the congregation's membership. Among the losses was John Harvey Kellogg, whose
name the church removed from its roll on November 10, 1907. Despite
all Prescott's agitation of the pantheism issue, the Tabernacle's leadership
did not cite doctrinal problems as the cause for termination of the doctor's
membership. Nonattendance, nonsupport, and antagonism to Ellen
White's ministry were the reasons listed.[56]

The conflict left many scars. It soured Prescott's relationships with
Sutherland, Magan, Haskell, and Butler for life. His nervous system also
suffered as a consequence, making it necessary for him to take an extended break for recuperation. But Daniells, for one, was exceedingly
grateful for the personal support Prescott had given him and for the role
he had played during the crisis. The professor's "hand at the helm" as editor of the Review had helped to steer the church ship successfully through
stormy seas, enabling it to avoid successfully the dangerous icebergs that
had threatened its bows.

The irony was that when the denomination had appointed Prescott
editor in 1902, the need had not been for a defender of the status quo but

for a reformer, a progressive finder of new paths. The publishing house was in trouble and needed a new direction. The remarkable thing is that he was able to combine both roles, even in the midst of a major church schism. His vital role in establishing the new Review and Herald in Washington, D.C., during this turbulent period, as we shall see in the next chapter, was a major achievement for the church. We might also view it as a major personal accomplishment for Prescott that has helped secure the professor a permanent place in the denominational hall of fame.

---

[1] Cited in R. W. Schwarz, *John Harvey Kellogg: American Health Reformer* (Ph.D. dissertation, University of Michigan, 1964), p. 394; AGD to WCW, Feb. 15, 1932.

[2] A one-time editorial colleague, Alonzo L. Baker, attributed the remark to Magan. "My Years With John Harvey Kellogg," *Spectrum*, Autumn 1972, p. 43.

[3] AGD to GAI, Dec. 12, 1902.

[4] JHK to OAO, Nov. 18, 1892; OAO to EGW, Dec. 4, 1892.

[5] JHK to OAO, May 26, 1893.

[6] JHK to EGW, [copy] 1903.

[7] WWP to EGW, Dec. 14, 1900.

[8] WWP "Circular to Presidents" [Dec. 31], 1901; HEO to WWP, Dec. 24, 1901; *RH,* Jan 14, 1902.

[9] WWP, "Circular to Church Elders," [Dec. 31], 1901.

[10] *RH,* Jan. 7, 1902, p. 5.

[11] *RH,* Feb. 25, 1902, p. 13.

[12] *RH,* Mar. 18, 1902, p. 16; WWP to AGD, Mar. 12, 1902.

[13] AGD to EGW, Jan. 8, 1904; AGD to WWP, Feb. 25, 1902; WWP to AGD, Mar. 12, 1902; *RH,* Mar. 25, 1902, p. 16; *RH,* Apr. 8, 1902, pp. 21-23; "Report of Council Meeting Held at EGW's Home," Oct. 19, 1902.

[14] AGD to JAB, Mar. 26, 1902; AGD to JHK, Apr. 14, 1902.

[15] The denomination was still using *Christ's Object Lessons* as a fund-raiser for the church's education program.

[16] WWP to AGD, May 19, 1902; WWP, "Suggestions on . . . 'The Living Temple,'" May 19, 1902.

[17] AGD to CWF, Nov. 6, 1903; AGD to GAI, Dec. 12, 1902.

[18] EGW to AGD, Sept. 5, 1902; AGD to EGW, Mar. 13, 1903; "Stenographic Reports of Fifty-third Meeting of GCC," Nov. 15, 16, 1902.

[19] *RH,* Dec. 9, 1902, pp. 6, 17; SDAPABdMin, Dec. 2, 1902; WWP to AGD, Jan. 18, 1903.

[20] WWP to B. F. Anderson, Feb. 18, 1904; GCCMin, Nov. 14, 1902, Nov. 22, 1902. AGD, *The Abiding Gift of Prophecy* (Mountain View, Calif.: Pacific Press Pub. Assn., 1936), pp. 335, 336.

[21] *GC Bulletin,* Apr. 3, 1903, p. 67; Apr. 6, 1903, pp. 73-82; AGD to WCW, May 17,

1903; JHK to WCW, Jan. 21, 1903; WWP to AGD, May 22, 1903.

[22] AGD to WTK, Sept. 2, 1903; AGD to IHE, Aug. 20, 1903; *RH,* Aug. 4, 1903, p. 4; *RH,* Sept. 17, 1903, p. 16; *RH,* Oct. 15, 1903, p. 3; WWP to AGD, Aug. 6, 1903; WWP to JHK, Aug. 6, 1903.

[23] WWP to WCW, Sept. 30, 1903; WWP to AGD, Sept. 1, 10, 1903.

[24] AGD, *The Abiding Gift of Prophecy,* p. 336. ALW, *Ellen G. White: The Early Elmshaven Years, 1900-1905* (Washington, D.C.: Review and Herald Pub. Assn., 1981), vol. 5, p. 331.

[25] AGD to WCW, Oct. 29, 1903.

[26] WWP to JHK, Oct. 28, 1903.

[27] AGD to WCW, Oct. 29, 1903; WWP to AGD, Oct. 13, 1902.

[28] WWP to WCW, Jan. 10, 1904.

[29] AGD to EGW, Jan. 8, 1904.

[30] GAI to EWF, June 26, 1904; WCW to WAS, Jan. 20, 1904.

[31] JSW, "An Open Letter to AGD and the General Conference," May 1, 1922.

[32] AGD to WCW, Dec. 24, 1903.

[33] WWP to JWW, Feb. 18, 1904.

[34] JHK to GIB, June 1, 1904.

[35] EKV, "The Berrien Springs Meeting (1904)." AUHR; EKV to GMV, Jan. 11, 1982.

[36] EGW untitled MS, May 24, 1904; WCW to EGW, May 30, 1904.

[37] JHK to SHL, June 13, 1904; AGD to GAI, July 8, 1904; WWP to AGD, May 27, 1904; WCW to WAS, June 6, 1904; WCW to WAS, July 9, 1928.

[38] Estella Houser to WAS, June 6, 1904.

[39] EGW to Union Conference Presidents, June 15, 1904; "The Berrien Springs Meeting," MS 74, 1904.

[40] F. M. Rossiter, *The Story of the Living Temple* (New York: Fleming H. Revell, 1902).

[41] ATJ, "Elder W. W. Prescott on God in Nature," p. 26. AUHR.

[42] AGD to GAI, July 8, 1904; JHK to GIB, June 15, 1904; AGD to GAI, July 8, 1904; GAI to AGD, Aug. 28, 1904.

[43] WWP to EGW, Dec. 14, 1900; EGW, *Redemption or the Temptation of Christ in the Wilderness* (Battle Creek, 1874), pp. 24, 81.

[44] WCW to SNH, Apr. 18, 1900; EEA to SNH, Nov. 12, 1900.

[45] EGW to AGD, Dec. 14, 1903; EGW to WWP, July 7, 1902; EGW, untitled MS, July 18, 1902; EGW, "A Change of Feeling Needed," May 24, 1904.

[46] WWP to AGD, May 19, 1904.

[47] WWP to EJW, Nov. 14, 1904.

[48] *Ibid.*

[49] WWP to JHK, Oct. 28, 1903.

[50] WWP, "Sermon at Healdsburg," Mar. 26, 1904.This sermon, preached with Ellen White in the congregation, strongly emphasized sanctification and the work of the indwelling Christ.

[51] 1919 Bible Conference transcript, July 13, 1919.

[52] 1919 Bible Conference transcript, July 14, 1919.

[53] JHK to SMc, Jan. 28, 1906; JHK to SNH, July 13, 1904; JHK to GIB, July 20, 1904; WWP, "The Philosophy of the Living Temple" (undated). GCAr.

[54] Bert Haloviak, "Pioneers, Pantheists, and Progressives" (unpublished manuscript, 1980). GCAr.

[55] Cited in WWP to AGD, Mar. 8, 1906; WWP to WCW, Aug. 7, 1906.

[56] Schwarz, *Light Bearers to the Remnant* (1979), pp. 296, 297.

CHAPTER XII

PUBLISHING AGAIN

SOMETHING MUST BE DONE "to allow the *Review* to call the church to reform," bemoaned Daniells to W. C. White in 1902. It had been exactly one year since the 1901 General Conference tide of reform had broken through the dikes of tradition. While much had happened in the interim, many places still needed to be "washed clean of the debris" of the past few years. The *Review*, as the church's leading publication, could be such an asset in the reform program, if only it would at least swim with the tide instead of trying to stem it. Something had to be done with the *Review*. And not just the magazine. As Daniells saw it, the whole publishing plant in Battle Creek was in trouble.

From the earliest days of the church the weekly *Review* had served as the church's preeminent periodical. For all intents and purposes it was the voice of the church. Its importance had in fact led the emerging denomination into establishing its own publishing establishment. Since 1852 church-owned presses had printed the *Review*. Publishing had become one of the denomination's most successful means of evangelism.

By 1902 the church's publishing house in Battle Creek, Michigan, had become one of the largest and best printers in the state. The four-story building encompassed more than 80,000 square feet and employed 275 employees. Annual sales reached about a half million dollars. According to 1899 figures, however, only about 20 percent of it was religious material. The rest was ordinary commercial printing: novels, Montgomery Ward mail-order catalogs, business directories, and the like. Both management and employees had come to see the whole operation simply as a commercial enterprise. Morale was not good. Sharp business practices prevailed, and management treated the work staff roughly. Many of the foremen and employees were not Adventists. As a result, church officials were not at all happy with the state of things.[1]

REFORMS GOING NOWHERE

During the closing years of the nineteenth century Ellen White had issued repeated calls for management to improve conditions in the publishing house. The church had made various attempts, but with little success. During 1893, for example, Prescott, as a member of the General Conference Committee, became very concerned about the business. He had worked closely with editor Uriah Smith; A. R. Henry, the manager; and Harmon Lindsay, the treasurer, in trying to improve the spiritual tone of the plant by conducting a revival series. Whatever results he achieved were short-lived.

Three years later, in 1896, he again wrestled with the problems, but they seemed intractable. What could be done when the institution had so many "unconverted and unconsecrated" employees staffing it? Perhaps it would be better to "cut down some of these large institutions," he suggested in a letter about the problem to Ellen White. Then, maybe, the working force would be more manageable.[2] Eventually in 1897 her repeated agitation produced some changes when the General Conference session that year removed senior management. But the end result was bitterness, lawsuits, and more dissatisfaction. Nevertheless, during the declining years of the century she continued her campaign for reform.[3]

Little had changed by the time Daniells came on the scene in 1901. To the new president, the publishing house seemed diseased, "a festering spot for a lot of evil." It was an "unclean place," and he concluded that it must be "cleansed from top to bottom."[4] He started with a week of revival meetings for the staff held during the regular December Week of Prayer. To his surprise, he found what he thought was a "responsive chord." There seemed to be a willingness to make changes. Before the end of the week the board had met and taken a decision to call the experienced Californian publishing house manager, Charles H. Jones, to put Battle Creek on the right track. The move failed because Jones was unwilling to come. But Daniells was not discouraged. Feeling that the board was at least "sincere in its efforts to reform," he believed it would press ahead.

But such transformation wasn't going to come quickly or easily.

Terminating the commercial printing and building up enough denominational work to replace it was obviously going to take time. And why the
need to transfer ownership of the publishing plant to the General Conference? Some of the board members objected to that.

Where the question came from surprised Daniells more than the
question itself. Uriah Smith, fellow board member and longtime editor,
evidently did not understand the General Conference president's push for
reorganization, or if he did, he just didn't like it. Quickly Daniells learned
that other church leaders such as Haskell and Butler were also not excited
about the implications of the 1901 General Conference reform program
either. Was it really necessary for the General Conference to assume control of all the various church agencies? they questioned. They had recently
been in touch with the editor and hoped that Smith would put forth their
point of view. He was certainly willing.[5]

Smith had reacted negatively to Daniells shortly after his Week of
Prayer meetings. The "responsive chord" the General Conference president thought he heard evidently resonated with dissonance as well as har-
monies. In an editorial in the *Review* Smith pointedly protested the
suggestion that the place smelled badly. How could Daniells insinuate that
"a heavy load of odium" rested upon the publishing association?
Defensively he repudiated charges that the institution had proved false to
its "corporate obligations." Yes, as "Laodiceans" the publishers had made
mistakes, as the Week of Prayer meetings had pointed out. But transferring ownership of the property to the church, Smith objected, would not
cure that problem.[6] The editorial troubled Daniells. With Smith so clearly
and publicly opposed to his reform movement, how would he ever succeed with the publishing house or even with the church? It was clear that
new blood was needed, and the General Conference president knew
where to get it.

At the stockholders' meeting about a month after the Week of Prayer
he persuaded his colleagues to elect Prescott to the board. Daniells seemed
to know where he was going. Three days later the new management board
set up a subcommittee of three to formulate new policies for the business.
It included the General Conference president and Prescott with the new
publishing house manager, I. H. Evans, as the third member.[7]

Daniells felt that Uriah Smith in his old age had become opposed to reform of any kind. For example, the 70-year-old editor followed up his protest editorial in early January by publishing a series of three articles by William Brickey that resurrected the old law in the Galatians controversy of 1888. According to Daniells, the "vicious attack" on the 1888 message had shocked and confused *Review* readers and thoroughly distressed the college Bible teachers. The General Conference present could not understand how Smith could avow confidence in Ellen White on the one hand and on the other hand "reject the Minneapolis message."[8]

Other aspects of Smith's work also gave concern. He had offended Black delegates to the General Conference late in 1901 with an indiscreet article on race relations. (The publishing house had retrieved the issue from mailbags at the railway station at the very last minute and the article withdrawn at considerable expense.) He had also offended church musicians at the Tabernacle by printing an article criticizing their performance. The musicians promptly threatened to resign, and Smith had to write a rebuttal to the critique.[9] The increasingly cantankerous editor, it seemed, was not managing things as he should.

By mid-February the General Conference Committee was ready to replace him. But with whom? The assistant was his son Leon, who was much like his father. Daniells recalled years later that the committee that met on a Saturday night to consider the matter felt "greatly perplexed." The situation was critical and the potential replacements so few. Finally the committee engaged in a "most earnest season of prayer." When they arose from their knees and looked at the matter again, the General Conference president reported, their minds were clear. "Brother Prescott should be elected editor."[10] The minutes of the meeting collaborate Daniells' recollection. Committee members clearly realized they were dealing with a highly sensitive situation. The recording secretary took the trouble to state that the group had "a remarkable unanimity of opinion as to the propriety of this action."[11]

Smith took the demotion extremely hard, especially since only 10 months earlier he had been reinstated as senior editor after having been relegated for three years to the role of an associate to A. T. Jones. According to his wife, Harriet, the news "cut him to the quick," and that night he suffered a stroke from which he never fully recovered. Although tempted at first to pull out of Battle Creek and retire to an orchard in the

South, Smith eventually decided to bear the decision gracefully and stay with the *Review*. A year later he was dead.[12]

Being appointed editor in chief was certainly not good news for Prescott, either. It "dumbfounded" him, and for days afterward he could not sleep well. Smith was a man for whom Prescott had the greatest respect, even though he did not always agree with him. He understood what the blow had done to the editor, and it embarrassed him acutely.[13]

During the week that followed, the much-troubled Prescott "studied" to find a way out of the difficulty. Finally he came up with a compromise. He shared his thoughts with Kellogg, with the Review and Herald manager, I. H. Evans, and even with Smith himself.

Perhaps the board could simply elect all three men—Smith, Prescott, and Smith's son, Leon—as editors without making any statement as to the relative standing of each. Then a separate action would appoint Prescott as managing editor and list him underneath the other names on the masthead. In this way, at least Smith's name would still appear at the head of the column.

According to Prescott, the idea helped Smith's feelings "quite a good deal." The board also saw light in the professor's suggestion and agreed that it was "in harmony with the spirit of the counsel received from the General Conference." Thus Prescott's editor in chief designation subsequently changed to managing editor. His role, however, would remain the same. He had reported to Daniells that the two Smiths clearly understood that "there could be but one managing editor." The action "will leave the editorial management in my hands," he assured the president. Would Daniells "waive the technical part of the question"? Prescott hoped that his letter to the General Conference president would reach him before he talked with Ellen White. She would then understand the situation "just as it is." He realized that it was an exceedingly delicate matter.[14]

It was probably inevitable that the move would cause controversy. People were bound to misunderstand. In fact, the feeling that the whole thing was a Prescott-engineered coup lingered for years. Kellogg, for one, made good capital out of the incident. The demotion was "one of the most cruel things" he had ever seen, he wrote with characteristic hyperbole in 1904. In his view, Smith had been "turned down square without a word of gratitude or appreciation," and the stroke he suffered as a result was "his death blow." Of course, the doctor had an ax to grind. Leon Smith was another who became quite a bitter Prescott opponent, at least partly because of the way he felt his father had been demoted at the *Review* because of his theological views.[15] F. M. Wilcox, who later served as editor at the *Review,* was yet another who, even 30 years later, harbored suspicions toward the professor because of the episode.

As usual, though, those closest to the situation and who knew the facts about what happened felt quite differently. Fellow board member S. H. Lane, for one, felt that Prescott had taken "a very wise course with Brother Smith." Sharing with Daniells his reaction to the painful events, he wrote, "The more I am associated with Brother Prescott, the more I am convinced that he is not only a Christian but a gentleman in the first degree. He is so free from anything like harshness. He tries to take a fair view of everything, so that one cannot but like him."[16] The testimonial was completely unsolicited. E. R. Palmer, another General Conference official, also later confirmed the "gentlemanly way" Prescott handled the matter and the "tender solicitude" manifested toward Smith. Ellen White, contrary to the rumors flying around Battle Creek that she had rebuked Prescott and Daniells over the matter, stated that she was pleased that Prescott had joined the *Review* and that Smith would not be bypassed or dropped from the masthead. Painful though the task was, the denomination's leadership obviously felt they had done the right thing. They had no regrets.[17]

Prescott assumed his duties immediately upon his appointment, his name appearing in the masthead of the very next issue, February 25. Obviously concerned to avoid stirring the waters further and wanting to give readers time to adjust to the changes, he waited six weeks before adding the designation of managing editor to his name. Furthermore, in deference to Smith's age and experience, Prescott continued to refer to his predecessor as senior editor. The transition went smoothly, with Smith accepting the inevitable. He did his best to make things easy for Prescott. "During the last year," the professor remarked at Smith's funeral in March 1903, he had done "all that a Christian could do to make my editorial work comfortable." He lauded Smith's gracious spirit.[18]

Other developments in Battle Creek during the transition period at the *Review* added to the trauma. In the same week that the editorship tangle occurred, the sanitarium burned down. Prescott's first issue carried extensive reports of the calamity, and a busy week of meetings followed. But he still found time to plan for new initiatives. Any changes he wanted to make, he realized, would best be made in the transition stage. Also, he knew that everybody was watching and that he needed to move with care.

Six weeks later the magazine appeared with several innovations. Page size shrank, but the number increased to 24. The publication introduced a brighter typeface, and the cover carried a full-page illustration. Prescott intended to make the *Review* truly preeminent. Within weeks the popular *Missionary Magazine,* the second string in Prescott's editorial bow, merged with the *Review,* and the circulation of the combined paper took a jump.[19]

The fresh, clean, lighter lines of the new *Review* matched its brighter editorial tone. It exuded confidence and a more definite sense of purpose. But Prescott found that he had to stay close by the office if he wanted to "still have things go . . . as I wish." He had to forgo speaking appointments elsewhere.[20] Evidently some in the office had not yet come up to the new editor's expectations. Anything less than technical perfection was unacceptable to Prescott.

Right at the outset he understood the role of the *Review* editor to be a primary influence in shaping the future of the church. Daniells had wanted the magazine to call the church to reform. It had to lead the way. Prescott saw that the paper must therefore be both visionary and informative, reviewing and heralding, and he must be an educator still. The articles he selected and the editorials he wrote he considered "a means of educating our people." Prescott was still a teacher at heart—the term *professor* had not stayed with him for nothing. Now the whole church was his classroom and the *Review* his blackboard. He grasped the opportunity with relish.

His first self-assigned task involved instructing the church on "what our gospel message really is."[21] He had in mind his new understanding of the importance of healthful living and its link with the message of the three angels. Thus, his first issues strongly promoted the Forward Movement and ran reports on health and the development of the church's medical program. The first issues also stressed the theme of Christ's mediatorial work. A long series on the latter topic ran during 1902. He intended the articles to complement the two-quarter series of lessons then being used in the Sabbath school that Prescott had also authored.[22] One of the themes the series developed was the unity of the health program and the gospel. But by December tensions between the medical wing of the church and the General Conference had become severe, and two weeks before the series ended, Prescott felt obliged to offer his first public alert against the teachings of Kellogg.

The cautioning was gentle, but it reflected the professor's increasing concern about Kellogg's theology. Prescott had begun to see that the doctor's emphasis on God in nature was tending to weaken faith in the ministry of Christ "by substituting a human conception of the presence of God for the reality of His presence in Christ through the Holy Spirit."[23] It was the first of many warnings he would make through the *Review* during the next five years.

By mid-1903 the conflict with Kellogg had become the preeminent item on the church agenda. When the Review and Herald board reappointed Prescott in June of that year, the specific mandate spelled out for him was "to keep constantly before the people, the distinctive doctrines of this denomination."[24] When, a few months later, Kellogg began publicly quoting Ellen White's writings in his defense, the battle was joined. Prescott felt an editorial duty to begin educating the church more thoroughly. Thereafter, discussions of "new theology," "higher criticism," "Christian pantheism," "speculative knowledge," and "the sure foundation" filled the pages of the *Review*. Between December 1902 and December 1907 more than 100 of Prescott's editorials related either directly or indirectly to the Kellogg crisis. "We purpose that our people shall understand," he wrote, outlining his editorial policy. "When the true situation is clearly understood, then an intelligent choice can be made."[25]

Kellogg sympathizers at times criticized Prescott for "pushing [the issue of] pantheism hard" through the *Review*. He responded by insisting that he was not overstating the problem. Besides, he claimed, Ellen White expected him to make a stand. Should anyone blame the church for "refusing to leave the original platform"? But at times Prescott did seem to overreact. Beginning to see hidden meanings behind every expression Kellogg used, he even questioned a popular Kellogg phrase, "miracle of life," which Prescott saw as a veiled catchphrase disguising sinister pantheistic notions. Was he reading into it more than the author intended?[26] In a state of war it was possible to become too trigger-happy.

Other things than Kellogg and his dangerous theology would also become grist for Prescott's editorials. The Sabbath, the Second Advent, and the fulfillment of prophecy were all common themes, as was the topic of religious liberty. Elsewhere in the magazine missions became a noticeable emphasis, with the subject receiving its own column called The Field. In it the professor attempted to shape the attitude of church members toward the advance of the denomination in foreign countries. The column highlighted cultures and customs and utilized photographs to help inform readers of the needs of a worldwide outreach. Prescott was much more liberal in his use of photographs than his predecessors had been (five per issue compared to one per issue previously). The professor saw them as a valuable communication and educational aid.

Beginning in 1906 he introduced a column specifically to help educate the ministry.[27] It presented source materials that supported important Adventist doctrines or prophetic interpretations. The enthusiastic response to the column eventually led the professor into producing materials for what the Review and Herald later published as the *Source Book*, a volume much valued by teachers and ministers alike. Writing books and editing magazines, however, accounted for only a part of Prescott's involvement with the church's leading publishing house. While Daniells wanted the *Review* to call the church to reform, he also sought to reform the publishing house itself. Prescott was his man for that job as well. From 1903 until 1909 the professor served as chief executive officer of the publishing house. In this capacity he supervised not only its transformation but also its relocation, first to downtown Washington, D.C., and then to Takoma Park.

TRANSPLANTING A PUBLISHING HOUSE

A change in editors was not what Daniells originally had in mind when he asked Prescott to transform conditions in the publishing house in 1901. But the editorial assignment proved to be a bonus. It placed him in a strategic position to accomplish reform. Within three weeks he had specific ideas to present to the board.

Prescott hoped to bring in a "better class" of young people to train as apprentices. He urged Daniells to scout the colleges for suitable talent. Also, he arranged for evening classes for the apprentices and a Friday night vesper service for employees. Ever the schoolteacher, Prescott went so far as to organize a residence hall complete with a preceptor for the young out-of-town apprentices. "We ought to change the atmosphere here permanently for the better, and this can only be done by educational methods," he explained to Daniells.[28] They were good ideas. Large institutions have a way of being difficult to reform, however, and Review and Herald was no exception.

How could the publishing house survive without commercial work? Mail-order catalogs and novels turned good profits, and the Review had to make its heavy investment in large presses worthwhile. If the equipment printed just church material they would be idle much of the time. Working conditions and morale were also difficult to improve. In fact, employee dissatisfaction grew noticeably worse. Repeated incidents of willful carelessness and vandalism caused the board enough concern for it to take action to increase the fire insurance coverage by $50,000 (the recent sanitarium fire was no doubt another significant motivation).[29] But by the end of 1902 Prescott felt that he had made little real progress. Was reforming the publishing enterprise a lost cause?

It was only a partial surprise to many church members to learn, on the last day of 1902, that the entire Review and Herald publishing house had burned to the ground the night before. It was an unforgettable interruption to the Week of Prayer meeting Prescott was about to start in the nearby Tabernacle. Some may have suspected arson, but the most readily accepted explanation of the calamity was that it was an act of divine judgment. Ellen White emphatically stated it to be so, and a majority of the local church members concurred.[30]

The fire proved to be very persuasive. At the first board meeting after the disaster Prescott succeeded in having two reform actions approved: (1) "That we do not expect to resume commercial work in the institution," and (2) "That our only interest is to care for the institution in reference to our denominational interests." Even then, while the spirit was willing, the flesh was weak. The publishing house continued to accept commercial contracts right up until 1906.[31]

One of the options opened up by the fire (a blessing in disguise?) suggested itself early to Prescott and no doubt to others as well. At last it might be possible to move out of Battle Creek. The more he discussed it in the office, he reported to Daniells, "the more the idea seems to be accepted in a general way here that in all probability the work will be removed to some other place."[32] But it was the publishing house stockholders who would have to decide.[33] In the meantime the management quickly found commercial printers in town to produce the *Review,* and Prescott commandeered Daniells' office for his editorial team. Deciding just how much equipment to replace immediately was a vexed question for the trustees. Purchasing all the essential machinery would cost $20,000, but that would necessarily mean staying in Battle Creek. Prescott did not like that option at all. If the publishing house should eventually relocate its plant, would it not be better to wait? The issue led to sharp disagreement. Finally management reached a compromise and purchased a minimum of equipment just to keep basic operations functioning.

The first formal airing of the proposal to move church headquarters out of Battle Creek took place three months later at the General Conference session in Oakland, California. Ellen White concluded the discussion by emphatically declaring that it was time to move. Exactly where, she didn't know, but somewhere on the Eastern seaboard would be best. A recommendation went to the stockholders scheduled to meet on April 20.

But anything from the General Conference, however, did not carry much weight with some of the stockholders. It was an eventful meeting. The fight was bitter and long remembered. In wanting to assume ownership of the publishing house, some argued, the General Conference was getting out of its depth. How could ministers successfully manage such a large business venture? Why should the fire be considered a judgment from God? questioned others. Were all fires divine judgments? In the heat of the conflict, opponents threatened to withhold stock and raise legal obstacles—threats that they carried out. But at the end of the day, the majority voted to accept the proposal of the General Conference and authorized a transfer.[34]

A search committee soon began inspecting sites in New York and New Jersey. Prescott, who figured that a New York dateline on the *Review* would be an advantage, had to stay behind in Battle Creek. He arranged for his elder brother, Amos, a former Adventist now caring for the family's shoe polish and household chemical business in New Jersey, to help with site investigations. In June letters from Ellen White in California and telegrams from Judson Washburn in Washington, D.C., suggested that the nation's capital was also a possibility that the leadership should check out. Finally a site at Takoma Park attracted the attention of the committee. Six miles from the city center, the site was "high," "healthful," with pure air, pure water, and "delightful shade." Best of all, the real estate brochure promised no mosquitoes. By July a group of key officials had made their choice. The denomination purchased a 50-acre lot in Maryland along with a small, attached adjoining property across the line in the District of Columbia. The latter provided the all-important postmark Washington, D.C.[35]

Arranging the legal transfer of the publishing business was a convoluted process. In July the publishing house board sold the two main magazines, the *Review* and the *Youth's Instructor,* to the Foreign Mission Board, at that time legally based in New York. The Mission Board paid $10,000 for them. In the meantime Prescott headed up a small subcommittee charged with legally establishing a new publishing association in Washington, D.C. They then secured temporary rented premises in the heart of the city, just one city block from the grounds of the Capitol, and set the office up with equipment. With the infrastructures in place, the Review and Herald then purchased the two magazines back from the Foreign Mission Board, and the new publishing entity was in business.[36]

Back in Battle Creek on the last Sabbath in July, Prescott and Daniells reported to the church the arrangements now made. They recounted the providential leadings of God along with the timeliness of Ellen White's specific directions. Slowly the hostility toward the move began to diminish. In the *Review* of August 11 Prescott informed the church at large. "The developments of the past year constitute a turning point in the history of this movement," he wrote. "Changes are now imperatively demanded which might have been avoided, and we must act accordingly."[37]

Some key players, though, still did not feel like cooperating. For example, former Review and Herald financier and manager A. R. Henry spoke for a group of disenchanted stockholders and insisted that the Review and Herald should buy their stock at what they considered a satisfactory price. If that did not happen, he said, they would seek a court injunction against the move. Daniells had not expected that. What was he to do? The litigation promised to be drawn out. Swallowing hard, the

General Conference president paid the inflated price, and the move was under way.[38] But not without some scoffing from those who stayed behind. They told those who made the transfer, Prescott reported years later, that "we had better save our packing cases to bring our things back." After all, "there was not anyone coming down to Washington that had enough business experience to run the thing at all, . . . and we were cutting ourselves off from our business connections of half a century."[39] Those who questioned the wisdom of the relocation would learn, however, that Prescott had not lost his inky thumbs.

By August 10, 1903, Review employees began unloading four railway freight cars laden with 46 tons of equipment in Washington. Prescott and his plant manager, S. N. Curtiss, were the first on hand to supervise setting up the new operation. The following day the men realized that they were making history as they signed the final documents for incorporation. A new era was dawning, but first they had to settle the bills, and the kitty was empty. Financially embarrassed by the stockholders' last-minute demands, A. G. Daniells, while on a camp meeting itinerary, had to beg for funds from the conferences to pay off the stockholders. Ten days after the unloading of the delivery wagons, the first issue of the *Review* appeared with its new Washington dateline. Four days later the premises, though temporary, were dedicated. In a short address to the congregation of 50 Prescott compared their work to that of Zerubbabel. Their buildings might not be so large or glorious as those that had existed in Battle Creek, but the important thing was that God was with them. That would surely make their work outshine the past.[40] It was a bold new start even if the mechanics of it all proved to be chaotic.

BUILDING AGAIN—"IN TROUBLOUS TIMES"

"The Review and Herald has passed through a terrific experience . . . but I am glad the Lord has not allowed it to go under," Daniells wrote to W. C. White in 1907. "I do not think that our brethren connected with the Pacific Press, or any other publishing house, have had any just appreciation of the tremendous difficulties Professor Prescott and his associates have been laboring under since the Review and Herald fire."[41] No one had expected it to be easy, but neither had they expected it to be quite so difficult.

To start with, housing had been difficult to find for the employees. In addition, the narrow six-story building on North Capitol Street was quite ill-suited to be a publishing house. It did not have enough room for the larger presses, and the Review had to contract work out to other firms in the city. With editorial offices on the fourth floor and the presses in the basement, the carrying of copy and proof sheets up and down five flights of stairs soon became a problem. Later, maintenance had a rope and pulley system, complete with bell, installed outside the windows.[42] The publishing house staff accepted the temporary arrangements, though inadequate, because everyone expected that a new building would be erected as soon as possible. Their hopes were disappointed.

Just a few months after the move, some stockholders refused to transfer their stock to the new association, crippling it. Repeated appeals through the Review failed to persuade the discontented group and, reluctantly, in 1904 the publishing house had to abandon plans for the new building in Takoma Park.[43] Further difficulties followed. Some raised objections to the purchase of the adjacent five-acre Thornton Estate that would provide the Washington, D.C., address. Court challenges and a series of appeals consumed precious resources and delayed a settlement. Not until the end of December 1904 was the matter eventually resolved and Prescott held the title deeds safely in his hands.[44]

The legal transfer of the old Battle Creek publishing plant finally concluded one month later. Prescott had to travel to Battle Creek to be actually present to bid for the old association at auction. It cost him $126,000 and, according to an almost gleeful Kellogg, a great deal of anxiety. The professor was not at all sure that the new association could afford to buy out the old. He was greatly relieved when the court decided to approve the sale, and the old company legally ceased to exist. As it so happened, however, Prescott's Washington company was too strapped for cash to effect an immediate transfer of operations under the court's conditions. The denomination, therefore, had to maintain the old entity for a further 18 months in Battle Creek, meaning a further frustrating delay in the start of the new building in Washington.[45]

The complicated situation also caused problems in the building of Prescott's own home. The legal delays on the Takoma Park property disrupted his original plan, and both he and Daniells had to settle on alternative lots near each other, but on other land not affected by the dispute.

Bad weather stretched out the building schedule for more than 10 months. Not until the middle of 1905 was he ready to take possession, and even then the house had "hardly a room ready to occupy." But he had had his fill of living in cramped rented quarters.[46]

As president of the new publishing association, Prescott was its chief executive officer responsible for the everyday conduct of the business. Much of the detailed work of production he delegated to S. N. Curtiss, his business manager and treasurer. (The office of "president" maintained administrative authority until 1911, when an action formally delegated his responsibilities to a "duly appointed manager.") His first concern as president was financial security. The business lacked operating capital, and he needed to build quickly to provide financial strength. Prescott also determined not to allow the publishing house to fall into the same trap it had tried to escape from by the move from Battle Creek. It was time for a new order of things.

In September 1903 at a meeting of the board called especially to establish policy, Prescott argued for the same five-day workweek he had instituted in his own large publishing business in Vermont 20 years previously. It had proved economical then, and he believed it would work now. Besides, the Review employees needed spare time for evangelistic activities. Sunday should be free as well as Sabbath. Frightened by the cost, the board demurred, with a decision to study the matter further. Balancing financial constraints and spiritual concerns was difficult, but Prescott was determined. Either the commercial approach must give way in favor of a more evangelistic basis or "we shall drift upon the same ground and our work will bear the same impress as before," he argued.[47]

"Molding the policy of the institution" and making it a "pattern" for others (do we hear echoes of the establishment of Avondale?) was one of the main reasons that W. C. White saw for having Prescott at the head of the publishing company. He knew of "no one else living who could give it such a high intellectual and spiritual mold."[48] It was not, by any means, the professor's first choice of work. Accepting the role reluctantly, he would have preferred to be elsewhere.

In early 1905, when plans were finally in hand to proceed with the building of the new plant, Prescott had tried to withdraw from leadership of the institution. The size of the venture and his preoccupation with its concerns were making it difficult for him to carry out his other pastoral and administrative responsibilities successfully. Experienced publishing managers such as W. D. Salisbury from Australia, C. H. Jones from California, or I. H. Evans from Battle Creek, he argued, were more suited to the task. But his colleagues disagreed. As W. C. White pointed out, Jones would probably not come, Australia needed Salisbury, and Evans was not well equipped for the special conditions in Washington. The new enterprise needed someone who could choose the right kind of personnel—a good judge of character. Prescott was the man. Could not the professor handle the work, White inquired, if he took care not to allow his editorial responsibilities to become all-absorbing? While the denomination could call other business and editorial helpers, it was important that Prescott himself study "the principles and plans upon which the [publishing] work should be conducted," and then present them "to faithful men who would teach others also." It was vitally important that the Review set a pattern, and no one else was so well suited to that task as the professor, White, who himself was an experienced publisher, concluded.[49]

It was a difficult decision for Prescott and caused him considerable anguish. He would "greatly prefer" not to have to spend his time on business affairs and was not at all sure that he would make "any flattering success of the work" if he did. But he realized that someone had to do it or the publishing house would "suffer greatly." Reluctantly he accepted the assignment and even more reluctantly decided to relinquish his vice presidential responsibilities at the General Conference.[50]

W. C. White, for one, was delighted. "There is no nobler work you could undertake just now," he encouraged. The professor would have before him "the greatest, grandest opportunity that will ever be presented in this cause to put a thorough mold upon the work such as it had in the beginning but which it lost in the eighties and nineties."[51] The prospect was enough to give Prescott the shakes. But he was not one to pass up a challenge. At the General Conference session in March 1905 the professor presented plans for the new building. A special fund-raising drive, endorsed by Ellen White, promised $15,000, and three months later excavations began for the foundations.

But Prescott quickly ran into a number of difficulties. One particularly troubling matter concerned the financial arrangements. The publishing house had counted on the $15,000 donation raised as an overflow of the special fund-raising drive for church projects in Washington, D.C. Thus, when Ellen White sent instructions that the overflow should go to help the church in the Southern states instead, it "troubled" and "confused" Prescott. Previously Ellen White had sharply reproved church leaders who had publicly appealed for an offering for a project in the South and then diverted it to some need in the North. If that had been "robbery" then, he didn't know how the new diversion could be made to "look straight" now. In his letter to W. C. White on the matter, he acknowledged that Ellen White's son was probably as perplexed as he was, but Prescott wanted some explanation because the publishing house now found themselves forced to transgress another cherished policy adopted at the urging of Ellen White: not to go into debt.[52]

There was no easy answer. W. C. White replied that he was just as puzzled. But there was, he pointed out, blessing in obedience. He was glad that Prescott had purposed to do as they had done in the past: "Follow the counsel which is given us, believing that the Lord knows more about his work than we do." It was a characteristic response for Prescott. His attitude to Ellen White remained unaltered by the apparent inconsistency.[53]

Financial problems occurred on every side, further delaying progress on the building. First, Frank E. Belden, a cousin of W. C. White, sued the publishing association for a huge sum over its misuse of one of his hymn-books. Somewhat embarrassed, W. C. White consulted with Prescott over the problems created by the unethical positions taken by former managers, but he urged the professor not to contest the matter. It would be better for all to settle Belden's claims out of court.[54]

Then, on top of everything, arrangements to sell the remaining equipment and the property at Battle Creek fell through as a result of the bitter conflict with Kellogg.[55] Consequently, the publishing house had to ship the entire inventory of large presses to Washington at great expense. The unexpected development meant that the new four-story building in Takoma Park, finally ready for occupancy in March 1906, was crowded from the very start.[56] But at least the *Review* had finally settled in a permanent new home. May 31, 1906, witnessed the publication of the first issue from the Takoma Park address.

Prescott worked hard at creating the right atmosphere in the new establishment. He selected new employees with great care and established a night school for them during the summer. By astute planning he was able to finally phase out commercial work in late 1906. Presses now kept busy printing just denominational material alone. Both Prescott and Daniells had worked hard to foster an "aggressive bookwork" and to recruit more literature evangelists. It had paid dividends. Sales were such that the printing plant would soon have to expand.

In fact, just two years after the completion of the building, space was so much at a premium that the board voted to approve a large addition for storage. Mindful of his painful 1893 experience with the enlarging of buildings at Battle Creek, Prescott was disturbed by a comment from Ellen White in an article protesting the accumulation of debt on buildings. Quickly he sent letters spelling out in careful detail the intricate financial circumstances of the publishing association to Daniells and W. C. White, seeking advice. This time he averted misunderstandings, and the building expansion proceeded. The Review and Herald was on its way to a strong position, but the cost had been high.

"So terrible" had been the strain during the previous three years, Prescott reported in mid-1905, that it had brought him "almost to nervous prostration." Daniells felt the same. At times it seemed all too much. After the rush of the 1905 General Conference session, which occurred in the midst of the busy building program, Daniells had, on more than one occasion, collapsed at a committee meeting, unable to carry on and obliging Prescott "to take charge of the meeting in order to finish up the business."[57]

Reports that Prescott had been overworking reached California and brought advice from W. C. White. The professor should take time out to "make a garden, . . . saw wood" or do "something that will make you sweat." It was good advice, but Prescott was almost helpless to do anything about it because of the constant demands made on his time. "Teachers are the hardest men in the world to teach," White had remarked, and Prescott would doubtless have agreed.[58] Nature finally took its course when Prescott had a nervous breakdown in 1910.

In 1909 he transferred from the presidency of the Review and Herald to other work. During the six years he had been the chief administrative officer and editor, periodical output alone had doubled to 50,000 copies per week. Staff on the payroll had increased from 31 to more than 100, and production had soared to more than $1,000 worth of publications per day—all of it denominational.

Prescott, of course, recognized that the success of the new publishing house was ultimately a result of the advance of the church at large. It was not simply "the special ability" of those who were "in charge" that made an institution succeed, he had stated in a parting speech.[59] True. But without that "special ability" and the willingness to spend oneself in the service of others, nothing succeeds either. Prescott had demonstrated both. In 1909 he left the *Review* reluctantly and hurting badly. It was work he had come to enjoy, and he would have preferred to stay, particularly as editor. But a theological controversy over how to interpret Daniel 8:13 had wracked the church during the previous two years. It was polarizing the ministry and, despite Ellen White's appeals, it would not quiet down. Prescott had been in the center of it, but with him out of the *Review* it just might fade away.

---

[1] *GC Bulletin,* Feb. 16, 1899, p. 8; GAI to EGW, Nov. 9, 1899; "Stenographic Records of the Fifty-second Meeting of the General Conference Committee," p. 35. GCAr.

[2] WWP to EGW, July 30, 1896.

[3] Many of these letters are published in EGW, "Selections From the *Testimonies* Setting Forth Important Principles Relating to Our Work in General, the Publishing Work in Particular, and the Relation of Our Institutions to Each Other" (Oakland, Calif: [Pacific Press], 1898).

[4] AGD to WWP, Dec. 28, 1901; AGD to WCW, Jan. 31, 1902.

[5] AGD to WCW, Apr. 14; Feb. 15, 1902.

[6] *RH,* Jan. 7, 1902, p. 8. Daniells recalled years later that neither Butler nor Haskell fully understood the reform program (AGD to WCW, Feb. 15, 1932); see also Eugene Durand, *Yours in the Blessed Hope, Uriah Smith* (Washington, D.C.: Review and Herald Pub. Assn., 1980), p. 43.

[7] SDAPABdMin, Feb. 14, 1902.

[8] *RH,* Jan. 21, 1902, p. 4; Jan. 28, 1902, p. 4; Feb. 4, 1902, p. 3. Brickey had been a staunch supporter of Smith's position in the post-1888 year. AGD to WCW, Apr. 14, 1902.

[9] GCCMin, Oct. 23, 1901; Durand, pp. 266-268.

[10] AGD to WCW, Feb. 15, 1932.

[11] GCCMin, Feb. 15, 1902. According to Prescott, a meeting on the following Sunday apparently reviewed and again confirmed the decision. WWP to AGD, Feb. 20, 1902; *RH,* Mar. 4, 1902, p. 14.

[12] Harriet N. Smith to My Dear Sister, Feb. 28, 1902.

[13] WWP to EGW, Apr. 22, 1902; *RH,* Mar. 10, 1903, p. 7.

[14] WWP to AGD, Feb. 20, 1902; The board was happy to endorse Prescott's more pastoral approach to the dilemma. SDAPABdMin, Feb. 20, 1902.

[15] JHK to GIB, Apr. 12, 1904; LAS to AGD, Jan. 17, 1908.

[16] SHL to AGD, Feb. 28, 1902.

[17] ERP to AGD, Mar. 26, 1907; EGW to WWP, Mar. 30, 1902; AGD to WCW, Feb. 15, 1932.

[18] *RH,* Mar. 10, 1903, p. 7.

[19] Prescott modeled the new look on another religious periodical, the *North-Western Christian Advocate.* SDAPABdMin, Mar. 24, 1902; *Missionary Magazine,* May 1902, p. 196.

[20] WWP to AGD, July 3, 1902.

[21] WWP to AGD, Apr. 10, 1902.

[22] Merlin Burt observes that although the series dealt with Christology, they did not seem to use the opportunity to actively promote the new Trinitarian understandings or use any of the clearer language on the "Sonship" of Christ that had emerged in the late 1890s. Prescott still needed to think things through more, and besides the church's agenda was too crowded with other issues to have safely opened new battlefronts ("Demise of Semi-Arianism and Anti-Trinitarianism in Adventist Theology, 1888-1957" [unpublished research paper, Andrews University, 1996], pp. 15-17). Prescott still needed to think things through more, and besides the denomination's agenda was too crowded with other issues to have safely opened new battlefronts.

[23] *RH,* Dec. 2, 1902, p. 6.

[24] SDAPABdMin, June 10, 1903; WWP to WCW, Sept. 30, 1903.

[25] *RH,* Dec. 28, 1905, pp. 3, 4; WWP to JWW, Feb. 18, 1904.

[26] *RH,* July 13, 1905, p. 3; Jan. 4, 1906, p. 24; Nov. 3, 1904, p. 3.

[27] *RH,* Apr. 5, 1906.

[28] WWP to AGD, Mar. 12, 1902.

[29] SDAPABdMin, Mar. 25, 1902; Aug. 23, 1902; Aug. 25, 1902; Dec. 2, 1902.

[30] WWP to AGD, Jan. 28, 1903. The December 8, 1977, issue of the *Adventist Review* is devoted to the fire and provides a good survey of the event.

[31] SDAPABdMin, Jan. 4, 29, 1903.

[32] WWP to AGD, Jan. 20, 1903.

[33] Early Adventist leaders adopted an "investment" approach to raising capital for funding the establishment and development of the first denominational institutions such as the Review and Herald Publishing Association, Battle Creek College, and the Battle Creek Sanitarium. Generally the church incorporated them as legally autonomous entities and encouraged members to "subscribe" by purchasing shares in the enterprise. Those who did were technically the legal owners of the institution and received voting privileges at the annual meeting of stockholders proportional to the number of shares they held. The stock was nondividend, and all profits made went to the institution or to charity work undertaken by it. Often people would donate the stock itself to the various enterprises. The system worked well in the early years. Then, during the first decade of the twentieth century when the General Conference absorbed the institutions as part of its reorganization, a

number of legal difficulties arose with stockholders who had become disenchanted with the church.

[34] "Stenographic Report of the . . . Meeting of the Stockholders of the Review and Herald," forty-third session, Apr. 23, 1903; Apr. 24, 1903.

[35] ERP to WCW, June 15, 1903; WAS to F. I. Richardson, July 27, 1903; *RH,* Aug. 11, 1903, pp. 5, 6; Aug. 20, 1903, pp. 4, 5; Sandra Kurtinitis, "Railroads and Real Estate Speculation: Takoma Park's Beginnings" (unpublished research paper, Takoma Park Public Library, 1977).

[36] GCCMin, June 18, 1903; SDAPABdMin, July 1, 1903; FMBMin, July 8, 1903; AGD to OAO, July 28, 1903.

[37] *RH,* Aug. 11, 1903, p. 4.

[38] AGD to EGW, July 27, 1903; *RH,* July 28, 1903, p. 24; AGD, *The Abiding Gift of Prophecy,* pp. 348, 349.

[39] *1919 Bible Conference,* p. 570.

[40] *RH,* Sept. 3, 1903, pp. 10-13.

[41] AGD to WCW, Mar. 29, 1907.

[42] WWP to AGD, Sept. 1, 1903; Estella Houser to I. J. Hankins, Aug. 28, 1903; WWP to WCW, Sept. 11, 1903. Sarah Prescott joined her husband at the end of September after remaining behind to sell their Battle Creek home.

[43] *RH,* Nov. 19, 1903, p. 24; Feb. 4, 1904, p. 24; Apr. 21, 1904, p. 24.

[44] WWP to WCW, Nov. 6, 1904; Dec. 8, 1904; Dec. 29, 1904; WWP to AGD, May 27, 1904; *RH,* Jan. 5, 1905, p. 17; *RH,* May 18, 1905, p. 19.

[45] JHK to GIB, Jan. 15, 1905; WWP to WCW, Jan. 19, 1905; *RH,* Mar. 9, 1905, p. 17.

[46] WWP to AGD, Sept. 4, 1904; WWP to WCW, Oct. 19, 1904; Nov. 6, 1904; July 13, 1905.

[47] WWP to WCW, Sept. 11, 1903. Whether it was possible to implement such ideals is not clear. Prescott had to modify a number of cherished ideals in the face of unexpected problems.

[48] WCW to AGD and WWP, Jan. 25, 1905. W. C. White felt that Evans, the most likely candidate, was probably better suited to the financial affairs of the GC and that he was not strong in the selection and education of foremen, journeymen, or apprentices.

[49] *Ibid.*

[50] WWP to WCW, Feb. 15, 1905.

[51] WCW to WWP, Feb. 23, 1905.

[52] WWP to WCW, July 31, 1905.

[53] WWP to WCW, July 13, 1905; July 31, 1905; WCW to WWP, Aug. 11, 1905.

[54] WCW to WWP, Nov. 3, 1905. White commiserated with Prescott on the issue but advised that it was better to avoid publicizing things that the Review and Herald ought not to have done. He was disturbed that Evans had considered engaging a non-Adventist attorney to contest the case.

[55] Rumors had begun to circulate that the Battle Creek people might also seek a takeover of the Tabernacle, and Daniells developed a series of articles for the *Review* on the

history of the Kellogg conflict. The church made appeals for Adventists to leave Battle Creek. These developments led to a breakdown of arrangements to sell the publishing house property, which, coupled with the exorbitant fees exacted by a hostile attorney, squeezed finances severely.

[56] WWP to WCW, Jan. 24, 1906; Mar. 20, 1906; July 19, 1906.

[57] WWP to WCW, July 31, 1905.

[58] WCW to WWP, Sept. 18, 1905.

[59] WWP to AGD, Aug. 7, 1908; *GC Bulletin,* May 19, 1909, pp. 71, 72.

CHAPTER XIII

THEOLOGICAL CONTROVERSY
AND A CHANGE OF JOB

COMPARED TO THE Kellogg conflict, the theological controversy in Adventism over "the daily" was a mere storm in a teacup. For *Review* editor Prescott, however, it was a serious and costly business. Without doubt, he had correctly followed the right denominational procedures required for dealing with matters of dispute, but that was of little consequence. To his dismay, he found that educating the church and attempting to broaden its thinking even on a minor doctrinal point could produce extreme hostility. Before the conflict ended, Prescott found himself out of office. Was the point in dispute, then, such a minor point? Had the denomination dealt with him fairly?

Prescott had returned, relaxed and refreshed, to Washington from his 1907 trip through eastern Asia and Europe. He had hardly had time to settle properly at his editorial desk again, however, when he found himself press-ganged into leading the forces on one side of a rapidly escalating controversy. Marshaling the opposition was Stephen Haskell, who had initiated the conflict with some saber rattling several months before. He had found "errors" here and there, and some were "very dangerous," he had warned Ellen White in June. "Leading brethren" had adopted positions that "undermine present truth." Then, casting caution aside, he openly declared, "There are many who know that Prescott and I differ and are really waiting to see how that will yet come out."[1]

The point over which Haskell and Prescott differed was the interpretation of *tamîd,* a cryptic expression in Daniel 8:11-13, and translated "the daily" in chapters 11 and 12. The term is a key word crucial to the interpretation of the prophetic passages.[2] To many twenty-first-century Adventists, the term and the convoluted technical arguments that swirled around it seem either quaint in an eccentric way, almost like a bizarre sideshow, or esoteric in the sense that it concerned highly technical details that only those who involved in the discussion could possibly understand. Some have occasionally argued that it was, and is, of no current relevance—quite removed, in fact, from the more important central business of Adventist Christian living. But in truth the dispute for the chief protagonists focused on a vital undergirding theological issue that the church needed to come to grips with—the relationship of Ellen White to the interpretation of Scripture. Though largely resolved by the 1940s, when debate over the meaning of "the daily" eventually died out, the methodological issue still has relevance, because even today it continues to raise its head in various places in the Adventist community.

In addition, the history of the conflict has importance in its own right as a significant episode in Prescott's life. It culminated in a great deal of personal trauma and a major change in his career. But the incident also significantly reshaped and redeveloped Seventh-day Adventist doctrinal understandings for a second generation of believers. And it is interesting for the intriguing insights it offers into both the strengths and weaknesses of Prescott and his protagonists.

ROOTS OF THE CONTROVERSY

William Miller in the 1840s, using a complicated series of biblical proof-text parallels based on his English text, had asserted that the expression *tamîd* in Daniel 8 referred to Roman paganism. The Papacy had "taken away" this paganism in the year A.D. 508, when England had supposedly been converted to Christianity. Joseph Bates, J. N. Andrews, and James White had all followed Miller in adopting the view, and Uriah Smith had set the interpretation in concrete through an extended development of it in his book *Daniel and Revelation*.[3] Several things made the disputed expression exceedingly important to Haskell. For a start, it was an integral part of the most important biblical passage used to substantiate the denomination's sanctuary doctrine. It also concerned what Haskell considered to be an important prophetic date. Further, the pioneers had taught the position. But most important of all was the fact that Ellen White had, in his view, stated clearly that the "old view" was correct. She had written in 1850, "Then I saw in relation to the 'daily' (Dan. 8:12) that the word 'sacrifice' was supplied by man's wisdom, and does not belong to the text, and that the Lord gave the correct view of it to those who gave the judgment hour cry. When union existed, before 1844, nearly all were united on the correct view of the 'daily'; but in the confusion since 1844, other views have been embraced, and darkness and confusion have followed."[4]

For Haskell, the statement was clear-cut. Further discussion was quite illegitimate. Ellen White had spoken, and that settled it.

The actual interpretation itself and the arguments for and against it were not that critical, Haskell explained. "Personally, it don't amount to a hill of beans to me." What did matter, though, was the authority of Ellen White. To adopt any interpretation other than that which she had indicated was to undermine her authority. Haskell saw no way around it.[5]

Prescott, on the other hand, understood the term *daily* to refer not to paganism but to Christ's mediatorial ministry. It was an expression drawn from the tabernacle services that clearly pointed to Christ. Through its doctrine of the Mass and its corollary emphasis on mediation through a human priesthood, the Roman Catholic Church had obscured or "taken away" the mediatorial role of Christ.

Such a "new view," according to him, harmonized better with the biblical context and with the facts of history.[6] Much more important than even that, however, it made the interpretation of the whole prophecy of Daniel 8 thoroughly Christocentric. It focused on the gospel rather than on dates, forgotten nations, and questionable events in the past. Daniells concurred with the professor. The matter of the correctness of a doubtful date of history "pales before the importance of the glorious truth . . . regarding the ministry of Christ," he would later write in defense of the "new view."[7]

Prescott recognized the difficulty presented by Ellen White's endorsement of the "old view." But he argued that the larger context of her 1850 article provided a way out. Clearly she was primarily concerned with correcting a problem of "time-setting" among a small group of early Sabbatarian Adventists.[8] One must consider the context and original intent of her *Early Writings* statement. Adventists now needed to reinterpret the "imperfect" statement on "the daily" within that larger setting. Again Daniells concurred. "It is a great injustice to your mother," he wrote to W. C. White, "for men to place an interpretation on her words that arrays her against all history. . . . Another interpretation equally as well founded can be given." Such an approach he was sure would save the church and Ellen White from "great humiliation."[9]

Although probably the most prominent American exponent of the "new view," Prescott by no means originated it. Louis. R. Conradi, president of the union conference in Europe, had been the first to publish the new interpretation in his widely circulated book on the prophecies of Daniel.[10] But that book was printed in German. The great irony was that its publication caused not a ripple either in Europe or in the United States—a perhaps unanticipated advantage of foreign languages. Before publication he had asked Ellen White to advise him if she saw a problem with his interpretation. Receiving no response, he had assumed she had no objection and had gone ahead with the printing.[11]

FOLLOWING "PROPER" PROCESSES

Prescott had tentatively raised the new interpretation with his fellow workers in England in 1899 (apparently following some conversations with Conradi) and found that the position troubled some of them. It disturbed E. E. Andross enough, for example, that he informed Haskell. Prescott also later discussed the idea with Daniells and Uriah Smith. Like Haskell and Andross, the interpretation did not impress Smith either. Apart from a veiled reference the professor made to the topic in his 1902 Sabbath school lesson series, however, he had avoided discussing the matter in public.

After 1902 Prescott and Daniells were too preoccupied with the Kellogg crisis to give the subject much attention, but whenever Prescott's mind turned to "the daily" he became enthusiastic. His rare discussions with Daniells and Spicer on the topic convinced him more and more that the new interpretation provided a vital prophetic mandate for the new Christocentric focus that he had been trying to encourage in Adventism. It would give the church a new impetus. But Daniells urged constraint, and Prescott waited. He hoped, however, that "at the proper time" and "in the proper way" the church would deal with the issue. Spicer would later comment in the professor's defense that Prescott had been "very conservative" and responsible in not agitating the question. "During all these years he has let the other side shout away, and he held in."[12] But by

October 1907 Prescott was convinced that the proper time had arrived.

In that month two former publishing house editors published a volume challenging the Adventist interpretation of Daniel 8. In the process they heavily scorned Smith's interpretation of "the daily."[13] When the General Conference Committee asked Prescott to write a rebuttal to the book in the *Review* affirming the traditional view (without, of course, naming the volume), he declined. Frankly, but in good conscience, the professor stated that he found it "impossible" for him to interpret the chapter as Smith had done. In fact, the venerable editor's position was indefensible! The committee, of course, apparently unaware of the Conradi volume, was immediately interested in hearing Prescott's view. The next question was how Ellen White would react to such a reinterpretation of her *Early Writings* statement. The committee requested the professor to write and ask.[14]

If Prescott could not defend Smith, others felt they could. Pioneer Adventist John Loughborough, for example, submitted an article of rebuttal for the *Review*. Prescott, however, felt obliged to reject it. "We are being attacked from various sides now," the *Review* editor explained. "I desire to use all care not to give anyone . . . ground upon which to successfully make warfare on our teachings."[15]

At the same time, Prescott had crossed swords with Haskell on the topic. The latter had asked the professor to review the revised manuscript for his book *The Story of Daniel the Prophet,* and Prescott had replied, suggesting changes to his presentation of chapter 8. In his letter the professor had remarked that it would be only a question of time before "the present teaching [on the daily] will be discarded" and incautiously added, "the sooner, the better." It was a bold but highly unpalatable prediction, and Haskell could not stomach it. "We ought to understand such expressions by the aid of the Spirit of Prophecy," he shot back. After all, God had given it for just "this purpose." In this way "all points are to be solved."[16] Prescott remained unconvinced. The battle had commenced.

Haskell, who at the time served as conference president in California and was a stalwart friend and defender of Ellen White, was sure she would not stand for such license in the use of her writings as Prescott now suggested. Ellen White, he reasoned with himself, had a great deal of respect for him as her fellow pioneer—and warm Christian affection.[17] She would understand—if only she knew. In fact, she needed to know. He anxiously pressed her assistants for an interview. But both W. C. White and C. C. Crisler were aware of what was happening and dutifully informed Prescott. The professor replied in haste that Crisler must arrange a "delay" in any presentation to Ellen White. It was important that "the whole subject" be "properly presented." Daniells would soon be at Elmshaven and could make the case.[18]

Two weeks later Prescott himself made the six-day rail crossing to the West Coast. Urgent requests had reached Washington. Ellen White's staff greatly needed his scholarly help in preparing a response to recent criticisms of her work by Battle Creek's Dr. Charles E. Stewart (the doctor had widely circulated a small blue-covered paperback listing a number of complaints).[19] The Elmshaven editors were also working on some manuscripts on the Ezra period, and they requested Prescott's assistance in preparing them for publication. Crisler wanted to make sure his chronology was correct. The professor's presence at Elmshaven would also allow opportunity for a roundtable conference on "the daily" question. Several others had written letters of inquiry to Ellen White that had been "pigeonholed" until she could consider all sides of the question. Making such a conference more urgent was the premature publication of an article boldly advocating the "new view" in a recent issue of the *Signs of the Times* edited by M. C. Wilcox in California. Prescott feared for the reaction and complained to Daniells about the lack of restraint on the part of "the *Signs* people." The two sides urgently needed somehow to find "common ground."[20]

Crisler and W. C. White were grateful for Prescott's editorial help during his trip West. He had worked through a mountain of manuscripts, written a new publisher's foreword to *Steps to Christ,* and given counsel on many problems. As a result, Crisler reported, Ellen White was very grateful. "Our future work will be done with more assurance and courage on account of the counsels we have received." It had been a "splendid" visit from W. C. White's perspective. Prescott wished he could feel as good about the conference that had been held on "the daily."[21]

The contending parties on the issue had met on Sunday morning, January 26, in one of Ellen White's offices. Haskell and his wife and J. N.

Loughborough had participated, along with Crisler, W. C. White, D. E. Robinson, Daniells, and Prescott. The outspoken and feisty Mrs. Haskell thought the meeting had been a disaster. "Brother Prescott," she wrote to Daniells, "is so sure he's right and everyone else wrong." He had talked for four hours and only then let Haskell and Loughborough respond. But the "two old men over seventy-four years of age" had weary heads by then. She felt that it was "hardly a fair chance."[22]

Haskell shared his wife's opinion. Next day found him writing what Daniells thought was a most "uncharitable attack" on the professor. Prescott had erred in the Anna Phillips case; he taught exactly the same things as Kellogg; and he certainly couldn't be trusted in the matter of "the daily," Haskell told Daniells. Three days later he sent a copy of the letter to Ellen White.[23]

The week following the conference Prescott continued to work at Elmshaven and had further opportunities to discuss the matter with W. C. White and Crisler. He also had the chance to talk to M. C. Wilcox and A. O. Tait, the editors from the *Signs*. The two Elmshaven staff members apparently felt quite comfortable with his approach to the problematic *Early Writings* statement (they had not yet received the copy of Haskell's letter). Prescott left with a clear agreement with W. C. White that he could now go ahead and write an exposition of Daniel 8 in the *Review*. The six-day trip back East provided him time to work out his outline. By the time he arrived home he had planned a whole series on the book of Daniel.[24]

THE OPPOSITION REACTS

Haskell, along with other *Review* readers, learned of the intended series from an announcement in the March 5 issue. He was determined to fight. If the editor went ahead with his series on Daniel, Haskell threatened to W. C. White, he would circulate an old 1842 chart supporting the "old view" of "the daily." Ellen White had explicitly endorsed the chart in the 1840s. He reported that he had already had the plates made.

The threat worked. Both White and Crisler wrote to Prescott urging delay. White added an apology, explaining that he had forgotten a caution he should have passed on from his mother. "About the time you left here Mother told me that there were some things presented to her that would lead her to caution you about publishing in the *Review* just now."[25]

Unfortunately, it came too late to prevent the mass circulation of an advertising brochure prepared by the circulation manager, Drury W. Reavis, announcing the Daniel series and promoting a circulation drive for the *Review*. The editor had taken "careful and safe counsel" and given "hard study" to "some contested points of our former interpretation," declared the flyer with a typical advertising brochure's attention-grabbing style. The series "would give *Review* readers some unusually interesting and highly constructive thoughts."[26] The brochure was ill-advised. Such high-powered marketing approaches might succeed in selling more magazines, but they would not help Prescott change church teachings. What that needed was less drama and fanfare, not more.

Upon receipt of the generalized cautions from Elmshaven in early 1908 Prescott expressed his willingness to withhold publication "for a time." But it disappointed and discouraged him to find so much resistance to "new light." Why should there be so much suspicion and bitterness toward him personally (a copy of Haskell's unpleasant letter to Daniells had somehow come into his possession)? Why single him out in such a personal attack? Other editors, such as M. C. Wilcox, had studied the matter for themselves and had reached the same conclusion.[27] Why was it that only Prescott was untrustworthy? And why not ban Conradi's book? It had been in circulation for years. The professor became almost totally despondent.

A family crisis compounded his discouragement. He had returned from California to find his wife, Sarah, seriously ill with cancer. She underwent major surgery, and for a time Prescott had feared she would not survive. Fortunately, the surgery was a success, and she slowly recovered. But the sobering experience drained him. "Poor man," wrote Daniells to Crisler, who had suggested Prescott check some further sources, "he is continually overworked, and his physical strength and vitality are so low that every additional burden seems like a mountain." His "anxiety" over Sarah's bout with cancer "proved to be nearly the last straw."[28]

In another letter written to W. C. White the same day, Daniells spoke much more frankly. The General Conference president, in fact, was deeply worried about his colleague. It seemed, he reported, that the professor "would definitely . . . retire from the work for a time." Prescott had told him "he did not think he would try to hold on any longer," having been working "close to the breaking down line" for a long time. Changing the metaphor, he noted that Prescott was so near to going under that "another ounce of weight would sink him." Daniells was distressed because he did not want to lose his colleague. A "keen scholarly man" with "keen vision," the church "greatly needed" him in the editor's chair. His "good perception" of what to leave out of the Review and what to put in—the latter being more important—was extremely valuable.[29]

As it happened, Daniells' fears did not materialize—at least not in 1908. With Sarah's recovery Prescott's courage also returned, and he managed to continue "pulling along." But the professor's nervous health remained precarious. He was walking an emotional tightrope.

While he waited for further word from Elmshaven, he met twice with the General Conference Committee to explain his views on Daniel 8. The response encouraged him. As he saw it, "there was an almost unanimous conviction" among the leadership that the approach he was suggesting was "warranted by both scripture and history."[30] Within the month Prescott received the green light. He could go ahead with the planned series on Daniel. Instead of just looking at Daniel 8, however, he would write an exposition of the whole book, dealing with the sanctuary questions simply as they came up in their "natural place." Beginning May 14, the series proceeded slowly. The professor hoped that by the time he got to the "theological portion" emotions would have settled. It was a vain hope.

Out in California, from his conference president's desk Haskell continued to stir up the dust, firing off protests in various directions. One salvo he directed at Crisler for Elmshaven's "unwise" course in encouraging Prescott. He would "not be responsible for the result," he threatened hotly, if Prescott published anything. Another salvo he directed at the two Washington leaders through W. C. White. White should consider arranging a change of jobs for both Prescott and Daniells. "Leading men," he claimed, were rallying to his side. The Washington men should be exceedingly careful. The best answer to Prescott's heresy, he concluded, would be to distribute widely *Early Writings* and the 1842 chart. Church members could then read and see for themselves the obvious error.[31]

Haskell found an eager ally in the Southern Publishing Association in Nashville, Tennessee. Yes, they would publish his chart, and editor L. A. Smith gladly advertised it in Southern's journal, *The Watchman*. It required stiff resistance from Daniells to prevent the arrangement from going through. Eventually, under General Conference pressure, SPA withdrew the advertisement and did not print the chart—at least officially. On a private basis, however, Haskell still had the chart published and circulated.[32]

Unfortunately for the California president, his other defensive strategy also failed. *Early Writings* was out of print, and in spite of repeated pestering, Elmshaven refused to give him permission to have it restocked. He felt very badly over this defeat and could not understand the withholding of what he considered vital ammunition. Why would not W. C. White defend his mother and uphold the authority of the Spirit of Prophecy? "It almost overcame me," he wrote later to her. The refusal by W. C. White possibly provides the context for a report circulated among the defenders of the old view by J. N. Loughborough that Ellen White had told him in private conversation that she had "let it [the daily] go" because "they have got Willie." The comment indicates how politicized the debate had become.[33] In the meantime Haskell did his best to besmirch Prescott's character and to persuade anyone he met of the terrible danger to the church.[34]

The professor's response to Haskell's provocation was predictably gracious, but he was clearly getting exasperated. "I have shown you plainly," he responded to one pointed letter from Haskell, "that your interpretation would make the Spirit of Prophecy contradict history." And there are, he continued, "from fifty to one hundred ministers in the denomination who I must think are as intelligent and honest as any of us, who think your interpretation . . . is incorrect." If Haskell wanted to argue ad hominem and raise personal matters, then he could do the same. After all, had not the older man also received several rebukes from Ellen White? Prescott could cite two or three incidents at least. But the professor did not "think it was kind or wise to watch for each other's failings and make charges of this kind."[35]

By late August, though, it was becoming clear to Prescott and other church leaders that it would be counterproductive for the *Review* to proceed with the exposition of Daniel. Misunderstandings had arisen on all sides. He therefore abandoned the series on August 27, even though he was still only dealing with chapter 3. From Daniells' perspective, Prescott had remained highly circumspect and had done his best to avoid controversy. He and the others who shared his views had "counseled quietly with their brethren" and had "taken with care every step pointed out by the Spirit of Prophecy as the right course in such a case." In fact, they were still "willing to counsel." But both Daniells and Prescott were becoming concerned about what kind of report Haskell was giving Ellen White.[36]

Sometime back in mid-1908 Prescott had received a letter of warning from Ellen White (his reply seems to indicate he received it some considerable time after she had written it). The professor had at times come near to making shipwreck of his faith, she said, and he was still in danger of making mistakes. He tended to place too much weight on minor matters. Sometimes silence would "reveal a spirit of wisdom and discretion."[37] The letter did not mention anything specific, and it puzzled the professor—at least until Daniells had a chance to talk personally with Ellen White later in 1908.

The General Conference president reported that he had eventually talked at length with her on "the daily." She had been seriously ill at the time, but as he related years later, he caught her on "one of those days when she was feeling cheery and rested." He felt he had been able to explain the essence of the problem to her "quite fully" with Haskell's chart stretched out on her lap. She comprehended the idea of the *Early Writings* statement correcting a time-setting problem. But when he tried to talk about the meaning of the expression "the daily," she "would go into that twilight zone right away."[38] She could not understand the points raised and stated that she had no light on the matter. Daniells' report led Prescott to believe that from "what Ellen White said" the way would "be opened" to deal with "the daily" when his series came to chapter 8 of the book of Daniel. Later again, upon the General Conference president's return to Washington, Prescott had learned "about the situation in California." Daniells had apparently informed him that during recent months Haskell had been in weekly contact with Ellen White and had at times entertained her as a guest in his house. He had misrepresented Prescott's position on "the daily" and had endeavored to "prejudice the case" against the new view. Ellen White had stated that she did not understand the argument.[39]

With the missing parts of the puzzle now fitting together, Prescott felt able to reply to the letter from her. Realizing that she was not well and that her staff endeavored to shield her from as many unnecessary burdens as possible, he directed his reply to W. C. White. (In 1908 neither W. C. White nor Daniells expected her to live much longer—her sickness seemed too serious. They were concerned to protect her "from the well-meaning intentions of her friends" as well as her enemies, so that her last days would be as tranquil as possible.) Choosing his words with care, Prescott noted that he had received a letter sometime earlier from Ellen White "containing some good counsel" and some things that he was "quite at a loss to understand." The sensitive wording of Prescott's correspondence suggests that he was dealing with an extremely delicate situation. He was concerned not to give offense and yet also needed to try to avoid being the victim of misunderstandings.[40]

In phrases that intimated that he was now privy to inside information that W. C. White also knew about, he explained that Daniells had informed him about "the situation in California." He thought he now understood more clearly what Ellen White "had in mind in writing to me" and was glad that she in turn "had a better understanding of the position" that he held on Daniel 8. Would W. C. White please convey to his mother that he would "try to profit by the counsel" she had written.[41]

LETTERS SENT TOO LATE

Unfortunately, however, Prescott did not have the opportunity to profit from two other letters that Ellen White wrote him shortly after her first one. The two later letters contained much more pointed and direct warnings. One was dated June 24, 1908, and the other a week later on July 1, 1908. Prescott was in danger of "making a mountain out of a molehill," she said in the first letter. In the second she specifically said he should not agitate the "daily" and raise questions in the *Review*. The whole issue would become a great mountain unless he determined to let it alone. He should focus on other things. But as the result of some uncertainty at Elmshaven, neither of the two letters got sent in 1908. Prescott did not receive them, in fact, until two years later. At that time he had withdrawn from denominational employment and was in New England recuperating from a nervous collapse brought on by the death of his wife and the trauma of his dismissal from the editorship of the *Review*. According to W. C. White, Ellen had been undecided about the letters and had amended them several times but never sent them. W. C. White had eventually mailed them at his own initiative and on his own authority in August 1910.[42] In the meantime, however, others, including Haskell, had become aware of their contents.

The late receipt of the two documents hurt and totally bewildered the professor. "It is a little difficult for me to understand why they were not sent to me at the time, if they were designed to be of any practical benefit." Circumstances had changed so completely since their writing, however, that he wondered what "difference" they could make in his "present course of action."[43] He had not been editor of the *Review* "for more than a year." Prescott had evidently underestimated the seriousness of Ellen White's concerns on the "daily." The letters would have corrected this. Why had they not gone out when really needed?

The easiest answer would be that the Elmshaven staff simply forgot to carry through on Ellen White's request and mail them. Other factors suggest, however, that the situation was more complex. She had asked someone to read her the letters several times as they were being readied. Just as the staff were ready to send them she would request them to read them again and then would decide against mailing them. Various handwritten amendments on the typed documents suggest that Ellen White felt somewhat ambivalent about the whole situation. Was Prescott really putting "new timbers" in the foundations, as some suggested? Was Haskell exaggerating and possibly misrepresenting the problem to her? She was not sure. Although she struggled to understand the complicated arguments, she could not. Since the Lord had not given her any light on it, it could not be a "vital question." Why did some church leaders persist in making such a big thing of it?

Evidently Ellen White, perhaps in the confusion of it all, eventually assumed that the warning letters had gone out. In her August 28 letter to Haskell rebuking him for circulating his chart she mentioned that she had specifically asked Prescott not to put anything in the *Review*. Here she referred not to the earlier May letter but the unsent July letter. Even W. C. White quoted key portions of the two letters in his correspondence to other church leaders on the topic of "the daily."[44] Whether copies circulated to others for information, as was her occasional practice, is not known.[45] Such use of the letters assumed that Prescott had received them and may have indicated to others that he was refusing to follow the counsel. It is no wonder, then, that Prescott felt bewildered and unjustly treated when others began to blame him for wrongfully urging "the daily" during this period.

A range of other misgivings between Washington and Elmshaven complicated the delicate political relationship between the two centers at this time. Associates in the General Conference leadership team, for example, were extremely worried over the large debts the Californians were accumulating in their drive to establish new health institutions. They knew that W. C. White was not an able financial leader and feared that he was stretching the church too far by developing new institutions too quickly. Some worried about his independent publishing endeavors that tended to upset the market. Exchanges of rather blunt correspondence went back and forth. In another matter, later in the year, some perceived White as being overly mercenary and heavy-handed with regard to royalties on his mother's books.[46]

On the other hand, the Californians were beginning to feel that the General Conference wanted to control absolutely everything. Why did Washington insist that all matters had to go through the General Conference? Why was the Review and Herald so grasping when it came to royalties, for example? All White expected was "simple justice."[47] Haskell, for his part, repeatedly complained of the tendency to centralization.[48] Was Daniells becoming too strong and independent? Was he slipping away from W. C. White? The reality was that strong leaders lived on both sides of the continent. A quiet unspoken power struggle began to simmer over the allocation of resources and over who should determine the direction of the church. The distance between the two places and the rapid development of the church seemed to highlight the feeling at Elmshaven that it might be losing its influence over church affairs. The fears brought a confidential letter of concern from W. C. White.[49]

According to White, his mother worried that Prescott and others such as I. H. Evans and E. R. Palmer were too much of an influence on the General Conference president. Daniells, he cautioned, should be careful of the weaknesses of such individuals.

The president was perplexed—he needed every good helper he could get, and these were valuable men. He waited three months before writing a very carefully thought-out response. Daniells realized that it had political implications, but his reply was a masterpiece of bold yet careful diplomacy.

Yes, the General Conference president was aware of Prescott's "failings"—just as aware as the professor's opponents in California and

Tennessee were and who would probably like to "set him aside." On the other hand, he had also "seen in him some of the rarest gifts possessed by any man in our ranks." The church needed those attributes. Was he being unduly influenced by Prescott? He did not think so. In fact, he noted bravely to W. C. White, "the man who has the greatest influence over me is the one I am now addressing." Many church officials, he reflected, were inclined to think that Ellen White's son held more of a sway over him than what was "good and safe" for the church. They were more aware of what they considered White's "weaknesses" and "dangerous tendencies" than they did his "strong, safe and valuable gifts." But Daniells highly valued W. C. White's gifts. All they could do as fellow leaders, he concluded, was to affirm each other's strengths and help each other's weaknesses.[50]

Daniells' response took a carefully balanced stance and at the same time was a loyal defense of his colleagues. Later he served as a bridge builder between Prescott and White over the royalties issue, and White apologized to the professor.[51] But it did not help Prescott in the long run. Feeling that he was losing the battle over "the daily," Haskell had busied himself with the ad hominem strategy, rallying support for his cause and actively campaigning to have Daniells and Prescott replaced. Unless the denomination made a change, he declared to W. C. White, "the cause" would be in trouble.[52]

A CHANGE AT THE REVIEW

During the middle years of the first decade (1900-1910) the General Conference had not made evangelism a high priority. The conflict with Kellogg and the struggle involved in transferring church headquarters to Washington had monopolized the attention of Daniells and Prescott. Furthermore, in response to Ellen White's earlier urging, the church had adopted development of the work in the American South as a priority. Daniells felt he had succeeded in "lifting the cloud in the south" by transferring "a large number of good capable men" to that region.[53] Overseas missions had also been a priority in terms of the personnel and resources assigned. But during 1908 Ellen White became increasingly worried that the rising debate over "the daily," regardless of the merits of either side, would further prolong the neglect of large-city evangelism. She determined not to let that happen.

At the 1909 General Conference session held in Washington (May 13-June 6) "the daily" intruded as an unwelcome visitor. Defying a mutually agreed "state of truce," an "old view" defender (O. A. Johnson) had provocatively distributed a privately published pamphlet around the tents. The publication portrayed "new view" advocates as undermining the prophetic role of Ellen White.[54] In response delegates decided to discuss the topic openly, setting aside two evening sessions for the purpose, with W. C. White appointed as chair. But despite his best efforts, he could not restrain advocates of the "old view" from descending to the level of personal attack, and the discussions became highly combative. L. A. Smith's paper, particularly, cast a large slur on Prescott and Daniells.

Ellen White fretted over the attitudes displayed at the meetings. During the conference session she had issued a strong call for the church to take up the task of evangelizing the nation's large cities. Now she worried that the waves of emotion generated by the conflict on "the daily" would drown out her pleas. Something had to be done to focus the church's attention on evangelism. It could not afford to get distracted by arguments over inconsequentials. Somehow the issue needed to be defused.

Three days before the session ended she told Prescott that the denomination needed his "ministerial ability" in the cities. He should unite with others "in seeking to bring souls to the light of the truth." Evidently she felt that a change would also help in his spiritual growth and advancement. At the moment he was "not where the Lord would have him to be."[55]

A week later, just prior to her leaving Washington, D.C., she met with the General Conference Committee and communicated her instruction. It should not hold Prescott in Washington "to do a work that another man can do." Recalling her experience with the professor years earlier in Melbourne, she stated, "He can stand before the people and give the reasons of our faith in an acceptable way. . . . He has a precious gift, and here he is employed in work that other men can do, while there is a dearth of laborers who can warn these large cities." While the professor could still prepare "special literature to go among the people," he should not continue as editor. It was instruction that caught the General Conference Committee by surprise. Not all could see wisdom in the suggestion. Some of its members did not "take willingly to the idea of losing Elder Prescott,"

Ellen White later recalled as she told the story to her son Edson. She had been obliged to speak "plainly" to them.[56]

The committee was reluctant to let Prescott go from the *Review* for several reasons. Its members genuinely did not know who could replace him. F. M. Wilcox, the newly appointed associate editor, had been with the *Review* for only two months. Nor did they consider the other associate, C. M. Snow, adequate. W. A. Spicer, the only other person of sufficient stature, could not be spared from his post as secretary of the General Conference.

Another consideration was that Prescott had just launched a new magazine at great expense to the publishing house, one designed to meet the newly aggressive moves of Roman Catholicism. Who else but Prescott could shepherd that publication along? A further consideration apparently bothered some committee members. They felt that although he had not been the aggressor, Prescott was being singled out—perhaps unfairly—for his involvement in "the daily" controversy. Would not this way of resolving the problem simply reinforce the wrong attitudes (and wrong theology) of the Haskell group? Should Prescott be the scapegoat? Although Ellen White had not mentioned this reason at any time in her public discussions, it seemed to some of the leadership that it was nonetheless part of the hidden agenda. Would not Haskell consider his campaign to have been successful?[57] Their hunch was apparently true, but not until later did her associates, Haskell and G. B. Starr, confirm it. The two men had traveled with Ellen White around the Eastern states after the conference. They had spread the word that, in alleged private conversations with them, she had expressed the fear that Prescott might lead the denomination astray.[58]

Prescott went quietly. In obedience to the counsel, he arranged for his board to elect a replacement for himself. They chose Spicer and asked Prescott to continue as an associate editor. He would also remain editor of the new monthly *Protestant Magazine*. A few days later he requested the General Conference Committee to provide direction concerning his evangelistic assignment. The committee appointed an advisory committee and established a budget for a tent and a stereopticon. The courageous and cheerful way in which the professor adjusted to the sudden change in his fortunes brought admiration from Daniells. "He has taken the counsel

Sister White has given him like a Christian and a whole-souled man, and has helped us in every way possible to make adjustments in the office," the General Conference president reported to a mutual friend.[59]

As we might expect, the Haskells rejoiced in the change. Mrs. Haskell claimed that she had not read more than two editorials in the previous five years because they had "very little charm" for her. "But since the late change," she wrote to Spicer, the editorials were "the first thing read." Her husband had also noticed the change, she said. "There is a different spirit, all through it."[60]

If the Haskells thought they noticed a new perspective, it was largely the work of F. M. Wilcox as office editor, not Spicer, who retained his secretary's post at the GC and simply added the editor's job to it.[61] As he pointed out to G. I. Butler, he was just "editor in the saddle." The associate editors actually produced the publication. His primary function was "to take the blame when we don't do something somebody wants us to do."[62] Two years later Wilcox received full command.

THE CONTINUAL CONTINUES

If Ellen White had hoped that removing Prescott from the *Review* would help quiet the disturbance on "the daily," she was disappointed. "Old view" exponents launched a major pamphlet campaign soon after the General Conference session. Johnson circulated his publication in every nook and cranny of the church, and L. A. Smith followed. Both called into question the General Conference leaders' loyalty to her prophetic role.

M. C. Wilcox, from California, urged Daniells to respond. "I know you have been rather hindered because you did not wish to do anything that would stir up division," he wrote, but was it not time now to frankly set forth the issue?[63] The only time the "new view" appeared in print in 1909, however, was a veiled allusion to the idea in the context of the Week of Prayer reading. The new *Review* editor, Spicer, called it their "opening shot." Spicer lamented to the European church leader, Conradi, that he envied his freedom to present the matter in Europe. "Take pity on us poor fellows who have to sledge along on this side." Would Conradi please keep a "wide-open door" for him, he requested, in case he needed it, suggesting jocularly that perhaps he should also fear for his job.[64]

Within a few months the skirmishing had again become a major battle.

The Atlantic Union Conference session in December 1909 put several questions to the General Conference delegates on the matter. Smith's pamphlet was raising disturbing questions. As a result, the General Conference officials held a private meeting with the union committee to explain the dispute. The committee in turn recommended that the General Conference officials speak to the rest of the delegates. Daniells asked Prescott to be the presenter. Even though already familiar with the concept, the General Conference president found himself impressed by the professor's explanations. Prescott gave "the finest series of studies on the prophecies" he had ever heard, he later enthused to a colleague.[65] Subsequently, he also arranged for Prescott to repeat the studies at other union sessions and at the college in Washington. On the latter occasion a stenographer recorded the talks, and they eventually developed into a pamphlet.

Daniells defended his actions to W. C. White. "I cannot believe that we are forever to remain silent while these men [Smith, Haskell, Johnson, and Loughborough] are printing and presenting what we believe to be error, to place us in a wrong light before our brethren. . . . Our influence must soon be destroyed." White agreed with the president. It was, he said, "only fair" to stand up for themselves. He asked for a copy of the pamphlet developed out of Prescott's talks. White also wrote a long letter to Haskell urging restraint and setting out the way the church should handle disputes. "The daily" itself was not now the real problem. The two bigger questions that W. C. White felt needed straightening out were (1) attitudes between leaders and other members and (2) how the church should or should not use his mother's writings.[66]

The personal attacks on Daniells' colleagues distressed the president more than anything. Smith, Haskell, and their cohorts, it seemed, were totally committed to destroying "the good name" and the "standing" of their opponents. In a handwritten note to W. C. White in March 1910, the General Conference leader reported on the character assassination that had gone on at the recent union conference session at Nashville, and he urged White to help the "old view" aggressors change their course. Daniells marked the note "for your eyes only." He did not wish W. C. White's aged mother to see it, for he knew it would only embarrass and distress her.[67]

"It hurt me very much," he wrote, "to hear the unkind things that were said about Brother Prescott and Brother Conradi. . . . Poor Prescott was handled terribly." What worried the president most of all was that the mudslinging had been done "in the name" of Ellen White and "on the authority of the hard things she said [about Prescott] here at the General Conference." Both J. S. Washburn and Edson White in particular had said "most cruel things" and vindicated themselves "by telling of their private interviews with your mother." Daniells considered it a "shockingly indiscreet" breach of confidence. "I would not have this get to Prescott for anything . . . ; it will stagger him and his friends."[68] The conflict over "the daily" had obviously gotten out of hand.

By mid-1910 Ellen White had heard enough of the troublesome fad. She could not understand it, had no "instruction" on it, and could see "no need for the controversy." "Not a subject of vital importance," it should in no way be made into a test of anyone's orthodoxy. And, furthermore, the church must not use her writings to settle the question either way. Contention should cease, she stated firmly in a general letter to the ministers involved. "At such a time silence is eloquence." The letter prompted W. C. White to have second thoughts on the wisdom of his advice to the General Conference leadership encouraging them to reply to the attacks made against them. He had now changed his mind, he soon reported to Daniells. His mother was rather "decided in the conviction that it had been a mistake [the decision to reply]."[69]

If they had made a mistake, W. C. White was not inclined to blame them. He knew that it was the old view supporters who had been the "unfair aggressors." It was primarily to these provocateurs, he stated, that Ellen White's letters applied. Furthermore, her instruction that the denomination must not use her writings to settle the matter was a plain denial of Haskell's all-important central argument. Without the *Early Writings* statement there would have existed no conflict to begin with.

Prescott would have had difficulty understanding that "the daily" was not an important issue. Rather, it was a significant hermeneutical key to Daniel 8 because it opened the door to a much more meaningful Christological interpretation of Daniel's prophecies. He saw it as providing the undergirding of the much-needed refocusing of Adventism on a Christologically centered presentation of its distinctive doctrines, an approach that Ellen White herself had many times endorsed.

But from Ellen White's perspective the church was perhaps not yet ready. If the new interpretation resulted in a serious rift in the denomination, then other concerns became more important. By endeavoring to play down the issue, she did not mean that truth was unimportant or that an idea was not worthwhile simply because it concerned the exegesis of only one verse. Rather, the need for the church to preserve unity and to focus its energies on the evangelistic challenge facing it in 1910 motivated her efforts at peacemaking.

Just as personality and political issues muddied the waters of the Kellogg controversy, so did they in the dispute over "the daily." Adventist leaders in the South had for a long time been dissatisfied with general administrative decisions emanating from Washington. How then, they questioned, could theological truth come out of the same place? Again, while most church leaders thoroughly enjoyed Prescott's confident, personal style, a minority thought him imperious and an overconfident know-it-all. If people reacted to Prescott, it tended to be a strong response either way. It did not help the cause of "the daily" either.

Prescott was an intellectual, an avant-garde committed to the pursuit of truth. Even when swamped by administrative assignments he still found opportunity to pursue his study, expand his mind, and somehow have the time to search for new insights. But a strong evangelistic drive also motivated him. Truth was for sharing. One might expect that his experience during the righteousness by faith debate of the 1890s would have made him more wary of the difficulties of educating a large community. Had he not learned that trying to change people's thinking, to reshape a community's understanding, was an enterprise fraught with hazards? Yes, he had, but for Prescott, that was not a reason to give up trying. Besides, on this occasion, he was sure he had done the right thing and followed all the correct procedures in introducing the "new view" to the church. And he had. He had a strong sense of pastoral responsibility for the church. Nor was he unconcerned about church unity, as illustrated by his protest that M. C. Wilcox, with his *Signs,* was going too fast in pushing the issue. True, by going more slowly, they would rock the boat less, but it was naive to think that the church could change its thinking without controversy.

"The daily" conflict illustrates more clearly than anything else, perhaps, that change and development in a church's thinking occur more from the number of funerals it conducts than by the number of Bible conferences it organizes or books it publishes. Does more progress result from the passing away of a generation than by the present generation accepting the change? This "storm in a teacup" thus highlights the point that conflict is inevitable whenever anyone proposes new directions in the area of religion. It also illustrates the fact that, despite taking precaution and waiting for the proper time, there is probably never a moment when a church is ready for change.

The conflict left scars on Prescott that never completely healed. The public, personal attacks, citing Ellen White's alleged conversations, made him suspect by conservatives for the rest of his days. The conflict also caused many to be suspicious of the General Conference. A key union conference resisted attempts at organizational reform by the General Conference even 20 years later because of lingering resentment over "the daily" issue. The counsel to back away from open conflict on the matter had much wisdom in it.

The passage of time ultimately vindicated Prescott's position. His interpretation of Daniel 8:11-13 eventually became the norm throughout the denomination. Indeed, the Christological interpretation of the passage continues to provide an important base for the gospel-centered understanding and presentation of the church's sanctuary doctrine. Furthermore, the episode also settled the nondeterminative role of Ellen White in establishing the meaning of Scripture, although not often widely understood or remembered, as later conflicts in the church and even present ones suggest. Prescott may have felt unjustly treated by the events and the outcome of "the daily" conflict, but his experience with Ellen White in the past had taught him the wisdom of submission even when he did not understand. He valued her counsel even when it was difficult to accept. Such an attitude helped him continue to be of use to the church.

---

[1] SNH to EGW, June 30, 1907.

[2] A brief discussion of the technical significance of the term *the daily* and a useful and comprehensive history of its interpretation in Millerite and early Adventist literature appears in the *Seventh-day Adventist Encyclopedia* (Hagerstown, Md.: Review and Herald Pub. Assn., 1996), vol. 10, pp. 429-433.

[3] *ST*, July 15, 1841, p. 41; U. Smith, *Daniel and Revelation* (Battle Creek, 1892), pp. 159-161, 260-268.

[4] EGW, *Early Writings* (Washington, D.C.: Review and Herald Pub. Assn., 1945), pp. 74, 75.

[5] SNH to WCW, Dec. 6, 1909; SNH to EGW, Feb. 25, 1908; Dec. 29, 1908; SNH to CCC, Mar. 30, 1908.

[6] Prescott argued vigorously that there existed absolutely no historical evidence that the English were converted in 508 and that therefore paganism was at that date taken away by the Papacy. WWP to JNL, Dec. 12, 1907.

[7] AGD to WCW, Jan. 3, 1910. The terms *old view* and *new view* were in fact quite inaccurate. See *Seventh-day Adventist Encyclopedia,* p. 433. Unbeknown to any of the parties, it seems, Crosier and others in the 1840s had advocated the position Prescott was endorsing. Prescott himself did not discover this until the 1930s as a result of LeRoy Froom's search for Millerite sources. WWP to AOT, Jan. 2, 1930. See also L. E. Froom, "Historical Setting and Background of the Term 'Daily'" (1940). GCAr.

[8] *Seventh-day Adventist Encyclopedia* (Washington, D.C.: Review and Herald Pub. Assn., 1976), vol. 10, pp. 366-370.

[9] WW to LHC, Nov. 27, 1906; AGD to WCW, Mar. 30, 1910.

[10] *Die Weissagung Daniels* was later translated into several languages and after 1905 even circulated in America among foreign-language groups.

[11] Bert Haloviak, "In the Shadow of the Daily: Background and Aftermath of the 1919 Bible and History Teachers' Conference" (unpublished paper, 1979), pp. 37-39. GCAr. Haloviak's paper provides an excellent survey of the contending positions on "the daily" and has a helpful discussion on the central question of Ellen White's role in doctrinal discussions.

[12] WWP to LHC, Nov. 27, 1906; WAS to JSW, Feb. 6, 1910.

[13] John Kolvoord and Moses E. Kellogg, "The Vision of the Evening and the Morning: A Study of the Prophecy of Daniel VIII" (Battle Creek, 1907), pp. 21-34, 82-86.

[14] WWP to CCC, Dec. 20, 1907.

[15] WWP to JNL, Dec. 12, 1907.

[16] SNH to WWP, Nov. 15, 1907; WWP to SNH, Dec. 1, 1907.

[17] In the 1890s when she was in Australia, Haskell as a widower had proposed marriage to the widowed Ellen White. She had thought and prayed about the matter for some time and then regretfully declined for a variety of reasons. HCL to AWS, June 2, 1947. She suggested he find another partner, whom she recommended. Through the years, though, there remained a close fellowship of the spirit between Stephen, his new wife, Hetty Hurd, and Ellen White. A photograph of the aging pioneer occupied a special place in her home at Elmshaven.

[18] WWP to CCC, Dec. 20, 1907.

[19] Known as the "Blue Book" but entitled *A Response to an Urgent Testimony,* the little volume raised questions about Ellen White's literary borrowings and inconsistencies in her testimonies.

[20] CCC to WWP, Dec. 14, 1907; Dec. 26, 1907; Dec. 27, 1907; AGD to WWP, Jan. 7, 1908; *ST,* Jan. 8, 1908, pp. 6, 7; WWP to AGD, Jan. 10, 1908.

[21] CCC to AGD and FG, Feb. 6, 1908; WCW to ERP, Feb. 7, 1908.

[22] Mrs. SNH to AGD, Jan. 26, 1908.

[23] SNH to AGD, Jan. 27, 1908.

[24] WWP to AGD, Feb. 4, 1908. According to Haskell, Prescott had remarked to him, "I see no other way now then [sic] we shall both be at liberty to teach what we regard as the truth on this subject." SNH to WCW, Mar. 1, 1908.

[25] WCW to WWP, Mar. 24, 1908.

[26] DWR to WAS [circular], 1908; WCW to AGD, Apr. 13, 1908.

[27] M. C. Wilcox did not feel in any mood to postpone his dealing with the subject simply to appease Haskell, though he was eventually persuaded to delay his series. MCW to CCC, Apr. 1, 1908.

[28] AGD to CCC, Mar. 18, 1908. Prescott had already checked the sources.

[29] AGD to WCW, Mar. 18, 1908.

[30] WWP to CCC, May 1, 1908. In the interim Prescott published other more generalized material supporting the church's position on the time prophecies in an effort to reply to Kolvoord and Kellogg's book. *RH*, Mar. 26, 1908, pp. 11, 12; Apr. 2, 1908, p. 12; Apr. 9, 1908, pp. 11, 12; Apr. 16, 1908, pp. 10, 11.

[31] SNH to CCC, Apr. 13, 1908.

[32] Daniells wrote to the manager of the press, I. A. Ford, asking him in the name of fairness and proper procedure not to proceed. He stressed that those who differed with Smith and Haskell had not used church journals to air their views. If SPA published the chart, he would not feel duty-bound to "restrain" the others. Ford, who viewed the "new view" as tearing up "the landmarks" and moving the "pins" and the "pegs," reluctantly agreed not to advertise the chart further. AGD to IAF, July 13, 1908; IAF to AGD, July 20, 1908.

[33] J. S. Washburn's daughter, Mrs. Grace W. Tewalt, who was disillusioned by the conflicts in the church, reported this interpretation. Eventually she withdrew her membership. Grace Tewalt to R. H. Adair, Aug. 29, 1955.

[34] SNH to EGW, Aug. 13, 1908.

[35] WWP to SNH, Aug. 2, 1908.

[36] *RH*, Aug. 27, 1908, p. 24; AGD to E. Arneson, Sept. 10, 1908; WWP to AGD, Aug. 28, 1908.

[37] EGW to WWP, May 22, 1908.

[38] 1919 Bible Conference transcript, July 30, 1919.

[39] WWP to AGD, Aug. 28, 1908; EGW to SNH, Aug. 29, 1908.

[40] WWP to WCW, Sept. 7, 1908.

[41] *Ibid.*

[42] WCW to WWP, Aug. 12, 1910.

[43] WWP to WCW, Aug. 23, 1908.

[44] WCW to PTM, July 31, 1910; EGW to SNH, Aug. 29, 1908.

[45] The risk always existed that letters could get put in wrong envelopes, as happened with a letter to F. B. Starr that went to Anna Ingels by mistake in 1896. But it appears to have been rare. Anna Ingels to EGW, Mar. 1, 1897.

[46] WCW to ERP, Feb. 19, 1908; WCW to CHJ, Feb. 7, 1908.

[47] White offended Prescott in the misunderstanding over royalties, implying that Prescott and the Review and Herald had been "unjust." WWP to AGD, July 27, 1908.

[48] SNH to WCW, Oct. 8, 1907; Nov. 13, 1908. SNH to EGW, Nov. 6, 1907.

[49] WCW to AGD, Mar. 22, 1908, cited in AGD to WCW, June 25, 1908.

[50] Ibid.

[51] He tried to correct the impression he had created: "I have a high regard for you personally as a friend, and a very high estimation of your standards of honesty, justice, and strict integrity." WCW to WWP, Aug. 30, 1908.

[52] SNH to WCW, Oct 22, 1908; SNH to EGW, Dec. 15, 1908.

[53] AGD to WCW, Feb. 10, 1909.

[54] O. A. Johnson, "The Daily: Is It Paganism?" (College Place, Wash.: n.p. [1909]).

[55] EGW, "A Message to Responsible Men," June 3, 1909.

[56] EGW, "Proclaiming the Third Angel's Message," June 11, 1909; EGW to JEW, June 16, 1909.

[57] SNH to WCW, Oct. 22, 1908; SNH to EGW, Dec. 16, 1908. Haskell had made known his view to Ellen White that if changes did not occur, "the cause" would be in trouble.

[58] MCW to AGD, Sept. 28, 1909; GBS to AGD, Aug. 19, 1919.

[59] RHPABdMin, June 15, 1909; GCCMin, June 29, 1909; AGD to GBT, June 29, 1909; RH, July 1, 1909, pp. 3, 4. Presumably the leadership retained Prescott as an associate to provide some mature judgment and a measure of continuity. His editorials appeared infrequently until the end of 1911 but became much more regular again after that.

[60] Mrs. SNH to WAS, Sept. 22, 1909; SNH to WAS, Sept. 27, 1909.

[61] RHPABdMin, June 15, 1909. Spicer did not want the job and voted against his own name. WAS to CPB, July 8, 1909.

[62] WAS to GIB, July 12, 1909; WAS to CPB, July 8, 1909.

[63] MCW to AGD, Nov. 14, 1909.

[64] WAS to LRC, Oct. 26, 1909.

[65] AGD to CFV, Dec. 2, 1909.

[66] AGD to WCW, Dec. 20, 1909; Dec. 31, 1909; WCW to AGD, Jan. 11, 1909; Mar. 13, 1909; Mar. 15, 1909.

[67] AGD to WCW, Mar. 31, 1910.

[68] Ibid.

[69] WCW to AGD, July 28, 1910.

CHAPTER XIV

THE TROUBLED YEARS

"PROFESSOR PRESCOTT IS IN need of help," wrote a concerned I. H. Evans to Daniells in April 1910, a year after the professor had left the *Review*. "He has surely had a hard year. What he has suffered no one knows better than yourself." And Daniells did. His colleague, at age 55, was burned out—his emotional energy completely spent.[1] He shared Evans' worry that the denomination would lose Prescott.

After the General Conference had asked him to leave the *Review,* Prescott's melancholic temperament had eventually gotten the better of him, and he had succumbed to deep depression. What was the use of carrying on with his reputation shattered, destroyed by his theological critics? How could he continue to work when rumors circulated everywhere that he had lost Ellen White's confidence? Why did he not have the energy to respond enthusiastically to his new assignment? His ministry was a failure.

How far Prescott had gone in seeking other employment is not clear, but he had talked seriously with Evans about the possibility. Finding another job would not be difficult, he reasoned. Lots of other publishing houses in Washington, D.C., needed experienced editors. Besides, he did not feel well equipped for his new work assignment anyway. Conducting evangelistic campaigns in big cities took special abilities. If he were to find other employment he would be under far less pressure and, more important, he would have more time at home to look after Sarah. His wife's cancer had returned. At the least, his critics would be happy that he was out of the way. Such were Prescott's feelings as he grappled with his depression in 1910.

Yes, Prescott had been effective in evangelism previously. In Australia, in England, and even in Washington, D.C., on a couple of occasions he had preached at large meetings. But the idea of working as a full-time evangelist was something new. Previously he had had little to do with the basic planning and organizing of such campaigns. Others had done the pitching of the tent, arranging the venue and the advertising, creating the interest, and actually organizing the meetings and coordinating the teams of Bible instructors. Prescott had usually just been the leading speaker. Being responsible for running the whole campaign intimidated him. He felt his lack of experience keenly. Not one to ignore counsel from Ellen White, he had intended to comply with her directions. The plan for his new work indicated that he was to maintain his home in Washington and to visit cities for meetings of several weeks' duration.[2] But carrying out the commission proved difficult, and delays complicated the process.

The first postponement resulted from an automobile accident shortly after the General Conference session of 1909. Prescott had had his Model T Ford sandwiched between two trolley cars and extensively damaged. His critics had pounced on the event, declaring it "an admonition from God" that he should begin his new work immediately.[3] But it took time to get the vehicle repaired, and then he needed to fit in his vacation in. During late summer he had to meet previously arranged camp meeting assignments. The year sped past.

Prescott planned to begin his city work after the late summer camp meetings. He had selected a venue and arranged the meetings. But in early September an ominous recurrence of Sarah's earlier illness disrupted the schedule. He hastily canceled the last of his camp meeting appointments and returned to Washington. Although nursing Sarah consumed much of his time, he managed to keep up his work on the *Protestant Magazine* and to take speaking appointments near the capital. By the end of the year her cancer was in remission, and things looked brighter.

Early January 1910 found Prescott in New York planning anew for evangelism, but people advised him that a tent effort during the harsh winter was out of the question. Instead, he now set up plans for the early summer of 1911. W. C. White expressed his disappointment that Prescott had not opted to run some campaigns in the Southern states during the winter. Daniells explained that the professor had asked for a tent, but the GC had been unable to provide one.[4] Subsequently, Prescott scheduled three meetings to run concurrently in New York with the advertising co-

ordinated. Preparatory work began with teams of Bible instructors organized to begin visiting interested people. The local conference president,
W. B. White, was excited. "A new era" had "dawned" for New York.
"Brother Prescott . . . seemed to be full of courage to take hold of the
work," he wrote to Daniells, who in turn reported the matter to
Elmshaven.[5] It was apparent to the General Conference president, however, that in spite of W. B. White's optimism, Prescott was dragging his
feet. Duty was not necessarily a good motivator. He had declined an invitation in early 1910 to be president of Union College because Ellen White
had said he should do city evangelism, but it was evident that the professor was working more from a reluctant sense of obligation than anything
else. Burnout seemed to be increasingly taking hold of him.

While he prepared for his summer meetings, the professor organized a
number of large public convocations in Washington, D.C., highlighting the
Sabbath and religious liberty issues. He also conducted evangelism in
Battle Creek. But by March, with the approach of spring, when his spirits
should have been lifting, his depression deepened further. Sarah's illness
had returned with a vengeance, requiring further surgery. By April it was
clear that if she was going to recover at all, it was going to be very slowly—
at least a year. She needed William at home, and he set aside the plans for
the summer campaign. The cloud of depression darkened, and discouragement settled over his future. He wrestled again with the option of seeking other employment so that he would not be a burden on the church.

The series of events embarrassed and perplexed Daniells. "I regret
very much that the way has not seemed clear to him to throw himself entirely into the evangelistic work in our cities," he confided to W. C. White
in May. The General Conference president knew just how discouraged
and hurt Prescott had been as a result of the fallout over "the daily," but
he had hoped that urban evangelism would have been "a stimulus and an
inspiration to him." The professor's inability to get "entirely" involved in
evangelism was also making it very difficult for Daniells.[6]

In April 1910 Evans had suggested that he ask Ellen White about the
possibility of Prescott picking up his work again temporarily with the
Review, given the dilemma caused by his wife's illness. It would take at
least a year for her to regain her health. Was it worth talking about with
Ellen White now that the situation had changed so drastically? Daniells

was visiting California when he received the letter. "We have but few men of Prescott's ability," Evans argued, even if the ability came with a "peculiarity of temperament." Given the fact that "we all have these peculiarities . . . each has to help the other," he commented. He knew he was on dangerous ground and did not for a moment want to "discredit" Ellen White. Evans made his suggestion tentatively and typed the letter himself, so that his stenographer would not see it. In it he also included a request for the General Conference president to destroy the letter if he could not concur with the idea. But even if Daniells had been attracted to the idea, he dared not, and in fact could not, talk about it with Ellen White. She had refused to grant him any interview at all.[7]

Ellen White had become extremely sensitive about the lack of attention given to city evangelism. She was also feeling "intensely" and "greatly exercised" because Daniells had made such a major issue of "the daily" at the union conference sessions. Every time W. C. White went into her room, he reported, she spoke about the matter.[8] She had sent several strong letters to Daniells—even suggesting that he needed to be reconverted. For his part, the General Conference president did not know what more he could do. He had set up committees to plan for evangelism, pushed through large appropriations, and had succeeded in transferring some prominent evangelists to the Eastern cities. He was certainly not ignoring her counsel. But he was puzzled as to what more he should do. Her son did not know either.

Rumors had apparently reached Ellen White that Daniells and Prescott were revising church books in order to introduce new ideas. In actuality it was her son who was coordinating the revision of *The Great Controversy,* but this was another period when the aging Ellen White was not in good health. Periods of depression clouded her days, and she was not able to cope well with stress. W. C. White had to be very diplomatic and sensitive with regard to the various problems he brought to her.[9]

Her letters to Daniells had been so strong that he thought that she was wanting him to resign as General Conference president. Then, when she refused to see him, he did not know what to do. He turned for counsel to W. C. White and Crisler. Together they came up with two extra measures to help city evangelism along. Daniells would personally conduct some meetings, and then he would write and also get others to write to inform

Ellen White of what was being done. He followed the suggestions and found before long that the "burden" had lifted from her. The personal involvement also opened his eyes as to how ill-equipped for evangelism the conferences really were.[10]

Aware of these dynamics, Daniells did not feel it an auspicious time to discuss Prescott's perplexities with Ellen White. She would certainly misunderstand Evans' suggestion that the professor edit the *Review* again. While he concurred with Evans' observation that the *Review* had deteriorated in quality, if Prescott should go back, "it would place him in a false and embarrassing light and . . . would result seriously for all of us."[11] Daniells was distressed, however, that Prescott had become so utterly discouraged. It "unnerves him for life's duties and makes it impossible for us to help him." What would become of the professor if he should lose his wife, the General Conference president did not know. He would soon find out.

Sarah deteriorated rapidly. Further surgery in May to remove the cancerous tumors was only partially successful, and the doctor could offer no further help. He gave Sarah a few months at most. Within a week, however, it was clear to Prescott and the medical specialists that the cancer was making "astonishingly rapid progress" and would "do its work very soon."[12]

William canceled all his appointments and took her home to make her "few remaining days as comfortable and pleasant as possible." Special seasons of prayer for healing brought comfort and support for the professor "in his sore experience," but they did not change the outcome. After a "terrible struggle," Sarah died on Friday morning, June 10. She was 54. Resigned at last to the inevitable, the couple had made their final arrangements. The funeral took place on Monday in the large front yard of the Prescott house on Blair Road. Offices and presses at the Review and Herald and at the General Conference closed for the morning, and the entire staff attended the service—a measure of the respect the couple enjoyed.

A telegram to Daniells on Friday morning quickly brought him back from the Pennsylvania camp meeting to be at his stricken friend's side. He found Prescott "brokenhearted" and struggling to bear up. "It is a most pitiful experience," he wrote to friends. Prescott felt the blow "severely." Expressing his own grief, Daniells noted that Sarah had been "a beautiful character, a bright-faced Christian, and a friend to everybody," and, according to neighbors, the couple had been "unusually devoted to each other."[13] During her last days she too had been discouraged, concerned for her husband and his work and struggling, as he had, with the sorrow of having lost the friendship and confidence of Ellen White. She too had heard the stories circulated by Haskell and Starr. It pained the General Conference president deeply to see his colleague so grief-stricken and desolate. Conducting the funeral service was no easy task. "I do not know of ever having had a heavier task assigned to me since I began my work in the ministry," he observed in his report to the Whites.[14]

Prescott, fragile though he was, managed to hold himself together until the funeral ended, but the effort completely exhausted his resources. Friends found during the days that followed that he simply broke apart. He "would burst into tears and could not control his feelings." He found it difficult to see anyone or even to write a letter. A return to work was out of the question. He was too "broken up and nervous."[15]

Doctors advised the professor to take leave for a while, and the sorrowing professor retreated to his brother's home at Biddeford, Maine.[16] There, where he and Sarah had spent the first happy year of their marriage 30 years previously, Prescott nursed his grief. Long walks along the beaches of Cape Porpoise and the support of family helped, but he was still restless and depressed when he returned to Washington six weeks later, but still earlier than planned. The cloud of depression would not leave him. At times he felt quite desperate as he swung between moods of cheerfulness and deep troughs of despair. The harsh things reported by Haskell and Starr behind his back kept crowding his mind, making him feel worthless, and he again seriously considered withdrawing from church employment.[17]

Colleagues in Washington, D.C., understanding the anguish Prescott was suffering, arranged another long sea voyage. September found him en route to India via London to attend annual meetings. He had grasped at the opportunity, as he explained to W. C. White, for it was "quite impossible" to "undertake any heavy work." Daniells thought he detected, just prior to the professor's departure, that Prescott was feeling a little more "hopeful and courageous." He had indicated that upon his return he hoped to "throw himself with all his heart into the city evangelistic work,"[18] but not in large cities where there would be a lot of fanfare, as W. C. White might have in mind. He did not want to be placed in any limelight. Instead, he would just go to some neglected city and work quietly, away from public notice. In spite of his courage, Prescott still felt hurt and humiliated.[19]

During the voyage out, the now beardless professor slept for long periods but still found it hard not to brood. "I could write much about my feelings, but that is useless. I must push on as best I can."[20] Three months on the Asian subcontinent, conducting meetings and visiting mission stations, helped him forget himself—for a while at least. He brought back to Washington encouraging reports of the church's progress. Glad for the break, he felt better, although he was still troubled by severe headaches. The prospect of returning to an empty house did not excite him either. "I can well understand that once again it tears your heart to think of coming to the old home," sympathized Spicer. "It is only by throwing oneself into the work, with eyes upon finishing it, that the heart can find rest."[21] And his future work? Somehow he still could not see himself as a city evangelist.

Struggling to know how to carry out Ellen White's expectations, and yet also to help find a place to make use of his friend's gifts, Daniells had organized a series of evangelistic field schools for early 1911, to convene in each of the union conferences. Ministers would spend the mornings together in classes and in the evenings conduct public meetings. Daniells and Prescott would work together. The first one at Knoxville, Tennessee, in March was an encouraging success, although some of Prescott's sermons were so deep they made Daniells' head "crack." The school had resulted in a renewed commitment to evangelism among the ministry, and the two leaders looked forward to the second program scheduled for Philadelphia in April.

During Prescott's absence Daniells had also arranged for the professor to spend the summer assisting with a tent mission in Boston. On the side he would also do some chaplaincy work at the Melrose Sanitarium. The General Conference president was "exceedingly anxious" that the professor "get hold of the city work" but realized that he was not yet at full strength.

Faithfully Daniells kept W. C. White informed of his plans. Trying his best to comply with Ellen White's instructions for Prescott, he asked the younger White to let his mother know "so she may understand what we are doing."[22] His effort was to no avail. The plans came to nothing.

While returning from India, Prescott had contracted a severe cold. He had been unwilling, however, to let it deter him from speaking at the Knoxville meetings. Daniells had gone to considerable trouble to arrange the meetings, and the professor did not want to let him down. By March he still had not thrown off the cold, and by April it had turned to pneumonia. The doctors feared consumption. The General Conference president went to the Philadelphia field school alone, leaving Prescott "suffering a great deal" and struggling about his house with the aid of a stick, "like an old man." Recovery was painfully slow, and finally, a few weeks later, the General Conference leadership on medical advice sent him north again to Maine "to engage in light exercise and work in the sunshine."[23] They also abandoned their summer evangelistic plans.

Three months at his brother's beachside cottage on Cape Porpoise with his son, Lewis, now 18, and his aged parents, proved to be a tonic. Relatives came to visit, and the professor even began to get a tan. "I have made a good gain," he reported to Daniells in August. "I am much stronger and . . . have tried to rise above my terrible depressions and to take a more hopeful view of things." He hoped to be "ready for earnest work" upon his return.[24] Just what that might be still gave Prescott cause for anxiety and uncertainty. He had suggested to Daniells that perhaps he could make the *Protestant Magazine* bimonthly and spend the extra time writing a book on the Papacy. The church needed to respond to the aggressive drive of the Catholic Church. If it became a dominant force in U.S. politics, it would lead to trouble for Adventists. Perhaps the Adventist Church could lead the way in developing such material to educate the public about the problem, he argued. Daniells was not sure. The October meeting of the General Conference Committee would decide. Prescott resigned himself to "whatever may seem best," hoping that his colleagues would come up with something satisfactory.[25]

The return to his home on Blair Road brought major changes in Prescott's circumstances. Although his aged parents continued to live with him, 19-year-old Lewis left home to study engineering. Quite unlike his father, he had developed an interest in things mechanical (and along with it, a reputation for fast driving around Takoma Park). In September he moved north to the Massachusetts Institute of Technology in Boston. But the Prescott home would not stay empty for long. A few weeks later, on November 27, Prescott married a new 32-year-old wife, 24 years his junior.

Daisy Estelle Orndorff was quite a contrast to Prescott's first wife. Not his intellectual equal as Sarah had been, nor as refined, Daisy nevertheless complemented him well. She was modest and retiring, but possessed a buoyant and cheerful personality—the needed counterweight to Prescott's melancholy. A trained nurse, she had been acquainted with the professor for some time. Her conscientiousness when she came to live with the Prescotts to provide professional nursing care during Sarah's last battle with cancer impressed him. Although initially reluctant to accept his proposal (was he too old?), she finally yielded to the professor's persuasion. He sorely needed companionship.[26]

Remarriage seemed to add noticeable new zest to Prescott's work. In December 1911 the Atlantic Union Conference president commented on the new enthusiasm the professor had displayed while preaching at the union session. "It seems to me I never heard Brother Prescott put so much lift, ginger, and good sense into his teachings as at our conference." His sermon was a "masterpiece" that "simply carried the union conference."[27] Prescott's editorials in the *Review* also evidenced a brighter, more confident tone. Even so, the kind of work Daniells now had in mind for the professor did not become clear until February 1912. The leadership made him secretary of the General Conference Religious Liberty Department. The appointment came to Prescott as a complete surprise. "I had no intimation that any such action was contemplated," he remarked.[28]

Many requests had come for the incumbent religious liberty secretary, K. C. Russell, to take up city evangelism. An experienced evangelist, he enjoyed the work. Prescott's role as editor of the *Protestant Magazine,* on the other hand, fell naturally into the religious liberty area. It would also provide him a base from which to conduct large-city rallies. At first he felt reluctant to accept the appointment for fear of what the reaction at Elmshaven might be and decided he should counsel further. Only after he heard from W. C. White in May 1912 did he feel comfortable. Daniells had talked the matter over with White and his mother. He reported that both saw light in the appointment as long as Prescott was not tied to his office but could give considerable time to speaking in the cities.[29] The past two and a half years had been a long night for Prescott. With these new opportunities, life seemed to become lighter once more.

America too was in need of light. Religious tensions were building throughout the nation. Catholics, with their increased numbers and fired by the Irish heritage of many of them, were becoming much more militant. Some Protestants wanted to join hands with the Catholics to enact laws to make America a Christian nation. Other Protestants felt the need to respond in order to protect their freedom. In this context the *Protestant Magazine* soon became known nationwide, and its editor found himself able to draw audiences in a way he had not dreamed possible when the church first envisioned the magazine. Prescott at last seemed to have found a happy blend for the use of his multiple gifts. Pulpit, pen, and chalk became his tools of trade. His scholarship and editorial skills combined to produce a quality magazine, and his gift of preaching augmented the publication. Prescott was in his element.

The professor's appointment as religious liberty secretary, however, did not last past 1913. That year saw the creation of a separate North American Division office that took care of such responsibilities. By that time, though, the *Protestant Magazine* had become a monthly publication. Catholic agitation had grown much more serious, and Prescott had more than enough work to keep him busy full-time on the publication.

---

[1] IHE to AGD, Apr. 29, 1910.

[2] GCCMin, June 8, 1909; TEB to AGD, Aug. 8, 1909; *RH,* Aug 26, 1909, p. 24.

[3] GBS to AGD, Aug. 29, 1909.

[4] AGD to WCW, Jan. 3, 1910; WCW to AGD, Jan. 11, 1910.

[5] AGD to WBW, Jan. 19, 1910; WBW to AGD, Jan. 26, 1910.

[6] AGD to WCW, Jan. 3, 1910.

[7] IHE to AGD, Apr. 29, 1910.

[8] WCW to AGD, Jan. 11, 1910.

[9] Age was taking its toll on Ellen White's health and abilities. Prayer was offered for her "in her great weakness" by her staff, and W. C. White had to be very cautious and careful in the way he introduced the matter of such things as the revisions to *The Great Controversy.* WCW to AGD, Jan. 11, 1910; June 20, 1910; Aug. 10, 1910; AGD to WCW, Jan. 3, 1910; Mar. 21, 1910; July 13, 1910; Aug. 3, 1910; Aug. 10, 1910; AGD to LRC, Aug. 12, 1910; WCW to WAS, Feb. 20, 1910. See also Ron Graybill, "The '1911 Revision' of *The Great Controversy*" (working paper [n.d.]), GCAr.

[10] A good general discussion of the problems of city evangelism at this time appears in Howard B. Weeks, *Adventist Evangelism in the Twentieth Century* (Washington, D.C.: Review and Herald Pub. Assn., 1969), pp. 11-60.

[11] AGD to IHE, May 13, 1910.

[12] WWP to WCW, May 23, 1910; May 29, 1910.

[13] AGD to WCW, June 9, 1910; Jessie K. Moser [Waggoner] to AGD, June 15, 1910; AGD to GBT, June 12, 1910.

[14] AGD to WCW, June 13, 1910.

[15] FMW to GIB, cited in GIB to EGW, Oct. 19, 1910; WWP to WCW, Aug. 25, 1910.

[16] AGD to WCW, June 13, 1910.

[17] The use of alleged private conversations with Ellen White that no one could verify had long troubled Prescott, and he had talked with W. C. White about the problem a number of times. It devastated him that such things had traumatized his beloved Sarah in her last days. The problem continued to cause perplexity and anguish during much of the next five years. WWP to WCW, Aug. 25, 1910; Mar. 15, 1915.

[18] WWP to WCW, Aug. 25, 1910.

[19] AGD to WCW, Sept. 26, 1910; WCW to WWP, Aug. 12, 1910; WWP to AGD, Aug. 28, 1910.

[20] WWP to AGD, Sept. 26, 1910; *RH,* Jan. 5, 1911, p. 9; Jan. 12, 1911, pp. 13, 14. Prescott had shaved his beard shortly after Sarah's death.

[21] WAS to WWP, Jan. 2, 1911.

[22] AGD to WCW, Mar. 31, 1911; GCCMin, Apr. 2, 1911. Daniells was clearly concerned to keep Ellen White informed—an anxiety suggesting that an effort was being made to placate or pacify. He presented the plans as positively as he could.

[23] AGD to WCW, Apr. 11, 1911; AGD to WWP, Apr. 13, 1911.

[24] WWP to AGD, July 25, 1911; Aug. 17, 1911; Sept. 3, 1911; AGD to WWP, Aug. 9, 1911.

[25] WWP to AGD, Sept. 24, 1911.

[26] Mrs. Alice Perrine to GMV, Feb. 21, 1981; Interview with Mrs. Mary Jane Mitchell, Andrews University, Feb. 11, 1981.

[27] WBW to AGD, Jan. 23, 1912.

[28] WWP to AGD, Feb. 6, 1912.

[29] GCCMin, Mar. 29, 1912; WCW to WWP, May 13, 1912; *RH,* May 2, 1912, p. 24.

CHAPTER XV

PROTESTING AGAINST ERROR— WITHOUT AND WITHIN

P ROBABLY THE MOST ably edited anti-Catholic publication in this country," the editor of the *Wesleyan Methodist* wrote of the *Protestant Magazine* in late 1915. Its utterances were "fair, its quotations authoritative and its deductions convincing."[1] Not everyone agreed, though, and as a result, the magazine had to struggle to survive. Three months after the editor of the *Wesleyan Methodist* offered his glowing commendation the magazine folded, and its editor, W. W. Prescott, received another job.

Why did the *Protestant Magazine* last for just five years? What caused its decline? Why had some Adventists come to feel uncomfortable with it? These are questions with interesting answers. The story of the journal, the only intentionally anti-Catholic paper ever published by the denomination, opens a fascinating window on the church during the years just before Ellen White died. It provides helpful insights into some of the problems Adventists grappled with during the period, and it also provides an insight into the role that Prescott had established for himself as a resident historian and scholar in the church.

The *Protestant Magazine* began because Adventists were becoming extremely concerned about Catholics. The American Federation of Catholic Societies, at first barely noticed by Adventists, began causing great concern in the church by the end of the first decade of the twentieth century. It had achieved marked success not only in molding Catholic opinion but also in influencing public legislation. Between 1906 and 1910 its membership had doubled from 1.5 million to 3 million, reflecting not only an efficient organization but also the heavy influx of Catholic immigrants from Europe. In New York alone, between 1903 and 1913, the number of Catholic communicants had increased by 69 percent and constituted 10 percent of the state's population. To many Americans, such developments were a threat to republicanism. Adventists saw them much more as a fulfillment of prophecy. They believed such things would lead to the formation of the beast of Revelation 13 and eventually to the destruction of religious liberty.[2]

According to Prescott, religious liberty had become "a dead issue" during the first few years of the decade.[3] In the church the Kellogg controversy had eclipsed almost everything else. Circulation of the religious liberty journal, the *American Sentinel,* had subsequently declined to just 2,500 per month. As a result, the denomination discontinued it in 1904.[4] Two years later, however, nationwide agitation over the enacting of federal Sunday laws and the introduction of religious instruction in the capital's public schools again quickened Adventist interest. Prescott became personally involved in making representations to Congress, and the *Review* reported extensively on the developments. The new threat led church officials to establish a new 32-page quarterly called *Liberty.* The masthead of the first issues of the new journal listed Prescott as an associate editor. Correspondence, however, indicates that he took the leading editorial role, investing large amounts of time in producing the magazine and in fostering its interests.

By 1909 church leaders perceived the increasing aggressiveness of Catholicism as a major challenge. As Prescott pointed out to them, Rome had decreed in 1908 that America was no longer a missionary country but a Roman Catholic Christian nation. Large Catholic congresses convened around the country, and a new Catholic weekly started with the specific purpose of influencing the public mind. It was the stated plan of the hierarchy in Rome "to win America for the church."[5]

Prescott argued that Adventists needed to make a response to this, but that *Liberty* magazine was not really well suited to the task. Another journal, designed especially to confront the challenge, seemed to be warranted. When Prescott presented the idea to his board in January 1909, its members were immediately enthusiastic and gave hearty approval. They felt that the first issue should be published as soon as possible. Four months later delegates attending the General Conference session received the first copies of the premier issue.[6]

"We make no apology for issuing the *Protestant Magazine,*" Prescott declared in his opening editorial. "No other publication, so far as we know, has the same purpose." In the tradition of the sixteenth-century Reformers and protesting German princes, the magazine would protest against the apostasy of both the Roman Catholic and the professedly Protestant churches and plead for "the faith which was once delivered to the saints."[7] The basic problem of Protestantism, he asserted, was that it had ceased to protest.

At the outset Prescott intended the journal to be both educational and militant. He would not pull any punches. Its style would be forthright and aggressive. "In dealing with the important subjects which will be considered . . . , it is our purpose to use great plainness of speech, and to permit others to do the same." While he would, of course, avoid misrepresentation and be kind and fair, he would not hesitate "to state actual facts." The magazine had "no sympathy with that sentimental Christianity" that was "ready to sacrifice essential truths" simply to preserve "an outward appearance of unity."[8] Prescott lived up to his word.

Features on justification by faith, the mediation of Christ, and the prophecies of Daniel and Revelation dominated the early issues. But they also carried articles analyzing Roman Catholic doctrine and outlining the history of the Papacy. Prescott prominently featured pieces illustrating the Papacy's involvement in politics. A special section in each issue presented notes and press clippings designed to keep readers up-to-date on the activities of the Catholic Church in America.

As the second decade of the century wore on and Catholic officials seemed to adopt a higher profile in American public life, Prescott's journal commented more frequently on people and events. For example, on one occasion he protested the fact that the United States president met with church officials and attended Catholic services in his official capacity. Large photographs illustrated the articles. On another occasion he raised concerns about Woodrow Wilson's appointment of a Catholic as his private secretary and published his exchange of correspondence with the president. One major scoop was an exclusive interview with former New York governor William Sulzer, who had had impeachment proceedings initiated against him as a result of public agitation on the part of the Catholic hierarchy. The national news services picked up both stories, thus giving them wider publicity. On another occasion *Harper's Weekly* reprinted two controversial articles from the magazine. Such reporting brought the *Protestant* (it was frequently referred to by its short title) and its editor to national attention.[9]

The public notice accorded to the *Protestant* provided Prescott with an excellent opportunity to carry out Ellen White's counsel in regard to city evangelism. He capitalized on the magazine's success in his advertising campaign. In some instances he was a guest speaker at campaigns, while on other occasions he ran short evangelistic series himself in the Eastern cities. As editor of the nationally known *Protestant,* and with a reputation as a respected defender of the Protestant cause, he found it easy to draw large audiences.

Generally the *Protestant* maintained a dignified and scholarly tone. But at times some articles tended to be sensational, such as the four-part series entitled "A Convent Tragedy." It told the story of a teenage girl concealed from her parents in a convent. Consisting largely of extracts from court records, the articles highlighted the influence of a lesbian nun and immoral priests on the girl. In another sensational piece, Prescott challenged a Washington-based priest to furnish a wafer from the Eucharist so that it could be chemically tested. The test would determine if the doctrine of transubstantiation was valid. Protestants applauded, but Catholics found such writing "outrageous."[10]

Such articles helped generate a large correspondence for the editor. Many of the letter writers wrote as patriotic Americans who saw the Catholic movement as a threat to the American way of life. They encouraged Prescott in his effort. Others saw him as a narrow-minded bigot. He responded courteously to all, although for some he felt that an acknowledgment was all he could afford to do. To one critic he replied simply, "A gentleman would not write such a letter as yours and you cannot properly expect that a gentleman would make any reply to it."[11]

Even if Prescott's usually dignified *Protestant* occasionally descended to sensationalism, Catholic editors still regarded it as a "respectable opponent."[12] In spite of its lapses, it was the epitome of propriety when compared with other anti-Catholic papers such as *The Menace,* a vitriolic "yellow sheet." The more than 20 anti-Catholic periodicals in circulation included a number of such examples. Catholics could hardly be expected to take all this mildly—and they didn't.

In 1911 the Federation of Catholic Societies decided to try to prevent the circulation of the "scurrilous and slanderous attacks" upon their faith. They sought to have anti-Catholic periodicals excluded from the U.S. mail by law. By 1915 the Federation had gained enough support to have two bills providing for the legislation presented to Congress. The move stunned Protestants and brought a vigorous reaction. So keen was the interest that a *Free Press Extra* published by Prescott achieved a distribution of 250,000—a record for the Review and Herald up to that time. The legislation went down in defeat.

CIRCULATION PROBLEMS AND AN UNTIMELY END

In spite of wide public notice and the large circulation of special issues such as *The Convent Tragedy* and the *Free Press Extra,* securing sufficient subscribers to make the magazine self-supporting proved difficult. At the beginning, Ellen White's endorsement of the magazine and W. C. White's support persuaded many church members to become subscribers. Frequent promotions in the *Review* also helped. By 1912 monthly subscriptions had climbed to 12,000, and with colporteur sales of single copies added in, print runs often reached 40,000. By March 1915 the number of regular subscribers had climbed to 23,000. With a sales price of only 10 cents per copy even this circulation was insufficient, however, to enable the magazine to pay its way. Prescott and his associates conducted several promotional campaigns and explored a variety of creative ways to achieve "a living circulation," but nothing seemed to work. The professor did not have to wonder why. He knew.

The saga of "the daily" continued to dog his steps. Although Prescott had been careful not to specifically raise "the daily" issue or even exegete Daniel 8:11-13 in the *Protestant*, the whole underlying theological rationale of the journal, nevertheless, derived from the "new view." Prescott's basic approach involved contrasting the Catholic Mass, which "took away" the need for Christ's high priestly work, with the true gospel, the "continual" mediation of Christ. The Adventist Church, with its emphasis on the priesthood of Christ, he asserted, had been raised up prophetically (Dan. 8:13) to restore this essential truth. The thrust of the magazine rested on that premise, and the professor's opponents understood it clearly. J. S. Washburn, for example, was particularly antagonistic and conducted a bitter personal campaign against the magazine and its editor throughout the

Columbia Union Conference. Even a summons to Washington to give an account of his divisive activities to the General Conference officers could not deter him. He was not afraid of the "inquisition."[13]

The outbreak of World War I in 1914 also hampered circulation. While other church journals were able to build up their struggling circulations with sensational stories on the war, church leaders wanted the *Protestant* to avoid such journalism. At the time, official contacts between the American government and the Papacy in connection with the war increased tensions between Catholics and Protestants, leading to riots in some places and even murder. Further heightening of tensions would be counterproductive to larger Adventist interests. As some leaders noted, the church did not wish to "precipitate a crisis before it is due."[14] Thus with stagnating circulation and further confrontation undesirable, there seemed to be no alternative but to stop publication. The denomination called Prescott to other duties in October 1915, and shortly afterward publication of the journal ceased.[15]

The closure of the magazine provoked a vigorous reaction. If the paper had had enemies in the South, it became apparent that it did not lack supporters in the North. The Northern Union Conference president, Charles Thompson, demanded to know why the publishing house had not consulted "the field." Did not the journal have favorable standing with the Protestant churches and the ability to deal with the issues of Catholicism in a "true and dignified way"? In his opinion "the field" wanted the magazine.[16] The Lake Union Conference committee felt much the same way and took the trouble to express themselves on the matter. A few months later they petitioned the General Conference to recommence publication. Spicer, who had been one of the associate editors of the journal, reported on the uproar to Prescott, who was in South America at the time. The *Protestant* "had a good many more friends than we appreciated, I think." He enclosed copies of some of the correspondence with the hope that the "ex-editor" would enjoy "hearing his friends fight for the journal."[17]

Reviving the magazine, however, proved difficult. Although the petitions received a favorable response at the Autumn Council in 1916, and the North American Division Council granted approval for the republishing of the magazine, the Review and Herald board was reluctant to act. The final vote at the Annual Council of the General Conference

Committee had been two to one in favor of starting again, but it was noted that several who did not vote had serious misgivings. If publishing a magazine specifically on Catholic issues was going to upset so many, and if its undergirding theology was going to prove such a continual thorn in the flesh to the fundamentalist ministers in the denomination, was it worth it? Without "united support" from the membership the board deemed it inadvisable to undertake such "a delicate and important work."[18] Thus at the end of 1916 the journal was officially buried, with Washburn and his allies celebrating the demise as a major victory. But although its life had been short, and in spite of the Columbia Union politics, its legacy to the church was invaluable.

THE LEGACY OF *PROTESTANT MAGAZINE*

As Howard Weeks' study, *Adventist Evangelism in the Twentieth Century,* has shown, the decade 1910-1920 was highly productive evangelistically. The sociological impact of the rising Catholic movement and World War I provided a fertile field for evangelistic endeavor. People, troubled by events seemingly out of control, looked for meaning and certainty. The *Protestant Magazine* helped to give an effective theological rationale with which to relate to these particular concerns. It served as an effective aid to evangelism.

And it had another side benefit. The focused attention and attacks on Catholicism and the resultant careful scrutiny given to the charges by Catholics and Protestants alike had an interesting result. Adventist writers and preachers found themselves forced to be more careful and accurate in their thinking and in their presentations. One incident that embarrassed churches in the Northern states illustrates the problem well.

In New York State a Catholic priest had found an official and widely circulated Adventist chart that made an extravagant claim about the change of the Sabbath and the papacy. Through a newspaper he challenged the local Adventist congregation in the town in which he lived to provide support for the claim. The local church appealed to the General Conference, which turned to Prescott for help. The search for documentation in the Library of Congress and in the library of the Catholic University in Washington proved fruitless, even with specialist help. No evidence existed for the particular claim, and church officials were embarrassed at the public disclosure of what the priest called "gross misrep-resentation." According to Spicer, in 1911 a number of similar incidents had occurred as Catholic magazines more frequently challenged Adventist claims about the papacy.[19]

Such events pained Prescott, with his scholarly thoroughness and his obsession with accuracy. In his own editorials and articles he exercised the utmost care. According to W. A. Colcord, one of the assistant editors of the *Protestant Magazine,* the professor would always seek advice and criticism from others before going into print. Prescott customarily read his editorials aloud to an associate, "footnotes and all." It was much better to have them "criticized before being published rather than afterwards."[20] He wished his ministerial colleagues would be at least half as careful, and on occasion he would try to educate them on the matter.

In 1911, for example, Prescott appealed through one of his *Review* articles for ministers to be more careful in their dealings with Rome. Two years later at the 1913 General Conference session he addressed the matter again. This time he exposed numerous facts touching the use of certain quotations that claimed to be authentic but that were actually fake. The talk produced an animated discussion and a strong endorsement.[21]

Another part of the legacy resulting from his work on the *Protestant* was the enduring *Source Book for Bible Students.* While checking the accuracy of quotations used by the church in its polemic against Rome, the professor discovered other authoritative statements on church history and doctrinal development that were helpful in defending Adventist teaching. He printed them regularly in the *Protestant* and occasionally in the *Review.* In 1913, at the request of the General Conference, he began to prepare the quotations for publication in permanent form for the benefit of pastors. Originally his plan was to revise and expand the already existing *Facts for These Times,* but various interruptions delayed the project. The completed volume finally came out in 1919 under a new title and in new format. While others assisted with the work on the *Source Book,* it was largely a Prescott production and helped confirm his role as historian laureate in the denomination.

RESIDENT HISTORIAN

The wide variety of sources utilized in the *Source Book* illustrates well just how broadly Prescott read. Graduation from Dartmouth had not meant the end of his education by any means. He continued to study, particularly in the fields of theology, biblical exegesis, prophetic interpretation, and church history. His learning accorded him considerable status in the denomination. For example, in the estimation of Asa Tait, the editor of the *Signs of the Times,* the professor was "certainly . . . one of the best educated men . . . among us. He is a good writer, . . . clear thinker and profound student."[22]

Ellen White's editorial staff also valued Prescott's education. For example, in late 1907, when C. C. Crisler was working on a series of Ellen White's articles on Ezra for the *Review,* he had urged the professor to assist them because of his expertise in the area. Although he was using "the best authorities" available to guide him in getting the chronology and names of the kings correct, he recognized the help that Prescott had been in preparing the articles for publication. Prescott, on his own initiative, had earlier edited some of Ellen White's sentences out of the articles before he printed them. They consisted of passages that disagreed with standard history books on the Ezra period. He had then written to W. C. White to explain his actions.[23]

It was Prescott's understanding that Ellen White did not intend her writings to settle matters of historical controversy. Statements in her articles did not carry that kind of authority. "Unless she has special light on these historical matters, I am somewhat at a loss to know how these historical controversies can thus be settled," he wrote to W. C. White.[24] His purpose in deleting the passages was to protect her "from unfriendly criticism and attack." Crisler was glad Prescott had taken the initiative, and urged him to continue deleting portions in the remaining articles that he thought might "do more harm than good." Before the series had been completed, however, the professor found himself pressed into visiting Elmshaven personally to give "critical help" in planning further Ellen G. White articles.[25]

The scholarly help he gave in the process of revising Ellen White's *Great Controversy* also provides an illustration of the professor's role as resident historian. W. C. White visited him at his home in Washington early in 1910 to urge him to assist with the work. But Prescott was reluctant to get involved. He was already overworked, but more than that, he feared that involvement would simply provide his critics with more ammunition against him should they hear he had any connection with changes in Ellen White's books. His reinterpretation of "the daily" passage in *Early Writings* had already incensed them. At W. C. White's insistence, however, he consented to go through the book and "write out his suggestions." White also pressed Daniells to encourage Prescott in the task. He desired that the professor "be free in his suggestions." The result was a 39-page document detailing 105 changes that Prescott thought would improve the book and make it more accurate. No doubt he could suggest other changes, he said, but he had been short of time. Thus his list was not exhaustive.[26]

White was grateful for the professor's work and treated it confidentially. He had said "very little [to his staff] as to who had pointed out the passages . . . as we thought you would wish us to do."[27] W. C. White did not regard Prescott as a renegade for proposing changes, as some studies have implied.[28] In fact, Elmshaven later asked him for further suggestions. W. C. White was also glad for the alternative quotations Prescott had supplied. The professor had sent across additional historical material as a basis for further revisions. Some of it eventually found its way into the appendices.

As might be expected, Elmshaven did not adopt all of Prescott's suggested revisions, though some leaders thought all of them should have been, and more besides. For example, in Spicer's view, Crisler, Robinson, and W. C. White had been too cautious and "hard to get along with." They, he thought, had turned down some of his own suggestions without good reason. Although the new edition would have "many things changed," Spicer wrote to Conradi, some things "should surely have been corrected further." Robinson's explanation of the reluctance to accept all the modifications was that Ellen White's staff felt sure the evidence to support certain positions she had taken had at one time existed, but they believed that Roman Catholics had intentionally destroyed many of the sources.[29]

W. C. White, however, had been working under considerable difficulty. The controversy over "the daily" had created an atmosphere of suspicion and mistrust, and it seems that he had not been able to tell Ellen White freely, if at all, about who was involved in the revisions. As already noted, during this period his mother had been "in great weakness" and suffered from depression for extensive periods. Longtime family friend

C. H. Jones reported that W. C. White had been trying to prevent her from "being perplexed by details which might remind her of former occasions" and "start her off on some line."[30] Eventually she became apprehensive about the book revisions because of rumors she had picked up at the Saint Helena Hospital concerning Daniells' and Prescott's role in the work. The rumors suggested that the two men were using the opportunity to change the doctrines of the church. W. C. White had planned to get the bulk of the revisions done quickly so he could show it to her in a largely completed form and thus ease her mind of any anxiety over the project. Most of the changes simply involved giving credit for quotations. The task of revision was not an easy one for W. C. White, and whether he was able to fully explain Prescott's part in a way that removed Ellen White's apprehensions is not clear. He was glad when it was finished and then could explain and illustrate just what had been done to put to rest some of the rumors. So high was the risk of being misunderstood that it was apparently not until the project had been fully completed in January 1911 that he was able even to mention the project to Haskell.[31]

The Great Controversy was not the only book revised during this period. Roman Catholic aggressiveness had heightened the need for more care in other leading church publications as well, and the need to replace printing plates provided an appropriate opportunity. Uriah Smith's Daniel and the Revelation and the widely circulated Bible Readings for the Home Circle were two that came under review. Prescott took a leading role here as well.

From time to time in later years Prescott continued to send W. C. White information on additional points for revision. For example, in 1914, he discovered evidence that The Great Controversy had not dealt correctly with the "Crush the Wretch" cry of the French Revolution and sent it across to Elsmhaven. White thanked him "most heartily" for the information and renewed his request to the professor that whenever he "found things of this character" he should be sure to pass on the "benefits" of his "investigation and study."[32] No further changes have been made, however, and the 1911 edition remains the standard edition of The Great Controversy.

A LONELY SCHOLAR

Prescott had pointed out a number of places where he thought that Ellen White and her staff could correct and improve The Great

Controversy. He did so at W. C. White's request, and it in no way indicated that he lacked faith in Ellen White's work, in spite of what his critics thought. "Just come with me and look at my books," he replied to those who had doubts about him at the 1919 Bible Conference. "If you think they do not help me, come and see how I have marked them."[33] Prescott had in fact spent a lot of time helping to defend her against the criticisms of such individuals as A. T. Jones and C. E. Stewart. In 1906 he had refused to publish an article in the *Review* "because it would give aid and comfort to those who are looking of opportunities to discredit Sister White and her work."[34] On another occasion the professor pointed out to W. C. White how he was demeaning his mother's role by overemphasizing the commercial aspects of publishing her books. Calling Ellen White an "author" and a "publisher" and listing himself as her "business agent," for example, offended Prescott's "sense of the propriety of things . . . in view of the peculiar character of her writings."[35] That some church leaders would think he did not believe that Ellen White's writings had the "peculiar character" of inspiration distressed him.

As previously noted, those who differed with Prescott on "the daily" had actively fostered the impression that the professor was an unbeliever or, worse, an apostate, because he had no confidence in Ellen White's writings. J. S. Washburn, G. B. Starr, F. C. Gilbert, Haskell, and others were particularly vocal. It also distressed Prescott that they would use statements Ellen White had allegedly made about him in personal conversations with them. Yet at the same time she had said nothing to him personally. Several years earlier the embarrassing misuse and misquoting of her statements made in private interviews had led her to conclude that it was not her duty to grant interviews to those who had "trials and difficulties" to present to her. It was in effect like gossiping with the prophet. In a conversation she might express an opinion about some person's action and then the inquirer would go and report the matter as they themselves wanted it to be understood. Letters would then come from the persons who had been misrepresented. Often she could not recall having said anything at all about the individuals concerned.[36] It was a problem she found difficult to avoid without becoming a total social recluse, and as a result the misunderstandings continued.

Prescott had brought a similar problem to her attention in 1908. J. A.

Burden, the manager of the Loma Linda Sanitarium, had tried to force his colleagues and the General Conference to follow a particular line of action because of a statement she had made to a small group of leaders. Others in the group, however, had heard exactly the same remarks and understood them in a markedly different way. An unpleasant confrontation had arisen as to who was right, and thus an argument developed over what the exact wording of the transcript should have been.

It was Burden's use of her statement as a club to force the consciences of others that distressed Prescott. "Such a course as this does more to discredit the Spirit of Prophecy, and to bring us into trial concerning it, than anything the Battle Creek people can say," he wrote to W. C. White at the time.[37] Both Ellen White and her son agreed, and W. C. White expressed his appreciation for the clear way in which Prescott was able to articulate the problem so it could be understood. Such things were damaging both to people and to the denomination. But what could they do to correct the problem?

In April 1915, toward the end of J. S. Washburn's bitter campaign to malign Prescott and shut down the *Protestant,* Prescott again raised the matter of the misuse of alleged "personal interview" statements in an agonized letter he wrote to W. C. White. He also mentioned that Ellen White's reported "unkind" statements had heavily clouded Sarah's last days.

W. C. White responded with two encouraging letters, trying to correct the misrepresentation. He had tried several times, he said, to talk to his mother about Prescott's "burden and sadness," but "she could not understand," and he had put the matter off, thinking that a "time would come when her mind would be led out upon this matter." Apparently it never did. He was positive, however, that his mother had "always had a very high regard" for him and had even in her last years manifested to him "a mother's love and tenderness." Concerned to "cheer the heart" of the discouraged Prescott, he urged him to "take that hopeful and trustful, and joyous view" of his lifework with which his "brethren" regarded it. He had no sympathy for the "misguided men" who were "ploughing up and down" on the professor's back, but he did not think he could stop them. "Not until the judgment will it be known how earnestly I have endeavored to persuade these men to drop their burden."[38]

For his part, Prescott was sure that a great deal of the hurtful criticism could be avoided if only both ministers and church members had a clearer understanding of the nature and role of Ellen White's authority. They needed to be more accurately informed about how she did her work. Had not his acquaintance with the process of preparing her books and articles for publication broadened his understanding? Had not his own involvement in the process as a guide on historical and doctrinal matters made it easier for him to understand the nature of her work? Ellen White's statements did not automatically make things rigid, final, and unchangeable. But who was to do the educating?

W. C. White reported that he had tried to do exactly that. He knew it was important. In 1913, at the General Conference session, he had made explanations intended to broaden the church's understanding of Ellen White's work, but the delegates had misunderstood what he said. As a result, he had become more cautious. How to broaden the church's understanding without destroying confidence in her prophetic gift was extremely difficult.

Spicer shared Prescott's burden. He had also urged W. C. White to make some clearer "explanatory statements" to the church. The issuing of the revised edition of *The Great Controversy,* he thought, would be a good occasion to correct many of the misconceptions. "It is firmly settled," he noted to Conradi, "that phrases and historical statements in these books have to be corrected just the same as in other books."[39] While the Elmshaven staff made some vague explanations, Spicer had been disappointed because they did not go far enough. No one, apparently, was willing to risk explaining it like it was, and the reluctance bothered Prescott.

"It seems to me that we are betraying our trust and deceiving the ministers and the people," he protested to W. C. White later in 1915. "It appears to me that there is much more anxiety to prevent a possible shock than to correct error." The same applied to ensuring that publications were accurate. How could church leaders knowingly allow books to continue to be published with "serious errors" in them and yet "make no special effort to correct them"?[40] Was he thinking of Uriah Smith's Arianism? Or did he have in mind Josiah Litch's mistaken prediction about the fall of Turkey in 1840, spoken of in *The Great Controversy?* Prescott had explained the latter problem in depth to the General Conference Committee in 1914 after working through the research with a task force with very good "conservative" credentials. Members of the committee had admitted the problem and acknowledged his arguments as sound, but nothing was done publicly. (Not until 1981 would the matter be publicly conceded as a problem.)[41] Prescott's obsession with accuracy and the high value he placed on integrity made him into a scholar who was extremely sensitive about "truth." As a result, he experienced considerable loneliness at times. He had few with whom he could share his burdens and few with whom he could present his insights and his attempts to resolve some of these intellectual problems.

The death of Prescott's aged father in early 1915 compounded his feelings of loneliness and discouragement. J. L. Prescott had been one of the few surviving pioneers who had witnessed the falling of the stars almost a century previously. His death caused the professor to wonder whether he, too, would not live to see the fulfillment of the church's proclamation, the return of Christ. The apprehension that the Advent hope might not be realized in his lifetime heightened his frustrations with the lack of progress he perceived in the church. Those who so easily criticized him for being progressive, it seemed to him, were going backwards. His confidential letter of April 6, 1915, to W. C. White reveals the depths of his frustration. He was thinking of giving up, having been almost overwhelmed by defenders of the old order.

"After giving the best of my life to this movement, I have little peace and satisfaction in connection with it and am driven to the conclusion that the only thing for me to do is to do quietly what I can do conscientiously and leave the others to go on without me." Although it would be a far from happy ending to his life's work, it was the best solution he could think of. He could not stop the criticism, nor could he stop the "false impressions" about Ellen White's work that were behind it all. "The way your mother's writings have been handled and the false impression concerning them which is still fostered among the people" caused him "great trial and perplexity." He could see no change coming, though he had talked about it with W. C. White for years. "No serious effort has been made to disabuse the minds of the people" of their wrong views. In fact, it seemed that what amounted to "deception" had been practiced in putting together Ellen White's books, although "probably not intentional" in nature. Prescott knew he was dealing with a highly sensitive matter and had typed the letter himself, as he did "not wish to dictate it to anyone."[42]

But he feared that the church was "drifting toward a crisis," and that in all probability it would come sooner rather than later.[43]

Prescott had been overly pessimistic. The problem of the misunderstanding of Ellen White's writings and of the nature of inspiration did not reach crisis proportions nearly as soon as he had expected. But nevertheless his words were prophetic. The crisis did come. During the last decades of the twentieth century it broke out in damaging ways that the church found exceedingly difficult to manage. Addressing the task of correcting the misunderstanding is an ongoing challenge for the church. While the problem festered away, however, people who held "narrow" and "fanatical" views of the authority of Ellen White continued to attack Prescott. Claude Holmes, a Review and Herald typesetter, was a notable example. In 1917, by deceit and misrepresentation, he had obtained from the General Conference vault copies of her private letters to Prescott and Daniells. He then published lengthy extracts in a slanderous pamphlet circulated widely in a campaign to discredit the two men. Holmes temporarily lost his job as a result of the incident, but that did nothing to repair the damaged reputations.[44]

Washburn and his colleagues rejoiced at the death of the *Protestant Magazine* in 1915. They thought they had at last silenced the professor and destroyed his influence in the church. Prescott was tempted to think so too, and fell into a fit of despair. He had never been so discouraged. But his enemies were mistaken. The professor still had friends in high places who felt that the church needed his rare gifts. Before 1915 had come to an end he had received important new duties in the General Conference that were to extend his influence once more beyond America. He might be 60, but his work was not nearly done yet.

---

[1] *Wesleyan Methodist,* Sept. 1, 1915.

[2] A. F. Gorman, "American Federation of Catholic Societies," *New Catholic Encyclopedia* (New York: McGraw-Hill, 1966), vol. 1, p. 400; *RH,* Aug. 23, 1906, pp. 3, 9.

[3] WWP to WCW, Jan. 15, 1904.

[4] WWP to WCW, Jan. 15, 1904; WCW to WWP, Jan. 26, 1904. The magazine had been losing $200 per month.

[5] According to Prescott, the decree had been issued on June 29, 1908. *PM* (1909), vol. 1, no. 1, p. 64.

[6] *GC Bulletin,* May 25, 1909, pp. 149, 150.

[7] *PM,* July 1909, pp. 2, 3.

[8] *Ibid.,* p. 2.

[9] *PM,* June 1914, pp. 252-263; *American Citizen,* Mar. 6, 1915. *Harper's* carried two articles of Prescott's on "The Pro-Papal Program." Some Catholic societies consequently threatened it with a boycott.

[10] *PM,* March 1913, pp. 102-111; April 1913, pp. 150-163; May 1913, pp. 203-217; June 1913, pp. 258-266.

[11] WWP to W. J. Kelleher, July 15, 1914.

[12] Cited in ERP to CHW, Jan. 4, 1931.

[13] JSW to CEH, Apr. 18, 1920.

[14] RHPABdMin, Nov. 30, 1915; Dec. 5, 1915.

[15] *Ibid.* The trustees elected Prescott pro-tem chair in the absence of the regular chair, and thus he presided over the action to suspend publication of his magazine. He evidently supported the action. Five days later the next meeting of the board considered the matter again and ratified the previous action. The general feeling seemed to be that it was the best thing to do under the circumstances.

[16] CT to WAS, Dec. 10, 1915.

[17] WAS to WWP, Dec. 28, 1915; WAS to CT, Dec. 21, 1915.

[18] RHPABdMin, Oct 5, 16, 1916. The dispute over the fate of the *Protestant* indicates how polarized the church had become over the matter of "the daily." Relationships between the Columbia Union Conference (the source of most of the hostility against the magazine) and the General Conference continued to deteriorate. JSW to AGD, "An Open Letter," May 1. 1922. AUHR. See also Haloviak, "In the Shadow of the Daily."

[19] WAS to WCW, Feb. 17, 1911. According to Spicer, some Catholic papers had Adventist magazines particularly as their target with a view to "smash our literature." *GC Bulletin,* May 28, 1913, p. 176.

[20] WAC to AGD, Feb. 13, 1911.

[21] See *RH,* Nov. 23, 1911, p. 10; *GC Bulletin,* May 18, 1913, p. 22; May 28, 1913, p. 176.

[22] AOT to TEB, Sept. 8, 1915.

[23] WWP to WCW, Dec. 1, 1907.

[24] *Ibid.*

[25] CCC to WWP, Dec. 14, 1907; Dec. 27, 1907. W. A. Spicer shared Prescott's conviction on such issues, noting that "it was not right to claim any extraordinary authority for matters of this kind" (WAS to LRC, Nov. 30, 1914).

[26] WCW to AGD, Apr. 20, 1910. His reluctance did not result from his particular view of inspiration.

[27] WCW to WWP, Apr. 20, 1910.

[28] A. L. White, "W. W. Prescott and the 1911 Edition of *Great Controversy*" (Feb. 3, 1981), p. 3.

[29] WAS to LRC, Nov. 30, 1914; 1919 Bible Conference transcript, July 10, 1919. Spicer and editorial staffer W. A. Colcord were others who also were requested to suggest changes. Source material provided by Prescott proved helpful in replacing passages with incorrect

credits. WCW to JEW, May 27, 1910; June 17, 1910; July 8, 1910; WCW to DAR, Apr. 4, 1910.

[30] CHJ to WAS, Jan. 27, 1911.

[31] WCW to AGD, Jan. 31, 1911.

[32] WWP to WCW, Nov. 30, 1914; WCW to WWP, Dec. 16, 1914.

[33] 1919 Bible Conference transcript, July 14, 1919.

[34] WWP to FMW, Mar. 2, 1906; AGD to WCW, May 17, 1906.

[35] WWP to WCW, Aug. 23; Sept. 15, 1912. White explained that he had the "business" letterheads prepared for non-Adventists but they had inadvertently been used for church correspondence. See WCW to AGD, Aug. 15, 1912.

[36] EGW MS 24, 1889.

[37] WWP to WCW, Mar. 10, 1908; WCW to AGD, Mar. 22, 1908.

[38] WCW to WWP, Mar. 12, May 7, 1915.

[39] WAS to LRC, Nov. 30, 1914.

[40] WWP to WCW, Apr. 6, 1915. The Review and Herald board and the General Conference Committee appear to have taken up some of the concerns raised by Prescott in his 1915 letter shortly after he wrote it. RHPABdMin, May 28, 1915; ERP to TEB, July 11, 1915.

[41] Prescott had demonstrated to the 1914 Annual Council that Turkey had never lost its independence and that Litch's chronological reckoning involved in arriving at the 1840 date was mistaken because it had ignored an important change in the calendar. WWP to AOT, Nov. 23, 1916. See also R. W. Olsen, *One Hundred and One Questions on the Sanctuary and on Ellen White* (Washington, D.C.: Ellen G. White Estate, 1981), p. 50.

[42] *Ibid.* Spicer also noted that a good part of the problem lay in the manuscript preparation process at Elmshaven. "The trouble is all in the book-making, and there has been too much of an effort on the part of the book-makers, I believe, to emphasize the fact that they do it all under observation, as though that would make sure of inspiration and correct work" (WAS to LRC, Nov. 30, 1914).

[43] Sixteen years later (in 1930) LeRoy Froom echoed Prescott's prediction. "It is my conviction . . . that one of the greatest crises that confront this movement is before us ere we come to a sound, rational, scriptural and historical understanding . . . of the Spirit of Prophecy" (LEF to WCW, Sept. 28, 1930).

[44] GCCMin, Feb. 16, 1917; Feb. 18, 1917. WWP to AGD, Feb. 25, 1917. Holmes became very bitter toward Prescott, who had the responsibility of dealing with the matter in Daniells' absence.

CHAPTER XVI

A NEW HARNESS

"YOU ARE ACTING FOR the president of the General Conference in the fullest and truest sense," Daniells wrote to Prescott in December 1915. The General Conference had just appointed the professor as its first field secretary, and he was about to make his first overseas visit in his new role. Daniells was concerned that he have the "greatest freedom" in order to do his job well. He was to "counsel with the men on the ground," the same as he would "were he the president." No one was more surprised at the appointment than Prescott himself.

Five years previously, when she had been concerned about the low priority given to city evangelism, Ellen White had felt that Daniells and Prescott ought not to continue working together so closely. Her worry that the two men might get sidetracked in book revisions formed an added reason for advising their separation. Subsequently, the two men pursued their respective responsibilities with less association, at least in public. The days of their virtual partnership, when Prescott was editor of the *Review,* were over.

Since 1910, however, circumstances had changed markedly. Evangelism had again become a priority, and overseas mission projects had grown so rapidly that Daniells found it difficult to keep up with the demands. As more frequent overseas visits became necessary and his schedule became more strenuous, the General Conference president found himself overextended. Predictably, it began to affect his health. In 1914 a serious complaint that Daniells had developed required surgery, but his schedule of appointments was so tight that he had to postpone the operation for several months. When he finally found time for it, he cut short his convalescence because of previous commitments, and consequently his health continued to deteriorate. At the Annual Council of the

General Conference at Loma Linda in November 1915 his fellow leaders concurred that if he was to cope he needed assistance, and promptly created the field secretary post to help him keep abreast of the expanding mission program. Daniells knew just the right man for the job, and the council agreed with him.[1]

"I want to assure you of the pleasure it gives me to have you as a very close associate and coworker," he wrote to Prescott after the meeting.[2] A surprised Prescott was at first not sure it was the right thing to do. His "experiences" in the past five years caused him some "misgivings." Would his critics raise objections on the basis of Ellen White's letters? There was no way of knowing. They could not ask her for advice. She had been dead now for almost six months. But Daniells was sure that changed circumstances required changed plans, and he encouraged the professor to accept. Prescott conceded.

"Your words of encouragement and the hopefulness you have expressed have done much to inspire the feeling that I may again be useful," he responded. He recalled the "genuine pleasure" of their "association of years ago" and looked forward to a "repetition of some of these profitable experiences." Prescott assured him that he would do his best and hoped that Daniells would have "no reason to regret" his recommendation.[3]

Less than three weeks after his appointment Prescott and his wife boarded a ship bound for Rio de Janeiro. The denominational structure in South American needed to be formally organized into a division, and Prescott would supervise the process and install the new administration. Daniells had given him a comprehensive job description. He was to become acquainted with the workers, inspect mission stations and facilities, and secure definite information so that "wrongs" might be corrected and "stronger movements" launched. The General Conference president would look forward to Prescott's reports.

The 16-day sea voyage south was Daisy's first trip beyond the U.S. Stormy winter weather at the outset made for rough seas, and she found that she was not a natural sailor. The voyage was more than half over before she could venture near the dining room. On the other hand, her husband, feeling quite robust, boasted that he had not missed a meal.

Prescott built his schedule of appointments around the usual union session meetings. A two-week-long workers' institute would be held in conjunction with each meeting. Prescott himself would lead the instruction. His themes, drawn from the *Protestant,* rested solidly on his "daily" theology, though he never mentioned the term. His hearers found them particularly relevant in a region in which the population was predominantly Roman Catholic. The "general purpose" of his studies, he explained to readers of the *Review,* was to show that the whole of Scripture was "a revelation of Christ and His gospel" and that the third angel's message was "the final presentation of that gospel."[4] The focal point was the work of Jesus as Savior, Mediator, and High Priest in the context of the prophecies of Daniel and Revelation. It was pure Prescott at its best, and the workers received it eagerly.

The first institute and session occurred in São Paulo, Brazil, followed by one at La Plata, Argentina. After the La Plata session Prescott inaugurated the new division and installed Oliver Montgomery as president. Prescott's party, accompanied by the new president, then embarked on an extensive itinerary that took in Uruguay, Paraguay, south Brazil, a cog railway journey over the Andes to Chile, and then Bolivia and Peru. The highlight of the trip for the professor was to see Ferdinand Stahl's newly opened work among the Lake Titicaca Indians. The warmth of the reception by the mission's recent converts more than made up for the daylong horseback ride the 60-year-old professor had to make just to get to the lake. He was not sure how much of his sermon was understood, however, after it had been translated first into Spanish and then into the local Indian dialect. Another high point of the trip was finding so many of his former Battle Creek College students holding leadership positions in the mission program.[5]

The South American trip concluded with Prescott again in Buenos Aires, Argentina, attending the first committee meetings of the new division. By late June 1916 he was on his way home to Washington, D.C., praying hard that the German submarines that trailed their ship would not initiate hostilities. The journey was a frightening reminder of the hazards of a sea journey in time of war.[6]

A heavy schedule of summer camp meeting appointments awaited the professor upon his arrival home. Prescott soon found, though, that South America continued to demand his attention. Finding personnel to fill the many requests that came from the rapidly growing church structure there was not easy, and many letters from the southern continent also required an answer. William and Daisy had made many friends there. He was thoroughly enjoying his new job.

MORE LITERARY WORK

If Daniells was happy to see Prescott using his gifts in administration once more, E. R. Palmer (the manager of the Review and Herald) was not. It chagrined him that he had lost his resident theologian and scholar, and he was exceedingly reluctant to give Prescott up "entirely to the General Conference." The publishing house had work developing all the time on which he needed Prescott's "criticism and help." Could he have the professor at least part-time?[7] Before 1916 was over he had his wish, and Prescott was back working on the *Source Book* and the revision of *Helps to Bible Study.* Other writing projects included a series of articles for the *Signs of the Times,* Sabbath school lessons, and a college Bible textbook.

As time went by, Prescott found that his field secretary's role provided him useful opportunities to extend his influence as the church's preeminent theologian and as watchdog for the denominational press. For example, in 1917 he wrote to his friend A. O. Tait about an article in the Signs that he considered particularly misleading. "I presume you would thank me more for keeping still than for writing," he began, "but I occasionally feel it would be a relief to express myself." The article had asserted that the Papacy had changed the Sabbath in the fourth century, when, according to Prescott's sources, "the Papacy" as such had not even "risen to power" or become "the Papacy" until the sixth century. "It is exceedingly annoying to me to have our publications allow such unhistorical statements, and such a perversion of fact to appear in them." Tait took the complaint in good spirit, but he responded that it was hopeless for an individual here and there to change the general trend of such things. What the denomination needed, he argued, was a general meeting by all the main leaders to straighten such things out.[8]

Evangelist C. B. Haynes was another who appreciated a note from the "watchdog" that pointed out that an article he had written in *The Watchman* had not presented "the facts as they are." On this occasion the topic was one of Prescott's "burdens." It was incorrect to speak of the Papacy ascending to power in A.D. 538, he asserted, even though it had been the church's traditional interpretation of the 1260-day prophecy of

Daniel 7, and even though Ellen White had endorsed it. The facts were that 538 marked "a most humiliating stage in the history of the Papacy." The dates 533-1793, he pointed out, were much more accurate. Haynes was grateful for the correction and asked for further help.[9]

On the other hand, A. W. Spalding, editor of *The Watchman,* resented Prescott's interference. In 1920 the professor wrote a semisatirical letter to him expressing surprise that *The Watchman* would still publish the "old view" of Daniel 11, which held that Turkey was "the king of the north." The satire stung, and Spalding appealed to P. T. Magan of Loma Linda to come to his defense. He enclosed a copy of his own reply to the professor. Unfortunately for Spalding, Magan was not inclined to see merit in either the old view or the new one. Still, having had his own run-ins with Prescott, Magan was not at all enamored by "the big voice." He sympathized with Spalding and enjoyed the editor's bold reply to "the great professor." It was a "masterpiece" and had "done up the great authority on theology" quite nicely.[10]

What bothered Spalding most was Prescott's aristocratic "Yankee" superiority. It reminded him of some lines from Tennyson:

> "Who shall call me ungentle, unfair;
> I longed so heartily then and there
> To give him the grasp of fellowship;
> But while I past he was humming an air,
> Stopt, and then with a riding whip
> Leisurely tapping a glossy boot,
> And curving a contumelious lip,
> Gorgonized me from head to foot
> With a stony British stare."[11]

To Spalding, to the Irish Magan, and, no doubt, to others as well, Prescott came across as cold and distant. Whether the professor was conscious that he gave such an impression to some people is not clear. If he ever communicated about it with anyone, it is not in any surviving letter.

"INSTITUTING"—AT HOME AND ABROAD
Palmer hoped that Prescott would be able to finish off his editorial

projects at an early date, but his hopes were dashed in mid-1917. An urgent request had come from the Asiatic Division for help in providing in-service training for its poorly educated ministers. Prescott was an educator with a great burden for ministerial education. Would he respond to the invitation?

In Daniells' opinion, it wasn't just the ministerial force that was weak. The division leadership itself was not particularly strong either. He had serious misgivings about the decisions the inexperienced men had been making. Ten years previously, the General Conference president claimed, Prescott had visited the region and had evidenced "a clear insight into conditions." But the church had paid little attention to the professor's extensive report. Daniells, after his own visit to China in late 1916, had concluded that it would have been wiser if the General Conference had appointed Prescott himself to take charge of the Asiatic field. "I am convinced," he wrote to the professor, "that you are blessed with a large executive ability. . . . The interests of the cause are safe in your hands."[12] If Prescott could visit the area again now, it would provide valuable help to the division leaders. Would he go for two years?

The idea appealed to Prescott. Ever since his days as educational secretary of the General Conference he had wanted to do everything possible to educate the ministry. His South American trip in 1916 had sharpened that interest. It had made him acutely aware that, while the ministers and others he met could ably present and defend church doctrines, they were not able to do so in a way that pointed people to Christ. They might change the thinking of those already Christian, but they were not able to "convert" the "unsaved." It concerned Prescott greatly that Adventist preaching still lacked a Christocentric, salvific focus.

He felt strongly enough to write out some positive suggestions on the question to Frederick Griggs, the General Conference educational secretary. Griggs, in turn, circulated the professor's letter around the Bible departments of the various colleges.[13] At the same time Prescott had begun work on a college textbook, *The Doctrine of Christ*. The book would serve as a basis for educating ministers to have a Christocentric understanding of church doctrines.[14] Now, as he thought about it, the opportunity of presenting the material at ministerial institutes throughout the Asiatic Division would give him the chance to refine and field-test it. On

September 27, 1917, after an impressive public farewell by his colleagues, Prescott and his wife set sail for China.

The program outlined for the professor let him know early that he was not going to be on a holiday. It called for more than 12 two-week institutes for 1918, with union conference sessions sandwiched in between. By the end of March he was already feeling the pressure. The lecture timetable required him to give an average of 40 presentations at each institute—approximately three lectures per day. Then he had to travel to the institutes, which had been planned for Manchuria, Korea, Japan, Shanghai, Canton, Hankow, and Singapore. In addition, the schedule set aside six weeks for him to give special instruction to the ministerial students at the China Mission Training School and three months for developing publications. By the time he completed his tour of duty every evangelist and Bible instructor in the division had sat at his feet.

According to D. E. Rebok, a longtime expatriate worker in China, the foreign missionaries greatly appreciated Prescott's emphasis on the Christocentric preaching of Adventist doctrines. His efforts for the indigenous pastors were not a success, however. Quite a number of the poorly trained ministers found his lectures simply "too deep." Even the translators struggled to find language to keep up with him. Adjusting his message to the comprehension level and educational background of his audience was not an easy task.[15]

Prescott did not find living conditions in China particularly easy either. Traveling was often by primitive conveyance and was dangerous because civil war had broken out in the interior. An epidemic of pneumonic plague in the country imposed severe restrictions as well. "It was a bit hard for him, and he put up with many privations," wrote division president I. H. Evans, "but he did it courageously, and was always most happy and content with his conditions."[16] One piece of news the professor received early in 1918 called for special courage.

Because of his assignment in the Far East Prescott had missed the 1918 General Conference session in San Francisco. It was the first he had not attended in 30 years, and he was eager to find out what had occurred behind the scenes. "What does not get into print is often the most interesting and sometimes the most significant," he had written to J. L. Shaw, his fellow field secretary. Shaw had little "inside" information to give about the conference, but he did have disturbing news concerning Prescott's only son, Lewis. The local Washington newspapers had reported him as "missing in action."[17]

WAR CLAIMS A SON

When the United States entered the war against Germany in mid-1917, it had enacted a general draft for military service. It had called up, among other Adventists, Daniells' own son, Grosvenor, and several stenographers from the General Conference. Hearing of the news of his friends, Lewis Prescott decided to enlist rather than get drafted, much to the distress of his father. Lewis explained that he did not wish to risk getting caught in the draft and being sent to the trenches. He had just graduated from the Massachusetts Institute of Technology in June 1917 and was a high risk for the draft. If he enlisted, he could at least choose his line of service. What could his father say? Because of his engineering degree the Royal Flying Corps of Canada quickly accepted Lewis. He had been in basic training at the time his father left for China, and a few months later he received his assignment to active service in France.

The news from Shaw was not clear. Prescott did not know whether Lewis had been killed or taken as a prisoner of war. For months he lived with the agony of uncertainty. Since the time when his son had first enlisted, he had feared for the worst, and now it had come true. What made the news such "a hard blow" was that at sometime during his late teenage years Lewis had ceased being an Adventist, and his father was deeply concerned about the boy's spiritual readiness for death. With no further word, the professor eventually gave up hope of ever seeing his son again. No memorial service was ever held. The family gravestone in Rock Creek Cemetery in Washington, D.C., simply lists Lewis as "missing in France, April 18, 1918."

His son's death confronted Prescott again with a spiritual dilemma. "I want to tell you frankly, my brethren," he confided during a candid moment at the 1919 Bible Conference 12 months later, "that I have had a tremendous struggle . . . in the last year." He could not fathom the will of God, he said. It had been difficult for him "to submit" to what had come. Lewis was an only son. He would have no grandchildren now to cheer his old age. But the tempest of grief had passed and, although it was still difficult for him to accept the loss, peace had finally come.[18]

1919—A YEAR OF CONFERENCES

Prescott did not complete two full years in eastern Asia, as originally planned. With the cessation of hostilities in late 1918, the church needed to make major administrative decisions delayed by the war. In addition, the General Conference had planned a series of important meetings that the war had also postponed. After conducting his last institute in Singapore in March, he headed home. Prescott was eager to be back at headquarters. The year 1919, in fact, turned out to be a year of conferences—six in all. The most notable and the most significant in retrospect was the Bible Conference.

Prescott missed the first set of meetings—a "bookman's convention" in early April. But he participated prominently in all the rest: the educational convention in late April (two days after he arrived home), the evangelists' convocation in May, the editors' convention in June, and the Bible and history teachers' council in July. Prescott led the convention for editors—a first for the church. It had been a long-cherished dream to bring denominational editors together to deal with the kind of issues that had arisen during his *Protestant Magazine* years. He also played a prominent part at the Bible Conference, which, as noted, was undoubtedly the most significant meeting of the year. Full verbatim transcripts (more than 1,300 pages of typescript) of the meetings offer valuable insights both into Prescott's preaching and into an important stage in the theological development of the church.[19]

Church leaders had felt for some years the need for a council of Bible teachers, editors, and administrators. Such a conference, they hoped, would permit theological discussions to take place without the rancor that had surfaced in the past. It could also allow thought leaders in the church to clarify their thinking and reach a greater measure of consensus.

Three weeks after Prescott returned from China, the Spring Council meeting set the dates for the Bible conference, and the professor found himself as the chair of the planning committee. The committee preferred Harbor Springs in Michigan as the site. Perhaps, some hoped, a return to the site of Prescott's landmark 1891 convention might help reproduce the same spirit. And maybe it might also lead to the same kind of revolutionary results. But it was not to be. The conference eventually took place in Washington, D.C., where reference materials and libraries were readily accessible. The two conferences met jointly. The Bible and history teachers' council convened in the evenings during the Bible Conference and continued for 12 days after the Bible Conference concluded. Sixty-five participants attended and discussed a number of topics that clustered around Christology and prophetic interpretation. Prescott himself was the major speaker. He gave more than a third of the 69 presentations and contributed largely in many of the discussion periods. His theme? As one would expect: how to give the Adventist message a Christocentric focus. His talks seem to have had as their basis the manuscript he had developed in 1917 and had used in eastern Asia.

The reaction to Prescott's presentations amply demonstrated the church's need to achieve greater clarity and a stronger consensus in its Christology. For example, on July 6 quite a number of delegates strongly resisted his assertion that Christ was without a beginning, was coeternal with the Father, and was therefore truly God. To say (as many Adventists did) that He had a beginning was to make Him a dependent being and therefore not equal with the Father. The professor ably argued his case from the Greek text, citing grammar and syntax freely. The church, he argued, needed to adopt a more scriptural, Trinitarian view on the eternal deity of Jesus. But when challenged over how to interpret the traditional subordination texts such as John 5:26 that spoke of the Father granting the Son "to have life in himself" and others that used the terminology of Christ as the "first-born of all creation" (RSV) and the "only begotten of the father," the professor stumbled. Adequate language eluded him. Subordination, he suggested, did not relate to "the question of attributes or of His existence." Christ, though eternal and self-existent, yet somehow was also "derived" (taking John 5:26 at face value), though he later backed away from the term, evidently uncomfortable with its connotations and implications. The centuries-old dilemma concerning what one might call "inner-trinitarian relations" was not easy to articulate clearly, and he struggled to make his point clear. He strongly asserted the full eternal deity of the Son, who was "equal with the father" and identified with the "I AM" of the Old Testament (very God), but yet at the same time he felt that there must be a "proper" way of somehow dealing with His eternal generation as indicated by the subordination passages.[20]

The debate wrestled with the same issues that had troubled the New England states from Jonathan Edwards through to Horace Bushnell during the anti-Trinitarian controversies a century earlier and that had led many churches into Arianism and then on to Unitarianism. Adventism had been born at the end of that anguished period. Many of its founders had come from Restorationist movements such as the Christian Connexion or the Freewill Baptists, churches that tended to be strongly anticreedal in their outlook, a perspective actually much more strongly influenced by Enlightenment-inspired rationalism in their doctrinal formulations than they would have cared to admit.[21] Such mid-nineteenth-century Christians in their anticreedalism and adoption of the "Bible only" interpreted Scripture in a strictly literal, "plain meaning of the text" sense and thus attempted to make sense of the biblical data in the light of the "common sense" philosophy of their day just as the ancient Greek fathers had tried to view the biblical data in the light of the "common sense" of their times. The "common sense" of the mid-nineteenth century had strong philosophical underpinnings rooted in rationalism.[22] Now, in the second generation and in the light of continuing study of Scripture, Adventism was painfully and slowly making its way back to a more orthodox Trinitarian view of the Godhead, although the word "Trinity" still remained essentially a no-no in church usage—probably because it was a nonbiblical word and was associated with the creeds.[23]

H. Camden Lacey, with his strong High Church Anglican background, came to the professor's defense with attempts to express the difficult truths in different language, suggesting that the term "second in rank" was a more appropriate expression.[24] If it is true that whether a people are "orthodox" or not is more clearly indicated by what they deny than by what they affirm, clearly Prescott was fully orthodox Trinitarian. And so the Seventh-day Adventist Church should be, because that is what Scripture taught. Christ was not a created being—He was coeternal with the Father. How then, challenged the professor, could the denomination continue to circulate Uriah Smith's *Daniel and the Revelation* with its clear Arianism and thereby leave itself open to criticism that it was a sub-Christian sect? He recalled the embarrassment of his time in Melbourne in late 1895 (see p. 120).

But how could you not maintain a punctiliar beginning for Jesus, responded those who disagreed, if you took the subordination texts of the fourth Gospel and elsewhere at face value? Furthermore, was not the doctrine of the Trinity really a Roman Catholic aberration, a product of the falling away of the church during the first three centuries? The clash with the dominant anti-Trinitarian sentiment produced considerable tension. At one point during the discussions Daniells also had to come to the professor's defense. "Let's not get a bit nervous or scared," he said. "Don't let the conservatives think that something is going to happen and the progressives get alarmed for fear it won't." Then he asked the stenographer to discontinue transcribing the discussion until tempers had cooled.[25]

Some participants also reacted to Prescott's strong emphasis on the indwelling Christ, because it sounded too much like Kellogg's teaching. The suggestion that he was teaching "pantheistic ideas" stung the professor and brought an angry response. How could people misunderstand so easily? The vital distinction between Kellogg and himself was this very Christocentric emphasis. How could one who was so strongly Trinitarian, who believed in the full deity of Jesus and the personality of the Holy Spirit on the one hand, be perceived as being pantheistic on the other? Again the meetings came to a halt. Prescott refused to continue with his lecture until the matter had been sorted out.

By and large, however, the delegates appreciated the professor's emphasis on the centrality of Christ as it became clear that his purpose was "not to present a theory about the person of Christ" but to bring people to a knowledge of Him. "The preaching of the gospel is not to persuade people to agree with me in my theological views," he asserted. "The preaching of the gospel, so far as I am concerned, is to bring people into personal association with that person with whom I have fellowship."[26]

Many of Prescott's presentations moved from teaching to impassioned preaching. Rich in Scripture quoted from memory, the sermons frequently struck home with his audience, prompting frequent and repeated "amens"—all faithfully recorded in the verbatim transcript. Delegates voted him a statement of appreciation at the end of the conference.

More gratifying to the professor than a vote of thanks was the recommendation that his material be published in book form. It appeared in two volumes as *The Doctrine of Christ* shortly after the meetings, with a second one-volume edition issued in late 1920. The first 13 chapters dealt with the person and work of Christ, while the remainder dealt with specific Adventist doctrines. It was not a systematic theology but rather the genre of a doctrinal class textbook, a format commonly used at the time. Prescott hoped the book would influence "the method of Bible teaching" in the church's schools and thus ultimately refocus the denomination's understanding of its doctrines and therefore its evangelistic outreach. It did, but very slowly. Interestingly, the book does not deal with the Godhead, nor does it mention the doctrine of the Trinity anywhere—strange indeed for a book of that title. The avoidance of the terminology indicates the extent of the aversion to the concept itself in the denomination.

After trying to move the ministry and theological leadership of the church into the new way of thinking about the doctrines through the Bible Conference, Prescott next received a request to direct his attention to the general membership of the church. In 1921 the same material appeared as a yearlong series of Sabbath school lessons. Again, while the lessons strongly affirm Christ's divinity and His status as the "I AM" of the Old Testament, the absence of any stress on the eternal existence of Christ or any exploration of the implications of this Christology for the understanding of the Trinity is striking. As Burt observes, "either Prescott was being sensitive to the concerns of a significant segment of the church, or the editorial committee expunged anything that would be controversial."[27] The church intended its Sabbath school lessons to build community, not divide it. The lesson material had a practical salvific emphasis and was the fleshing out of an approach that Prescott had been refining since 1888 and his Battle Creek evangelistic meetings in the Opera House. And it was the focus he had used in Australia that had so thrilled Ellen White. Christ, rather than the Sabbath doctrine or the doctrine of the judgment, should be the unifying and the distinguishing feature of Adventism. A profound paradigm shift, it saw bringing people to a saving knowledge of Jesus as the purpose of every doctrine.

According to LeRoy E. Froom, who as a new editor in China in 1917 was thoroughly impressed by Prescott's studies, the book failed to "sweep the field." The professor's "lofty concept" was "like a great breath of fresh air" for some teachers and administrators, but for others it was too much of a departure from the traditional prophetic-doctrinal emphasis. The latter "strongly opposed" it and "derided" the approach as "the New Theology," largely because the book advocated the "mediation of Christ view of the 'daily.'" In Froom's opinion, Prescott was right in seeing "the daily" theology to be a direct follow-up of the "underlying principles" of the 1888 message. Those who resisted one also tended to reject the other. Prescott was "ahead of his time—many years ahead," but, according to Froom, his seed sowing was not wasted. It bore a rich harvest later, although the professor did not live to see it.[28]

Prescott's four presentations on prophetic interpretation at the 1919 Bible Conference also indicated that he was ahead of most of his colleagues. He also believed that prophecy must be understood as Christocentric. His basic approach, together with a careful noting of context, would save preachers from making foolish interpretations such as applying Nahum's chariots to modern railway trains. Furthermore, prophecy was capable of repeated fulfillment. It meant, for example, that Antiochus Epiphanes could be a fulfillment of Daniel 7 as "a wheel within a wheel." Some, such as editor M. C. Wilcox, teacher H. Camden Lacey, and missionary F. W. Field, also saw light in this viewpoint. So, too, did Daniells. The latter hoped, however, that people would not widely discuss the concept outside the conference.[29] He feared its divisive potential.

As already noted, the Bible and history teachers' council ran concurrently with the Bible Conference. Its meetings at first convened during the evenings. They then continued on for a few days after the Bible Conference concluded. Prescott gave two lectures during it. His extensive remarks in two other freewheeling discussions on Ellen White's writings, however, brought him more notoriety than anything he said in his formal presentations. The two main topics listed for discussion indicate that church leaders were making a serious attempt to set some sensitive issues out in the open. The topics were "The Use of the Spirit of Prophecy in Our Teaching of Bible and History" and "Inspiration of the Spirit of Prophecy as Related to the Inspiration of the Bible."

Prescott's burden in the two discussions was to have teachers understand that Ellen White's writings needed to be placed "under" the authority of Scripture and that they were not inerrant. They needed correction. He substantiated his point by illustrations from his work on the revision of *The Great Controversy*. The kind of questions that came from the dele-

gates indicated that many were uncomfortable with his "liberal" viewpoint, and Daniells again found himself supporting his colleague. What
Prescott was saying was true to the facts, the General Conference president asserted, even if it did make people nervous. He appealed to delegates not to misrepresent the professor but to think about what he had
said. They should also remember that he had firmly asserted his personal
confidence in Ellen White's gift.[30]

Since Adventism's earliest days its writers had strongly affirmed the
teaching that Scripture was "verbally inspired." They meant by this that
the Bible was inerrant in its autographs. For example, Moses Hull's popular book *The Bible From Heaven,* published in the 1860s, and Canright's
later plagiarized version by the same title both affirmed such a view.
Furthermore, just a month prior to the 1919 Bible Conference, the *Review*
had carried a series of F. M. Wilcox's editorials strongly supporting the
declarations about the "inerrancy" and "verbal inspiration" of Scripture
made at the recent interdenominational conference on Christian fundamentals. Wilcox had asserted that such an understanding was the "historic" position of the Adventist Church.[31]

Most ministers and Bible teachers in the denomination strongly shared
the position. It was extremely difficult for them, therefore, to acknowledge
the possibility that Ellen White could write something that might need correcting. But corrections were necessary, Prescott insisted, not only in the
choice of words or in expression but also in "thoughts," as illustrated by
some of *The Great Controversy* revisions. For example, how else could the
editors in 1911 add the word "alone" to a sentence and thereby actually re-
verse the meaning of the passage? Prescott knew the particular example
well. He had suggested it, and Elmshaven had adopted it.[32]

The sensitive nature of the discussion on the Spirit of Prophecy and
also the emotion-laden reaction by delegates to presentations on the
"Eastern question"—a disputed reinterpretation of Daniel 11 that removed the focus from the nation of Turkey—persuaded Daniells to
change his mind about circulating the transcript of the conference after it
ended. Originally it had been planned to make the transcript into a permanent public record of the proceedings of the conference, as had occurred with earlier educational conventions. Conference organizer
Prescott had hoped that the document would serve as a helpful educa-

tional resource for college teachers and pastors. The General Conference president's wisdom prevailed, however, and the transcript remained locked away and forgotten in the General Conference vault until Ron Graybill found it 55 years later.

Reactions to the conference varied widely. On the one hand, F. M. Wilcox spoke for those who thought that "a good brotherly" feeling had prevailed, even though most delegates probably remained just as persuaded of their own views afterward as before. On the other hand, N. J. Waldorf (a conservative pastor) thought the session had conceded too much to the "progressives." In spite of the fact that the "new views" had largely prevailed, he for one was resolved to "stand by the old landmarks, sink or swim." He would gladly be known as a dissenter from the "Prescott-Lacey theology." J. S. Washburn, whose information about what was said in the discussions at the conference was only secondhand, had some choice descriptions for the event. He labeled it a "Council of Darkness" and a "Diet of Doubts," the "crowning act in the program of doubt and darkness and criticism . . . enveloping Washington." It was the "omega" of apostasy that Ellen White had been talking about. Washburn determined to stamp out the "new theology."[33]

Two scurrilous pamphlets circulated widely in the early 1920s by Washburn and C. E. Holmes focused strongly on the 1919 Bible Conference. They bitterly attacked Daniells' administration and figured largely in making the 1922 General Conference session in California one of the most politicized sessions in denominational history. A deadlocked nominating committee held up the business of the session for many days, giving rise in the meantime to sensational reports in the newspapers. Eventually the denomination formally repudiated Washburn's and Holmes's pamphlets as "un-Christian propaganda." A vote of the 1922 session publicly condemned the efforts of the two men and their supporters to "destroy the good names of honored officials." Nevertheless, it replaced Daniells as General Conference president, naming W. A. Spicer in his place and appointing Daniells as secretary.

The disastrous 1922 session with its fallout from the 1919 Bible Conference scarcely touched Prescott, who at the time was in Australia safely serving as president of Avondale College. The delegates reelected him in absentia as field secretary. As it had 26 years earlier, the island continent again provided the professor with a place of refuge.

---

[1] *GC Bulletin,* 1915, p. 2. GCCMin, Nov. 21, 1915. Spicer as GC secretary also received an assistant at the same time.

[2] AGD to WWP, Dec. 9, 1915.

[3] WWP to AGD, Dec. 20, 1915.

[4] *RH,* Mar. 23, 1916, pp. 15, 16; May 11, 1916, p. 15.

[5] *RH,* May 18, 1916, p. 11; WWP to A. W. Kelly, Aug. 1, 1916.

[6] WWP to CMS, Aug. 1, 1916.

[7] ERP to WWP, Aug. 18, 1916.

[8] WWP to AOT, May 6, 1917; AOT to WWP, May 28, 1917.

[9] WWP to CBH, July 3, 1917; CBH to WWP, Aug. 6, 1917.

[10] WWP to AWS, Nov. 18, 1920; AWS to WWP, Nov. 22, 1920; AWS to PTM, Nov. 23, 1920; PTM to AWS, Nov. 29, 1920.

[11] AWS to PTM, Nov. 23, 1920; PTM to AWS, Nov. 29, 1920.

[12] AGD to WWP, Nov. 12, 1916.

[13] WWP to FG, July 26, 1916; OAJ to HCL, July 1, 1917; OAJ to WWP, July 1, 1917.

[14] Teachers first used the book *Doctrine of Christ* in manuscript form, and then later in 1920 the Review and Herald published it. Its objective was to familiarize ministers with the doctrines of the church and a way of presenting them as a "revelation of Jesus Christ and Him crucified."

[15] D. E. Rebok to GMV, Feb. 3, 1981.

[16] *RH,* May 29, 1919, p. 32.

[17] WWP to JLS, Mar. 21, 1918; JLS to WWP, May 9, 1918.

[18] 1919 Bible Conference transcript, July 11, 1919; WAS to WWP, June 18, 1918; WWP to JLS, Aug. 5, 1918.

[19] The document, forgotten in the General Conference Archives, came to light only in 1974. See Donald E. Mansell, "How the 1919 Bible Conference Transcript Was Found," July 6, 1975. GCAr.

[20] Merlin Burt has a helpful discussion of these tensions in Prescott's Christology and an insightful analysis of the theological development in the church in this area. See his "Demise of Semi-Arianism and Anti-Trinitarianism in Adventist Theology, 1888-1957" (unpublished research paper, 1996), pp. 26, 27, 31. AUHR.

[21] A good recent discussion of the central issues in New England anti-Trinitarianism may be found in Bruce Stephens' *God's Last Metaphor; The Doctrine of the Trinity in New England Theology* (Chico, Calif: Scholars Press, 1981). Also useful is Frank Foster's *A Genetic History of New England Theology* (New York: Russell and Russell, 1963).

[22] Although William Miller had renounced the deism of his earlier years, the Newtonian rationalism that had undergirded it still largely infused the philosophical atmosphere he and most of his fellow North Americans breathed.

[23] 1919 Bible Conference transcript, July 6, 1919. See Jerry Moon's two chapters on the historical background of this area of Adventist theological development in *The Trinity* (Hagerstown, Md.: Review and Herald Pub. Assn., 2002), pp. 190-231. The book is coau-

thored by Woodrow Whidden, Jerry Moon, and John W. Reeve. Even though F. M. Wilcox had published in the *Review* in 1913 that Adventists believed in the divine Trinity, the statement avoids discussion of inner-trinitarian relations, stating that Jesus is "the Son of the eternal Father" rather than the eternal Son. *RH,* Oct. 9, 1913, p. 21. Semi-Arians such as Washburn could live with it.

[24] Lacey had been with Prescott in 1896 in Australia when together with Marian Davis they had studied ways to express the concept of Christ's divinity and eternal sonship clearly in the right language when assisting with the editing of *The Desire of Ages.* See chapter 8.

[25] 1919 Bible Conference transcript, July 6, 1919.

[26] 1919 Bible Conference transcript, July 2, 1919; July 10, 1919.

[27] Burt, p. 30.

[28] L. E. Froom, *Movement of Destiny* (Washington, D.C.: Review and Herald Pub. Assn., 1971), pp. 348, 377, 380-391. Froom gives a close analysis of the contents of Prescott's college text.

[29] 1919 Bible Conference transcript, July 2, 1919; July 3, 1919.

[30] The transcript of the two discussions appears in *Spectrum* 10, no. 1 (May 1979): 27-57.

[31] *RH,* June 19, 1919, p. 2.

[32] Some confusion on the meaning of terminology used contributed to the difficulty of resolving the tensions in the problems of the inspiration of Scripture. To say that Scripture was "verbally inspired" did not necessarily mean "mechanical dictation," although many understood it that way. Many often employed the term simply to mean that Scripture was given in words and that inspiration guarded the meaning. Words, of course, could be changed and better words found, but the meaning was reliably the same. In this sense, inspiration referred not to the process but to the result. Sometimes Prescott used the term *plenary inspiration* to express the idea that Scripture was wholly trustworthy. His difficulty was that what he saw with Ellen White's writings was that sometimes the meaning needed to be changed to make them accurate. But it was not the way he viewed Scripture and was a problem he struggled with. Was the inspiration different? Alden Thompson's *Inspiration: Hard Questions, Honest Answers* (Hagerstown, Md.: Review and Herald Pub. Assn., 1991) offers a better solution to the dilemma.

[33] FMW to WCW, Aug. 19, 1919; NJW to LEF, Oct. 24, 1922.

CRAPTER XVII

CAMPUS TROUBLESHOOTER

ONLY DORA CREEK LOOKS the same," Prescott reported to W. C. White on his first visit to the Avondale campus after 26 years. He had not been at all impressed in 1895. It had had no buildings, no roads, and no gardens—just a sawmill and a few tents in the bush. Now he was amazed at the "marked transformation" on the estate. He was also agreeably surprised to find individuals still on the campus who had heard him preach during his first institute back in 1896.[1] But he had little time for nostalgia, however. A backlog of work awaited the professor.

C. H. Watson, the Australasian Union Conference president, had gone to the spring meetings in America in early 1921 for the express purpose of securing somebody to help remedy the ailing educational program in Australia. Avondale was in trouble and in need of the "strongest" leadership he could find. Two years previously the school had dismissed a number of department heads because they were encouraging "commercialism" (unionism?) in the college. Frequent changes in the principalship (10 in 24 years) had not helped strengthen the program either. Henry Kirk, who served as principal in 1921, was a man of integrity and highly conscientious, but he had had little teaching experience and was not much older than many of his students. Discipline was lax, and the "rowdiness" in the dormitories was getting out of hand.[2]

An economic recession complicated Avondale's difficulties. The school had raised tuition to offset the increasing operating deficit and had suspended payment for the 12-hour-per-week student work program. As a result, enrollment had tumbled by 43 percent—down to 143 students— and the deficit had grown larger than ever. Whoever came to lead the school would have to know what he was doing. The General Conference had just the man, and Watson was delighted at his success in snaring him for the job. The *Australasian Record* trumpeted the coup. Professor Prescott was one of the "foremost educational leaders within our ranks."[3]

William and Daisy arrived in Sydney in early September accompanied by the professor's younger sister Belle and her convalescing minister husband, A. J. Bristol. Prescott's mother, Harriet, had died 15 months previously, and Belle, who for years had been caring for her in Washington, was now free to travel. It was rare that Prescott had time to enjoy family.[4]

Although it had been 26 years since Prescott had served as a college president, his views on education had not changed. Nor had his style altered much. As he figured it, the purpose of an Adventist school was still primarily to prepare workers for the church. The curriculum, therefore, needed to be thoroughly Christocentric. In his previous schools he had employed the daily chapel as his chief means of imposing his "stamp" on the student body. At Avondale it was the same. Only the daily 15-minute feature updating students on "important world events" seemed to be different. The professor was not sure that Australian newspapers were sufficiently broad enough to cover the really important news, so he had his trusty Springfield *Republican* sent to him from North America. He needed to keep himself and his students abreast of the times.[5]

In spite of the marked transformation Prescott had first observed on his return visit to the campus, it soon became apparent that much still needed to be done. Such things as screen doors for his house, new furniture for his office, and new classroom areas for sewing and cooking were quickly attended to. But when it came to new kitchen facilities for the students and a new sewerage system, the board balked. What particularly disturbed the polished American was the fact that a quarter of a century after it started, the school was still using Australia's traditional "backyard" nonflushing toilets. By the time he left Australia two years later he had persuaded the board to change its mind and install a flush system.

Prescott had more success in improving the morale and the image of the school than he did in reversing its economic fortunes, even though he at least made a good start on the latter. The school stemmed losses in its student industries by more careful supervision and by dismissing several inefficient staff. The professor also persuaded the union conference to hire a number of his teachers as colporteurs or clerks during the summer vacation to help reduce his expenses. It was a difficult time for the staff. In spite of the belt-tightening, however, Prescott was still able to build morale. Students quickly "measured up to Prescott's expectations" and, according to J. E. Fulton, the union secretary, the future of the school began to look hopeful once more. It was strenuous work, and Fulton noted that the 66-year-old principal "felt the strain a good deal."[6]

Other men normally retired at 65, but not Prescott. He might be predisposed to become weary more quickly, but he had lost none of his intellectual vigor or his keen judgment. Early on he recognized that a stopgap president was not in the best interests of Avondale. The school needed a head who could implement permanent policies and plan for a long-range upgrading of the institution. It would require four or five years to get the place firmly on its feet. The person who he thought could do the job best was Lynn H. Wood. Wood was someone, Prescott assured the committee, who was determined "to follow fully the instruction given in the Spirit of Prophecy." The union committee followed his advice. Wood was at Avondale by graduation in November 1922 to take over Prescott's duties. The professor had been at Avondale a little more than a year, but Wood found that he had left behind "a real spirit of consecration and earnest devotion to the scriptures" among the students.[7]

Although he left Avondale, Prescott did not depart Australia for another year. In the interim, both men continued to work together to improve the school. By September 1923 Wood had developed a long-term plan, and Prescott joined him in trying to have the Australian church leadership commit themselves to it. The plan called for the appointment of strong departmental heads "to strengthen the college faculty," a large increase in facilities, and a student recruitment drive. In spite of Prescott's support, all the Australian leadership could manage to approve was the student recruitment drive. It was the only thing that did not cost money.

Prescott's labors, even while serving as principal, had not confined themselves to Cooranbong alone. Shortly after his arrival in Australia the union committee appointed him as its educational secretary. The union committee intended that not only should he supervise and develop the scattered junior schools, but that he would also conduct institutes for the ministers in each of the state conferences. The professor's "long . . . experience" was too valuable a resource to keep just for the students at Avondale. The whole field should hear him. Thus by September 1922 a temporary Bible teacher had been arranged to care for the professor's classes at the college while he went elsewhere conducting the first of his field schools. During the following 12 months ministerial institutes and camp meeting appointments eventually took Prescott from west Australia to New Zealand and to every conference in between. Fortunately his energy levels and health were sufficiently robust. Nevertheless, at 67, he increasingly found the work of camp meeting preaching (congregations of 500 to 1,000 without a public-address system) and the many hours of personal interviews that went with it a "hard pull."[8]

At the end of his appointment the Australian church leaders urged the professor to stay longer but could not persuade him. He and Daisy felt that after two years down under they had had enough. They returned to the United States at a most fortuitous time. Just weeks after his return his younger brother, Charles, died in Maine. Prescott managed to visit him just prior to his death.[9] His sister, Belle, died later the same year. Few of his large family of siblings now remained.

A TURN AT UNION COLLEGE

Avondale was not the only college in trouble in the 1920s. Union College in Lincoln, Nebraska, also faced a major crisis with shrinking enrollment and increasing deficits. As Union College historian Everett Dick has astutely noted, it was an era in which church leaders reluctantly paid deficits after they had been incurred but could not bring themselves to allocate an operating grant in advance. Neither had they yet learned that a college could not survive on tuition income alone. Union's problems intensified in 1922 when long-serving president H. A. Morrison resigned in protest over his board's refusal to accept his recommendations for moving the school toward senior college accreditation. Other faculty left with him, and school morale plummeted.

With the deficit ballooning toward $100,000 at the end of 1923, the frightened trustees put the college on the market. A new start out in the country, they hoped, would be much more economical. But no one wanted to buy Union College—at least not at the price the board attempted to sell it for. General Conference adviser C. W. Irwin came to study the situation and recommended a host of cost-cutting measures that included reducing teaching staff, cutting back on dormitory heating, and selling off the uneconomical dairy herd. The school implemented the recommendations, but as a result, its morale worsened even further, and the deficit still increased. In March 1924 a marathon four-day meeting of the board considered closing the school. But that was not the best option either.[10]

At the time Union College was the only Adventist school that enjoyed state recognition for its teacher-training program, thus making it a "keystone in the arch" for the system of schools in the Central Union. A number of secondary and elementary schools depended on the college at Lincoln to provide certified teachers. Closing the institution would also mean shutting down the rest of the schools. Union would have to keep going no matter how painful it might be. It would have to make further stringent budgetary reductions, the only way out of the dilemma. But at that point the new president, Otto M. John, balked. Unable to live with the program outlined by the board, he also resigned.[11]

Finding a new president was not easy. After several unsuccessful attempts to secure a suitable candidate, the trustees turned to the General Conference for help. Was there anyone it could send? As it happened, the General Conference had a good troubleshooter right at hand, and he was available. Prescott had just returned from Avondale. By early July 1924 the professor was once more behind a president's desk. Board chair S. E. Wight was delighted. Within just a matter of weeks Prescott had taken "hold of the school in a masterly way." A strong charismatic leader was just what the institution needed to steer it through the greatest crisis in its history.[12]

From the General Conference treasurer's perspective, the reason financial matters at Lincoln were so grim was simply that they had been "sadly neglected for years." Hard economic decisions had to be made and done quickly, he pointed out to Prescott. To make sure the tough decisions actually happened, Prescott had himself appointed as business manager. The college soon made staff retrenchments, sold off the dairy herd, and obtained vital loans and grants to keep the school operating. It was a busy start, and General Conference treasurer J. L. Shaw was glad Prescott was there "to hold the line." But the professor soon became convinced that Shaw's grasp of the situation was too simplistic. The treasurer's expectation that the institution could turn itself around quickly with only tuition income to rely on was unrealistic and overly optimistic. If a car driven downhill at full speed attempts to negotiate a corner too quickly, the professor warned, it goes into the ditch. Prescott wanted to turn the corner, but he did not want to be the one to "ditch the car."[13]

By January the following year, however, the trustees felt that they had no choice. In spite of the economies affected by Prescott, deficits continued to mount. Again the trustees decided to put the school on the market. And again no buyers came forth. After several months it became evident that the school would have to stay where it was and would just have to tighten its belt further.

Rebuilding student morale was one of Prescott's major concerns. For the professor, the way to do that was to return to the old ways he knew so well. He had assigned seating for students in the cafeteria reinstituted along with a courtesy campaign. Students should dine "like ladies and gentlemen." Chapels again became the focus of the daily program, with faculty required to attend as well as the students. Punctuality was a must. The doors closed at 9:30 a.m., and the monitors took roll. Former students of the period recall that Prescott personally donated a new organ for the chapel. Most of the talks he gave himself. He was even known to go around the chapel as the students were assembling and set all the window shades at the same level. When it came to detail, he was meticulous. The impact on students was profound, and they vividly remembered it years later.[14]

"Prescott . . . was the epitome of dignity. His bearing, his manner demanded respect," recalled former student Opal Wheeler.[15] Students who dared to study during chapel period or whisper to a friend received a withering look from the president. He also expected staff to measure up. Rochelle Kilgore, a teacher at the time, recalled that at the moment the first faculty meeting for the year was scheduled to begin, the professor quietly walked to the door and turned the key. "Needless to say, everyone was on time for the next faculty meeting." But, according to Kilgore, the faculty appreciated Prescott's "definite plans," and "everyone knew just what was expected of him."[16]

On the academic front, Prescott's strategy also consisted of a return to the old ways. While every student had to take a class in Bible each year, it did not mean any lowering of standards. The professor rarely gave A grades in his own classes. The school encouraged reading outside the Bible but monitored it carefully. The president himself led an inspection committee through the library holdings. It removed 60 titles from the shelves, thereafter to be available only to teachers.

While absolutely committed to quality, refinement, and dignity, the professor was not at all enthusiastic about the trend toward cap-and-gown ceremonies. "You'll not get me in one of those" was his response to those who tried then and later.[17] Nor was he excited by the push for external accreditation. He preferred to be "entirely free from all outside entanglement." Only then, he felt, could schools devote themselves to the work for which they were "first established."[18] In early 1925, therefore, when the North Central Association threatened to drop Union's junior college accreditation because it lacked a regular endowment, Prescott was halfway glad. His board, however, saw things differently, and the professor dutifully complied with their instruction that the college should do everything possible to secure a continuation of the recognition.[19]

Six months in the president's chair at Lincoln was all it took to convince the 69-year-old Prescott that the task really required the energies of a younger man. As at Avondale, he realized that his best contribution to the institution would be to help find a suitable long-term replacement. Subsequently, Leo Thiel commenced his duties with the new school year in September 1925.[20]

The trustees, however, were reluctant to lose the professor, who in the space of one year had in fact succeeded in turning the school around. According to General Conference associate secretary C. K. Meyers, Prescott had brought "a new spirit into the experience of the school" with his "straightforward . . . Christian leadership." It was "a new day as far as its possibilities were concerned."[21] But one year was not enough. The college then asked if he would stay on as chair of the Theology Department. The school needed to retain the "confidence of the constituency," board chair Wight argued, and Prescott's presence on campus would "count for much" in that direction. Persuaded, the professor eventually stayed for two more years.

BIBLE TEACHER "WITHOUT A PEER"

Prescott had first taught Bible classes for ministers at the Winter Bible School in 1889. Since then he had instructed at institutes around the globe. But institutes were informal "in service" type classes, not full-fledged college courses. Not until 1921, when Prescott went to Avondale, did he begin to present formal full-length classes. Staying on at Lincoln in 1926 gave him the opportunity to continue that practice.

Students seemed to relate well to the heavy-jowled 70-year-old professor. His thorough familiarity with Scripture and his ability to quote lengthy passages accurately from memory inspired them. He would follow careful notes, but would not tie himself to them, and Christ was always the focal point in every class. "I have never heard anyone present the gospel message of salvation so clearly and so penetratingly as he," E. G. Sauer, a student from Prescott's Union days, later recalled.[22] Prescott also impressed people outside the classroom. According to George Hutches, another student, just the sight of the professor taking his noon-day stroll arm in arm with his wife around the campus "inspired and challenged" the student body.[23]

To some students, Prescott could seem stern and forbidding. His aura of dignity seemed to make him unapproachable. Alfred Kranz, a young graduate from Avondale in 1921, found him that way. Kranz happened to be traveling to New Zealand to take up his first teaching appointment and chanced to be on the same trans-Tasman steamer as the professor. Each day during the journey Prescott and his wife took their exercise, walking the deck arm in arm, but the professor "took not the slightest notice" of the young graduate who was too shy to speak first to a superior. It was as if "he [Prescott] lived in a different world," Kranz noted.[24]

Others, however, who were able to bridge the gap, found him congenial and friendly, although not given to a lot of small talk. No one dared to crack silly jokes in his presence, although he was not short of humorous stories of his own to relate from his travel experiences. Numbers of former students report that, in spite of his reserve, he made it a practice to invite them to his home.

Sometimes the invitation was for a meal—always a formal occasion. Prescott never came to the table without a coat and tie, recalled Alice Perrine, who felt that dining at the Prescott home was a lesson in dining graciously.[25] The silverware was always carefully set on the table. Afterward it was gently washed first and then laid on a dish towel to avoid scratching it unnecessarily. Sometimes the invitation to the Prescott home was just to listen to the "wireless." In the days when crystal sets were the norm, Prescott was one of the first to purchase a radio. Although they more often heard static than music, students felt honored to be invited to enjoy an evening of listening.[26] Many of Prescott's students were able to discover the warmth of a genuinely kind nature beneath his stern exterior.

One of the reasons Prescott was happy to stay on at Union as chair of the Theology Department was that it provided an opportunity to achieve a long-cherished goal. For many years he had talked about revamping Bible courses and restructuring the whole ministerial training program to make it more Christ-centered. Here was his chance. The professor's physical energy might be diminishing with age, but his mental acuity certainly wasn't, and his burden about helping ministers to be more Christ-centered was as great as ever.

During his short term as president the professor had received permission from the General Conference to redesign the ministerial training program, but he had not been able to get started on the project. He had also tried to attract the young H.M.S. Richards to join the school as a Bible teacher. Prescott had met Richards in Canada and realized that he was the kind of minister who could make classes Christ-centered. He would be a good help in revising the course offerings. However, he could not coax Richards away from his evangelistic work, and there was no one else Prescott could think of. The professor would have to do it by himself.[27]

The new "Analytic Bible" classes designed by the professor during 1925 were structured around his textbook *The Doctrine of Christ.* He modified other classes to provide a good blend of practical and theoretical training. Overall, as Prescott noted in his bulletin, his purpose was to give "the dominant place" to the study of the English Bible, with the distinctive aim of presenting "a comprehensive view of the everlasting gospel." At the same time, instruction would focus on "the special message for the last generation." The college offered a regular four-year-degree program as well as a shorter two-year course for those who wanted to train just as "gospel workers."[28]

Prescott's associates in the Theology Department soon began to catch his vision and became enthusiastic about the fresh approach. Along with the students, they also marveled at the professor's great knowledge of the Bible and his ability to quote it so extensively. As a Bible teacher, Prescott was "without a peer," according to fellow Union religion teacher Homer

Saxton.[29] In his opinion Union was fortunate indeed to have the professor, and the department was definitely headed in the right direction.

Restructuring the curriculum kept Prescott extremely busy for most of 1925. Serving as department head, teaching nine hours a week, and developing lessons for others stretched his resources. But still he found time for extracurricular interests. One of them was a pioneer one-hour religious radio broadcast that went on the air every Sunday evening over Lincoln's new station, KFAN 319. The college music department provided the music, while Prescott organized the program and preached the 20-minute sermon. The station boasted a listening audience of more than 1 million, and that may well have been right. Prescott received letters of appreciation from many parts of the United States, and by 1928 he was mailing 250 topic outlines each week to listeners. But to the professor's dismay, the station abruptly canceled the program in April 1928. Prescott's Sabbath presentations and some anti-Catholic remarks had apparently riled some influential listeners. Hostile letters to the station's management forced them to terminate the program. Prescott had not learned to soften his rhetoric.[30]

Other problems besides the cancellation of his radio program troubled the professor in 1928. "The grind of regular classwork," particularly "the writing part," had begun to wear on him. More bothersome than that, however, as he explained to Spicer, now the General Conference president, was his unhappiness with the administration of the new college president. Leo Thiel had relaxed social standards, was inefficient in his management, and, according to Prescott, was not committed to Ellen White's philosophy of education. Prescott felt frustrated at seeing "the ideals" he had tried to establish "so easily ignored."[31] He had been tempted to withdraw from the school during the previous year to avoid the tension, but then had decided to stay on with a reduced teaching load. The smaller teaching responsibility had at least enabled him to finish a book he had been working on for years. Released as *The Saviour of the World* in 1929, the book gave Prescott considerable satisfaction in publishing in popular form what had been the burden of his ministry for years, though it did not solve his other problems at Union. But Prescott was not alone in his dissatisfaction, because Thiel troubled a number of others.

Discontent over the president's administration continued to simmer until in 1928 the Central Union Conference became involved in the problem. At that point, according to pastor-observer George Hutches, the matter developed into one of the more noteworthy political scandals in the history of the conference. At the 1928 Central Union session several conference presidents conspired to have S. E. Wight replaced as union conference president. When the nominating committee presented its Friday afternoon report, it had M. L. Rice in his place. The delegates accepted the report by a margin of two to one. Rice offended many S. E. Wight loyalists, however, by immediately attempting to take over the remaining proceedings of the session. Traditionally the transfer of power occurred at the conclusion of the session. According to Hutches, a most "unrestful" and agitated Sabbath followed.[32]

Immediately after sundown on Saturday evening, Prescott, the senior General Conference representative, convened a special session to reconsider the nominating committee's report. Heated discussion followed, and then Prescott called for another vote. Again the delegates adopted the report, this time by a slightly narrower majority of 91 to 55. In a highly irregular ruling, Prescott declared that the minority was "too big to ignore" and sent the report back.

At his direction the nominating committee went out again with a request to reconsider its report. But the opportunity for further discussion did not help. The committee declined to change its report, whereupon, in the midst of high tension, Prescott dismissed the committee and ruled that a new one be appointed. He figured that any new president was going to need wider acceptance and support by the constituency. How could any leader function knowing that more than a third of his constituency did not want him? The new nominating committee proved no better at reaching a solution. Even after several days of deliberation it could not agree on a name for the presidency. Finally, as a compromise measure, the session returned S. E. Wight to office for six weeks, and the session instructed the union executive committee to seek wider counsel and to find an acceptable new president within that time. The mandate was eventually fulfilled by the appointment of J. J. Nethery from the Southern Union, but S. E. Wight was indignant.

In the interim, still as chair of the Union College board, Wight succeeded in removing Thiel, who he suspected had been a leading figure in the coup against him. No doubt the board had other reasons to approve such a move. To the trustees, "bobbed hair," "rouge," shorter dress lengths, and freer social relationships were symptomatic of a general decay. Thiel was letting down on standards. As far as Wight was concerned, it was poetic justice. Whatever Prescott may have thought of Thiel's role in session politics or of Wight's personal maneuvers, he was sure that college president's removal was a good thing for the school.[33]

Of course, the students did not agree. The relaxation of social regulations, in their thinking, was an improvement rather than a downward trend. They felt that Wight had succeeded in stopping the clock. The march of progress had ground to a halt. On the other hand, Prescott cherished the hope that the new president, P. L. Thompson from Pacific Union College, might even turn time backwards. Some things, he felt, needed to be undone. As it turned out, Thompson met the board's expectations. He was a social conservative. To the chagrin of the trustees, however, they found that theologically he was also an independent thinker. The president lasted only a year before resigning.

Troubled about the integrity of Ellen White's gift of inspiration, in view of her "borrowing" and her "shut door" theology, Thompson abandoned denominational employment to accept a position at a Baptist college. Fortunately for the school, Thompson's theological difficulties did not become a public issue on campus. He left quietly. But the issues he grappled with caused problems for Prescott during the next few years. In fact, during the 1930s theological questions became a major problem for the church. By then, however, Prescott was far from Union College.

AN ORACLE AT EMMANUEL MISSIONARY COLLEGE

If Prescott thought he had finished with classroom teaching when he left Union in 1928, he was mistaken. Four years later he was back in the classroom again, helping out his old friend, Lynn Wood, who had by now transferred to Emmanuel Missionary College. The Berrien Springs school was on its way to senior college accreditation, which required that a teacher with at least a master's degree should head up its Theology Department. Even in the 1930s such qualifications were still scarce.

Prescott declined Wood's first invitation in 1931. The prospect of 12 hours of classes each week plus the attendant administrative duties daunted the professor, now 77. Eighteen months later the General Conference urged the professor to accept the appointment when the North Central Association of Colleges threatened to cancel EMC's accreditation, even as a junior college, unless it upgraded. When church leaders finally realized during the early 1930s that Adventist youth were turning to secular universities and would continue to do so in increasing numbers unless denominational schools received accreditation, the accreditation issue was more or less resolved, albeit reluctantly and with reservations. By now Prescott had also adjusted to the inevitable and willingly contributed his Dartmouth degree to help solve the problem at Berrien Springs.[34]

It was a hazardous time to be working in a college Bible classroom. During the early 1930s theological disputes concerning some of its key doctrines had wracked the church, and some prominent leaders such as L. R. Conradi in Europe and William Warde Fletcher in Australia had defected. A strong conservative reaction had followed the theological disturbances, making it difficult to attract qualified teachers.

According to LeRoy Froom, editor of the new *Ministry* magazine, many of those available as Bible teachers were so "orthodox" they were leaning "backwards." They constituted a perplexity to the leadership "and to the reverent body of scholarship in the movement." Others were too "mechanical and doctrinarian." The church needed teachers with a "vision" and a "forward look." But there were precious few of the latter.[35] The "progressive" H. Camden Lacey, for example, who had been a teacher previously at Washington Missionary College, had declined the position at EMC because he did not want to face "the constant small criticism" that came from the church membership. Such criticism would arise "on some minor point of truth," usually stirred up by some student "who did not understand his viewpoint." Lacey had found administration reluctant to support a teacher in such situations, and therefore he did not feel it worth the risk to teach Bible. In view of the chilly attitude in the church toward people who thought, Lacey preferred to stay quietly in pastoral work. Wood had invited five others and had been unsuccessful in getting any of them.[36]

Prescott was no doubt aware of the risks that Froom and Lacey had spoken about, but he was more concerned about the amount of work he would have to do than its dangers. He probably thought that with General Conference credentials he was safe. After all, he would retain his appointment as field secretary, and his salary would continue to come from the General Conference. For President Wood this was the real "coup." Running a school in the midst of a depression was not easy. The rest of his staff had just voted themselves their third 10 percent reduction in pay to help the college cope with the economic crisis.[37]

Although he had not planned to carry a "full" load, Prescott soon found himself busily involved in the program. A department head could not skip administrative councils, library and discipline committees, and faculty meetings, even if he was not far from 80 years of age. But however many birthdays he had had, the professor's personality would simply not allow him to be just a spectator at such meetings. He often led with a prayer or a proposal. Prescott stood the strain well, according to Wood, although the professor tended to be rather intense in his thinking and was "a bit inclined to carry the load of the school." Wood could cope with that. In fact, he appreciated Prescott's "counsel" and his "presence."[38] So did the other faculty. According to one colleague, Prescott's being around "was like having an oracle on campus."[39]

By the end of his first year Prescott prided himself on having not missed a class. His health remained steady, and he enjoyed the stimulus of being among young people. With his advancing years, the number of family relatives whom the professor could rely on for support was diminishing quickly, and he found himself depending more and more on church friends and acquaintances. Students helped fill the gap, and he frequently opened his home to them. At the end of 1933 board chair W. H. Holden reported that the professor was "greatly loved and respected" on the campus. He was delighted that Prescott had agreed to continue teaching for a further year.

Prescott enjoyed his second year in the classroom. He felt he was making a significant contribution. But the year did not end as happily as it had begun. Before it was over, the professor had felt the biting chill of the theological ice age that had temporarily descended on the church.

As we have already noticed, the early 1930s were years of tension and perplexity for denominational leaders and teachers. An atmosphere of suspicion and distrust in the church had arisen out of the theological turmoil, and school administrators discovered it extremely difficult to attract good Bible teachers. W. H. Holden, for example, had found himself frustrated

at not being able to find a suitable person for EMC in 1932 and had complained to the General Conference, "This lack of confidence in men is a
terrible thing." He was "alarmed" about the future because each year the
problem was becoming worse.[40]

Froom shared his anxiety about the atmosphere of suspicion and "reactionism" that had recently "swept over" the church. "Men who think, no
matter how reverently and loyal," he observed, found themselves feared.
The denomination had adopted a "policy of evasion of fundamental questions," and "the hard dogmatism" of such fundamentalists as Benjamin G.
Wilkinson, an ultraconservative Bible teacher from Washington, was preferred by too many church leaders.[41] Such a policy, in Froom's opinion, was
"unworthy of this remnant movement." Theological positions "which have
to be protected by ecclesiastical legislation and popular sentiment . . . are
weak indeed." The trend to "codify and creedalize" church teachings
alarmed him. It would only result in Adventism's becoming "rigid and static
as other reform movements before us." The ideal Bible teacher, he argued,
should instruct their students "how to think safely and soundly," but the
prevailing and widespread climate of distrust prevented that.[42]

We see the correctness of Froom's assessment well illustrated by the
trouble that descended on Prescott at the end of the 1933-1934 academic
year. The professor's difficulties arose not from what he shared with his
students in or out of class, but from what he said in confidence to his
General Conference colleagues. During a Michigan camp meeting apparently some time in late 1933 he had remarked to W. H. Branson, a fellow
General Conference officer, that he had waited for years "for someone to
make an adequate answer to Ballenger, Fletcher, and others." The questions about the church's sanctuary doctrine that the individuals had raised
were serious, he said, but he had not yet "seen" or "heard" an answer.[43]
Coming from one who was still regarded as the resident theologian emer-
itus it was a significant comment. But what did Prescott mean? The
General Conference official was not sure, but he was worried at what he
thought the professor had in mind.

Branson may or may not have been aware that it had been Prescott himself whom church officers had requested to counsel with W. W. Fletcher in
the late 1920s. He probably did not know either that it was Prescott who
had received the task of making a formal response to A. F. Ballenger at the

1905 General Conference session. And he may not have realized then that the professor was reflecting on the adequacy of his own answers as much as on that of others. In Branson's ears, Prescott's observation simply sounded like an admission that Ballenger and Fletcher were right.

What particularly disturbed him was the professor's suggestion that Christ had served as a priest in the heavenly sanctuary *before* His incarnation. In Branson's view that meant that Prescott was undermining the traditional teaching of a two-apartment ministry of Christ beginning in A.D. 31 at Christ's ascension.[44] The professor had apparently also mentioned similar things to I. H. Evans and other leading men who he thought were mature enough to wrestle with the difficulty. Unfortunately, he had misread his colleagues.

Already uncomfortable with Lynn Wood's rush to accreditation, Branson, who would have liked to overturn the recent decision approving it, now also feared for the college president's orthodoxy as well. He did not want Wood "imbibing" any of Prescott's "variant views." The General Conference officer tended to see things only in black or white and had difficulty accommodating anything but the most strict views on doctrine. He reported his conversation with Prescott to his fellow leaders and determined that it was time for a new president and a new Bible teacher at EMC.

Across in California, W. C. White was troubled during this period by Branson's (and Evans') approach to administration as well in other areas. In mid-July 1933 he had framed a careful letter in which he "spoke plainly" to the General Conference president, C. H. Watson. He intended the letter for Watson's eyes only and marked it "personal and private," because in fact, it was highly political. White knew that if what he wrote "was made public many would misunderstand it."[45]

He lamented the fact that Watson was planning to be overseas in South Africa and Australia for several months in early 1934, and he pleaded with the president to change his plans. Watson should not depart the country at this time, he urged, because it was simply "not safe" to leave leadership in the hands of his vice presidents. "The work in the U.S. needs the kindly leadership which you are able to give it," he stressed. In White's opinion the vice presidents elected to serve with Watson had been exercising "the old spirit of imperialism" during the past two or three years. Two of the vice presidents, he alleged, had been unsuccessful as division presidents in their overseas postings and had had to be brought back home because of their "spirit of domination." But White would not allow them to dominate him. "People are praying for Christian leadership in the place of businesslike domination," he wrote. He asserted to Watson that he had been commissioned by his mother to meet "tyranny and oppression as it would come up in our work from time to time."

A few weeks earlier Watson himself had had to administer a letter of rebuke to White for some of the latter's independent activities, and it was this that provided the occasion for White's confidential comments. He did not think that this was the real Watson. The General Conference president did not seem to take offense at White's outspokenness. In his reply he chose not to comment on "some of the things you have stated," he noted, "for they have to do with my brethren who are assisting me." He simply observed that his associates were all "very loyal, helpful comrades to me in this work."[46]

Watson's response was gentle and gracious and exuded the maturity and confidence of an experienced leader. But it is clear that a number of his associates were perceived as heavy-handed as well as quite conservative. The president himself does not appear to have been involved in the Prescott matter.

At Branson's initiative plans soon formed to replace Wood with Thomas Steen, and board chair Holden received instructions that he should not continue to employ Prescott. But Holden did not see things the way the General Conference officer did. Nor was he anxious to have blood on his hands or to do other people's dirty work. Prescott was a friend. Furthermore, the professor was a General Conference employee. The General Conference itself should take formal action with regard to Prescott. The ball bounced back into Washington's court.[47]

On January 29, 1934, Branson struck. A letter jointly signed by Branson and Evans on behalf of the General Conference officers asked Prescott to withdraw from Berrien Springs, because he was "not in full harmony with the denominational beliefs." If he was "out of harmony" with "certain vital points, especially the doctrine of the sanctuary," it would be "inconsistent" for him to continue teaching. They hoped that Prescott would see the response as "fair and proper." The officers would be happy to interview him in Washington if he desired.[48] But this time it was Branson's and Evans' turn to misread a colleague. The professor would not let anyone deal so casually with him. The action also stirred Wood. The matter seemed neither "fair" nor "proper" to either of them.

Prescott's ire was up. His integrity was at stake, and he valued nothing higher. How could Christian leaders flagrantly violate Christian principles so easily? How could they condemn a person without a hearing, and how could his colleagues talk behind his back to others without first discussing the problem with him? And why should they dismiss him first and then tell him to come to Washington to "confer" afterward? "It is axiomatic in a court of justice," he wrote, "that an accused person should have the opportunity of facing his accusers in court, and be given a fair chance of disproving the charges against him." But here the General Conference officers were going to be both his accusers and the judges to try him. Where was the justice in that? the aggrieved professor asked. It was plainly unethical.[49] Both Holden and Wood agreed. They feared for the reaction from both students and staff if word got out.

For Prescott it was a matter of honor that he had not discussed "controverted questions" in his classes. In any case, his private views did not clash with what he presented in them. Lacey might have been "unwise" at times in discussing things with his students, but not so with Prescott. Surely discussions with "leading men" were quite proper. The professor had not raised any issues with students. It was a matter of integrity.[50]

A week later further word on Washington's "unethical" proceedings reached Prescott and rankled him even more. He would prepare to defend himself. Would the General Conference officers please put their charges in writing? "Do you claim that I do not believe in the work of Christ our High Priest in the heavenly sanctuary?" he asked. Or was it that they thought he no longer believed that Christ was "doing His closing work corresponding to the work of the typical high priest"? Just what were the charges?[51] The officers remained silent.

Three times Prescott pressed his request to have the accusations set out for him in plain language. "It is no light thing to tell a worker who has held a good record for fifty years that he is unfitted to go on because he does not believe certain 'vital points' of our message."[52] But the officers were reluctant to press formal charges. They preferred just to "talk." Would Prescott please come to Washington to discuss the matter? The professor complied and visited with them March 2-4, but he adamantly refused to discuss theology.

In a series of two interviews the General Conference leaders expressed their desire to save the church "from drifting into theories like Ballenger's" and discussed the impropriety of Bible teachers holding differing views, even if they did not teach them. Prescott sidestepped the discussion. He was certain, according to Evans, that were he to start into it, he would be "misunderstood, misquoted, or otherwise misinterpreted."[53] His sole concern was with the clear injustice of their procedures. Taylor G. Bunch, the Bible teacher at Loma Linda, could hold variant views (Bunch was the first to use the term *phase* for Christ's ministry instead of *apartment*). Why single out Prescott and why in such an unethical way? Did they, he asked, have some "personal element" against him?[54]

Pushed into a corner, the officers conceded that their procedure had been "unusual," and they sought the professor's forgiveness. They were still adamant, however, that "one who differs on the sanctuary question" should not head up a college Bible department. Thus they did not want to drop their recommendation that he withdraw. Prescott was also determined, and he threatened that he would appeal to the whole General Conference Committee for a formal hearing. Only then did the officers agree not to push their recommendation further.[55]

As noted already, from the start I. H. Evans apparently had serious misgivings about Branson's handling of the episode. He had hoped his fellow leader would let the matter rest. Now sorry that Prescott had been so deeply hurt, he sought to be a peacemaker and to persuade his fellow officers to withdraw the offending letter of January 29. He found sympathetic listeners who agreed that the professor had "cause for grievance." But Branson, who was out of Washington at the time, remained unmoved. If he should back down, he asked Evans, how would he explain his reversal to the EMC board members he had spoken to?[56]

Branson might have talked to some board members, but he apparently had not spoken to all of them. Six weeks later, when Prescott tendered his resignation for health reasons, it dismayed the board. The majority, it seems, had not heard of the professor's difficulties with Washington, or, if they had, they sympathized with him. The board took the unusual step of explicitly recording its collective judgment that "it would be one of the worst things that could happen to have him leave at this juncture." Disregarding Branson's wishes, they urged the professor to stay. Even if he reduced his teaching load but remained "to exert his influence with the young people and have his name at the head of the Bible department . . . it would mean everything to the school."[57] But Prescott had been too deeply hurt. His morale had crumbled, and he had lost the burden. In the summer of 1934 he returned to his home in Washington, D.C., discouraged and depressed.[58]

By the time of Prescott's return, Evans had become quite distressed over the whole messy affair. If the January 29 letter could not be withdrawn "because others are involved," he would at least remove his name. On May 9 he wrote contritely to Prescott, apologizing for some of the expressions the letter had used and asked forgiveness. "I know of no man whom I would trust more than you or in whom I have fuller confidence as not teaching in the classroom what is undenominational. . . . I have always held you up as a model Christian . . . and a man of high ideals. I still have the same feelings toward you that I have held for you through many long years."[59]

Evans was an old friend, and his apology gladdened Prescott. He recognized, though, that the younger leaders in the General Conference still distrusted him, and thus he refused to participate in committee meetings or officers' councils after his return. Also, he knew that the Adventist grapevine was working, although he had not talked to anyone himself or given the church's opponents "any opportunity to make capital" out of the affair. He was very concerned about the continuing shadow cast on his standing in the church.

In September he attended an officers' meeting to seek clarification. Explaining why he could not participate with them in council, he stated that he was surprised that the leaders had not withdrawn their formal January action "expressing their lack of confidence." Prescott's attitude was neither arrogant nor confrontational. He appeared as a suppliant, but he believed in honor and fair play. Furthermore, he valued his reputation. If they were going to let their action stand, then it was now only "proper" that he should receive an impartial review to determine "what standing I have in this denomination."[60] They should arrange a formal hearing.

The professor's patience and persistence eventually paid off. Four days later the officers conceded their error, formally apologized, and asked forgiveness for the way they had proceeded. They still held the view that Bible teachers should be "in the fullest accord with our leading denominational points of faith," but they confessed that they had acted wrongly. With "one mind" they wished to withdraw their January 29 letter.[61]

Prescott was too much of a gentleman to rejoice, but he was quietly grateful for his vindication. He responded with appreciation and suggested that both sides should now just drop the matter. As a gesture of goodwill and a statement of their confidence, the officers invited the professor to preach a devotional sermon at the forthcoming Annual Council. Fellowship had been restored. Before the month was out Prescott celebrated his eightieth birthday, but he was not ready to retire yet. His mind was still fresh and his health good. He could still be of help to the church. Thus his name stayed on the door of his office in the Takoma Park headquarters.

---

[1] WWP to WCW, Dec. 19, 1921.

[2] Interview with Mrs. E. A. Reye, Nov. 20, 1981; Dorothy J. Robson (nee Kirk) to GMV, Apr. 21, 1981.

[3] *Record,* June 27, 1921, p. 8. Watson was fortunate. Five days earlier Prescott had been requested to take the presidency of Oakwood College as an emergency measure. The GC Committee then reversed itself to accommodate the needs at Avondale. GCCMin, Apr. 6, 11, 1921.

[4] *Record,* Aug. 21, 1922, p. 8. Belle had studied at Battle Creek College when Prescott was president and had met her husband there. They married in 1892.

[5] WWP to JLS, Dec. 18, 1922.

[6] JEF to JLS, Dec. 11, 1922.

[7] LHW to FG, Sept. 12, 1932.

[8] Thirty were baptized at the Queensland camp meeting at the conclusion of his preaching series. *Record,* Aug. 27, 1923, p. 8.; Oct. 22, 1923, p. 1.

[9] JEF to JLS, Feb. 21, 1924.

[10] UCBdMin, Mar. 4-6, 1924.

[11] *Ibid.;* E. N. Dick, *Union: College of the Golden Cords,* pp. 158, 159.

[12] SEW to JLS, Aug. 6, 1924.

[13] JLS to WWP, Aug. 20, 1934; WWP to JLS, Aug. 25, 1924.

[14] E. N. Dick to GMV, Jan. 22, 1981; L. H. Lonergan to GMV, March 1981; Howard G. Welch to GMV, Mar. 2, 1981.

[15] Opal Wheeler Dick to GMV, Jan. 28, 1981.

[16] Rochelle P. Kilgore to GMV, Mar. 18, 1981.

[17] W.C.G. Murdoch interview, May 4, 1981.

[18] WWP to CKM, Feb. 23, Mar. 1, 10, 1925.

[19] Dick, pp. 97-99.

[20] UCBdMin, Jan. 26, 1925; *Educational Messenger,* January 1925, p. 17; February 1925, p. 15.

[21] CKM to WWP, Mar. 1, 1925.

[22] EGS to EKV, June 3, 1979, cited in "William Warren Prescott: Administrator." AUHR.

[23] George E. Hutches interview with GMV, Feb. 11, 1981.

[24] A.F.J. Kranz to GMV, Feb. 5, 1981.

[25] AP to GMV, Feb. 22, 1981.

[26] Pearl Gaitens to GMV, March 1981.

[27] UCFacMin, Apr. 11, 1925; UCBdMin, April 1925; HMSR to GMV, May 21, 1981.

[28] *Annual Calendar of Union College,* Second Quarter 1925, p. 45; *Union College Catalogue* 1926-1927, pp. 89, 93.

[29] HFS to CHW, Aug. 28, 1932. The comment occurred later when Lynn Wood was trying to recruit him to teach at Emmanuel Missionary College.

[30] WWP to WAS, Apr. 27, 1927; Apr. 22, 1928; *Golden Cords, 1928* (College View, Nebr.: published by the students of Union College, 1928), pp. 78, 79.

[31] WWP to WAS, Apr. 27, 1927.

[32] G. E. Hutches interview with GMV, Feb. 11, 1981.

[33] E. N. Dick to GMV, Jan. 22, 1981.

[34] GCOMin, Sept. 25, 1934.

[35] LEF to LHW, May 11, 1931; June 7, 1931.

[36] LHW to CWI, May 25, 1931; LHW to LEF, June 3, 1931.

[37] GCOMin, Aug. 8, 1932; Aug. 9, 1932; EMCFacMin, Mar. 19, 1933; Apr. 1, 1933.

[38] LHW to HFS, Nov. 29, 1933.

[39] EKV, "William Warren Prescott: Administrator," p. 28.

[40] WHH to MEK, Mar. 6, 1932.

[41] Wilkinson, for example, held that the King James Version of the Bible was the only reliable version. He was the firebrand who, according to J. S. Washburn's daughter, hid behind her father and "used" him unscrupulously to promote the anti-GC propaganda that circulated in the church at this time. Mrs. Grace Tewalt to RHA, Aug. 17, 1955; Aug. 22, 1955; Aug. 29, 1955; Sept. 14, 1955; Sept. 17, 1955. GCAr.

[42] LEF to LHW, July 3, 1932; July 31, 1932; LHW to LEF, Aug. 5, 1932.

[43] WHB [undated handwritten note], Special Files, GCAr.

[44] Branson had apparently not read Prescott's 1928 article published by Froom in *Ministry,* which advocated much the same idea.

[45] WCW to CHW, July 19, 1933.

[46] CHW to WCW, July 28, 1933.

[47] IHE to CHW, Nov. 21, 1933. Evans seems to have been somewhat fearful of Branson's handling of affairs. WHB to WHH, Jan. 4, 1934; WHB to IHE, Jan. 4, 1934.

[48] WHB and IHE to WWP, Jan. 29, 1934; GCOMin, Jan. 22, 1934.

[49] WWP to WHB and IHE, Feb. 2, 1934; WHH to WHB, Feb. 12, 1934.

[50] Edward Heppenstall, a student of Prescott's, reported that the professor assiduously avoided controversial matters of any kind in his classes. E. E. Heppenstall, interview with GMV, Feb. 20, 1981.

[51] WWP to WHB and IHE, Feb. 9, 1934; Feb. 13, 1934.

[52] *Ibid.*

[53] GCOMin, Mar. 2, 1934; Mar. 4, 1934; IHE [memo] to WWP, Mar. 5, 1934. The memo was not sent to Prescott and seems to be for Evans' own records.

[54] JEF to TGB, Aug. 8, 1932; GCMin, Mar. 2, 1934; Mar. 4, 1934.

[55] WWP, "Statement Made to the Officers of the General Conference," Sept. 14, 1934.

[56] GCOMin, Mar. 4, 1934; Mar. 5, 1934; Mar. 8, 1934; Apr. 18, 1934; IHE to WHB and JLS, Mar. 9, 1934; WHB to IHE, Mar. 15, 1934.

[57] EMCBdMin, Apr. 15, 1934; see also EMCBdMin, Mar. 15, 1934; May 17, 1934.

[58] EMCBdMin, Mar. 15, 1934; Apr. 15, 1934.

[59] IHE to WWP, May 9, 1934.

[60] WWP, "Statement to Officers," Sept. 14, 1934.

[61] IHE and WHB to WWP, Sept. 18, 1934; GCOMin, Sept. 14, 1934; Sept. 18, 1934.

CHAPTER XVIII

WRITING TILL THE END

"THE LORD HAS GIVEN Brother Prescott a studious, spiritual, logical mind, and the ability both to write and to speak very carefully and correctly," Review and Herald manager E. R. Palmer declared to General Conference president C. H. Watson. Palmer wanted him to assign the professor to write books for the church. In 1931 Prescott was in Washington, D.C., still serving as field secretary. Palmer conceded that he was obviously still strong enough for field work, although speaking appointments were tending to dry up because of the professor's "comparatively heavy style" and his "fearlessness in attacking what he believed to be wrong." It would be a better use of Prescott's energies if he could direct his efforts to writing. The doctrines of the Bible in the setting of the life and ministry of Christ, and the Papacy, with its counterfeit gospel, were two topics of outstanding importance. Prescott, he felt, would do justice to both. "I know of no man who can either write or speak more clearly or with more authority . . . on these two subjects than Brother Prescott," the publishing house manager concluded.[1]

Watson was persuaded, but how could he convince his fellow officers? Prescott was developing a reputation as a battler, particularly in the conferences of the Columbia Union that surrounded Washington, D.C. Its strongly fundamentalist presidents and their friends who supported the Wilkinson-Washburn line in theology at the General Conference would not take to Palmer's idea easily. "The daily" was as big and as contentious an issue as ever. To write on any topic that related to that might not be wise. Was there another more neutral topic either Palmer or Prescott could suggest?

The publishing association leader had no opportunity to respond. Shortly after he had made his proposal he suffered a bout of influenza.

Driven by his workload, Palmer felt unable to allow himself sick leave. The influenza turned to pneumonia, and he never recovered. His death on February 12 at age 62 shocked his colleagues. Twelve months passed, therefore, before anyone decided on a more neutral topic for Prescott, and then Watson had to make sure he called only a select group of the officers in order to get the matter authorized. A book on archaeology and the Bible would be timely and would contribute much to the education of the church's clergy. The officers agreed to underwrite it.

With approval granted, the professor buried himself in the manuscript, and by July 1932 he had finished the bulk of the writing. The general nature of the topic suggested the possibility of a wider market, so an interdenominational publisher was sought. Fleming H. Revell had the volume ready by the end of 1933. *The Spade and the Bible* was the first book on the relationship between archaeology and the Bible by an Adventist writer.

His approach to the topic was to discuss the abundance of evidence "from the rocks and dustheaps of ancient lands" that supported the historical reliability of Scripture. He was careful, however, not to claim that archaeology actually proved the Bible true. Archaeology might confirm some historical facts and provide a reasonable basis for faith, but it could not "take the place of the voice of God speaking to the spiritual man."[2] Prescott, of course, was not an archaeologist and did not write as one. Thus the book was heavy with citations from authorities in the field. It served as a useful reference tool and was widely read, at least among the Adventist ministry.

The professor had barely started on his next manuscript on the papacy when his teaching stint at Emmanuel Missionary College interrupted it. After his return Prescott sensed that the prevailing attitude in the denomination toward research and scholarship would probably prevent the publication of his manuscript, even though the General Conference officers had approved the topic. He knew that his standing with the new generation of leaders in Washington was not high. In mid-1936 the officers confirmed his suspicions and advised that the book committee would probably not accept a manuscript on the papacy under the prevailing political conditions. He therefore abandoned the project. In the interim he assisted L. E. Froom with the translation of some original Latin materials that the latter was assembling for his Adventist Source Collection.[3]

Prescott had developed a warm friendship with Froom. They shared a similar vision for the ministry, and both men possessed broad minds. Froom had appreciated the materials the professor had developed for his classes at Union. "I have seen some of his studies," he commented to Daniells. "If our men could be encouraged in systematic Bible study such as he has given . . . it would do them a world of good" and would "lead them into channels of thinking that would revolutionize their presentations of the message."[4] He was aware that Prescott's preaching had sparked Daniells' own renewed interest in righteousness by faith. As far as Froom was concerned, the professor was well and truly on the right track.

Froom also appreciated the articles that Prescott had contributed to his new magazine, *Ministry,* as well as his keen support of the Ministerial Association and the occasional personal counsel he offered. "It is my opinion that that which appeals to him," Froom wrote to Daniells, "is surely of some worth. He is scholarly and critical in the right and friendly sense, and with his personal spiritual vision, I have great confidence in his judgment." To Lynn Wood, Froom commented, "One of the reasons why I always love to hear Professor Prescott address us is because of the impressive instructional feature of his sermons. They are food for thought."[5] The professor clearly impressed Froom. They were both on the same wavelength. During the 1930s, however, even Froom's friendship did not help Prescott much. Both had to tread carefully, and Prescott was not used to doing so.

During his spare time in late 1936 Prescott developed another series of manuscripts, this time on the subject closest to his heart, the person and ministry of Christ. The reaction to the draft copies that he circulated among his colleagues confirmed that the climate in Washington had indeed chilled. While both M. L. Andreasen of Union College and Northern Union Conference president Charles Thompson appreciated the material, Milton Kern, the General Conference secretary, did not like it at all. Prescott's emphasis on the contrast between Christ's heavenly ministry and Catholicism's earthly counterfeit did not sit well. Why did the professor continue pushing his "daily" idea?

Kern was also suspicious of Prescott's view that Christ had a "pre-cross priesthood" (he must not have known that Froom had already published the idea in *Ministry* in 1928). Such an idea, he felt, would be "detrimental in its effect on many readers." It was hardly "the accepted view of the denomination," he observed. "Under the existing conditions" it would not be wise to publish it. To do so would be to have the book "play into the hands of Ballenger, Conradi, and Fletcher." Prescott should write on other things if he wanted his books published. "There is so much that is fine and helpful outside of the things on which you seem to differ from your brethren."[6] Some, it would seem, would forever perceive Prescott as part of the opposition.

The professor quietly took Kern's advice and turned to another topic. His next manuscript dealt with the general topic of "the reality of Christianity." But still he was in trouble. The old guard had passed on, and now the name Prescott had become a liability. When he submitted his document to the reading committee, they rejected it. What irked the professor most was not that they turned the manuscript down. Every committee had the right to do that. He himself had chaired reading committees for years. But why should they question his orthodoxy in the process? Some members of the reading committee had complained that the manuscript taught "Sabellianism," "Theosophy," and a number of other heresies, even nullifying the second coming of Christ. This time Prescott appealed. The leadership established another committee of four to review the document, and their report gave it a clean bill of health. In the main it was "sound" doctrine, including the Trinity! With some minor editing, it could be published.[7] But it never was. The publishers could not see a market for the book, and it never got any further.

The negative response that Prescott received to his manuscripts was not entirely because the church had entered an era of "fear of men who think." True, a wave of "reactionism" had swept over the denomination, as Froom had observed, but there was also another problem. Part of the difficulty was of the professor's own making. He had been too easily drawn into church controversies, too ready to try to correct error, and too vigorous in defending truth. In the process it had fostered a deep animosity among his fundamentalist adversaries, particularly B. G. Wilkinson, J. S. Washburn, F. C. Gilbert, and those who followed them.

THE VERSIONS CONTROVERSY

Prescott's public falling out with B. G. Wilkinson occurred in late 1928, just a few months after the professor concluded his term of service at Union College. Wilkinson, the academic dean and Bible teacher at Washington Missionary College, had launched a vigorous attack on the American Revised Version (ARV) of the Bible in a series of public lectures in Washington, D.C. Advertised in the major newspapers, his first meeting drew a large attendance. The next day the Washington *Post* carried the headline "Dean of Washington College attacks American Bible."[8]

The ARV, according to Wilkinson, originated with the Jesuits and attacked the Incarnation, the deity of Christ, the Sabbath, the law of God, and atonement by blood. It was the product of higher critical scholarship and sought to undermine the fundamentals of Christianity as well as the distinctive Adventist message. Prescott, who attended the first session, could not believe his ears. He felt ashamed for Wilkinson "and for the denomination." Never before had he heard such "a display of arrant ignorance." The next day he protested to the General Conference officers.[9]

The church leadership did not do anything to restrain Wilkinson, however, until he distributed another batch of "sensational" advertising. Again protests bombarded the General Conference, Prescott's as well as others. This time W. A. Spicer, the General Conference president, wrote to Wilkinson and his superiors requesting that they not discuss the subject.[10] Subsequently, the public advertising ceased. According to Prescott, however, Wilkinson "kept on slamming the ARV at every turn." Students had come to him and complained that they had had "nothing else in their Bible classes for nine weeks except an attack on the ARV."[11] During the summer Wilkinson kept up his campaign around the camp meetings but was careful not to refer specifically to the ARV by name. He simply included it as the featured version in an attack on several modern translations.

Concerned about the impact Wilkinson was having on the ministerial students he was training, Prescott sought to discuss the matter on a personal level with him. Three times he tried to arrange an appointment between June and November of 1929. Each time Wilkinson declined. According to Prescott, his excuse was that he had no time to prepare.[12]

Meanwhile, in California G. B. Starr and F. C. Gilbert were also giving the Revised Version "quite a black eye." A. O. Tait, editor of the *Signs,* reported that he had personally heard Starr relate an alleged conversation with Ellen White in which she supposedly said "that she would like to know who was responsible for the Revised Version's being used in her later writings." According to Starr, she had stated that "she had never given authority for anything of that sort."[13] Unaware of the debate raging in the Columbia Union, Tait published an article in late 1929 on the relative merits of the King James and Revised versions of the Bible as a corrective to what he was sure was misinformation from Starr. To his surprise, he received a note of caution from Spicer, who urged him against publishing anything further on the matter. The letter was too late. Tait had to inform the General Conference leader that he had been planning a series on the history of the Bible for some time and, in fact, the first articles had already been set in type. Furthermore, the author was none other than Prescott.[14]

If Tait is to be believed, he had been trying to get someone to write the series for the past three years, but the contributor he had commissioned had not been able to help. When his associate, Alonzo Baker, had approached Prescott during the summer five or six months previously, the professor had happily agreed and, in fact, already had some materials prepared on the topic. With some rewriting and further research in the Library of Congress, the first five of his articles were ready for press by early November. Notices announced the series as beginning December 3.

Just the advertisement alone was enough to cause a ruckus. Before even the first article appeared, telegrams from presidents in the Columbia Union urged Tait not to proceed with the series. It would only bring controversy and unsettle the youth. The same presidents protested to the General Conference, which also urged Tait to exercise restraint. But the pleas fell on deaf ears. Tait had been involved in editorial work for a long time, and the arguments and actions of the Columbia Union leadership reminded him more of the attitudes he had seen in Battle Creek during the 1890s than anything he had observed in recent years. He had been "intimately" associated with Prescott in the "difficult struggles" at that time as well. "Astonished beyond measure" at the "spirit of the papacy" that some in the Columbia Union were now manifesting, he protested vigorously to Spicer. The church should not allow their "spirit of self-centered domination" to succeed.[15]

The Pacific Press board considered the matter carefully on December 2, noted that the only protests came from the Columbia Union, and then voted to proceed with the series "as if there was no controversy at all." The comparison of the two versions was "incidental" to the larger theme of the history of the Bible as a whole. Why should they withdraw the articles? But in an effort to be conciliatory they would get Prescott to revise the last three in the series to avoid possible misunderstandings.[16]

Tait was sure that an ulterior motive lay behind the clamor. He had previously observed to Spicer that F. C. Gilbert opposed the new version mostly because he did not like its translation of "the daily." Prescott later confirmed that the same reasons also motivated Wilkinson. "For ten years or more Wilkinson has been strong in his opposition to my teaching on Dan. 8, and, of course, if he can discredit the ARV he thinks he has won a strong point against me." According to the professor, he had not written the articles as a specific response to Wilkinson but simply as the story of the Bible.[17]

Simply the story of the English Bible though they might be, by the time the fourth article in the series appeared Spicer felt constrained to write a letter of rebuke to the professor. He was careful to note that he had composed it in the "regular course" of his "administrative duty." Spicer was in a hard place. Knowing what he did, he could not for a moment side with the Wilkinson school. He himself had submitted some of the revisions for *The Great Controversy* and thus understood the issues. But now he was president and had to wear a president's hat, one that was sometimes uncomfortable. Quarrels in the church made his work more difficult. Given the circumstances, he argued, the discussion of "the faultiness of Bible manuscripts" was "ill-timed and harmful."[18]

Spicer's problems were bigger than just a quarrel over Bible versions. That was just the tip of the iceberg. The General Conference found itself locked in quite a struggle with the conferences of the Columbia Union. They had "dominated" and "defied" the General Conference for years. Small—usually less than 2,000 in membership—but outspoken, their membership was strongly conservative. When the time came for the annual *Signs* promotion campaign, the presidents showed their true colors. The union conference president informed Tait that he was not welcome in the Columbia Union Conference territory. The Ohio president also announced that his conference did not want any promotional materials. It would boycott the *Signs*.

Baker, who was in charge of promotion, was indignant, but he tried to be tactful in his reply. How could the Columbia Union single out the *Signs* for an embargo when the *Review* of January 2 had taken a positive position on the ARV? Did not the standard college textbook also observe that the ARV was technically superior to the KJV? "These things have been taught for years in our denomination," the associate editor pointed out.[19]

It was clear to Tait, Baker, and the Pacific Press board that the opposition to Prescott's articles was really a highly personal antagonism stirred up by Wilkinson, Washburn, and others over "the daily." This became even clearer when the West Pennsylvania Conference president later objected to another series of Prescott articles in the *Signs,* this time on Daniel. He feared that Prescott might say some things different than those of Uriah Smith.[20]

Wilkinson was not going to be outdone by the *Signs.* Four months after Prescott's series concluded, he published a 258-page rejoinder entitled *Our Authorized Bible Vindicated.* Greeted with derision and mirth by the California editors and Bible teachers alike, the book, according to Baker, lauded the King James Version "as the only inspired Bible in the English language."[21] Teachers and editors appealed to Prescott to get the General Conference to take some action on the matter. But there was little the General Conference felt it could do, even though it was hearing plenty from the field about the book. Vice president J. L. McElhany wrote to union and local conference presidents, giving some background, and suggested that circulation of the book "would be of no particular help to our work."[22] The General Conference simply wished the issue to go away.

Watchdog Prescott thought that the situation called for a stronger response. In his opinion the book was quite damaging, particularly because on its title page it identified itself closely with the church. Furthermore, the Columbia Union was defiantly "advertising and pushing the book." Wilkinson also continued to agitate the matter, contrary to the advice of the General Conference officers. According to J. S. Washburn's daughter, her father and his friends considered it an enormous triumph when he with the help of his supporters in the United Kingdom was able to give a copy to the queen of England while he was on a visit to the country in

1930.[23] Prescott had prepared a critical review of the book and Watson had used it as a basis for discussions with Wilkinson. It was clear to the officers, however, that any response with Prescott's name attached would not carry any weight at all—at least in the Columbia Union. Instead, they commissioned L. E. Froom and education secretary W. E. Howell to write up a formal review of the book (a task made easier by the material already submitted by Prescott).[24]

Froom and Howell concluded that because the book did not "represent the Seventh-day Adventist viewpoint or sound historical . . . fact," the church should attempt to stop its circulation. Wilkinson defended his position vigorously, but that did not change the minds of the General Conference leaders who reaffirmed their recommendation. Although copies of the book continued to circulate, the issue slowly faded away. The conflict inflicted scars on Prescott, however, that took some time to heal. Some prominent leaders became increasingly wary of him.

666 AND A WRONGLY TITLED POPE

Another illustration of Prescott's educational efforts that resulted in his image as a troublemaker and suspected heretic concerned the interpretation of the number 666 in Revelation 13:18. Early during his time on the *Protestant Magazine* the professor's research on Catholic issues had led him to conclude that the church's traditional application of this number to the phrase *Vicarius Filii Dei* was incorrect. He had shared his findings with the General Conference Committee and found a sympathetic response.

Sometime later Prescott again brought the matter to the attention of the committee. This time he had reason to be seriously disturbed. He had asked evangelist C. T. Everson of England to visit the Vatican museum and to take photographs of the tiara used at the pope's coronation. Prescott wanted the photographs to illustrate an article. The title *Vicarius Filii Dei* did not appear anywhere on the tiara or on any other crown used by the pope. The pictures were still useful enough for Prescott to publish anyway. Sometime later, when the Southern Publishing Association released the revised edition of Uriah Smith's *Daniel and the Revelation*, Prescott was horrified to the core to find that the house had used his photographs and that an artist had added the words *Vicarius Filii Dei* to the coronation tiara. Confronted with the incriminating evidence, the General

Conference gave immediate orders to stop the printing of the book until the publishing house had removed the fraudulent photograph. Such forgery, Prescott argued, was just as bad as anything the Catholic Church itself might have attempted. "When we are driven to such conduct as this to prove some of our theology, we had better stop."[25]

The episode did not become widely known and was soon forgotten. Unfortunately, *Vicarius Filii Dei* was a neat fit to Revelation 13:18, and it continued to be the popular interpretation. But in 1935 the matter raised its head again when F. D. Nichol, editor of *Present Truth* magazine, received a challenge from *Our Sunday Visitor,* America's most popular Catholic magazine. Nichol had published an article alleging that *Vicarius Filii Dei* was the pope's official title. The *Visitor* alleged in reply that Adventists relied on biased and dishonest anti-Catholic sources to make their claim. One correspondent went so far as to claim that by using Adventists' "ingenious method of reckoning" one could make the number 666 apply to almost anything, including "Ellen Gould White," and he demonstrated how.[26]

Nichol had asked Prescott for any proof that he knew of to help him justify the claim. The professor had responded that there was none. He had studied the issue carefully when he was editor of the *Protestant.* His renewed study in the six weeks since Nichol had written only confirmed the fact. The claim, he said, rested on a discredited forgery, "The Donation of Constantine" published in *The Decretum of Gratian.* The actual title of the pope was *Vicarius Christi,* which could not be made to apply to 666. Furthermore, although gematria (the practice of expressing numbers by using consecutive letters of the alphabet) was employed with the Hebrew and Greek languages, it was not the case with Latin. It, therefore, did not work when used for a Latin title. And in this case the Latin title was not even correct. He observed to Nichol that Adventists would complain bitterly if their opponents made claims about their church beliefs based on what their critics or opponents said. Adventists, therefore, should treat others as they themselves would like to be treated.[27]

With the matter out in the open again, Prescott requested an opportunity to make a presentation on the topic to the General Conference officers. He had to ask several times because the leaders were busy. His careful research and weighty evidence convinced at least Watson and

Evans, but others (predictably) thought the issue needed further study. The matter was shelved, but with the understanding that in the meantime "the interpretation should not be repeated."[28] It seems that very few ever heard anything about the decision. The use of the number continued to be popular, and right up to his last days Prescott was still corresponding with authors who advocated it. He felt deeply disturbed that people would put the credibility of the church at stake by continuing to apply 666 to a nonexistent title of the pope.

No doubt some leaders, burdened with administrative responsibility, wished that Prescott would not respond so vigorously to such problems. If he would not take them so seriously, maybe they would just go away. Prescott, of course, was not inclined to share the viewpoint. As he saw it, if no one spoke up, the denomination would go backwards, and he could not allow his church to do that, even if it was over a minor point of prophetic interpretation. Not all of Prescott's reinterpretations were considered to involve minor points, however. Some things the leadership took much more seriously.

RESHAPING A DEFENSE OF THE SANCTUARY

There was no question what Prescott believed with regard to "the daily" or the counterfeit Catholic doctrine of the Mass. Everyone knew. His position on the church's central teaching on the sanctuary, however, was somewhat of a puzzle. Leaders recognized that Prescott had his own thoughts on aspects of the sanctuary teaching—or at least that he appeared to. But did these views really just concern minor points? Leaders were not sure. The fact that Prescott should be a little bit different at all was unsettling. As European Division president L. H. Christian reportedly observed at one point during the 1930s: "Nobody quite knows where Prescott is."[29]

Whether the professor had adopted such vagueness as a deliberate defense mechanism, or whether it was simply that fellow church leaders were too limited in their thinking to understand the problems and solutions he wrestled with, can be debated. Carlyle B. Haynes tended to think it was the latter. Prescott was "one of the greatest men in the denomination," he remarked to W.G.C. Murdoch on one occasion and then added unflatteringly, "Unfortunately he had to contend with a lot of peanuts."[30]

Whatever the reason, Prescott's reflections on the church's sanctuary teaching caused quite a number of the younger generation of leaders to be apprehensive about him.

Having taken a special interest in the doctrine of the sanctuary, he recognized its importance to the church and was especially interested in seeing that it was explained and defended correctly. In 1905 the General Conference had appointed him one of the committee to hear Albion F. Ballenger, and four years later he had written a series of articles replying to his interpretation of Hebrews. He had declined in 1911 to write a critical review of Ballenger's book challenging the doctrine, however, because he was not free to answer the problems on a "broad basis," that is, from the perspective of "the daily." When E. E. Andross ventured a reply, it dismayed Prescott. He had reviewed Andross' manuscript before publication and criticized it heavily because it denied "the efficacy of the new covenant previous to the cross, . . . a very serious perversion of the gospel." It disturbed Prescott that in order to answer Ballenger, Andross had reverted to the pre-1888 theological position of the church. Daniells agreed with the professor and noted that Andross's arguments would be "repudiated by a large number of our ministers."[31]

Eighteen years later, while visiting Australia Daniells was shocked to find that the vice president of the Australasian Union Conference, W. W. Fletcher, had adopted views similar to those of Ballenger. He advised Fletcher not to present them to church committees too quickly but to consult with Prescott first. Quite an exchange of correspondence followed between the two men, but Prescott was unable to provide any satisfactory answers, even though Fletcher appreciated his "kindly endeavors." The Australian church leader later spent time visiting with Prescott in Washington, D.C., but still the professor could not resolve his dilemma.[32]

Fletcher was not the only one in difficulty around 1930. At the same time, L. R. Conradi was wrestling with some nontraditional interpretations of prophecy that had arisen in the course of his research on the history of prophetic interpretation. Again Prescott received a request to help, and while visiting Europe he talked at length with the division leader. Again he met with little success. Conradi had detailed his research in a lengthy manuscript that Prescott was asked to review when he returned to Washington. The professor dragged his feet over the assignment, causing some to speculate that he was actually in basic agreement with the document and therefore did not know what to say. Eventually he produced a 22-page review that primarily consisted of a summary of some of the manuscript's "outstanding features." He offered no comment as to their merit, except to suggest that the manuscript not be published because it would not interest the average reader. Also, he said that a representative committee would need to review it first. College libraries might find it useful as a teacher's resource, he suggested.[33] The professor's rather favorable reaction triggered further rumors. Was it true that he agreed with Conradi? He was asked to issue a denial in order to protect himself and to help the European church give a clear answer.[34]

Prescott could not come up with any easy answers to the questions Fletcher and Conradi had raised. Neither, it seemed, could anyone else. In fact, considerable confusion marked the effort to respond to the problems. For example, in 1931 denominational leaders asked W. E. Howell to write a series of Sabbath school lessons on the sanctuary to help counteract Fletcher. The lessons turned out to be so badly flawed that the Sabbath School Department had to withdraw them and substitute another series. But as Flora Plummer, the General Conference Sabbath school secretary, pointed out, it was better for the church to receive a "blast" from Ballenger's followers for its failure to respond than to present a series of lessons that they could attack with some success.[35]

C. H. Watson also made an attempt to provide an answer in his 1934 book *The Atoning Work of Christ*. It too met with considerable criticism, because many felt that Ballenger would be able to get good mileage out of it. The church would "eat the bitter" over it, they predicted.[36] In these efforts Prescott stood on the sidelines. All he could say was that one could not dismiss the criticisms of the church's teaching lightly.

In 1937 the professor became more vocal after Branson had written a manuscript for a series of Sabbath school lessons on the sanctuary. Prescott succeeded in getting a two-session hearing with the GC officers to present his critique. Perhaps he thought he might be able to educate at least some of the leadership as to the complexity of the issues. He had done a good deal of reflecting since his encounter with Fletcher and Conradi, but his main point was the same one that he had raised about Andross's book 20 years before. Adventists should not deny that Christ had served as a priest *before* Calvary as well as afterward. He was a priest "forever" after the order of Melchizedek. Prescott believed that Christ's priesthood was inherent in His sonship. Also he suggested the significance of the 2300 days related to the "restoration of the sanctuary perhaps after the modern Babylonian Captivity"—a more flexible approach to the chronology. Other criticisms concerned the misuse of Scripture in Branson's manuscript, such as using Acts 3:19 to apply to the end-time.[37]

Prescott demonstrated his intimate acquaintance with the topic in his vigorous rebuttal of the charge that he had openly disagreed with *The Great Controversy* statement that Christ had begun his work "after His ascension."[38] The next day the professor produced four other Ellen G. White statements that clearly asserted that Christ had begun His ministry before Calvary. Why, he asked, should people refer to the one in *The Great Controversy* and ignore the others? The committee acknowledged many of his criticisms of the lesson manuscript as valid but, nonetheless, very few changes, if any, were made. Whether a shortage of time was the problem or whether the author had more persuasive power because he was a General Conference vice president is difficult to say.

Prescott had no sympathy at all for Conradi's schismatic activities nor for E. S. Ballenger's *Gathering Call.* It disturbed him that church leaders seemed to be more interested in simply replying to the critics than in permitting themselves to discuss their substance. The professor believed strongly in the church's distinctive mission, and he retained firm confidence in it, even though his efforts to sharpen the theological acumen and the Christological focus of his fellow leaders sometimes resulted in their misunderstanding him.[39] If only his colleagues could be broad enough to recognize that sometimes critics might have something to teach. He wished they could see that doctrines were capable of being expanded or modified in order to express truth more adequately. It was absolutely necessary, he personally believed, if one was to allow for continuing new insights derived from an ongoing study of Scripture.

During the 1930s, though, church leaders had more to think about than just theology. The financial trials of the Depression occupied much of their time. Furthermore, the church was growing rapidly, and administration was becoming ever more complex. Independent movements continued to emerge, and sorting out an appropriate organizational relationship with the White Estate at Elmshaven all cried out for urgent attention.[40] Of necessity, the new leaders had to be strongly oriented to pragmatics. It was not always easy to grant the time for the long interviews on theological matters that Prescott requested. Interview transcripts indicate that some leaders were coming to regard him as an elderly man who was sometimes becoming a bother. In fact, M. R. Thurber, a Review and Herald employee at the time, reported that during the late 1930s a rumor went around "the park" that vice president James. L. McElhany had called in Prescott and asked him to stop "pestering" the leaders. They had "work" to do.[41] Was Prescott outliving his usefulness?

Invitations continued to come for field work, and he was still in popular demand at camp meetings. In mid-1936 he spent considerable time on the West Coast preaching at camp meetings and at Loma Linda. Camp meetings in the Lake Union finished out the summer. Prescott's age manifested itself through his increasing tendency to reminisce during his sermons. He found that his acquaintance with the pioneers and his stories from his early years in denominational service kept his audiences interested. However, he could not long wander away from his theme: the centrality of Christ.

By the summer of 1937 the professor was feeling that camp meeting appointments had become a strain. At 82 his lung capacity and his stamina had so far diminished that he no longer enjoyed the challenge of making himself heard in the large canvas pavilions. He sensed that it was time for him to seek retirement. The 1937 educational convention at Camp Blue Ridge and then a stint at the Indiana camp meeting were his last official appointments. Thus concluded 52 years of denominational service.

RETIREMENT AT LAST

Even though Prescott had stopped going to his office and to camp meetings, he could not stop reading and studying. That had been his life. Most of his days he still spent in his library, and his articles still continued to appear in denominational journals. He had more time, of course, to work in the immaculate flower garden that graced the home on Carroll Avenue. Also, he could indulge in relaxing visits with old friends and with younger workers who had become his friends. Denton E. Rebok, a teacher from the nearby seminary, was one, for example, who used to spend hours visiting with the professor. "I loved to probe into his mind, his heart, . . . then listen intently as he poured out his thoughts in a flow of rich delightful language." According to Rebok, it was Prescott who taught him to think. He was "an intellectual giant, a prince in Israel."[42] Rebok was apparently not the only teacher at the newly established seminary in Washington, D.C., that the professor impressed.

Such "powerful influence" over the younger teachers at the seminary stirred J. S. Washburn, who, even in retirement, could not let go of his old animosity toward Prescott. He found an opportunity to strike once more at the dangerous "progressive" when in late 1939 the professor preached a sermon in the Takoma Park church. Prescott had spoken of Christ as the "Jehovah-Jeruh" of the Old Testament and had commented on the doctrine of the Godhead and mentioned that Scripture clearly implied the doctrine of the Trinity. He had observed that Christians should be careful with the word "person" when they used it to speak of the Godhead. The term had its limitations and if used improperly could convey the sense of three Gods. "There are three persons in the Godhead, but They are so mysteriously and indissolubly related to Each Other that the presence of one is equivalent to the presence of the other," he said.[43] According to Kern, the doctrine of the Trinity had been a matter of quiet discussion around the seminary for some years.[44] Was it because he was now retired that Prescott felt safe to actually use the term *Trinity* from the pulpit? If so, he had miscalculated.

The sermon, published as a tract, brought forth the most vitriolic attack by Washburn that Prescott had yet experienced. According to Washburn's pamphlet, the doctrine of the Trinity was "a cruel heathen monstrosity, . . . an impossible absurd invention, . . . a blasphemous burlesque, . . . a bungling, absurd, irreverent caricature." Christianity had adopted it "direct from heathenism." The professor was introducing a "Roman doctrine" into the church that was "wholly foreign to all the Bible and the teachings of the Spirit of Prophecy." If you accepted what Prescott taught and believed the doctrine of the Trinity, in reality, Washburn declared, "Christ is no longer your mediator." The doctrine denied the law and led to dictatorial attitudes. Alluding to the troubles in Europe and the spread of totalitarianism, he pointed out that Hitler, Mussolini, Stalin, and Franco all came from a background of Trinitarian belief. They were, he alleged, what the blasphemous doctrine led to.[45]

The last half of the pamphlet was a personal attack on Prescott himself. The professor might be "a courteous, cultured, educated gentleman . . . , but his teachings are thus the more dangerous and destructive. . . . However kindly or beautiful or apparently profound his sermons or articles may be, when a man has arrived at the place where he teaches the heathen Catholic doctrine of the Trinity . . . , is he even a true preacher of the Gospel?" Furthermore, Prescott used the Revised Version (deceitfully because he did not always say which version he was employing), had worked with Waggoner and Jones and Kellogg, had gotten ideas from Conradi and continued to teach the new view of "the daily," had suggested that 666 did not apply to *Vicarius Filii Dei,* had revised *The Great Controversy,* and did not believe in the Spirit of Prophecy, and had moved "nearly all the prophetic dates of the prophecies." The catalog of sins Washburn listed together showed clearly once and for all that Prescott was no longer a Seventh-day Adventist minister. Washburn thought he had the ear of at least some church administrators. He thanked God "that a number of our leading brethren have seen the terrible danger of his ruinous teaching."[46] Just as war raged in Europe, now war of a different kind descended again on the tired professor. The tragedy was that some still responded to such venomous material. One conference president from the Columbia Union even requested 32 copies to distribute to his ministers.[47]

In a spirit of conciliation Prescott invited Washburn to his home twice to discuss matters and to seek to find common ground, but the visits were unproductive. The 77-year-old Washburn felt that the professor was on the verge of going down into darkness, and he felt duty-bound to continue his campaign. He was deeply concerned that Prescott seemed to have such a "powerful influence" over some of the teachers in the seminary. That sway, he argued, had "done more to make it difficult to establish the theological seminary than anything else."[48]

Washburn's propaganda greatly upset Prescott's friends at the seminary, and, according to Washburn, "some serious threats" apparently came from "men high up." Was it not time to rescind Washburn's ministerial credentials? the seminary faculty argued. But nothing happened. No official rebuke materialized. D. E. Robinson of the Ellen G. White Estate, however, came to the professor's defense. With careful documentation from Ellen White's files he demonstrated that Washburn's charges were far off the mark. In fact, it was Washburn himself who now held "variant views." "Scores of Bible teachers, editors, and ministers" now held Prescott's ideas.[49]

Such slander and lingering personal animosity thoroughly distressed Prescott, but he could do little about it. But happier events did cheer his declining years. Founders Day celebrations at Emmanuel Missionary College on May 24, 1941, honored his contribution to the church by the dedication of a brass plaque. It read:

> "William Warren Prescott
> President of this College 1885-1894
> Author Educator Friend of Youth
> These Words of Tribute
> Raised to His Honor in Carven Bronze
> Are but a reflection
> Of a greater memorial engraven in the
> Hearts and Lives of the Generations
> Of students to whom he ministered.
> Founders Day 1941"

Prescott's health did not permit him to be present to enjoy the occasion. Surgery in 1939 had made him an invalid, but he was probably glad for the excuse not to attend. Such things embarrassed him.[50]

Confined to home by his health, Prescott enjoyed the visits of former colleagues and students in his last years. Details of happenings in "the cause" continued to interest him. "How his eyes would brighten as bits of information came to him," reflected Lynn Wood, a frequent visitor. The professor was disappointed that he had had to curtail his church attendance, but he was still able to visit neighbors, some of whom, he reported, were in poorer health than he was. But time was running out.

Influenza spoiled the professor's Christmas in 1943. It was a harsh winter, and his physical resources were depleted. Pneumonia followed, and Daisy arranged for him to go to the Washington Sanitarium in early January. But medical care could not rally him. He died peacefully in his eighty-ninth year on Friday, January 21, 1944. The Associated Press reported the news of his death across the nation, and obituary notices appeared in many places where he had labored.[51]

Lynn Wood preached the funeral service in the Takoma Park church and presided over the burial at the family grave site in Rock Creek Cemetery. It was a simple service. According to Wood, the professor, "in the modesty of his soul," had asked that no mention be made of his work or of the positions of trust that he had held. "Could he now speak he would but beckon us on." Alluding to the war then raging in the Pacific and in Europe, Wood compared the professor to a soldier who "when shot and shell are bursting around him . . . catches an inspired vision."[52] Prescott had caught such a vision—a vision of the victorious Christ. It had transformed his life, and it had helped in powerful and enduring ways to refocus and reshape his church.

---

[1] ERP to CHW, Jan. 4, 1931.

[5] WWP to CHW, July 19, 1932; *The Spade and the Bible* (New York: Fleming H. Revell, 1933), p. 214.

[3] GCOMin, Dec. 9, 1934; Nov. 13, 1935; July 23, 1936.

[4] LEF to AGD, May 16, 1927.

[5] LEF to LHW, May 11, 1931.

[6] MEK to WWP, Feb. 24, 1936. The officers were divided and apparently took no action. GCOMin, Feb. 23, 1936. The manuscripts received the general title of "Triumphant Christianity."

[7] GCOMin, Sept. 25, 1937.

[8] WWP to WAS, Sept. 13, 1929; GCOMin, Nov. 13, 1930.

[9] GCOMin, Nov. 13, 1930; WWP to WAS, Sept. 13, 1929.

[10] WAS to Brethren Robbins, Martin, Hamilton, and Wilkinson, Nov. 10, 1929, cited in AOT to WAS, Nov. 25, 1929.

[11] *Ibid.;* WWP to AOT, Dec. 3, 1929.

[12] WWP to BGW, Dec. 3, 1929; WWP to AOT, Dec. 3, 1929.

[13] AOT to WAS, Nov. 25, 1929.

[14] WWP to AOT, Dec. 3, 1929.

[15] AOT to WAS, Nov. 27, 1929.

[16] ALB to CVL, Feb. 11, 1930; ALB to WMR, Feb. 13, 1930; WWP to AOT and ALB, Dec. 11, 1929. The possibility that Tait would yield to the "papal combination in the Columbia Union Conference" disturbed Prescott.

[17] WWP to AOT, Dec. 3, 1929.

[18] WAS to WWP, Jan. 14. 1930.

[19] ALB to CVL, Feb. 11, 1930.

[20] AOT to WWP, July 14, 1930. Although Tait considered the articles were "mighty

good stuff," he didn't want to "start another big furor" and so thought it the better part of wisdom to delay their publication. The series did not begin until March 1934, but even then only 17 of the 26 articles saw publication. The series ended with Daniel 7 on September 18, 1934. "The daily" was still a highly emotional issue.

[21] ALB to WWP, July 14, 1930; W. G. Wirth to WWP, July 30, 1930.

[22] JLMc to Union and Local Conference Presidents, July 27, 1930.

[23] Mrs. Grace Tewalt to RHA, Aug. 29, 1955.

[24] W. G. Wirth and O. F. Frank had also written critical reviews of the book. GCOMin, Nov. 30. 1930.

[25] WWP to FDN, Oct. 16, 1935; "Meeting With Elder W. W. Prescott," Apr. 16, 1936.

[26] *Visitor,* June 2, 1935; June 30, 1935; *Commonweal,* Aug. 16, 1935.

[27] WWP to FDN, Oct. 16, 1935.

[28] "Meeting With Elder W. W. Prescott" (transcript), Apr. 16, 1936; GCOMin, Dec. 18, 1938.

[29] W.C.G. Murdoch interview, May 4, 1981.

[30] *Ibid.* Murdoch noted that though Prescott had been hurt, "he never wavered in his confidence in the brethren" and remained loyal.

[31] WWP to EEA, Dec. 5, 1911; AGD to WCW, July 10, 1912.

[32] WWF to AGD, June 5, 1929; WWF to WWP, Aug. 29, 1929.

[33] GCOMin, Nov. 11, 1930; E. Kotz to H. F. Schuberth, June 19, 1931.

[34] WWP, "Report on Elder L. R. Conradi's Manuscript," Sept. 3, 1931; WEH to WWP, Oct. 14, 1932.

[35] Flora Plummer to CHW, Feb. 2, 1931.

[36] IHE to WWP, Aug. 25, 1933. Howell had also prepared a manuscript that Evans thought had conceded too much. It is possibly in this context that Prescott made his alleged remarks to Branson and Evans while he was at EMC. The Australasian Division had called for another Bible conference to discuss the issues. The church planned one for 1932, but economic pressures led to its cancellation. CHW, "Information Concerning the Australasian Petition to the General Conference," July 12, 1948.

[37] GCOMin, Mar. 5, 1937; Mar. 6, 1937. The officers kept an abbreviated transcript of the presentation and included it in the minutes.

[38] EGW, *The Great Controversy,* p. 420. Branson's manuscript had cited the statement. The other passages Prescott quoted were *The Desire of Ages,* pp. 625, 680, 751, and *Fundamentals of Christian Education,* p. 403. GCOMin, Mar. 6, 1937.

[39] Taylor G. Bunch received similar criticism for using "phases" instead of "apartments," but this has become a standard position for the denomination. JEF to TGB, Aug. 6, 1932.

[40] I deal with this extended conflict between the General Conference and the Ellen G. White Estate in my forthcoming book, *Struggle for the Prophetic Heritage: 1929-1939* (Berrien Springs, Mich.: Andrews University Press, 2005). It took some time to resolve the complicated power struggle and the theological and administrative issues involved in the search for an appropriate form of relationship for the management of the heritage left by Ellen White.

[41] Interview with M. R. Thurber, Mar. 24, 1981. GCOMin, Nov. 13, 1935.

[42] D. E. Rebok to GMV, Feb, 3, Nov. 18, 1981.

[43] WWP, "The Coming One" (printed sermon given at Takoma Park church, Oct. 14, 1939).

[44] MEK to J. L. Jones, Feb. 24, 1938; MEK to JLMc, Feb. 27, 1938. Kern had referred to the protests from the Columbia Union as "foolish pratings."

[45] JSW, "The Trinity" (1939, 1940), p. 10. Washburn's theological difficulty with the doctrine of the Godhead related to the same questions that gave early Adventists such difficulty: what happened to deity when Christ died on the cross? How could Jesus be a true mediator if He was of one "substance" with the Father?

[46] D. E. Rebok to GMV, Feb. 3, 1981; Nov. 18, 1981.

[47] JSW, "The Trinity" (1940); JSW to JLMc, June 2, 1940; June 9, 1940.

[48] WWP to JSW, Apr. 24, 1940; JSW to JLMc, June 2, 1940.

[49] DER to JSW, Apr. 25, 1940.

[50] The plaque is not on public display on the campus but resides in the Andrews University Heritage Room.

[51] *Nebraska State Journal,* Jan. 21, 1944.

[52] LHW, "Funeral of Professor W. W. Prescott." AUHR.

INDEX